"*Arctic Twilight*, Claudia Coutu Radmore's fine collection of letters from Leonard Budgell—Arctic adventurer, radio and naval expert, fur trader, raconteur, life-long "Servant of the Bay," and a whole lot more—provides an illuminating portrait of life in the changing Canadian North during much of the twentieth century. Budgell's account of his well-travelled life, at once autobiography, history, and yarn, ranges from the riotously funny to the deeply moving. It is the fascinating story of one of twentieth-century Canada's true pioneers. *Arctic Twilight* deserves a wide readership."

A.B. McKILLOP, *Professor of History, Carleton University, Ottawa; author of* Pierre Berton: A Biography

"*Arctic Twilight* takes us into the mind of a gentleman of another time— a man of high intelligence, good sense and deep loyalty to The Hudson's Bay Company. Providing a thousand rich details regarding day-to-day life in the Arctic, Leonard Budgell's letters will delight history lovers, students of the North and fiction writers in need of background material. We should be grateful to Claudia Coutu Radmore for this valuable collection."

BERNICE MORGAN, *author of* Random Passage *and* Cloud of Bone

"Len Budgell's letters are one of the greatest legacies anyone could have left Canada and its people. With incredible insight and sensitivity he painted a remarkable picture, particularly of the aboriginal peoples of the Canadian north and their humanity. This work is extremely powerful in what it says about the humanity of first nations peoples, about the negligence and racism of mainstream Canada. It puts real life to the conditions of the north."

DR. FRITS PANNEKOEK, *Professor of History and President of Athabasca University*

"Of all the books I've worked on, this is my favourite. Len Budgell's letters are filled with wonderful stories—stories full of feeling, humour, wonder and courage—and descriptions of such beauty that you have to stop and re-read them. I want all my family and friends—everyone—to read it."

DOMINIC FARRELL, *editor; author of the forthcoming book* The Flag and the Pole, *Canada's experience in the northern archipelago*

"Over the years I've become so jaded by manuscripts that have come my way, even by those on the verge of being published. In *Arctic Twilight* I surely wasn't expecting to find (a) excellent writing, (b) subjects that touched me directly, or (c) glimpses of simple, unaffected, literary genius. But all three are here, in abundance.

"Len's letters to Claudia Coutu are abundant and sparkling, original, engaging—how completely wonderful. What a blessing that these two formed such a bond, and I think the fact Claudia is now sharing a manifestation of that bond with the world, is tremendous.

"In short, I am enchanted, riveted even, but the kind of 'riveted' where one wants to proceed slowly, to relish each bit. I confess I've taken to bringing the manuscript for *Arctic Twilight* with me from room to room, to have it close by for moments in between other occupations, snatches of time when I can pick it up again.

KAREN MOLSON, *historian; author of* The Molsons: Their Lives and Times

ARCTIC
TWILIGHT

Leonard Budgell and
Canada's Changing North

Edited and with
an Introduction by

Claudia Coutu Radmore

Blue Butterfly Books
THINK FREE, BE FREE

Blue Butterfly Book Publishing Inc.
2583 Lakeshore Boulevard West, Toronto, Ontario, Canada M8V 1G3
Tel 416-255-3930   Fax 416-252-8291   www.bluebutterflybooks.ca

Complete ordering information for Blue Butterfly titles is available at:
www.bluebutterflybooks.ca

First edition, hard cover: 2009

LIBRARY AND ARCHIVES CANADA CATALOGUING IN PUBLICATION

Budgell, Leonard, 1917–2000.
Arctic twilight : Leonard Budgell and Canada's changing north /
edited and with an introduction by Claudia Coutu Radmore.

Includes bibliographical references and index.
ISBN 978-0-9781600-1-2

1. Budgell, Leonard, 1917–2000—Correspondence. 2. Radmore, Claudia Coutu,
1943– —Correspondence. 3. Hudson's Bay Company—History—20th century.
4. Labrador (N.L.)—History—20th century. 5. Canada, Northern—History—
20th century. 6. Inuit—Canada—History—20th century. 7. Fur traders—
Canada, Northern—Correspondence. 8. Hudson's Bay Company—Biography.
9. Labrador (N.L.)—Biography. 10. Canada, Northern—Biography.
I. Radmore, Claudia Coutu, 1943– II. Title.

FC3963.1.B83A45 2008   971.9'03092   C2008-905563-2

Design and typesetting by Fox Meadow Creations
Text set in Fournier
Printed in Canada by Transcontinental-Métrolitho
The paper in this book (except photo sections) contains 100 per cent post-consumer fibre, was processed chlorine-free, and was manufactured using biogas energy.

No government grants were sought nor any public subsidies received for publication of this book. Blue Butterfly Books thanks book buyers for their support in the marketplace.

CLAUDIA COUTU RADMORE began a written correspondence with Leonard Budgell in the early 1980s, which continued even when she was training teachers in the South Pacific nation of Vanuatu for several years. Claudia recognized the educational and historical value of the wonderful stories Len related in his letters of his experiences living and working in Canada's North. *Arctic Twilight* makes Len's stories available to all.

Photo: Claudia in 1987, in an aluminum runabout on the way to the island of Mota Lava in Vanuatu. J. PATTERSON

LEONARD BUDGELL was born in 1917 in the remote Labrador settlement of North West River and grew up 80 miles to the east in Rigolet, where his father managed the Hudson's Bay Company trading post. Officially joining the Company himself in 1935, Len remained a "Servant of the Bay" until his retirement in 1982. He and his wife, Muriel, whom he met when she went to Labrador as a nurse, raised a family of four. Len Budgell died in 2000.

PHOTO BY ARTENA BABAIAN (1998)

CONTENTS

• Wolstenholme

Baffin Island

Hudson Strait

Ungava
Peninsula

N

| 0 | | | 100 miles |
| 0 | | | 100 km |

Ungava Bay

QUEBEC

Torngat Mtns

Cape White Handkerchief

Saglek Bay
• Hebron
Cape Mugford

Atlantic

Ocean

• Davis Inlet

LABRADOR

L Melville   Rigolet
North West River •
Hamilton Inlet
Mealy Mountains   Cartwright
Dove Brook   •
Muddy Bay

Gulf of St. Lawrence

Fogo Island

NEWFOUNDLAND

LEONARD BUDGELL
Servant of the Bay

In the first letter from Leonard Budgell in this selection, Len writes from a St. Boniface Hospital room in Manitoba. He has had a "spell," which eventually would be diagnosed as a heart condition too dangerous for the bypass surgery recommended. If this had been diagnosed when he was a child, he would have been advised to lead a sedentary, careful life, and yet Len would lead a life in which he guided small boats into hazardous waters, wintered in famine conditions close to the North Pole, and hunted in snowstorms in the treacherous Torngat Mountains. He would marry, raise a family of four, and manage Hudson's Bay Company posts in North Labrador and in the eastern and western Arctic. He would know ships, native peoples, the workings of outports, dogs, the habits of northern animals and birds, and sea animals. He would become one of the pioneers in radio in the North, and in time, be acknowledged as a primary source on the North for historians, with his oral and written resource materials held in The Hudson's Bay Company Archives.

I met Leonard Budgell in Winnipeg in 1979 when I was thirty-six years old. Len was sixty-three, still employed by The Governor and Committee of The Hudson's Bay Company, and too close to retirement for his liking. My partner, Thomas E. Brown, and I were hosting a historian from Ottawa for a conference. Len knew her well, and offered to drive her to our home from the airport. After a pot of tea together, it was only natural to ask him to visit again, and so began a long and wonderful friendship that included many hours over countless more pots of tea, walks at Hammock Marsh, and family lunches. In 1981, when I moved to Kingston to pursue a Fine Arts degree, a correspondence began consisting of several thousands of pages, most of them written by Len to me.

Once they began to arrive, in packets written on yellow foolscap and in sets of anywhere from ten to seventy-seven pages, I eagerly checked the mail for each brown envelope. As it turned out, not only was Len a faithful correspondent, he was a marvellous writer. Comments on daily and current events swung easily into adventures and stories from his Hudson's Bay Company postings, memories of people he had admired all his life in Labrador or on Fogo Island or reflections on Inuit life and the animals of the Arctic. The letters were so interesting I felt compelled to read parts of them to anyone who was around; they begged to be shared. Len was pleased at the thought that his family and others might enjoy his experiences. He supported the project from the start.

Of the 4,000-odd pages I received between 1981 and 1992, over half would keep me up to date with happenings in the family, everyday encounters, comments on current events—the stuff of personal letters. Len was so close to his family; I was kept up to date on how Muriel was, especially once she was diagnosed with Alzheimer's; I learned when a grandchild's new tooth came in, how small fingers planted beans, or of a New Year's Eve spent enjoying a tiny grandson. In general, such material is not part of this manuscript, but that it cannot be is an injustice to readers. His love for his family, his accounts of everyday life and those friends he kept in touch with, his meetings with other long-time Labrador and Arctic traders, his long walks and travels are every bit as important and entertaining, full of the sadnesses and joys of his life. Despite the severe editing required to keep his letters to a manageable length for publication, despite the removal of personal material and content to preserve the family's privacy, and mine, what remains is nevertheless an exceptional treasure trove.

Leonard Gordon Budgell was born in North West River, Labrador, a Hudson's Bay post roughly forty kilometres east of present-day Happy Valley, on the northern shore of Lake Melville. His father, George Budgell, was the post manager for The Hudson's Bay Company at Rigolet, farther east from North West River. His mother was Phyllis Painter of Dove Brook.

The post journal for the day of his birth is in George Budgell's standard format of weather, daily projects, and happenings, followed by a list of arrivals: For August, 1917; "Tues. 7, Fine in a.m. One short shower in p.m., otherwise fine. Wind strong, from N. West. Servants packing fish brought in by Mr. Lescadron. Arrivals: One baby boy, born to Mrs. B. in a.m." The child would be named Leonard Gordon, after Reverend Henry Gordon, an Anglican minister who later established the Labrador Public School at Muddy Bay.

Len would grow up in Rigolet, where George Budgell was the Hudson's Bay post manager for most of his career, although he was manager at Davis Inlet for one posting and at North West River twice. The family also spent a year's furlough on Fogo Island, Newfoundland, the island off the northeast coast of Newfoundland where George had been born, and where he had spent his first few years.

Can a love of ships be inherited? Len's niece Phyllis Fawcett wrote in an e-mail, "Re: Uncle Len's ship building genes: I think he comes by them honestly." His maternal grandfather, Silas Painter, and great-grandfather George Painter, who had come to fish, also built boats and schooners for The Hudson's Bay Company. There are records of Painters employed as fishermen by the Slade Company of Poole, England, that date back to 1784, with John Painter, 1784–9, and Joseph in 1792. Though these early Painters returned to England, it is likely that they, or relatives of theirs, returned to the area in the mid 1800s. Len's great-grandfather George eventually went back to England.

Grandfather Silas continued building boats until the company had no further need for schooners. His brother, Len's uncle Tom, had a mill at Dove Brook where they sawed the lumber to build the boats and schooners. From family stories, it seems they had tinsmith skills as well, which would have allowed them to work in the fish canneries.

Len remembered this grandfather well, remembered his stories, knew details about ships that would have interested few children. In these letters Len tells of seeing the clipper *Saladdin* come into harbour at the Turnavik Islands when he was five years old. His account shows how he already knew about, and truly loved, anything to do with ships. He idolized ship captains. In an essay about the ships of the Revillon Frères Trading Company, Len wrote of a journey when he was ten on the *Fort James*, captained by his idol "Uncle" Isaak Barbour. As Len puts it, "the captain said at breakfast, 'Take some parritch, bye, t'will put fat on your ribs.' I would rather have had the new-laid eggs we had brought on board, but hero worship being what it is, I accepted a bowl from the cook, and manfully slathered it with blackstrap while my brother ate eggs and toast and regarded me with puzzled bewilderment."

You will read of a young boy's elation, while at the top of a schooner topmast, having successfully replaced a flag halyard at the request of Captain Barbour. Some of his happiest times with The Hudson's Bay Company after he left the Labrador posts were on *Nascopie* and *Fort Severn*, doing repair and renovation, as motorman, and as chief engineer. Shirlee Anne Smith, former Keeper of The Hudson's Bay Company Archives, says she delighted in going upstairs to see Len and the other "old timers" at Hudson Bay House if she needed any information about ships. She says Len "knew everything about ships, of sailing ships and riggings. If I wanted to know [anything about ships] I would just ask Len."

Len's parents were not typical of the people of Rigolet, or of anywhere else on the Labrador coast. According to Richard Budgell,

Len's nephew, the Budgell home was filled with books. Doctors and clergymen—Dr. Harry Paddon, Dr. Lester Burry, the Reverend Henry Gordon and Dr. Wilfred Grenfell among others—would stay at the post when travelling, or stop by to visit. George Budgell was a good intellectual match. From this nurturing setting, Len and his older brother Max were sent to the Labrador Public Boarding School at Muddy Bay, started by the Reverend Henry Gordon, when it opened in 1923. Len was, at six years old, the youngest boarder. The Labrador Public School was ahead of its time. Non-denominational, the school encouraged its students to hold on to languages used at home, to hone skills learned there, to respect their roots, and to learn new skills relevant to their lives.

One year when George Budgell took his family to stay on the island where he had been born, ten-year-old Len went to school on Fogo Island. When the family returned to Labrador, the children went to the Yale School, funded mainly by Yale University, and built in 1925 by Dr. Harry Paddon for the Grenfell Mission in North West River. When the Budgell family was based in Rigolet, it meant that the children boarded at the school. Later, Max and Len were sent to Newfoundland for schooling, possibly in St. Johns, as Len states in one letter that when he was thirty he had only seen one city. He always returned to Rigolet for holidays.

However, Len learned best, and enjoyed learning most, by watching, by listening, by practising hands-on activities outdoors, or in workshops. He could recall not only the way a hand tool was used, but who was using it, and the way the hand looked itself with its "great knuckles," and how the stroke should be made. It seems he remembered every single thing he learned from Will Shewak, the Hudson's Bay carpenter; from John Blake, fur trapper and skipper of the *Fort Rigolet* and other HBC vessels; James Dickers, the Hudson's Bay cooper; Aunt Bella; Aunt Mary Harnett; Inuit hunters Albert and Coonera, among others, for these are the teachers he sought out.

The availability of books at home had fostered a love of reading in all the children, inspiring them to go on to further education and successful careers. Perhaps because of books he read at school, or from his personal choice of reading, references are found in Len's writing to literary characters such as Mrs. Malaprop, from Richard Brinsley Sheridan's 1775 play *The Rivals*. It was natural for him to extend a description with a quote from literature or the poetic canon, or from the Bible. Where in the letters Len seems to misquote, he probably would have done so intentionally.

His younger brother Jack told me that Len had a photographic memory, but he had a great memory for stories as well, inherited from his mother as well as his father. Jack said that Len was content to yarn for hours with his mother, even when very small, and that Len remembered these stories. Len could also recall nuance of language, dialect, and turn of phrase, word for word. Years later, he could retell stories read to him by his earliest school teachers, complete with specific details and dates. Particular traits of many of the local clergy and teachers would come out later in his stories.

When he was twelve, Len started working unofficially for The Hudson's Bay Company after school and in the summers. He was content, whether helping in the store, doing general chores or working eighteen-hour days on the salmon nets. At fourteen, he started taking nurses and doctors to outlying settlements by dog team in winter, by boat in other seasons. He acted as cook one summer, and as deck hand and engineer for several years, with Skipper John Blake on the *Fort Rigolet*, which plied the mail run between Rigolet and North West River. They would also pick up salmon, as well as fresh and salt cod. If life had gone as he wished, Len would have preferred a life on the sea, but jobs on ships were scarce. His father introduced him to the experience of being a Company clerk in the store when he was about fifteen.

For a man known to have made so many friends, Len had been a shy child, and was an extremely shy young man. He had not enjoyed being an apprentice clerk in his father's Hudson Bay store in Rigolet, according to his brother John. Len would do anything to get out of it, to be able to have a more private life outdoors. Though shy, he had a strong temperament, preferring to choose the company he kept rather than having people imposed on him, and associating with those who were like himself. When Len was first posted to Cartwright, he found that training in radio telegraphy suited him. He had to spend a good deal of time on his own in order to master the skills which would be a necessary in later postings.

When he was very young, it took a long time for Len to make the leap into friendship, especially with those his own age. In our long talks over our pots of tea, he shared some of the experiences from his early years, which, he said, contributed to the distance he once tended to keep between himself and others. He was especially sensitive about jokes played on him, and took personal slights seriously. Such episodes drove him further into his own company and away from those who might offend him.

While it took time for Len to allow others into closeness, he remained open to it. He was especially willing to learn everything he could from the Inuit, forming many of his most valued friendships among them. As a child, Len had grown up with aboriginal peoples around Rigolet and North West River. He respected them and their way of life which was interwoven with the life his parents had chosen. Native and part-native trappers and fishermen, komatiks, dog teams and canoes were all part of his early days. Young Len spent as much time as he could with Will Shewak, John Blake, and other Inuit Company employees. He believed that Will Shewak was a genius. These experiences gave Len a life-long sense of the abilities and intelligence, the wit and adaptability of native peoples. Len wrote about many of these men whom he admired. These accounts have been published, for the most part, in *Them Days*, the magazine of Labrador oral history, as well as in the anthology *The Labradorians: Voices from the Land of Cain*, edited by Lynne D. Fitzhugh.

In 1935, when Len was eighteen years old, Ralph Parsons, district manager for The Hudson's Bay Company at that time, hired him as an apprentice at Cartwright for $180 per year. Ralph Parsons, who had once been a clerk under Len's father at Rigolet, would later go on to become the fur trade commissioner for the company. Len wrote: "He told me that he had refused to allow me to go to sea on one of the HBC ships because, one, I was more valuable ashore, and two, there were certified captains looking for third mates' berths. He told me he was planning to send me north as I already had a lot of experience."

Because Len had "some original knowledge from a chap who oper-ated a radio station for the Grenfell Association in North West River, Jack Watts" and from Bill Moores of Cartwright, an arrangement was made so that he would learn the Marconi procedure as well as The Hudson's Bay Company code. Len spent many hours at Cartwright at the Marconi station when they needed a replacement for one of their operators. In the tapes recorded by Ms. Jocelyn McKillop, Len tells how he had to be sworn to secrecy over the radio, and that he was the first person in the British Empire to be sworn in that way. At the same time, he had a full-time position as HBC accountant, an indoor desk job that he hated. The radio skills were most useful at such later postings as Hebron, Wolstenholme, and other northern posts.

Once Canada entered World War II, even though Labrador was not yet part of Canada, Len was bent on joining the Royal Canadian Navy. The Hudson's Bay Company, however, felt that with his experience and radio skills he would be more useful on northern outposts. It was "suggested" that he remain with the Company rather than enlist. Loyal to the Company, Len stayed.

On the tapes, he says, "Ralph Parsons sent a telegram saying I was to go to Hebron to establish the first Hudson's Bay Company radio station on Labrador, and, in addition, to be control station for all the Ungava Bay stations. I was to pick up all traffic and shoot it down to the Marconi people on Labrador. The rest of Arctic traffic went to

Nottingham Island to the Canadian Ministry of Transport and went out that way. I was a very happy guy when I went."

Not only would Len's radio background be called upon at Hebron—and at his later postings—his skills in accounting, writing, carpentry, maintenance, boats, engines, guns, cooking and survival would also be of great use to him. Sharon Babaian, of the National Museum of Science and Technology, met with Len in 1993 in order to mine his expertise for an exhibit on the early years of radio with the Company. She had the opportunity of having lunch with the "old timers," the men Len had lunch with regularly after retirement. Several of them had been in the fur trade division, or had been at northern posts. "They were like that," she says, "the best fur traders of the Hudson's Bay. They all seemed self reliant, knew how to build things, service things, from ice huts to cleaning and using rifles, repairing, cleaning and installing engines in airplanes, all about radios.... If they didn't know how to do something, they taught themselves. They understood objects in themselves, were encouraged to do that."

At Hebron, Len could have stayed mostly in the store, or at the radio, but instead he used every opportunity to further explore the nature of the Inuit. Since he was ten years old, he had been given responsibility. He had been entrusted by his parents with undertaking long difficult journeys, with hunting and fishing, and with taking care of others. By the age of fourteen, he had demonstrated that he had the skills to sustain himself in a difficult environment, and so, though he was only twenty, he plunged headlong into the new adventure

The lessons learned never left him. In *The World as the Crow Flies*, Anne Marie MacDonald expressed so well Len's attitude towards others: "It's simple, really. If you like people, they will probably like you back..." Len's own take on that could have been expressed as, "... if you place trust in people, you will earn their trust and respect."

From that time on, Len developed broad connections with many people whom he would call friend, and many others whom he respected. Some were native people, others those with whom he shared history as a Company employee, a Company Servant. If you knew your job, did it well, and upheld the oath that was inherent in Len's mind once you had agreed to become a "Servant of The Bay," you became a friend for life. Len always used the capital "S" when writing of that relationship.

From Hebron, Len went to Wolstenholme, where for the first time, he was alone at a post, though there was a Roman Catholic mission nearby. He found the native people around Wolstenholme very different from the people at Hebron. Whereas at Hebron there was work making seal oil as well as hunting, trapping and fishing, people at Wolstenholme relied on hunting, trading fox fur, sealskins and walrus tusks. They were not as well off. Most trading happened at night, as daytime was for hunting and travel. Len knew little about Wolstenholme and learned more about the area, and about the fox or seal situation, when he encouraged the Inuit to stay with him through the night in the warm trader's house instead of in the unheated store.

Although Len was posted to Igloolik after a year at Wolstenholme, due to changed circumstances he never got there. He ended up doing what he loved best for the next three months: working as motorman on the *Nascopie* under Captain Thomas Smellie. It was at this time he encountered photographer Lorene Squire. These weeks provided some of his happiest memories.

After a furlough, and then temporary postings on McKenzie Island and at Red Lake, Len was assigned to Cartwright to help overhaul the *Nascopie*. It was at Cartwright he met Muriel Watson, a quiet young nurse from Saskatchewan, who was with the Grenfell Mission. He would stay in touch with her, court her, and marry her after the war.

Meanwhile, he was once again posted to Igloolik, again rerouted to Lac la Ronge. After the la Ronge posting, when he was finally "allowed" to join the army, Len taught radio communications at the military base in Kingston.

In 1946, while waiting to be released from the army, Len was asked to relieve a trader and his wife at Repulse Bay, at the extreme northwest corner of Hudson Bay near the Arctic Circle, in an emergency situation. The flight in itself was a memorable experience, especially when the four-seater canvas-covered Norseman caught fire at Repulse. That winter, Len was alone on the post with the radio and an old dog, and without firewood, food, furniture or trade goods during famine conditions. The few natives he saw were starving. He had nothing except ammunition to give them, and wildlife was scarce. During these eight bleak months, he met Father Pierre Henri, the Oblate missionary priest from Brittany known as Kabloona. Henry de Poncins wrote of this selfless priest who went out to King William's Island near the magnetic pole by dogsled, and who lived as completely like the Netsilik natives as possible. Leonard Budgell's nature was much in tune with that of Father Henri; there was nothing material he wanted or needed. Len's account of this experience, Mercy Mission, will be included in a future publication.

Len did not seek loneliness, but he did not find it a threat. He was quite happy to be on his own early in life. For the most part, he did not crave companionship, yet he was a young man with normal yearnings and normal passions. Len worked his way through the difficult lonely times in positive ways. In these selections from his letters is a story of an unusual rite of passage from youth to manhood with all its difficulties, particularly acute for a young man who longed for love and companionship, but one who was committed to a life in the North, often alone in the critical years, sometimes for months. What he chose to keep from those experiences was a lifetime of memories to hold and to share with anyone who was interested. It is a unique legacy, the story of the changing era in the Canadian Arctic, its twilight of transition.

Len took up postings for the Company in Saskatchewan, Manitoba, and Ontario, several of them Arctic postings; a timeline is recorded in an appendix. For several years following these postings to specific communities, the spring, summer, and fall seasons took him to Moosonee in the transportation branch of The Hudson's Bay Company. After he formally retired from the Company, he continued to manage Moosonee Transport, later known as Federated Shipping, a

Hudson's Bay subsidiary that supplied the communities of James Bay
with supplies by barge. In Moosonee, though his home base was St.
Boniface, Manitoba, his wife Muriel and the children could join him
during school vacations. At this time, he was officially associated with
Hudson's Bay House, the main HBC headquarters in Winnipeg, and
kept an office there.

Len was much too interested in whatever life gave him at any particular moment to be a career-conscious employee. Advancement was
never his first concern. His career was decided by the Company, and
never once, in either written word or in conversation, did he express a
wish to be other than a good and faithful "Servant" of The Bay. That
is what he signed on for, and as long as he could serve the Company
well, he was content. In one of his very last letters, written when he
was well over eighty, he quotes the precise words he agreed to when
he started with The Hudson's Bay Company. All his references to the
Company letters show how well he took that oath to heart. Len even
chose to marry Muriel on May 2, the anniversary of the grant date for
The Hudson's Bay Company's founding charter!

Some would say he wore the thickest of rose-coloured glasses
where The Hudson's Bay Company was concerned. Len would be
the first to say that with the circumstance of membership in the Company family, or with "the birthright," came the responsibility to speak
up when necessary, to take action when the family was threatened in
any sense, as well as to defend it when it was unfairly threatened or
maligned. Headquarters would promptly know Len Budgell's views
if an employee had not been treated properly according to his lights.
He would insist that an elderly Indian who had been an employee
receive a fair pension; an article printed with incorrect information
in *The Beaver* would be criticized in letters to the editor; he would
condemn the most popular of authors if he could prove that the truth
had not been written about The Bay, when facts might have been easily checked.

In a letter written early in the year 1999, he told me that some of his experiences were included in a recent history of Labrador, which included the writings of many Labrador people. He liked Lynne Fitzhugh's *The Labradorians* very much, but disagreed with some of the conclusions reached by its editor about the handling of the welfare of trappers and hunters in Labrador by the HBC. Len wrote: "...I don't dispute that some traders may have dealt unfairly with their customers, but some traders were very fair. Many HBC store managers, my father included, shared their income with any who needed it. I remember Mr. Ralph Parsons saying to my father once, when the Company was losing a good deal of money on the salmon fishery, "Skipper Garge, so long as you and your fishermen did their best, then HBC will bear the loss.'" Len made the same comments in an unpublished letter, almost word for word, to Doris Saunders of *Them Days* magazine. He continued, "I hope my remarks...don't offend Ms. Fitzhugh...She can write me off as hopelessly indoctrinated by the HBC." Doris Saunders, the originator and then editor of *Them Days*, became one of Len's close friends.

And to me, Len wrote: "...I know, Claudia, that it is the policy of the HBC not to reply to unjust criticism, but I hope the facts are made public. I have access to some very old records in the Archives, and it is astonishing how much credit was given to customers over a period of time and how little was ever paid. For the ex-Moravian posts alone, there were practically no profits, and losses were made year after year...For the Great Company survived the hard depression years, and in doing so helped native people to get through those years. The trappers' incomes had been almost completely wiped out by the decline in fur prices, and for the fish, and seal products such as seal fat. They knew they could come to my father."

John Michelin, a trapper from the area, agreed, telling Len's brother John that "...The Hudson's Bay Company took care of you, but eventually trapping died out. Many trappers were left with debts at The Bay, which it carried for years, eventually dropping them, but not forgetting in all cases." That it was so is proved by the fact that, according to John, "The Hudson's Bay was in charge of the commissary when Goose Bay was being built. Many from North West River worked on that project, and when they came to the Hudson's Bay to cash cheques, the old books were brought out, and the workers were asked to start paying the old debts..." It was probably felt to be a fair request. It should be no surprise that the then-retired George Budgell, who had been asked to run the commissary, was the man who decided to open the old books.

And to Len, it seemed only natural and right that the Company should be paternalistic. Walter Dickers wrote in his article "Christmas at Rigolet," published in *Them Days* magazine, that "... Old George Budgell was going around with his Hudson's Bay black rum, having a few drinks, then moving on to the Will Shewaks and the Jesse Flowers, HBC employees." which meant every family, as only HBC people lived at Rigolet at that time.

Len was not always pleased with decisions the Company made, or impressed with every Company Servant. He did feel that the best Servants were those who upheld the oath they took when they signed on with the Company, and that if every Servant, from the administration on down, had always acted in good faith, The Hudson's Bay Company would have remained one of the most important corporations ever to have existed in Canada.

Len handled his own positions of trust in the Company with the same clear-sightedness as when he drove a dog team in the snows of a winter Labrador, with the needs of passengers, fellow travellers and employees uppermost. The Hudson's Bay subsidiary that Len managed in Moosonee consistently made a lot of money for the Company, which was continually surprised that so much money could be made with so little investment. Len was an excellent businessman, but it was mainly his manner of working with people, of choosing the finest for the job, and then trusting that they would do their best without his poking his nose into every operation that got those results. To Len, that was the tradition of the Company he had grown up in, but based on his upbringing, he would likely have held the same views whether or not he had stayed with the HBC.

Len, like George Eliot, strongly felt that the growing good of the world is greatly dependent on unhistoric acts, and that the reason things are not as bad as they might have been is "half owing to the number who lived faithfully a hidden life." Len was fascinated by those who lived these hidden lives, how they acted, what motivated them; he believed that it was these men, especially the native people, who were the guardians and strength of the North. He was impressed by the direct interaction native people had with their world, their acceptance of life as it was.

In the natural wisdom of native people he found answers—specifics about hunting, survival skills shared over a *kudlik** in an igloo, or common sense responses to the white man's way of life. He thought about the concept of time, contrasting ours with the aboriginal's. To his list of things to ponder, Len added contemporary culture: bureaucracy, experts, managers, politics, TV announcers, clothing styles. Somewhat puzzled by a world gone crazy for material things, by people who seemed to have no common sense or sensibilities, by those who seemed to have little sense of morality, or who let others lead them, he agreed that there was much he did not know. To the lasting benefit of others, he knew how to express his thoughts.

One of the strongest reasons to make a selection from the letters of the late Leonard Budgell is that their content is of compelling interest to such a wide variety of readers. According to Shirlee Smith, "Leon-

---

*A *kudlik* (qulliq) is a crescent-shaped lamp carved from stone and fuelled by the oil from animal blubber. A wick made of moss or Arctic cotton draws the oil to make a type of liquid candle, and the open stone lamp was used by the Inuit to light and heat tents or igloos, melt snow for water, dry clothing, and cook food.

ard was a man of many facets, the kind of man who, because of his background and upbringing, we will see no more. He had a wealth of information on so many different subjects, and total recall ... of things that were so important, especially of his early days in the fur trade." His story and experience, his insights about places and people and a now disappeared way of life make a book for historians, for those interested in the North or Labrador, but also a book for readers of adventure, for those interested in nature, in human nature, in the sea, in ships, in the business of the fur trade, for those who like to read humour, or simply enjoy writing that sparkles.

As he was not writing for publication, there is none of the stiltedness that comes with self-conscious writing. They are wandery things, these letters. Describing a fine fall day at a nature reserve near Winnipeg will lead to a fall day in Labrador; a child on an airplane will bring a story of a native child; visiting an elderly friend in hospital will remind him of an old Inuit woman dying of hunger and cold, then to watching muskrats with a Nascopie child. When he tells of Coonera and Albert, Inuit hunters at Hebron, of the hours spent travelling with them, hunting with them, or just sitting and taking in the world of the day, we become part of that long-ago world.

From his early years, Len treasured the women in his life. His memories of his mother, of the older women who birthed babies, of his sisters and of one particular young girl, were memories of warmth and sharing. He loved to be with them, talk with them, help them in any way possible. While the men he met were suspect until they proved themselves, women, simply by virtue of being women, were immediately on what he considered to be well-deserved pedestals.

Len was used to the women in his life being strong and independent. His own mother capably fed and clothed her large family, as well as the Company employees, with help from local women. The "grans" of his childhood "borned" babies, and spent every moment in useful, community-oriented activities. His wife, Muriel, came to

Cartwright from a Prairie farm to nurse fishermen, ship builders, hunters, and trappers at Cartwright. It must have felt to her like the edge of the world. Len knew how trappers' wives were left on their own every year, often in complete wilderness during long winter months. Max McLean, in a tribute given when the first bronze statue in Labrador, *The Trapper*, was unveiled in North West River in 2004, spoke of the trappers' wives as being at the heart of the trappers' culture, "... strong women of British, French and Aboriginal heritage who kept the home fires burning when the men were away." These women had to hunt, cook, keep a woodstove burning, bear, feed and clothe their children under the most difficult circumstances. And Len also knew how important it was for Inuit men to have women in the family group in order to survive. These experiences gave him a great respect for, and at times fear of, women he encountered, especially when he was younger.

It's interesting that in later life, Len had difficulties appreciating the "new woman" who paid for a man's meal and opened her own doors. Some things should be sacrosanct; to Len women always were so. Women were to be respected and encouraged, and though he often thought them to be wiser, stronger and more capable than he, he felt that for reasons not of their own making, they were to be protected and taken care of. On the other hand, constantly amazed by women's abilities, he chafed at the awareness of how women were viewed in the "man's world" of business. Len made it his mission, whenever possible or necessary, to make sure that women were given their due, and if possible, were well paid for it.

In *Creating Minds*, Howard Gardner explores qualities found in the makeup of great people, insisting that they, in varied ways, value children and childhood. From Len's point of view, time spent with children was never considered wasted, whether they were his own, the offspring of co-workers, those he met on planes or in the supermarket. Edited from this manuscript are hundreds of pages of what exactly a child had said or seen, or asked about. Children were treasures. He was astonished by them, and the small ones could instantly steal his heart, especially his own children and his own grandchildren. He was fascinated by how the world looked through a child's eyes. While rejoicing in their spontaneity, he took them seriously, and would do anything to please, interest or entertain a child, to better a child's life.

Len's love for children was illustrated perfectly by his reaction to the children that employees at Hudson's Bay House would sometimes bring to the office. Len loved it when employees or former employees dropped in to his office with babies, though the practice was not universally appreciated. He wrote, "He [one executive at Hudson's Bay House in Winnipeg], as executives go, is okay, but short-sighted. He doesn't say anything when I invade his domain with the latest baby to visit Hudson's Bay House, but he looks disapproving. Can't understand that people go back to work happier and more productive if they've just held a tiny warm baby and felt its gossamer hair on the top of its head...."

From his own childhood, Len kept a great sense of whimsy and fun. As his "Aunt Bella" had done when he was small, he sent leprechauns to watch over friends and to carry messages on moonbeams. He believed in believing in leprechauns. In an unpublished letter he wrote:

Do you believe in leprechauns? They have the gift, the gift of magic. They are small and merry and will repair shoes. The forest daisies grow where they walk and you can follow them but they never allow you to see where they live. I know one personally. Dear old Aunt Bella gave him to me when I was little. He helped me through many a night when my dog was sick or I had a problem at school.

Once I thought he was Will Shewak during the day because Will's hands were so gentle and yet so capable. Smooth sensitive hands, that could do anything, even sew. Nothing was too difficult for him to try: men's work, women's work. If it could be done and needed doing, he would do it. I was hit in the face once by a dog whip, which is a terribly cruel weapon, and Will put his hands on my face and turned it to the light because he feared for my eye. His hands were as tender as my mother's would have been. We were not near home and he put a little spruce balsam on the cut to stop the blood and he took the whip from the boy who had accidentally hit me and hung it in a tree. It never came down. All he said was, "Don't touch it."

I asked Aunt Bella if Will might be a leprechaun and she said no, but I was never sure.

The Irish, but also the natives, believe in spirits, grand and small: the Inuit in Labrador feared the *torngaks*, after whom the mountains were named; there were fairies that were frightening...

Len gave me a leprechaun of my very own named O'Halloran, and I have come to know how precious the gift of a leprechaun can be, and what one can mean to a friendship. Certainly if the poet and artist William Blake could witness a fairy funeral at the bottom of his garden in West Sussex, then an O'Halloran can exist to take messages to a friend faster than trains, planes, or Canada Post, at midnight or at dawn.

Len innately understood the value of myth in our lives, of fantasy. He particularly enjoyed anyone who was "fey" or anyone who would be brave enough to express a different view of the world. Len had such a way of stepping back into his own childhood, into his "child shoes" and of speaking in that voice filled with a child's refreshing wonder.

That same wonder, combined with the sense of responsibility and initiative built into most of the youngsters from that environment, cemented the foundation of the man he would become. Though, as Len's niece Anne Budgell put it, Len was confident, capable, comfortable at many levels of authority, and not easily intimidated, the ability to reach deep into fantasy would help keep him going on many a long Arctic night; it would also lighten the heavier parts of life, sustain him when he realized that some of the wishes closest to his heart would never be realized.

For Len always wanted to return to the Labrador. Some part of his heart was always there. When I spoke with his daughter Shelagh while editing the letters, she said, "To me, my dad is Labrador." She knew how he had longed to go back, not just to North West River where he was born, or to Rigolet which he felt was his home, but to Hebron especially, and a valley near there called Tororak, back to Saglek Harbour, to Natchvak Fiord, to the Torngats, to Cape Mugford, to Watch (Watchman's) Island. If there was to be a hereafter, and Len was not so certain that there would be, these are the places, he wrote, that he would liked to haunt. His letters are full of North Labrador, especially the fall, spring and winter seasons. In twenty years of letters to me, the only stories and descriptions he repeated were these seasons in these places. Len did get back to visit his brothers in North West River, as the last letter shows, but he never got to revisit the more northerly shores that he longed for.

Len stayed in contact with many people, not through personal need, but because he truly valued his family and friends. Friends were the only commodity, he wrote, on which he would willingly pay tax, and old friends were the most precious. Len agonized especially with those who were coping with memory loss and illness. He was there for them until the end. He visited and wrote volumes, letters of twenty or thirty pages, to those he knew from Labrador and the northern posts, or from any other of the places he travelled and worked, perhaps with the exception of the army, but he also kept in touch with secretaries, their children, people he met no matter how casually, especially if children were involved. He knew they contributed so much to his life.

It was comforting after all these years for me to meet with two of Len's brothers, and to talk again with his daughters. All I had known of him in twenty-five years, all I had proof of, had made him, in my mind, impossibly faultless. His children enlightened me, saying that their father had strong opinions, had prejudices common to many of his generation or background, and that he wasn't always the easiest person to get along with. He was a parent like many others, who felt he always knew the best for his family. It was also a relief to hear from his brothers that he had a temper, that he could use language unsuitable for ladies' ears, that he was considered to have been overly eager to please his father. Len, after all, was human.

Some of his brothers did think that he only saw the good side of his father, not the overbearing man that his father could be, and against whom some of the boys rebelled. But he wrote, "I do know my father had a sharp tongue, and if a thing had to be said, he said it." He told the story in *Them Days* of how his father had bodily thrown a stubborn trapper off a wharf. Len saw all sides of his father, as he saw all sides of most things, but chose to overlook certain of them, tolerate others, and only tell and commemorate him in the areas in which he was great, or in which he was a guide, and loving. It's true that he did follow his father's path completely where the Hudson's Bay was concerned, and he stayed with the Company until the end, as his brothers did not; it must have appeared as if he looked at his father and HBC issues in a rather haloed light.

Like his father too, Len claimed, and was fiercely proud of, his Scots and Irish heritage. There is a preponderance of red hair in the family, and the Irish in his language, whether written or spoken. He admits to an Irish temper like his father's. Emma Jane Foote, who married Len's grandfather John at Wild Cove on Fogo Island, came from the Outer Isles, the islands between Ireland and Scotland, home of the Scots-Irish. The surprise was that while Len revered his father, and wanted so much to become like him, he never took up two of his father's enjoyments which were common to traders who spent long solitary months on faraway posts. He loved the smell of pipe tobacco and associated the smell with his father, and fondly remembered the example of his father taking a small drink with each employee at Christmas, but he never smoked, and he didn't like the taste of alcohol.

One gift came naturally from his father. Len's nephew Richard read George Budgell's Company journals from Rigolet, finding them beautifully written; I agree. Len's older brother Max also inherited this talent, writing of his travels in the wilds of Labrador under unusual circumstances. Len wrote as if he were simply there in the same room as his correspondent. The words flow like water onto the foolscap in beautifully phrased passages, in language that can be spare, specific and genuine, and is at times quite poetic. Landscapes are so particularly described, the wording so exact, that images are transmitted without interference from one brain to another. Since the letters were not written for publication, there is no sign of the writer's agony, of editing, re-editing or rearranging.

Determining the final form of this book was a challenge. Len and I began to plan this book in 1991. His support meant that we received a Canada Council grant so that the letters could be entered into a computer. He was familiar with early drafts, and comfortable with publishing the material in this book. Muriel died in 1999, and Len passed away on December 21, 2000. Though illness, shock, and grief slowed the momentum of the book project, all members of his family have been wonderfully supportive of this celebration of his life.

The selections here are from letters written from 1981 to 1991, though we corresponded for nine years more, and are only from letters written to me. After that time, his pages were more concerned with the joys and upsets of family, small babies and grandchildren particularly, and Muriel's health, as those in his family were the most precious to him. I also saw him fairly often, considering that I was living in southern Ontario, while he was in Winnipeg and Moosonee. He travelled to Ontario to visit family, and to Montreal for Company reasons. We would link up whenever possible. I was fortunate enough to visit with him in Moosonee. We spoke more frequently by phone. Even so, thousands of pages had to be whittled down to a manageable size.

Len's letters to me were usually more than twenty pages long, written in a small, tight, readable script. The longest was seventy-seven pages. Every letter included family happenings and personal matters that Len, or I, was not comfortable with publishing. Therefore, in the majority of cases, just partial letters are reproduced here, along with enough material for smooth transitions. It was important, at times, to include his stream of thought, to know how he arrived at a story; it was equally important that a reader would not be left hanging after an abrupt ending.

However, I have tried to keep the essence of Len by including certain threads and themes to which he returned again and again over the years concerning family, friends, work and work partners, each of whom Len considered equals, never simply employees. In the very first excerpt, Len is in the hospital, yet by some fortuitous accident, he can see the Hudson's Bay flag flying over Hudson's Bay House from his window. In a novel, such a device would seem all too precious, but it was only natural to Len that the Company flag should be there for him, neglected as it appeared, in this ridiculous health-related situation, that it was visible and flying for him as it had in so may other spheres of his life.

These stories encompass a lifetime. Many are serious; many are full of fun. Some are expressions of anger or frustration. To some extent, there is a sense of "what comes, will come, what happens will happen. No need to worry. *Aingnamut*, things are as they are." In general, these are relaxed and easy-going letters meant for the pleasure and for the information of the reader, which fortunately for me, happened to be me. Some of Len's stories that do not appear here will be in a future publication. They are a pleasure to read, but seem somewhat more formal than the letters.

Everyone in Labrador can tell a good yarn, but few have the skills to write about their experiences in so explicit a manner. Few had as many correspondents and contacts and connections. Very few cared as much about the whole picture, about the traditions and reputation of the Company, about how a way of life can be was saved through yarns. Len had the ability to perfectly remember words, phrases, colours, details, feelings, faces, expressions, dialects and languages, directions, personalities, sounds, motors and engines, tools, stories, moments, a quality of light. In praise of writers such as Alice Munro, Joyce Carol Oates, writing in the *New York Times Book Review*, said that the best of writers make us see how other people are "dangerously like us ... (giving) ... voice to the voices of their regions" and Len does this so well, whether those he writes of live by the sea, survive famine, build igloos or live next door.

After an evening of listening to and telling stories when he returned for a few days to North West River in 1993, Len wrote, "I realized what the yarns mean to the people, and to me. Times change so fast. Where are the capable hands, the sensitive minds to capture these whispers from the past? Perhaps after I am gone, my child or grandchild ... Perhaps the tales will die with those who can remember them. If so, something will be lost that can never be replaced or recovered."

The same could be said of the places he loved, that can never be recovered. Today the battles for mining rights continue. The new park in the Torngats will bring tourists, and oil will be drilled at Hebron; iat would have broken his heart. He would not go back to Rigolet. Too much was lost, especially after the army was stationed there during the war. But he had them in memory, could return whenever he wished. He could share them with words. In writing so perceptively of their humanity, Len has made the people in his letters come alive again, ensuring that they will not ever die. The more people who read of them, the more alive they will be. In giving his people and places to us, we, his friends, his family, his readers are granted the gift of knowing Leonard Budgell, Servant of The Bay.

—*Claudia Coutu Radmore*

October 22, 2008
Carleton Place, Ontario

ARCTIC TWILIGHT

ONE

From April 1981 until June 1984, I was a Fine Arts student at Queen's University in Kingston. Len is writing from St. Boniface Hospital, St. Boniface, Manitoba.

April 5, 1981

Dear Claudia,

I was touched by your call, but there again is something you would do and the lump in my throat wasn't hospital food.

As Mark Twain said, "The reports of my death have been greatly exaggerated." The Grim Reaper didn't pay a visit.

I don't know what happened. I was painting a ceiling at home, got down from the ladder feeling fine, and suddenly got a pain, not hard, in my chest. Felt a bit disoriented, and irritable. Muriel took my pulse and as it was not regular she called Dr. Bartlett who told me to go to emergency just in case.

So I came here and had more people fussing around. I felt like a chicken on the assembly line. I expected to see Colonel Sanders with his herbs and spices any minute. Forgot that he was already gone where all the chickens went, well not all the way either. He never would have qualified. At his age, more the boiling type, I'd guess.

By the time I was all trussed up, I was feeling as well as always, but I was shot up into intensive care, put on a monitor which had a little TV sort of screen with dinky little bleeps dashing backwards and forward which squealed (the machine, not the bleeps) every time I moved and if it squealed too often, the nurse came in.

After a few days they told me that I had not had a heart attack but I'd had an accelerated beat for some reason. So now I'm in another ward all disconnected from my TV (never even got to see MASH) and waiting for the results of tests. They have taken a lot of my old and rare blood for the tests which will make the Red Cross mad because I promised them some this very day, April 5.

Today I was slated for a stress test to see if the problem was caused by exertion (how dumb can they get). From what I'm told, I stand on a treadmill and run, like a squirrel in a cage, till they decide, acorns, nuts and pine cones gratefully accepted, also unbuttered popcorn. By the way, my writing is not the result of illness. This table wiggles if I breathe. It was supplied, so a label informs me, by Eaton's Contract sales, and whoever would expect an Eaton's table to stand still for an HBC writer.

When I was young, I had my tonsils abducted. Nurses were older people (could that be because I was only ten?) and they wore white things that crackled, especially in the night. One in particular had a face of vinegar, a heart of gold, and the voice of an angel. She also whistled like a spring lark which damaged the angel image for some people, because in them days angels didn't whistle.

Nurses don't rustle any more. They are nylon and polyester, which makes them seem a little different shaped to Miss Austin. They are also very, very young (could that be because I'm a little older now?), and they are incredibly patient and compassionate and their faces are tender and concerned especially when they are working with some of the really sick and elderly people.

Muriel comes every day and spends what must be a boring time, but I tell her that she'll get her reward in Heaven unless she decides to follow me in the other direction. My daughters come every day and relay messages from all over, including Kingston. Miss Preston[1] and Mrs. McKillop[2] sent a card. My steno keeps in touch with my home and will come when she can.

I'm wondering how the word got to you. I intended to write as soon as I was liberated from the green-screen. I expect that you must have heard from Miss Preston. There are a lot of nice people around.

From where I sit, I can see across two rivers and there is Hudson's Bay House, with a tattered corporate flag on the south end. I try to be The Bay's conscience in this regard. I would like to see that all HBC flags are taken down at night and put up again in the morning and are always clean and tidy. Anyhow, at present we are sporting a tattered flag. Perhaps an irate letter from a St. Boniface patient would do the trick.

I see that it is time for stress test. If you don't hear from me later, you'll know I failed it and have gone wherever they send weary squirrels.

Back from Stressville. I went with some apprehension because everyone told me it would be terribly hard. There was a lovely elderly nun there, and I knew from her face that it wouldn't be so bad and it wasn't. I went the full course, and passed. The doctor told me everything was negative and while it indicates the old ticker to be in, as the Old Book Collector says, fair or better condition, we still don't know why I am here.

1   Carol Preston was a staff member of *The Beaver* magazine. Although Len had known her since she was a teenager who had done babysitting for his younger children, he always addressed her as Miss Preston.

2   Jocelyn McKillop was a historian with The Hudson's Bay Company Archives.

All this hullabaloo on the eve of Moosonee[3] is a bit wearing. I hope to be away on time, but if not, I'll bring Ellsworth and Cal here and we'll talk about it.

Did I tell you my Maureen is now senior systems analyst for Hydro and some of the men in the division won't speak to her, but they have to listen and that's what counts. The male sex can be a mite tetchy when their pride is disturbed, bless them.

The first day I was here I saw five lonely geese plodding north against the wind, and it was about sixty kilometres per hour at the time. Guess they just came by to say hello and remind me that "these things too, shall pass."

Much later and on a more stable table, well, you know what I mean. I fell asleep over a recent *Manitoba Nature* magazine and woke to see Dr. Miller standing there reading my magazine and waiting for me to awaken. He said he was letting me go home with a twenty-four-hour tape recorder to monitor my ticker for a while. Kids who go to visit at farms hear strange things. That night, after I had told Mrs. Lowe[4] on the phone about the monitor, she was telling her husband about it. Young Adam, who will be five, heard part at least, and some time later he asked why Uncle Budgell had to have a tape worm for twenty-four hours.

The rest you know. I'm home and feeling fine, and I realize that while I knew about all the nice people in my world, I didn't really know how nice they all were.

So, 73's[5]

Len

Written from Winnipeg, Manitoba, the Budgells' home base when Len was not in Moosonee.

December 4, 1981

Dear Claudia,

Just a note to say I should have put a note in the little parcel of Moosonee high bush cranberry jelly I posted a day or so ago. I hope a little on your Christmas turkey will be what's needed to get you headed that way next summer.

I'm listening to the *Messiah* and writing. I remember so many years ago I heard it in Notre Dame in Montreal. That was the first time I'd ever seen as well as heard it, and it left a great impression. A war had just ended and I'd returned from a rather hard time at Repulse Bay where the only music we had was an ancient recording of the *Messiah*, which old Father Henri used to play for me. He is described in De Poncins' book[6] as a saint, and if I have ever been privileged to meet one, I will call Father Henri that man.

He used to start the incredibly old phonograph and reverently sit with his hands pointed like a steeple against his chin, and he hardly moved except to change the records. I don't think I knew what rev-

3 Len was manager at this time of Moosonee Transport Limited (MTL), which was operated by The Hudson's Bay Company out of Moosonee, Ontario. MTL took supplies by barge to several communities on James Bay and Hudson Bay. Len went to Moosonee each spring and stayed until fall. Ellsworth and Cal, from Newfoundland, were MTL employees.

4 Mrs. Phyllis Lowe, Len's secretary at Hudson Bay House.

5 A symbol used by radio operators, meaning "regards."

6 Jean-Pierre Gontrain de Montaigne de Poncin, *Kabloona* (Reynal and Company, Paris, 1941; reprinted by Time Life Books, 1965)

erence was till I met Father Henri. For sure I never before met a clergyman who lived his religion quite so completely. Perhaps I cannot believe as he did, but I can admire and respect someone who can believe so completely and who can live a life of poverty and hardship in such enfolding faith.

We spent a very hard winter together. There was no food to be had except what we got from the land and not much of that. There was hunger. People died. There was no air relief in those days. One day I helped the father and a young boy lay a poor old lady to her rest in the usual tomb of stones. She had been ill a long time and no doubt would have died, but I saw her in an igloo which was completely unheated the night before. I had no means of heating my own place but I was young, healthy and not suffering. I knew that far to the south, the Canadian army was spending untold money on Operation Musk Ox,[7] using ground and air equipment without heed to cost or quantity, and I was frustrated and furious that this small group of people must suffer so through no fault of their own.

And the father, while he agonized for them and had given them every comfort he had, and while he wept at every death, had a serene belief it was the will of his God and that good would come.

When I was at Repulse Bay there was a wonderful old man. He was still in good shape but his legs were failing and he could not see himself getting slower and slower and finally sitting around an igloo or in front of a tent for the rest of his time.

One day he came to see me. He had his winter's catch of fur, mostly white fox, beautifully cleaned and dressed, even though it was a bad year and we had no fuel. He paid a small debt he owed the Company and he bought a few things. He left a balance on the books, and said when the ship came in summer, I was to see his wife got a new tent.

---

7   Operation Musk Ox (February to May 1946) gave the Canadian military experience in living and moving over long distances in the icy conditions of the Arctic. The 3000-mile expedition in capped armoured snowmobiles studied "winter operations generally in the Arctic weather zone."

That didn't sound right, so I asked him if he was going away, perhaps to hunt for a long period. He said only, "I will walk." Claudia, he took the things he had bought and dropped them off at his igloo, and walked out into a dreadful storm, straight across Repulse Bay. His wife, much younger, sat in the igloo and said never a word. He knew and she knew that she could stay alive, she could easily re-marry. She didn't want him to go but she would not try to prevent him. The priest, too, he knew, and he prayed to his god, but he never condemned the old man to hell for suicide. It took tremendous courage on all sides, terrible cold courage, magnificent courage.

When the storm died, we went out hunting for him but it was weeks later that he was found, many miles away. He had found a piece of pressure ice about waist high and he had rested his arms on it and waited for the enemy that he had tested so often to come to him. And when he came and the old man could no longer hold his head up, he threw his hood off and laid his face on the hard ice and died there, fully aware all the time that what he did was for the better good. One less mouth to feed in a starvation camp, one less man that would soon be unable to sustain himself. In all his concern, this was the one thing he could not face, having someone support him, being a burden.

When they brought him in, Father Henri was there with me and he laid his hand on the old man's sightless eyes in a gesture of simple love. He said no words but they were not needed. He welcomed him home. The old man had been one of his flock, and even in the priest's strict code, he would not have it that the man had sinned. Does it not say "Greater love hath no man."

Father Henri is dead, buried in the barren country he worked in most of his life. I hope his mission saw fit to mark his grave with "Well Done."

I talk too much. Today I got up before daylight and drove up to the Shoal Lake area. The water birds have all gone but I sat near a huge windrow of trees that have been slashed in a land clearing operation.

There are hundreds of snowshoe rabbits there enjoying the shelter and the food. They are white as snow, though there is no snow on the ground, so they sit there with complete faith in their invisibility while rough-legged hawks circle above...

There were two eagles, golden adult birds, and four or five hawks. The air boundaries seemed to be definitely defined, each bird barely intersecting but never overlapping the other, the hawks perhaps a hundred feet higher than the others.

The eagles banked gracefully and aloofly away. They looked as though they were not moving a muscle, just gliding around, but with binoculars I could see the minute adjustments of wing and tail feathers which formed the perfect air foil, and all the while their heads turned and their lovely fierce eyes searched the ground.

One reason I went to Shoal Lake was to see deer. The hunting season was just over and they are very shy, but at sunrise two came out of the trees and stood perhaps a hundred yards away. The frost from their night breathing had coated the long guard hairs on their backs and they stood between me and the sun in a most delicate halo. Have you ever seen how they can activate each and every muscle separately? They stood there missing the warmth they had enjoyed from one another while they rested, and I could see the little shudderings and could almost feel the delicious content they were feeling in the warm sun. Then a ray hit the lens of my binoculars and they were gone, leaping high over the stumps and windfalls but more in high spirits than panic.

I found their beds still warm and steaming, and in the crushed swamp grass I could smell that attractive musk that jumping deer have.

When I was young I spent days watching wildlife in the most beautiful valley I ever knew, Tororak, in North Labrador. There was so much land, so much space, and thank God, that space still exists there. But a day here shows how the space here is shrinking, and soon there will be an ugly aluminium smelter near Shoal Lake. There will be cars and people and bottles and cans, and the church will not be allowed to die quietly. There will be paved roads and fences and the eagles and mink and deer will be forced to move farther north so the people will have prosperity and will take their children to see deer and eagles in the zoo.

And the old and cranky people like me will be ungrateful and perverse and not see that it is good.

Later:
After my time in the woods, I got an axe and split a bunch of firewood. It was a bit frosty, and wood splits easily when it's cold. There is not much to do with one's head but think, and watching white wood split cleanly easily brings all sorts of thoughts crowding around. I like to split wood. In my time I must have split several thousand or more. I wonder how close I got to a million at a time when a million was a top number, because no one counted split hunks of wood, or capelin, or smelts, herring even. I'll never know.

One nice old man used to count a lot of things, like the number of times he'd jig a hook up and down, the number of oar strokes to go from his fishing station to Rigolet. Once he counted our strokes from North West River to Rigolet. He and Hannah, his wife, rowed it, ninety miles. Couldn't add it up because he could barely read and write, so he counted one hundred for every finger on his right hand, and made a mark on the thwart. Then his left hand and same thing in a tally, like so, 11. When he'd gone around five times, he had 11111, which of course equalled five hundred, but he couldn't count that far. So he rowed and marked and marked and rowed for ninety miles, and when he got to Rigolet, he had one of the Eskimo boys figure it out, but it was no good because he had absolutely no conception of the final figure. Too bad. Old Uncle Tom Blake was a great old man. Another time he tallied the loaves of bread his wife baked in a year...

Len is in Montreal at a Hudson's Bay board meeting. O'Halloran is the leprechaun Len has "given" to me.

January 18, 1982

Dear Claudia,

I'm on the twenty-sixth floor of the Hyatt Regency and my room looks south and west. The snow has stopped and the lights are all spread out for me as far as I can see. I am happy. There are ways I could be happier, but these you'll get to see.

To begin at the start, it was a good day. I think you and O'Halloran were there in two of the empty chairs in that big boardroom that looks over the St. Lawrence and the Seaway and the docks from thirty-eight storeys up. Makes it hard to attend to the business at hand, but one must. We have had an exceptional year and it was nice to listen to congratulations and hear the figures come off the accountant's tongue. Mr. Bell, who likes to jest, asked me how I felt, getting the company involved in a profit tax situation, so I said I'd never been criticized for that before and put it down to inexperience.

I told him, too, that I had had very adequate help and the Queen's picture is always a nice reward. I had asked for a bonus for the boys who don't get overtime, and at Christmas they got an extra $2000 to add to the first $3000, so no one is unhappy. I was very pleased that all my requests were given the green light. I'm not sure till Arctic gets their wage recommendation in exactly what increase the boys will be getting, but it will be over 10 percent. That brings my men up to, even a bit beyond, the oil country people and that's what I have been shooting for. Also got money to revamp a trailer for a recreation area for them, and a TV and possibly electronic games. We'll also have water and sewer and showers etc. and if there is room, we'll move our coffee shack over.

They have agreed to confirm Jackie[8] in her job at a man's wage. Makes us the first equal opportunity employer in Moosonee. The accountant said, "Are you sure that's wise?" and I said, "Tell me why not. If I gave the job to a man, he'd get equal wages with the other men and possibly wouldn't be of much use to me." He said he got my point, but I know he still wonders.

I also asked that all accounts payable be handled out of Moosonee and they agreed. Another job for Jackie which will make her happy.

I left the place pretty well satisfied when Mr. Bell suggested that since Cal and Ellsworth are key men and vital to the operation, that we pay them the winter retainer. I probably looked like the cat that had cream on its face at the end of the session. What do I gotta do in return? Just promise to be around a while longer, which I had planned anyway. Oh yes, and take a young executive to Moosonee as required, to show him a bit about the business.

Back in Winnipeg:
Seen from the air, you have a lovely white carpet in your country,[9] which complements the dark water. The water shows all sorts of interesting patterns of small ice looking like they are clustering together to keep warm. Lake Ontario looks big and severe and impersonal from way up high, but it's only a pretence because as the plane moves along, the sun skips across the water creating a smile Lake Ontario wide. I was sorry for a minute when we lost the lake and headed up toward Sudbury, but the trees were nice, all dressed up in brand new snow. I could imagine them on the hills and in the valleys modestly trying to keep their skirts down against the winter wind that blusters around and really is too careless about the prim little trees. The little streams, a lot of them still unfrozen, slip quietly along in their twisty paths and

8   Jackie Stevenson. Len had known Jackie since she was a child growing up in Moosonee. In 1982, she became the office manager at MTL.

9   When Len was flying back to Winnipeg from his meeting in Montreal, the plane was low enough that he could see the landscape of the area around Kingston, where I was at university.

now and then two come together and hold hands. It's nice to see them snuggle down quietly when you know it's only a matter of time when nature will take away the white blanket and they'll laugh and tickle one another through another long warm summer.

But Claudia, in the dark of winter even, it's possible to follow a brook and listen as you go. After a while you'll hear a subdued gurgle away under the snow, and it's so nice and companionable to stand there in a completely silent world and hear that little chuckle away down deep in her chest. You feel she knows you are there and is playing hide and seek and giggling because you can't find her, never dreaming that you don't want to, that all you need is her voice that contrasts so sweetly with the cold silence above.

I like white on trees, on the ice, in contrast to the black leafless skeletons of the poplars and birches, dressing and accentuating the green conifers. Yes, white is nice. White is a feminine colour: white dress, chubby knees of a four year old, little knees that are scratched and marked but exquisite, on a pretty girl in warm summer, on my lovely old Aunt Bella, covering a long black dress, a snowy apron. Aunt Bella of the smooth apple cheeks and soft lips, who was always there when I was little, who helped me through so many childhood heartbreaks which are funny and poignant now, who was there to smile when I brought home my first goose, who held my hands in her tiny cool ones when I left home and made me realize that no matter what, she and my mother would always be there. I haven't gone back for many years, but they are there, Claudia, waiting.

I used to love being in the office at Rigolet when they were making up mail to go by boat or dog team to the far ends of the earth as far as I was concerned. St. John's mostly, but now and then Winnipeg or London, England, and every letter had a drop of red sealing wax on the flap and it was pressed with a round stamp with the Company's coat of arms.

I would be given a pile of envelopes and a box of Sea Dog Matches (made in Sweden and showing a sea dog on the box which looked like a tuskless walrus, while the brightly printed cards in every huge wood case showed a parrot—he had a match in his beak, and for many years I wondered about the connection). I'd spread out the envelopes and drop the hot wax on them and take care to get a good impression on each one.

That wax had an incredible smell. Very infrequently now, in a lawyer's office perhaps, I see the hot wax drop on a document and smell that odour. I just need to close my eyes and I'm back in that office with my father and his clerks, feel the heat of the big iron box stove and the faint scent of smoke and deerskin and newly dried fur, tobacco, and birch wood, and over it all the exotic smell of the hot wax.

I'd come in after bringing wood for the office stove, and because I was small, I could squeeze in between the desks with my back to the stove to do my stamping. It got so hot there it's a wonder I didn't catch fire or melt to a little spot of grease on the floor. The thought used to come that if I did melt one day, all that would be left would be buttons, my big bone-handled pocket knife, and the brass HBC stamp.

It was good to be there just helping and enjoying that particular time of day when the store had closed. It was dark outside and the clerks would stand around the stove and warm up after a day in an unheated store and talk. They nearly all smoked pipes and I'd watch the different ways they prepared the pipe and how they smoked it. I probably had lungs black as Satan's Sunday boots early in life.

They used to make dog harness and make and repair nets while waiting for the supper bell. I learned very early from Will, the foreman, to splice rope, and usually it was an art the clerks didn't have. So any splicing got tossed over to me, and I'd work so hard to get it exactly right so that neither my dad nor Will could pick up an item and say, "Who thought he spliced this?" Every evening after school I had all the pups to feed and put in their shed for the night, kindling to get for the house stoves and wood for the office, so old James, the cooper, would have all he wanted for the night. Then I'd go to all my favourite places. Out to the dog food house where Edgar and Fred were cooking the huge cauldrons of meal and fish or meat over the open fire while fifty or sixty tired and hungry dogs lay with their noses on their paws outside waiting. Then to the net loft where Will, and whoever his helper was, were repairing the huge salmon nets against next year's fishery.

They each had a big kerosene lantern on a nail, and they would reach up, never looking, and unhook the lantern as they moved along and hook it up on another nail near the work. They used two fingers to lift the nets so that the light fell on any small rents, which they'd cut into a three lead and repair in seconds. They were so deft and so sure and the lantern would not have stopped swinging, when it was unhooked and moved again.

Will had wonderfully even, white teeth and they'd gleam in the soft light as he looked at me and smiled. He was strong and gentle and a master with tools or machinery. He was mostly, I guess, Eskimo, and one of the most handsome people I ever saw. When Peter worked there, he was black and silent and hook-nosed, and always had a big crooked stem pipe clamped in his teeth, nearly always unlit. He'd smile but hardly ever speak, and when he did it was a rumble away down deep. Our Newfoundland dog always growled when she heard Peter speaking. I'm sure she understood his growls. Will did too. I didn't.

Last of all I'd go see James in the cooperage. No workshop anywhere could have more for a boy than a cooperage. Then to the office to stay with my dad and the boys till Mrs. Flowers started the huge brass bell clanging and everyone went to supper. I would like to sit you down in those days to see and smell and finally sit at the crowded table. After my dad muttered the grace, which I never did understand, we could eat. The little fellow near the end of the oval table that sat twelve or fourteen, with the red flushed face, stained hands and broken nails, that's me.

My mother would frown at the way I managed to destroy clothes, but she knew how I loved everything about that magic place and she never came down hard on me. Sometimes I'd have to wash my hands a second time, that's all. I think I must have been an odd-ball kid.

Written from Moosonee. I was planning to visit Moosonee later in the summer.

April 1982

Dear Claudia,

This pad had forty pages of instructions for Bob Brydges who will relieve me when I leave on holiday. If you get detailed instructions on how to make a payroll for Mike Blueboy and Robbie Koosees and others, don't worry. One way or another they'll get paid.

Robbie is someone special. He has a dozen or so words of English and a most heart-warming grin. He is five foot and a little, almost the same wide, and is exactly what the traders used to look for in canoe-men: strong, tireless, and good tempered. He works steadily at whatever he is given to do and leaves nothing unfinished. When the geese come in the fall, his soul hears them and he has to be away out there on the mud flats. Robbie could have free board and lodging in Loblaw's but he'd still have to go goose hunting. You'll like Robbie, I promise. Jimmy Sack too, he likes birds and knows where the robins' nests are.

Speaking of birds, and your sandpiper-like one with the funny walk? Was he a yellow legs? Did he have a long bill and a curious bobbing walk? We'll find one here and you'll tell me. I hope we can see our osprey take his thrilling dive into the water and come up holding a fish. We have a few nests here but they rear fewer and fewer young birds. The DDT they get in the fish down south in the winter makes the egg shells paper thin and they won't stand the weight of the bird. It would only mean a few more mosquito bites for tourists and we could still have our ospreys.

A pair nested for thirty years where my father could see them from his office window, and it was worth a stinging rebuke to go too close during nesting time. Many times I have seen him sitting watching a graceful form gliding slowly back and forth over the cove, then suddenly the wings would fold and the bird would hurtle to the water and it was rare indeed that he missed. My dad would clear his throat and maybe wipe his eyes and go back to his work. I knew that each descent was like a fierce untamed hand on his heart, creating a desire to be one with that wonderful free being in the sky.

The nest was in the top of a big tamarack, and over the years they had laid layer after layer of sticks and grass till it was about six feet high. One spring someone carelessly let a huge sheet of brown paper (that used to line the inside of sugar casks) fly away in a wind and it became entangled in the branches near the nest. The birds hadn't laid their eggs yet but they had returned. My dad worried and worried so I said I'd try to go up and clear it away.

He went with me and we paddled across and landed just in front of the tree. It was huge and the bottom branches were twenty or more feet up. The trunk was too massive for me to reach around but we had a light line and by tying a rock to the end we managed to get it over a limb and I climbed up. Once in the lower branches it was easy going and I soon reached the nest.

As I said, it was six feet high and built in a fork of the tree. It was more a platform than a nest, about eight feet in diameter and secure from any predator except an eagle. There were literally hundreds of fish skeletons there. I guess the parents could pick up and drop off a fish any time, so the youngsters never had a worry about food. There were also fair-sized stones that must have been brought there by the birds, I can't think why unless for the young ones to sharpen or wear away the beaks if they grew too fast. There was a thin sliver of wood which said "HBC–UI–Outfit 260," which delighted my dad when I told him. I asked if he wanted it and I know he did but he said don't disturb a thing.

I gathered the paper up and rolled it into a ball, threw it down, and was carefully climbing back out of the nest, when I saw a shadow and there was the osprey. He was balancing on a current of air, hardly moving, but I could see the minute adjustments of wings and feathers. He'd side-slip a bit and the lower feathers would become erect and hold him. It was exquisite. And his eyes, wide and yellow and unblinking; he just stared at me. I was in his territory and for a moment I thought he might strike. His big, partly exposed claws looked dangerous, as did his savage curved beak, but he meant me no harm. He just hung there while his mate circled a hundred feet away. Such a lovely sleek bird, the epitome of power and grace. Soon, if we don't help, they'll be gone and I'll have an ache where there should be joy. There are lots of lovely things left but it's human to mourn the things we have lost by our own carelessness. Must go, someone at the door.

And I never did explain 73's. It's a symbol used by radio operators, meant to be sent all in one. (Operators don't say dot and dash, they say dit and dat.) The symbol goes *dat, dat, dit, dit, dit, dit, dit, dit, dat, dat.* Say it fast, it has a swing, looks long but can be sent in a second. Broken down it can be -- ··· (7) ··· -- (3), so we send the symbol when we talk on a key and write 73's when we write a letter. What does it mean? I think the best word is "regards," but if you know your friend, it's a comfortable, friendly way to end a conversation or a letter. 73's (See what I mean?),
Len

June 4, 1982

Dear Claudia,

Did I tell you we were going up into Quebec? Now Montreal tells me the plan is to leave here Monday, go to Rupert's House, where Mr. Radisson wintered so many years ago, then to Paint Hills, then Fort George, then back here, to start all over again and go back as far as

Rupert's, East main and Paint Hills. At least the weather has warmed up again.

The breakfast dishes are looking reproachful so I'll be away. The weatherman says you are going to have a nice weekend. Enjoy it with your family, spend two minutes listening to a tree grow. They talk all their lives even as long as they stand as masts in a ship. They do, honest. I knew a lovely old ship, the *Saladdin*.

Can I tell you a little bit about the *Saladdin*? I won't take long, I promise. She's always been special, since I was five or six when I saw her first.

We were travelling on North Labrador on a little ship, a steamer, called the *Senef*, and my brother George was born on board. We ran short on coal and were anchored at a place called Turnavik Islands. It's a corruption of a delightful Eskimo word.

There wasn't a lot of space on the *Senef* and my parents were busy with the new baby and my two little sisters, so I didn't get out on deck as much as I'd have liked. Then one calm sunny day my dad came down and asked me if I wanted to see a square-rigged ship come in.

The *Saladdin* (I wonder about the spelling too) was coming to bring salt to the fishermen and load dry fish for Spain. When we got on deck, I could see her four tall masts over a low island but couldn't see her hull yet. There was absolutely no wind on the water but a bit aloft, and she was moving slowly with all her lower sails clewed up and only topsails and royals drawing.

I could see the crew away up in the masts and on the yards waiting to clew the upper canvas when she came to anchor. Captain Burgess of the *Senef* said to me, "There's a Cartet for you if you can name the sails she has down." Cartet was a huge raisin and dark chocolate bar from England. I could reel the names off instantly, after all, she only had the uppers on, and it was like the names of car parts to a modern kid. I got my bar.

And, Claudia, I can still feel the joy that was in me when her hull came around the island. She was partly loaded with salt. Moving so gracefully and without a sound, she turned and came slowly towards us, and as she came abreast her topsail yards were level with the top of the *Senef*'s bridge.

There was a sailor standing casually on the foot rope at the end of the royal yard and leaning against the huge spar. He was filling his pipe and gave me a wink and a smile as he passed. Perhaps I never envied anyone as I did that man, standing on a thin rope hooked under the heels of his leather sea boots and filling his pipe as though he was standing on solid ground, not forty feet of thin air to the next yard.

She was a clipper ship and her steep and lovely bow was complimented by her long bow-sprit. She had only one jib up, and as she turned it fluttered like a bird's wing. She was salt-stained and tired-looking, all the way across the miles of water from Cadiz, but she was lovely. At one time she had been a grain ship from Australia to the Continent and got into the salt trade when steamships took over the grain.

As she came closer and closer, her bow-sprit came almost on board of the *Senef*, and there, on its very end, was the tail of a shark, nailed there on her maiden voyage years before for good luck. That was sixty years ago come August, and if I had your gift I could draw from memory every detail of that dry, shrunken object. I'd heard so many yarns about shark's tails on bow-sprits but had never seen one. Now I had, and one more memory was put safely away.

Her figurehead was a dignified Eastern potentate with folded arms. He ignored the sooty little *Senef* but I think his lip may have curved in a smile at the little boy almost breathless with joy hanging on to the bridge sail. I never forgot that ship.

Years later, when I was on another ship and we went into St. Anthony, there by the wharf was the *Saladdin*. She was old and run-down, hauling the most unlovely of cargos, coal, but her lines were still beautiful. She was waiting to sail and no one was around when I went on board. Her rigging was ragged and uncared for, her bright work was scarred and bruised, her decks were splintered and covered with coal dust, her sails were poorly furled and the reef points had cows' tails in them. Her spars were innocent of paint or dressing. I climbed up and walked out on the same tall bow-sprit that had filled me with joy and saw the big wrought nail heads that had held the shark's tail. It was gone, probably into the uncaring sea some dark night as she battled along under low canvas.

She was dying, Claudia. I stood by her tall, straight main mast and put my ear near the fife rail and I could hear her suffering. There is sound in all sail ships; the little noises that tell you she's sound and strong and the comforting squeaks and creakings that let you know she is elastic and can give to the sea and survive any storm. But there are sounds too that tell you her heart is broken, that she has lost the will to fight, and the *Saladdin* had those sounds.

I stood there and remembered when I first saw her, and when her sails were white and her masts and spars were trim and beautiful, and I knew they had killed her with heavy loads of coal because it was war time and any bottom could get cargo. The faster steamships got the clean goods and went in convoys, the wind ships took the coal and ore and sailed alone. I knew she would not last much longer and I hated the people that had brought her to that state and who, when it suited them, would abandon her on a smelly mud flat some place to rot.

All the little sounds told me she would soon die. That's what I mean when I say a tree talks all its days, whether as a straight spar or a curved plank deep in a hull.

A few days later in Halifax the papers said that the "coaster" *Saladdin* had gone down off the Newfoundland coast in a storm. I was glad she didn't have to suffer the indignity of a wrecker's yard. I phoned the radio station and asked them to say the "clipper *Saladdin*" if they repeated the broadcast and an understanding man promised they would. Some beautiful things live forever—some die.

June 8, 1982

Dear Claudia,

Spent a lovely morning wandering around. Mr. Radisson might be surprised at what has happened to his Fort Charles. The Quebec government, via the Hydro, has spent eight million dollars on a settlement of perhaps 1500 people in two years and is still spending. The result is a horrible scar on the landscape.

It's a planned development for people who don't really want it and who don't know how to live with it, where garbage disposal is out the door or window. When they were nomads or semi-nomads that worked because there were only a few tents in each group and they weren't in one place long and they didn't have the tin can. Can you imagine a street paved with tin cans? They have the money and we saw people waiting in line to buy soft drinks by the case at a buck a can.

When I first saw Rupert's, a number of years ago, it was a tidy little settlement, mostly HBC buildings with a few tents on the river bank. Most of the population lived out on the land and made their own living. Now no one is on the land and the settlement lives on relief and Hydro compensation. I'd like to know how anyone can justify what's happened.

We got back around 7 p.m. or later. Old Ash Cutler, our cook, had two steaks ready and when we got back to the trailer, they were in the pan, so all's well that ends well.

The bay is full of ice, a lot of it broken up into the world's biggest jigsaw puzzle. It was calm and clear and we were at fifteen hundred feet which is a bit lower than Air Canada's average. There was the odd seal lying in the sun on his piece of puzzle and perhaps wondering how to put it all back together. Or maybe he wasn't and was sleeping quietly while the world went to pieces all around him, which I suppose brings him up, or maybe down, to a level with some humans.

Anyway we had a lovely day. Didn't accomplish much but found that a small puppy had arrived at the trailer, captivated old Ash, and was warm, sleeping on the porch on what looked to be a pair of Bill's coveralls. He looked as though he had found his niche and was prepared to stay on. Ash gave me a long, acted-out story, of how the "pore little feller" almost crawled up to the door, and with an expiring breath, scratched weakly on the step and barked feebly for help. He could have been telling the truth too, but I'll have to say that the pup made a remarkable recovery on that one meal. Ash looks like Uriah Heep but isn't a bit "'umble." He is a great mess hall cook, though. You'll eat one of his meals when you come. He feels that no part of a plate should be visible when he serves a meal. You know the plate has to be there. Your job is to shovel the grub away and find it. Now I think of it, Ash looks more like Punch than Uriah Heep, but you'll like him.

He told me last night the boys play so many tricks on him that "I'll go right off my eid," but he loves every minute of it and the boys would massacre anyone who tried to take advantage of Ash.

Looking forward to your visit. Take care, have fun. See, I can leave a few lines blank...

Len is in Winnipeg to complete paperwork for his retirement. I had visited Moosonee and returned to Kingston. His birthday is on August 7.

August 6, 1982

Dear Claudia,

Your letter and card came today, special delivery... I am truly fortunate to have a friend like you and while I am well aware of the affection we share, I am also very happy to have it confirmed. You are a very special person.

Perhaps in some traditional way, this should be a birthday for reflection, for thinking, because it will sure precipitate some changes in my life. I'm very happy with things the way they are, with the people I know and love. Perhaps old tradition will hit me one day, but I'm not too worried. As I told you in Moosonee, I'm content with my world, very content, and more than happy about the special people in it.

So today I shall appear before the bar and sign up for the rocking chair money. Then I'll have lunch with Miss Preston and Mrs. McKillop, and I wish you could be there. I'll tell them about your trip, we'll talk about you.

Coming home on the plane the other night, I sat next to an eighteen-month-old charmer, who soon climbed onto my knee because I had a window seat and she liked the wing light she could see blinking. She ate my dessert and drank most of my milk. Her mother said they had eaten in Toronto, but the baby didn't remember that, so she sampled Air Canada's cheese and crackers too. The mother was tired and put her head back and closed her eyes while we read books, put shoes on when they fell off, and for a while we bundled in a pink blanket and almost fell asleep. She was blonde and blue-eyed and so infinitely precious. I passed her in the airport and paused to say goodbye and she put those small arms around my neck and said, "Goobye, Poppy," and there was a bursting feeling in my heart that Doctor Miller couldn't diagnose that caused the terminal to be terribly blurry, and I, straight from a week of happy memories, was glad again, so glad that there is so much pleasure to be had in this world.

Yesterday I went out to Maureen's to help her mark a trail for a ride, in aid of a children's ward. There were a lot of trees across the path and we removed them with Stuart's help and his brother's four-wheel drive truck. Then Maureen and I went back to mark the various turns so the riders won't get lost. I went one way and she went another. It was the first time since I came home that I'd been alone for any length of time. It's nice seeing everyone and talking and catching up but I needed some space, some quiet time.

The Interlake is crowded with deer. Everywhere I saw the delicate prints of their feet. I went in to the north pasture quietly and I saw them like brown ghosts, here and there, glimpses of brown smooth skins, long graceful legs, the occasional white flag of an alarmed animal. After it grew quiet, I rested on a pile of hay bales that was very close to the thick bush and after a long while, two young deer came very close. They were last year's animals that had apparently not mated, or if they had, they had not produced a fawn, or had lost it. They had no idea I was there and they stood close together and she put her head across his neck and he tipped his head back till he was looking directly at the sky and he gently imprisoned her head against his back with his horns which were still small and immature looking. They stood that way for quite some time, just being together. When he released her, they caressed one another's faces with their tongues, and they copulated briefly, not in the fiery impetuous way they do during mating. More as though they were giving expression to some great feeling. It was much too early for them to be mating and I would guess that there will be no fawn. There was an aching beauty in the almost ceremonial act that I wish you could have seen. I felt as though I had witnessed the conception of Bambi. I had no idea that deer could or would mate outside the regular season, but they did, almost as if it were a familiar happening. I will have to talk to Lands and Forests about it.

I've seen many animals mate but never before with such tenderness and apparent feeling those deer exhibited. I could not disturb them by leaving so I waited till they had gone, side by side, into the forest. I was late getting home, but I was very happy.

TWO

Moosonee, August 31, 1982

Dear Claudia,

Good morning, the coffee's on. It's dark outside. In one month the mornings and evenings have drawn in, and fall is here. The swallows are gone, their little apartment houses on the poles down at the office are empty. Their summer rent of pleasure has been paid and we miss our little tourists. Jimmy says, "I miss him, the small birds, when he go home." They are all gone, the warblers and robins and the rest. The blue heron who lived on Butler picked up his long legs and trailed them south a while ago. A few blackbirds squabble over the mountain ash berries and a disconsolate crow or two caws without conviction in the mornings.

The emperor of fall and winter, the snowy owl, sits in the trees around the sanctuary, remote and aloof, while his dusky chamberlain, the raven, soars over the river on ebon wings, waiting to claim the territory that will be his when winter's long cold fingers grip the land. He has no insulated feet like the ptarmigan, no heavy down like Ookpik the owl. He has no apparent protection aside from his thin feathers. He is almost a tropical being, but he stays in the Arctic and survives. He is a carrion eater in a land where carrion is hard to find. He has a beak to tear putrid flesh, and for months he subsists on frozen food in minute quantities. Many, many are the days in the winter his hoarse croak and his incredibly musical "clink" are the only sound in a frozen sterile world, his black shadow the only visible moving thing on a dead planet. I don't believe nature meant him to live this way but he does, alone.

Once I was travelling in a fierce blizzard and saw, almost felt, his presence as he flew silently by. He was close enough to touch, close enough to see his stark profile, see his head turned to observe my dogs, myself, then with an imperceptible twist of his primary feathers, he was gone. Where? No one knows. A being of mystery and strength.

I must tell you... Jackie went for the mail yesterday morning and a few minutes later burst into the office: "There is a white whale near the barges."

And there he was, Claudia, alone, a big fellow, and we stood in the window and watched for half an hour or more. He'd go up almost to Hennessey's dock then back down past ours, then back. He would surface every half minute or so, except when a canoe went by, then he'd stay down till it had passed.

The air was cool enough so you could see his little jet of steam as he breathed. It was calm, and standing outside we could hear his breath as he exhaled. He was so graceful. Now and then he'd lift as he surfaced, perhaps to give himself a better view. Then the lovely, graceful flukes would be exposed. The men working outside were silent and stood watching, each and every one under the spell of that white body, perhaps each in his own way envious of the freedom and strength of that white wraith of the waters. When he had finally gone, Jackie sighed and left the office without a word.

Of all the white creatures that inhabit the world, I love the Arctic fox, the ptarmigan and the hare who usually live their lives out in a relatively narrow circle. But the three wanderers, those white spirits, the owl, the polar bear, and the beluga make their ceaseless pilgrimages across the frigid sky, over the sterile land and under the frozen water, never stopping except to rest. Those solitary white ghosts carry all the mystery of three elements and all the secrets of the remote places they have seen. Silent, unagressive, they come and they vanish. From where to where? The land is big, there is room yet. But if the day ever comes that we humans leave them no room to follow their trails of mystery, then we shall have done a harm that can never be expiated and we shall have damaged our own souls. I wish you could have been here to see him.

The last day of August, the last day I shall work for HBC, August 5, 1935–August 31, 1982. When I was young I could look at my dad's record, at Jimmy Dickers', at Will's, and at John's, and wonder what it could be like to spend so many of one's years in the service of one firm. They spent theirs on Labrador. I was even luckier perhaps. I was permitted to spend mine in a much wider circle—so many places, so many things, so many joys, and enough disappointments to preserve a balance.

I think now that the highlights had to be the people all along the way—the wonderful people—so many, some just touched, some with whom the bonds are stronger, and some, the few, the individuals, loved. Somewhere it says, "Lay not up treasure on earth." If that is a commandment, then I have failed, because while my trail has certainly not been over roads of gold, I have laid up a treasure on earth, precious gems. I think I'm happy with my life. I know of no one I have deliberately harmed, I know of one only whom I cannot meet and speak with, and I do not hold myself to be wholly responsible.

So, today I'm freed from my forty-seven-year contract and I don't really feel much of anything. Quite a few scraps of paper, the parties of the first and second part etc. Some I have, some lie on the bottom of Hudson's Strait.[10] But at the moment I must pick up a few dishes and head for the office. Perhaps I can beat Jackie to the broom this morning. It must be my turn by now.

Reminds me of a yarn my dad used to tell. One spring he hired Willie Skey, an Eskimo, to help repair boats and bark nets. He also hired Willie's wife, Mary, to cook for the men. One of Mary's duties was to ring the bell to get up, to come to breakfast, to go back to work, etc. all day till quitting time at six. The bells never varied, except Sunday, when they were only for meals. Any bell out of schedule meant fire.

So, on Mary's first day, my dad explained it all to her, with the help of a clock. Ring here for breakfast, etc. About mid-morning, bang went the bell. Fire!! And men went all over looking for fire, couldn't find any. So someone rushed up to the men's kitchen to ask Mary, how come the bell. Mary said, "Willie must be hungry now." My dad had to explain all over, the bell was rung by the clock, not Willie's stomach.

Many times I heard my dad say when things got sort of tangled, "Willie must be hungry now." How does that refer to Jackie and the office broom? I dunno, just reminds me is all. Have a good day.

You mentioned my dad in your letter. Yes, we are a lot alike. He was short, red-headed when he was young, but I only remember the little halo of white hair above his ears. He was a Company man, a fair man, a man with a temper that flared, especially when he saw cruelty or carelessness. He was outspoken and hated pretension. He was

---

10 The *Nascopie* was a 2500-ton steamer-icebreaker named after the First Nations people of Quebec and Labrador. Built in Scotland in 1911, by 1912 she set sail on the first of thirty-four voyages through the Hudson Strait to supply The Hudson's Bay Company northern posts. She also played key roles in both world wars. In 1947, the *Nascopie* sank, with many of Len's belongings, after striking a sharply rising uncharted reef off Beacon Island at the entrance to Cape Dorset harbour, Baffin Island.

Irish and Scots and Royalist and many times was torn between them. I knew him in all his moods and I've seen him terribly angry, and perhaps like me, like a lot of us, unjust in the heat of anger, but I've seen him looking into a robin's nest and wiping his eyes.

He loved nature, especially birds, and over the years allowed a valuable pile of wood to rot because a horned owl chose to nest there and come back year after year and he could never allow himself to disturb her. I remember his face when an American collector asked permission to take two eggs for display some place. That particular bird never laid more than three. That someone would destroy two he couldn't understand. He invited the man for dinner because, as he told him, "...you are about the strangest fellow I ever did see..." That was a part of my life that was very significant to me, then and now. My dad was a bit of a mystic. He'd have understood you in the leaves. He dreamed dreams too. He would have taken you to all his favourite haunts. He liked people and saw so much in them.

Sometimes if I catch a sudden glimpse of myself in a mirror, I see him and I feel good. People say that I look like him and it pleases me. I was at the retirement dinner of a highly placed HBC man and he said in his speech that as a green clerk, he was sent to Rigolet where George Budgell taught him how to be a Company man, how to be a good trader and how to the King and the Flag. He said that in all his time he had never met a man who was more convinced of the value of those things.

Moosonee, September 3, 1982

Dear Claudia,

Have often wondered where that salutation came from. We say it on all sorts of letters and it's only a word, but only when it's written to a friend does it seem to have its real meaning.

The trees are turning. Maidments Creek is, for some reason, usually first. You should see the splashes of colour there. Right now there is still a lot of vivid green, but there are blooms of sharp red and yellow that almost affront the eye in their brightness, and soon they will tone down and the rest of the trees will change their dress to conform.

Have you ever paddled up the Rideau in fall? I went alone by canoe from Kingston to Ottawa in 1946 just before I left for Repulse Bay. My ideas of beauty had been Tororak and perhaps the mountains and valleys in southern, wooded Labrador, but spring on the Rideau was almost more than I could comprehend, there was so much. I paddled among the thousand Islands and in the Lower Rideau, then, when I had a furlough, I went up to Ottawa again. I had lots of time and I just soaked along, but how I enjoyed it.

Ever get up in the middle of the night just to think or talk? Crazy, I agree, but once in a while interesting. I pity people who have insomnia and lie awake and hate it. I lie awake sometimes but it's almost at will, so many people and things to think about for a while, then sleep comes again. Last night I thought about other times, other places when it seemed my life was controlled to a great extent by the wind. Living in an Arctic environment, the wind dictates many of one's moves. The other elements don't seem to matter so much but wind, what did the poet say about, "Maiden's skirts a twirl?" He talked about kinder climates. In our world, maiden and all would twirl if she wore skirts.

The priests used to wear soutanes when bishops or important visitors were around, and they struggled to walk or work because the thing was like a sail. Fr. Choque was tall and had incredibly skinny legs. His gown always looked, in the wind, like a sheet caught between a pair of gate posts. Cape Wolstenholme is about as windy a place as you could find, and I remember the bishop, Fr. Cartier and Fr. Choque all working to unload their year's supplies from the mission boat, their gowns flapping in the breeze and disclosing glimpses of sturdy breeches and high sealskin boots which sent the Eskimo women into giggling fits. Finally it was done. They accepted the bishop's blessing, and as soon as he was a little way offshore on his way to the ship, off came the gowns and collars.

We have been getting a few gradual degrees warmer but fall is here, no question. The red currant bushes are brilliantly scarlet now and they contrast with the willows and raspberries in a sort of an electric jolt that you'd like. They hide under the other people's skirts all summer and make their berries, then suddenly they jump out in those scarlet leaves like a pretty girl whose old-fashioned mom kept in unattractive clothes as long as she could. They are bold and lovely at the same time and the first to say goodbye to summer.

Red is such a brave colour, especially to shy people who would never wear it. Long, long ago there was a teacher, not in my grade, who, to me at least, was lovely. She walked as if her feet and legs enjoyed it and she played games with her kids and had as much fun as they did. She wore a bright red blazer and a pleated tartan skirt some days and it was pure pleasure to see her go by. Don't suppose I ever spoke to her and I'm sure she didn't know the admiration I gave her.

She used to come to our house for meals and because my mother knew how shy I was, Miss Sampson always sat on the other side of the big table that sat fourteen. I'd have died if she ever sat next to me but I'd have died happy. I never see a bright red jacket but I think of her. She'll be over eighty now if she's alive. Wonder how much admiration and affection remains locked up in little boys' hearts, perhaps never released. Sad, because the object never knows. Worst thing in the world to be shy, so much love goes to waste...

Back to red, do you mind, for just a minute. Told you I admired red but could never have worn it? Well when they put me ashore at Cape Wolstenholme long years ago, I was alone for nine months, never saw a soul. In the store there were some men's pullover sweaters, English and probably priceless now. There was a red one, colour of a fox's mane, and because I was alone I wore it and I'm sure I got an enormous amount of pleasure from it.

It was a wonderful year, in spite of being alone and a lot of things are still in my memory: the sweater; an old black dog who came from nowhere and stayed. A day that I was crossing the bay on thin ice (a stupid thing to do alone), and a big old walrus suddenly bumped his wrinkled old head through the ice a few feet in front of me. He turned his red eye on me and blew out his breath through his whiskers and I could smell the fresh clams he'd been eating. Then he turned his head and stared out to sea, ignored me as though the rifle I was holding was a Mars bar. After a while he took a deep breath and just sank.

I can close my eyes and see the pattern the little blocks of ice that he thrust up made as they lay there. What I can't do is tell you the feeling I had to see him appear. From where, going where? In that frosty ocean, the feeling that it was a dream, the impression of terrible loneliness to see that patch of water. Wonder where that solitary creature went. Those little blocks of ice, arranged so neatly around the hole, that hole a mile away from any land, in a bay covered with ice.

What living creatures existed under that thin coat, would continue to live there as the months went on as the ice thickened, as the snow fell and covered it. For ten months it was covered and nature went on without hesitation. I can't tell you what I felt as I walked across it day after day, wondering where the little blocks were. Only my eyes ever saw them, and then only for moments. Lonely little blocks, lying there to mark the spot where a huge warm blooded animal had surfaced to breathe the same air as me, the air neither of us could exist without.

It happened before you were born, but I wish you could stand there and see the beauty feel the loneliness and revel in the beauty. The high, high hills, the flat ice, the lovely fresh crystal standing high on the salt water ice, like huge snow flakes on edge and as transparent as glass. You have probably never seen the incredible frost crystals that form only on the sea ice, a dream pattern at your feet for you to see. All so wonderful not because I wore a red sweater, but in some way connected.

Strange how one remembers things, probably years since I thought about that sweater. The boys were yarning at coffee time about memories, and they all said they couldn't remember a lot about when they were kids. It's because those memories are not valuable yet, they will be one day and then they'll be there. Nice isn't it?

There was sleepy horned owl on Pilgrim Island the other day, just minding his own business and the chickadees were hurling all sorts of insults at him because he was near the berries I guess. A couple of rabble-rousing Canada jays were there too, but they had to keep an eye on us. The owl never moved a feather. He just sat there; when it comes to minding one's own business, Mr. Owl has it made.

Some of us ate at the Moosonee Lodge yesterday. Heard some hunters complain that the weather was bad all through their hunt. One American said he had to charter a plane as Air Canada restricts hunters to seven pounds of ammunition. That translates into an average of one hundred shots each to collect his limit of five geese per day for two days. One thing for sure, he's not the world's greatest marksman. Reminds me of old Simon Quill at Pikangikum. He said one day that if I gave him a few shells, he'd get me some fat mallards. He seemed slightly stunned when I gave him a box of twelve gauge. I got my mallards, one or two a week that fall and they were good. Next fall I asked him for the same arrangement and he said sure, but he didn't need any ammunition, he still had lots from last year. There are hunters and hunters, you might say.

Angus and I met Simon out moose hunting one day. Angus said jokingly, "Get me a moose too." He had a large family and could use the meat, would be glad to tote it home. Simon explained that he only had one shell, therefore was sorry that he couldn't get Angus's moose. Imagine a man so confident of his own ability that he had one shell only to go out hunting and only a tea pail and tea.

Another canoe happened by going to Poplar Hill with their fall supplies. More as a joke, Angus bummed a shell from Totay and presented it to Simon who smiled and accepted it. Couple days later he came to Pikangikum. Yes, he had Angus' moose. Sorry he was late but he wanted to get it where Angus could pick it up by canoe. So he had waited two days at the rapid calling, and finally enticed a moose to the right place where he shot it and butchered it ready for pickup.

Yes, sure, he got his own moose too. He didn't want anything for his trouble and when Angus insisted he take a full box of shells and tobacco and tea, he went away shaking his head about crazy people.

He and his family lived on meat and fish. Simon was an expert in the collection of game. The main ingredient is patience. If you have enough to keep you waiting there possibly all day, one shot will secure ten or twelve birds. Sportsmen hunters who shoot on the wing destroy vast amounts of birds in the cripples they let get away. Every fall there are hundreds of wounded geese in sanctuary here, none or almost none from Indian hunters, all from the valiant city nimrods who didn't want the birds they shot. They seem to want to wear heavy khaki pants and high boots for a couple of days to pretend that they are big tough he-men. That's right, hide my soap box...

Moosonee, September 21, 1982

Dear Claudia,

Here we are taking the cellophane off of the first day of fall. Time does go by. Doesn't seem that long since we came here. Only a while since you were here and now the brave ones here are preparing to look old man winter square in the eye. The rest will, like me, sneak the odd look at him around the corner, and pretend he's broken his leg. But he's there, right enough, and he'll be around.

Someone said we cannot regret summer when we know the glory that is fall. Our seasons may lack something at times but no one can complain of what they give the spirit.

Where I grew up the hills are high and the water frightfully deep. It used to be a scary feeling when I was little to push off in my boat and let a line and jigger down and watch hundreds of feet of line run out and never reach the bottom, to think that I was perched on top of a tower of black water, that I would sink for a long time before reaching the bottom and what moved and lived in the black depth. I thought of a lot of things like that while I wandered around fishing and sailing, not only when I was small either. When I was at Hebron I once sat under the black face of Cape Mugford, an unclimbable wall of granite that rises sheer from the water for four thousand feet and continues down into the depths for who knows how many more feet. Even in a ship one feels so very small there. In a kayak as I was, it was possible to see how small one is in the general scale. I was a paddle's length from the rocks and there was an unfathomable amount of water under me. Easy to feel humble there, Claudia, very easy. But as you will notice, I have recovered. Perhaps it's the Newfie in me. Ever see a humble Newfie? Me neither. There isn't one. Well, maybe Joe Smallwood.

Maybe I sound like I ran around being scared and awed about the things I saw and experienced, but that isn't so. There were a lot of fun and games too. Guess I was a bit of a loner but there were lots of people. I think I related to the men who did the things that made our life: the carpenters, the coopers, the sailors, the fishermen. I wanted to know what they did and how they did it, and baseball or hockey took second place. We all hunted, from necessity, and I won't say I didn't enjoy it. When a kid of nine or ten can look at a huge platter of partridge or duck and think, "I got that meal," there is a lot of pride to fill his small chest.

September 22, 1982

Dear Claudia,

The second day of fall and a lovely day and the clock, that old spoil sport, says time to go to work. The calendar and the clock. We come under their influence when we are little and they never let us go. They give us enough anticipation to keep us in line, then they show us their authority.

What, if for a time, we were to move away from our regulated existence where, before we eat, we have to look at a little round object which also dictated when we started to cook. If we stopped sitting down for today's meal at the exact time we did yesterday, hungry or not, that would be the first jolt.

Our companions would not be hungry either. For a few days we would be terribly disorganized, and some might never recover, but go on to write bitter things about native shiftlessness. Some of us might break the chain and forget about the clock. We'd discover that time rolls smoothly if no longer broken up into hours and days. No more starts and stops for midnight so we can say Monday and Tuesday. It becomes simply day or night. The calendar falters and the clock stops and becomes what it is, a plaything for kids.

Remember once, stopping at old David Kadusak's place. They had an alarm clock which, according to my watch, was about eight hours wrong. I was the local radio operator, and my weather contacts had to be dead on, of course. I pointed out to David that the time on the clock was wrong, and he laughed and showed me how the hands went around in a circle and he could turn them to any position he chose, but did it make the sun change its position or make his belly demand food? Just a toy. When the sun was right on the water he would hunt for seal; when the sun melted the snow he'd fish in the open rivers. Takes a long time before one can wake from a long sleep and wonder about everything else but never about what we shall call this period of time. Sunday? Monday?

We had a bad time once,[11] short of food, terrible weather. Millik, Sammie, the policeman, and I. Things looked grim. No wind, and fantastic snowfall, snowfall the like of which you only find on the

11 In Hebron, North Labrador.

eastern slopes of the mountains. If there is wind, snow hardens and travel is easy. No wind, and one flounders and the dogs practically swim. It wasn't the custom to discuss the possibility that we might not make it, but we were all getting very tired and hungry, and I watched my uncomplaining dogs work their honest hearts out, and accept the very little food we had for them, then sleep to gain strength for the next day.

Through it all the policeman kept his diary. Millik asked me why. The policeman said, for one reason. We would not lose track of time. Incomprehensible, but okay.

Why write something every day? So that the people would know, if anything happened, when and why. Two big grins. If we starved and were found, the people finding us would know that it was a place and time that could only be found on a piece of paper, that people would know exactly what we did, maybe even said. Millik and Sammie grinned at one another and me, and several times I heard Millik snort as he lay in his robe.

We found a caribou, finally got to the coast, rested and ate, and took to the smooth ice of the fiord. Millik thought awhile, then asked me, what now? Will the policeman throw his paper away?

I said no, he'll keep it, and some day, send it to his headquarters and they'll read it. I can still see him. He shoved his hood back from his round good-natured face and howled with laughter. Away down south some place, a man will read about the day we didn't die, and he shook every now and then all day.

Millik was big for an Eskimo, good looking, and competent and honest and powerful. It took nothing for his face to break up into a hundred heart-warming smiles. Nothing bothered him, a hard day, an easy one, danger, hunger, nothing. In the great 1918 epidemic on Labrador, he was found, a tiny baby alive in a house of dead people. How long he had been there, no one knew. He was just walking, and surely able to know that something was very wrong. But he survived and grew to be a good hunter, a specially gifted traveller and a wonderful person to know.

Once he and Rena's brother and I were caught out on the water late in the fall. Ice was forming everywhere and our boat was forced to land by the ice on an island. Our only possible means of survival was to save the boat, and he tore the ceiling out of the boat. (That sounds as if the boat had a cabin. It didn't, it was open. The ceiling covered the timbers...) We slid lengths under the boat so that the ice, when it pressed together, lifted the boat, and we were adrift in a storm, a blizzard, moving with the ice, heaven knew where. I felt that things were serious indeed.

It was dark. The wind tore at us and the spray froze on our clothing. Nothing to do but wait. We sat in the boat, our backs to the storm, and I'll never forget Millik. He put his face close to mine, and I could imagine, more than see, his grin, but I could hear his chuckle at us for getting ourselves into such a pickle. Why worry, we could meet every situation, and if one came that we couldn't handle, "*Aingnamut*," it couldn't be helped. He was a special man among a special people.

The clock again. Jackie will have beaten me to the office for sure.

Later:

There is a lovely half moon tonight. This is the time of the year when the winds get up in the morning and run about all day, then sit in the edges of the forest and along the beaches to rest their legs at night. The sunset will glow for so long, and when it's gone, the sky will blacken to a purple velvet and all the little creatures will be still for awhile. Then one by one the stars will come out some timid and shy behind the blaze of our fire. But one by one they are there, and we can look up and see them, to wonder about them, so remote, so far away from us.

I felt that there was a little desecration when man walked on the moon, I didn't want it to happen. She's been up there so long, she's shone on me in so many places, through so many windows, over so many tents, igloos and uncovered camps.

When I was alone at Cape Wolstenholme, once for a long time, every full moon was like a visit from an old friend.

There was a radio program from Europe on short wave, a girl singing and announcing her own songs. All I had of her was a voice, but I could imagine her face, see her smile. She was, of course, beautiful, slim, beautifully dressed, and she sang to my heart, just for me. I wonder how many isolated people knew her, loved her. She was the moon, lovely, unreachable, but mine.

The bay at Wolstenholme faces to the northeast. The two high black hills run down on each side into the water, like two huge portals. The moon rises in the centre and slowly climbs until she is shining down into the bay, over the black water, over the ice in winter, when she makes millions of jewels in the frost crystals on the ice.

And I saw her as that beautiful singer entering, to be with me till the world turned. She would be gone a while, only to return as beautiful and remote as ever, and how I yearned to touch and hold as that voice sang, sometimes the sad and desperate songs of the boys and the hidden heartsick men of Erin, sometimes the fierce martial songs of the Scots lamenting their prince, sometimes the soft and tender love songs of the Celts. But my solitude was my refuge. I could never have spoken to that singer. I could never have told her what I felt.

That winter I wrote pages and pages to a friend I never had, to a person of imagination, the perfect person. Pages and pages of all the things that fill a solitary person's mind, and the next year it was all lost in the cold water when the *Nascopie* went down. I would like to see that paper now. I think I longed for companionship, but perhaps didn't realize it.

And, Claudia, in spite of the longing, in spite of the isolation, I was content. Strange isn't it. I wish you could read all those scribblings and understand the person, see his fumbling attempts to understand beauty, feel the compelling urge to talk to someone who would know.

I am no longer the kid who wrote at Wolstenholme. I've aged, changed, but the moon hasn't. In my memory, the building in Eric Cove is the same as it was then, even though the site has long been abandoned. The buildings are gone, but the moon still rises out of the sea, and climbs above the bay night after night. And the boy stands there to welcome the princess of the night who smiled, stayed a while, and went her way, leaving him content. It's a long way back to that boy and his dreams, my friend.

As predicted, Jackie got to the office before I did and took the radio sched, then we agreed it was too nice to do floors. So we decided to take her girls[12] and go to a beach and cook steaks. It was cool on the water and nice on the shore and the kids climbed trees and hunted fossils and ran miles with the tiny dog. We sat by the fire and talked more.

Jackie is a good listener. She loves to be our mascot, burrowing into our affection and comradeship like a starved puppy. She's been too shy and it's easy to hurt her. Not criticism; she will take that, or correction. There is no bother there, she'll smile and go happily on. She just wants to do it right. She takes her place naturally in any discussion and the boys listen to her contributions.

At first they were a bit indulgent, as perhaps I was. We had never worked with a young woman here before, but the men relate well to her where the business is concerned. At first she'd stand quietly during our discussion, never venturing an opinion. Now she perches on the outer office desk, disgracefully and unladylike, and puts her contributions in, while I usually stand by the window and the boys walk around the office like two socks in a washing machine. Her grasp of what we talk about is excellent.

It's scary to think of all the good ideas locked up inside the people like Jackie as they pass out pens and notepads around conference tables, silent efficient people who are mute because nature gave them a different composition. We are incredibly stupid, are we not? In Newfoundland too, the little woman has always been second man (the word is second hand, but means second in authority) and many a family succeeded because of a strong second hand. I suppose Cal and

12 Jackie's daughters stayed with her in Moosonee during the summer.

Ellsworth and I were not much better, not much worse than the rest of our gifted sex in our opinion of a girl's place in our man's world.

But our Ninety-Seven Pound Weakling, which happens to be her current title, has opened their eyes more than mine. They listen, but what warms my heart is the way she just naturally assumes her place, her right. She always says "Going to the railroad, airport, store, post office," wherever, but never asks any more, "May I take the truck?" She doesn't assume that the coffee table is her sole responsibility, though she usually does it because Cal and Ellsworth leave it worse than before, but if the phone rings, she'll toss the rag to the nearest one and be gone. At first they'd look astonished and gingerly dab at the table. Now they don't even stop talking and polish away.

Claudia, a terrible thought, are we building a monster for some executive one day?

Next day:

We talked about the walrus and loneliness, and you came up with the thought that it must be dark and terribly cold down there. What must it be like to be down in the sea with an uninterrupted ice cover? What sort of image would he see as he breaks through the ice? He isn't looking for enemies because very early in life he knows that he has no natural enemies. Man, yes, but he doesn't often see man. He looks dull and slow, reflective. What enters his big brain as he bursts through into the sunlight? What does he think and feel as he descends to the bottom to grope in total darkness with his strong tusks for the clams he needs to exist? He is in a void, a cold, dark void. The flounders see him coming and scurry away, and in clear sunlit water, one is astounded at the speed with which he turns and catches the alarmed fish. He returns to his slow deliberate pace. I've seen him swim under my boat with a flatfish in his mouth, almost dreamy in his slow progress, so that one almost refuses to believe he has that speed and agility in the water. I've seen him surface with a huge ball of mud tucked under his chin and held by his tusks. He'll lie on his back in the water and slowly pass the mud through his jaws, separating the clams, shelling them with his tongue, and spitting the broken shells away.

His table manners are atrocious, his disposition is mean and irritable, and he grunts and slashes at his companions if they intrude on his sleep. He is uncouth, smelly and ugly. His mating is a preposterous mime of a usually gracious act. His partner is grotesque and their union is only possible through the equally grotesque equipment that nature was forced to give him that his species might be preserved. He hates his offspring and once his mating frenzy is over, he ignores his mate, except to demonstrate to any other bull that she is his. And yet, when you see him as I did, looking sombrely out over the ice, when you see him deep under your tiny kayak in his own element, graceful in a ponderous way, he becomes a new being, a being of such intense loneliness that only the silent polar bear, in his ceaseless wandering, can compare.

And you wonder. Does he have yearnings? He is warm-blooded. Why couldn't he have a memory and instincts like a dog, who can be lonely, and sad, and hurt and so very glad. All wild animals play at times. They show tremendous affection. I don't see any reason why he cannot feel what a fox must feel as he sits on a hill looking at the warm spring sun. It just seems that walrus, thick-skinned clown, must have feelings that are not apparent to us.

You mentioned birch-bark pictures. Have you ever seen the ones they make in northern Saskatchewan? Of course you have, in *The Beaver*, Angeline Merasty's. I knew her at Île à la Crosse, and it was amazing how she could fold a piece of birch bark, bite here and there and you had a face or a moose. She was a sad, likeable person, and she lived in three worlds, Cree, Chipewyan, and English, and none was kind to her.

She lived in a little house mid-way between Natural Resources and the Company dwelling, which was on the far side of the lake from the settlement. While we had nice trees and high, dry, comfortable ground, Angelina was in a swamp. Willows by the million but no firewood.

In those days before oil, wood was a scarce commodity, and we were always hard put to get enough for our store and dwelling. But the RCMP had a Bombardier (snowmobile) and we had two, so on frigid Sundays (and Île à la Crosse is the coldest place I've ever lived…) when we could hear Angeline's hopeless axe crashing into the bony willows, the three police and my three Scots clerks and I would go way down the Buffalo Narrows trail with my gang. There would be Muriel and Pat and Maureen, the police wives and a friend, and we'd build a huge fire.

We'd throw up a shelter and the women and kids would picnic while we loaded the three Bombardiers with nice dry wood for Angeline. There was work involved to be sure, but the look on Angeline's tired, sad face was enough, and I sometimes had a guilty feeling that we had such a good time getting the wood.

She had a small child, I think adopted, and couldn't leave the house to go far, but one day we had a big surly Chipewyan girl with us and she was persuaded to come. She ate a bit, drank some strong tea, but had a purpose in mind. In a very short time, she stepped into her snowshoes, and we could hear the axe ringing away in the woods. Then the crunch of her snowshoes, and she was back with a log on her shoulder. She gave us a brief, almost apologetic smile, and was gone.

We soon got busy too and in a short time had three loads ready. The clerks and the police wanted to enjoy the fire and we tried to get Angeline to sit down too. However, the fear of missing an opportunity had seized her and she was back, silently and quickly chopping down trees and stacking them, tepee fashion against another expedition when her work in advance would save us a little. I think perhaps a widow in northern Saskatchewan living in limbo between worlds could tell us about insecurity and despair, but Angeline never asked for help. She was dour, moody, almost totally silent, and independent. I'm not exactly sure where her original home was. She and her husband came to Île à la Crosse before I did. He died and she never went back. They had a certificate, which I had to see before the welfare people would agree to give me lumber and roofing to repair her house.

Yes, she had to be legally wed or widowed to receive aid. Guess non-widows and outcasts don't get as cold as those in more holy bonds.

She was not in favour with the church because of the circumstances of her marriage, but the dear little Mother Superior and her twelve little nuns would pile into my Bombardier and I'd take them to Angeline's to visit.

Mother Superior was little and chubby and had a desperate heart ailment. She could have gone any time and she knew it, and in her indomitable way she sort of defied the rigid old priest, and by golly, the doctor. She cared nothing for the important world of commerce, believe me. Because of her health, the mission would refuse her the use of the Bombardier to go some unimaginable distance out in the bush to see a patient, so she'd call me and suggest I must have a trip planned up that way to deliver supplies or pick up a load of fish. And if not, what the heck, God would pay me.

I used to phone the doctor, a timid German chap, no match for his head nurse, and he'd say, "Not her again! Look after her as well as you can and get her back soon." So Pete or I would go, pick her and another sister up. She'd get into the machine panting and seeming about ready to die, but laughing, always laughing. Once she asked me seriously, "Where does the gas come from when you take me away like this?" and all I could think to say was, "From the bottom of my heart, Mother." She didn't say a word, just patted my head.

The superior of her order came in the spring and came to see me. Told me she had had a talk with the priest and the doctor and Sister was to be allowed to go her own way. She didn't call me so much after, but now and then she'd ask me to go some place in our truck or boat because she knew how I wanted it.

Back to Angeline. I wanted to tell you that when I was getting ready to leave Île à la Crosse, she came to the storeroom one day and asked to see me in private. She showed me a gold watch, very, very old, one I'd give an eye to own and she wanted me to take it, and I couldn't. She said there was a name inside but the case was stuck, the catch was slightly damaged. She couldn't remember the name, English or Scots she thought. I held it in my hands, Claudia, and I felt the history and the romance, but I couldn't own it. I had no right. I gave her the address of the HBC Archives and asked her to try to have it go there when she died.

She laid it on the desk and sat spinning it with her finger while she abruptly told me the story of her life. Nothing much, a lot of poverty and suffering, a lot of travel, a lot of discrimination, sorrow, fear. Not much of a life, no material for a romantic novel. She said, "I told you but you won't tell anyone, anyone..." She would owe no man and she thought she owed me. I hope I convinced her she did not.

Years and years later, I was at Fort MacMurray on my way to the western Arctic. A plane came over from La Loche and Île à la Crosse with a party of fish filleters for the plants on McInnis and Crackingston Lakes. Angeline was there with the girl, now nearly grown.

I expected a reserved smile and was completely startled when the face I never saw animated broke into a thousand pieces of welcome. I felt, as never before, that there was one heart that would never forget. We ate in a grubby little café and she talked, the girl sitting silent and watchful beside her, and soon she was gone.

Jackie's husband might be transferred form Elliot Lake and that could mean the end of Jackie's job here. She doesn't want that. She told me today that this job is vital to her.

She brought me a telegram listing the permanent salaried employees of MTL, and her name was on it. I had told her long ago I was putting her on permanent staff. She handled the paper like it was something holy. "I know you said you would, I never dared believe it." How many times did I see her look at that telex. She wants another year with us, and we want her.

September 30, 1982

Dear Claudia,

It is almost midnight, and almost October 1st There is a huge full
moon and the shadow that just crossed its face is that of a tiny man
in a top hat, buckled shoes and a short pipe. I hear you ask, what is
he doing awake at this hour? Well, I'll tell you. That old moon is a
charmer. She wouldn't let me sleep, and I didn't want to anyway. I
feel like walking, but where? We've had rain and mud is everywhere.
The thing to do would be to go down, get in the canoe, set its bow on
the silver dazzle on the water and follow. I would do it but Ellsworth
is going down early tomorrow to replace a couple of beacons that
have fallen and has all the tanks filled and ready to go. Better not
change things around.

The moon's charm, the moon's mystery. Makes me think of the
mystery of people. I like watching people and wondering about them.
And I like people, by the individual or building-full. When I was
in the army, I used to look at rows and rows of motionless bodies,
lines and lines of expressionless faces and wonder what's behind that
facade, that wall each man stands behind, and wonder how many will
live, or die, and how many fear it?

I would wonder what moves a man to take up a weapon and fall
in to be drilled and marched, drilled and marched, until he became
a fully trained soldier, a robot, a tool of war. We are not really very
bright, you know. I was probably the army's worst at drill, but I stood
there, and in my mind I ridiculed and resented the posturings and
salutes and stamping, the intricate steps and turns so that five hundred
men could be passed in front of one man, so that they could give him
the "eyes right" as they marched past.

As a radio operator, I was exempt from call-up, but I volunteered.
Why? Don't ask me. I guess, among others, I wasn't very bright. One
thing the army did, it put me in touch with people. Practically all I

had known in my grown up life were the kindly, honest, native people. The army showed me all the meanness and avarice that people are capable of. Some of what I saw, of course, was the result of the army's own de-humanizing process that seems to be necessary to produce the perfect cannon fodder, a process that allows a vindictive little man with three stripes on his arm to victimize a highly educated person that has no stripes.

I guess I was lucky. I had no drill skills and no one wanted me. I was a better radio operator than their instructors. Not because of brain or dexterity. I had had better teachers, the best. So the army left me alone, more or less. There were four of us and we sat in little cubicles and listened to Morse. The thing was that signals officers must have some qualifications, so they had to go through a form of testing every so often. We tested them. They entered their side of the booth unseen by us. The army cannot allow an officer to fail at anything, especially to be recognized by lesser beings such as us as having done so.

As to drill, there is a sad story. Consider, I already said I was no good at drill. I also said I wasn't very bright.

Some day when you are passing Barriefield and the Vimy Signals Camp, look inside. There should be several big white buildings with a huge drill square in front. That's where it happened.

It was Sunday. I was off duty and about to retire after a night's work, just waiting till the din of hundreds of men preparing for church parade was over. A friend, who had less brains than I, he was a drill sergeant..., came streaking through. He had a parade to call and his marker was AWOL. My brain must have been marjed (as Ash would say...:) because I allowed myself to be persuaded.

Now, Claudia, this was summer. The dress of the day was shorts and shirt. I was a comfortable few pounds heavier than I am even now, and I have fat legs. That fact is important, as I shall show you.

So, when markers were called, I followed the other markers out onto that wide field of horror. I finally stumbled to my correct place and stood at attention, my toes on the little white line. In due time, the parade was called and the thunder of hundred of feet moving in behind me inspired a kind of panic, but I refused to bolt. The expected thunder wasn't exactly sounding like thunder, so I sneaked a look. Now, if the army catches you at that, the penalty is too horrible to mention, but I did it, and my blood, which was already cold, froze. I could hear the little ice cubes rattling around my ventricle and dropping on the spot where my stomach used to be. The section heading neatly and correctly for my trembling posterior was composed of about three hundred, looked like three thousand, army women. They are famous for their drill. They had at least part of a precision squad in their midst. I could hear her giving quiet orders.

To the brass standing at the review stand, the operation appeared completely silent. They came to a halt behind me, and the click as they halted sounded like just one click. I heard the brass say, "Well done!" at the exact same time I heard the foremost girl who had halted behind me say, "My God!" and I knew I was the reason for that remark.

The rest of the deal was pure nightmare. I was slow to step off and she said, "Hurry it!" I was too close on a turn and she snarled at me. These women are very defensive about this drill. I finally staggered past the frowns at the stand and numbly took off up the long, long road to the drill hall where I could be relieved of my incubus, my quarter-mile long tail of elegant marchers.

The instant we stepped off the drill square, my torment was increased tenfold. Discipline was relaxed. The remarks and whistles flew, my legs and my whole personality was commented on, and that fiend of a precision caller... She would give an order and the bystanders would be treated to the spectacle of a large section in perfect step, but the marker would be out of step. I'd shuffle through a change step, not something I do well, I assure you, and by the time I got my feet pointed front again, she'd have changed the step again. No one can say I didn't try. I hop-scotched all along that eternity of a tree-lined avenue, died a thousand deaths, and when we came at last to the drill hall where their own officers were waiting to direct them to their seating area, I marched in one door and out the other. I don't know who marked them home. It wasn't me. I was probably in the shower trying to drown myself.

Couple or three days later, I poked my nose under the post office wicket and mumbled my H 30865, Budgell L., to the figure seated there, and there was a delighted squeal, "It's him!" and a dozen postal clerks came to look and chuckle and exclaim. I said, "Have your fun, but tell me who that infernal girl was because I'd like to kill her slowly with my bare hands and bamboo slivers." They howled for half an hour before they'd even give me my mail.

Did I volunteer ever to mark a parade again? You must be joking... I shall tell you that if the only way out of the army was via a parade, I would still be there, the oldest probably, but still there. On the day when the trump will sound and we will stand for judgment, I shall wait for one voice to say "Present," and with the Angel of Doom hovering overhead, with St. Peter pursing his lips over my record, I shall fly at her with such a frenzy and tread on her infernal twinkle-toes. I shall indeed.

THREE

Monday, October 4, 1982

Dear Claudia,

I used to like camping in the late fall. At Hebron we used to set up a tent over a big motor boat and go along the coast hunting. There were lots of lovely bright windy days, enough frost to make the ground hard. Hunting would be impossible because of the frost which made all the little pools noisy to walk on, and because of the sharp wind that affects the animals. They get spooky and run at any other movement.

It's not really winter weather and they seem to be having fun. I've watched foxes and wolves race one another till they fall panting on a dry sand bed where they wrestle and play fight for hours.

Those are the days when a person's stamina seems endless. One can walk and climb all day, to explore, to think. I guess I went to blow away the cobwebs of a busy summer. Usually there were three of us: Millik who left early and ranged far and wide setting up his area for the winter hunting; old Coonera who left his robe in the tent every morning saying he was going to make a big hunt today and who spent it in the lee of a big boulder smoking his black pipe and contentedly remembering the days when he would, "wear out a new pair of boots in one day"; and me.

Once I had the absolute delight of Coonera and Albert for a week. They were small men, even by Eskimo standards, immensely strong in their backs, legs and arms from years of handling kayaks and carrying loads. They sat endless hours watching the fiord for a seal and muttered together about old things, old people, all the tales that had been implanted so many years ago. Their stubby hands, broken and disfigured from years of hunting and fishing, lay on their knees in the immemorial fashion of men telling tales, and when they lifted them to express a point, they were as graceful and light as a ballerina's— hands that fashioned their kayaks, their hunting tools, almost everything they used. Scarred, thick of nail, not entirely innocent of the blood of their last victim perhaps, but hands that one could admire, hands that had served their owners well, hands that would serve me if I needed them. Hands that told a story.

I would sit near them and listen to their talk, short sentences, long pauses, every word thought over and stripped for brevity. The old tales are condensed, why burden memory with words? Two small figures whose time was rapidly coming to an end; they never gave that dark person who watched them a second glance. They had outwitted him times without number and there comes a time when a man can let go without a murmur. Times too when the enemy comes in and is sent reeling back, having overestimated his advantage. Those old men say a wolf is not dead till his teeth show. If his lips are closed he can still bite, so it is with little incredibly tough men.

One day they had been sitting in comfort until nearly dark when Millik arrived with a load of caribou meat. He had made his kill many miles inland. Two little men gathered up their equipment and stood grinning at me while they drank a last cup of tea. The invitation was plain, and I, many years younger, left with them.

Their pace was slow, almost ambling, and we took little detours to avoid rock slides and bogs. It grew dark and there were no stars. The hills looked all alike as we twisted and turned following the valley inland. In a short time I ceased to think about where we were going and left the trail to them while I stored up memories and impressions for this day. I have perhaps not thought about that night for thirty years, but it has been there, a night to remember.

Their pace increased as the night went on. The road got rougher as we climbed toward the top of the mountain. It was intensely dark and now and then a word or a touch would warn me of an obstacle or a dangerous place. Once we stopped, our backs to a steep wall of rock, and two black pipes were lit. In the light from the coals I could get flashes of their eyes and teeth as the pipe bowl alternately glowed and faded.

I said we must be high on the mountainside and close to the edge. One small man gathered a tuft of dry moss, and in the dark, found some dry grasses which he bound around it to make a little torch. He lit it and tossed it in front of us, and by only craning my neck a little, I could see it drop for a hundred feet or more. There were two quick chuckles and a little pat on my arm.

We went on and on. I was lost in the drama of it all. Those men, engrossed in the age-long supply of meat, they hardly spoke to one another. Occasionally they would stop and say quietly, "*narla*" (hark), and faint and clear we would hear the sound of a wolf singing, far, far away, an almost intolerably lovely song, and perhaps an answer miles away in another direction. The night was more precious as we listened.

Once we stopped. Not a word was spoken, and one man gently chafed the legs of his sealskin boots together to make a small whispering noise. We were rewarded by an enquiring bark from a fox and saw a shy shadow melt into the darkness as he passed close and got our scent. Two amused gurgles and we went on. Many things they showed me in that darkness, Claudia. It was almost like travelling in bright light. The complete adaptation of a man to his environment. Old gentle, tireless men. How I wish it were in my power to give them to you, the way I saw them.

We came at last to the meat cache, how I'll never know. We loaded ourselves with the meat, large loads. Only bones and offal were left behind for the creatures that were close to us, circling and waiting till the human presence, the deadly killer, was gone. They knew exactly where we were and my guides knew to a degree where they were.

We carried our loads a short distance away and we heard a light scuffle, no more, as what we had left behind went to sustain another creature and its band. Amused chuckles told me that darkness might hide the scene but their memory told them exactly what was happening.

The pace increased, and through that long limpid night we carried our loads. There was no pause to take breath, no slow down for mountain or valley. They were hunters returning and their strength and endurance was amazing. I, the youngest, who should have been leader, was last. Perhaps they even slowed their pace for me. On and on we went. My shoulders felt like they had hot irons in them, my back ached, my legs protested, and on we went.

In the cold early light we again reached our camp. We had been walking from dusk to dawn, over rough high land, unable to see where we had placed our feet, carrying heavy loads. I was tired, but I stayed out of my robe to watch two small men eat the meat they had brought, smoke a pipe each, and because it was almost day they ignored the tent and slept sitting up outside. I lay down and slept as the sun rose. Later, I was dimly conscious of Millik as he prepared for another day.

I woke somewhat later and glanced out of the tent where two small figures sat side by side, looking out over the fiord and apparently not the least tired, talking slowly and earnestly. Two men who had made a hard journey by darkness, who had slept only briefly and who were cheerfully looking at a new day, to sit and yarn, but to be ready in an instant to be gone again. Tough, tireless, admirable men. The angry, dark spirit would bide his time a long while before he collected one of those.

Then there was a war, and white-faced beings from tall caves in the city took them from their land to suit their plans. Why did we do it to them? Why is the land still there empty of people, yet full of all they need to survive. I admired those men because they were what I could never be: "Inuit."

You would have loved them with their short bodies, thick arms and legs, their faces open and frank and, beyond belief, friendly. They are polite by nature. Albert would raise his hand to his brow and crinkle his visage into a smile. His small bow was beyond description. He would touch your hand with his stubby fingers in the most gentle, friendly way possible and he would beam in a way that took you by the heart. Two gentlemen.

And we took those people from happiness and complete freedom to houses, rubber boots, linoleum, and the horrible racket of the radio and the alarm clock. Our race has a lot to answer for.

We are about ready to go home. When we went out to get the buoys last week, we had to pass close to the sanctuary, and there are a lot of geese there now. It was a nice clear day and they stood there, rank on rank, and wouldn't move. I think some are heading south. I can hear them at night and the song they sing is the goose version of "The Open Road."

The last barge sits at the dock. She leaves at 6:30 tomorrow morning. It will be the beginning of the end of the season. By evening there will be signs that we are closing down. Special boxes for equipment and delicate instruments come out. Jackie's eyes get a bit apprehensive; her summer is ending too. I took Jackie down to the tug to give them their last manifest. She feels it. She's been part of a close group. She wants to get back to the everyday life of daughters, school and breakfasts, home and school, and breakfasts with her family, but there will be a call that hasn't been there before.

We will work harder now, longer hours to get things done that we must, but we'll relax too. The jokes might disappear for a while, until the last day when they will be a buttress against the lonely little feeling that will not be denied. The last day after breakfast they will throw themselves on their beds with an air of "I've waited all summer for this, ahhh, great!" and in ten minutes they will be walking down for a last look around the tugs, the buildings, and they will scatter all over town, only to meet again in the Lodge window to watch the river run past as it has done for every October for hundreds of years.

Finally, Bish[13] will arrive with his little bus. That's tradition too, his final gesture that says thanks to all the boys for endless help during the summer, and everyone will be animated and kit bags and sea bags will be thrown carelessly into the bus. Everyone will say their last goodbyes to Mrs. Drudge at the Lodge, and no one will say much as we speed past the lonely looking tugs on their slipway. Someone will say, "So long you rusty old so and so," but the laughter will be perfunctory, and the eyes will turn to watch the hooded wheelhouse, the dead eyes of the hawses, and we will all think of her as alive, sentient and ours. We are glad to be going but sad that we must. And this year, a little extra bond, Jackie, who will be there, perhaps with a very strong feeling of belonging, proud that she has been tried and not found wanting, very much part of a solid world, secure in the affection of her fellow workers, and that will make me feel good as it will the other eleven. Very good indeed.

We will be different in the airport. The men are mostly big. Their hands show the signs of work. They plant their feet firmly and the government clerks with their briefcases take sidelong looks. Who are these big men? Why must they crowd on the plane that has been ours all summer? They are a bit noisy, a bit rough as they play their final jokes. Every one of them will watch Jackie's luggage when we get to Timmins but they'll all defer to me, the "old man", who will see her ticket through and walk her to the door and be the first to say goodbye, only to be overwhelmed as the rest crowd in to shake her hand, rumple her hair and proffer all sorts of advice about air sickness,

13 Bishop Hennessey, owner of Two Bay Enterprises, Moosonee.

because they'll never let her forget the trip out the bay last week, and when her plane leaves for Elliot Lake, there won't be much said until perhaps Ash says, "A wonderful fine maid."

Moosonee, October 1982

Dear Claudia,

It's almost seven, and the sky shows no light as yet. It's clear over head, but the lovely early morning lights of spring and summer belong to another memory book now. The fall light is steely and sharp when it comes, the horizon is clear and defined.

Claudia, how I fear the loss of sight. There have been more than 23,000 sunrises since I was born, no two alike. Memory has recorded an impression to cover them all and without sight, I suppose one could see the sun rise and set in the imagination. But one would lose those infinitely precious impressions that are covered in the corner of one's eye on a spring morning which is carried all day in a sort of tremulous privacy in one's heart, because it is too small, too fleeting to be shared, but lies there like a pink pearl on velvet.

Travelling in Saskatchewan, with his wife, Muriel, who was born there.

October 30, 1982

Dear Claudia,

We drove from Winnipeg to Wolseley, Sask. It's a little town, a couple of elevators, a machine sales, a few stores, perhaps one thousand people, an old folks' home and a small bright hospital...

You'd like the valley. It is brown and dry now, waiting for the first snow and the hand of winter which will lie heavy. The roads will block with snow and there will be no traffic because very few people winter in the valley these days. Most of them have moved to the towns at the tops of the hills, on the roads and railways. The days of sleighs and horses are gone and autos cannot travel the blocked roads or climb the steep hills, so the valley lies quiet and secure till spring, and the farmers and their families curl and go to school in comfort and the foxes and porcupines have the valley to themselves as they have for centuries. I think it would be nice to pass a winter in the Qu'appelle and remember the days when the HB packet went through on its way west. Until recently there was a section of the old HBC cart trail quite visible, but a man called Olive moved his fence a bit more year by year and finally ploughed the old trail for a few more bushels of grain. I'm afraid I could never like a man like that very much.

Speaking of moving fences, at Île à la Crosse I knew a man named William. Irresponsible, happy and lazy, he hardly ever worked, but he was an excellent mink skinner and flesher and was in demand among the many mink ranchers in the area. Willie wouldn't help raise the mink but would always be available at pelting time. I didn't know him very long because, to make a long story short, he froze to death one night on the way from Île à la Crosse to Beaver River and when we found him he was very dead.

Because he had lived apart from his wife for some time, the old father at the mission refused him burial in consecrated ground, and that hurt his old grandmother. So the corporal of the RCMP assured her that something would be done.

It was a well-known fact that the mission regularly took down a section of fence on their property where the cemetery was located and just as regularly moved it a few feet east on Crown land.

So, one stormy day, Al and his special constable, Vital, and my clerk and I dug a grave for William as close to the fence as possible and William was laid to rest there.

A blizzard soon removed all traces, and since the soil is sand, there was no vegetation to be disturbed. Come spring, who knew where Willie was? We marked his head with an inconspicuous metal peg and lo and behold in two years Willie rested in consecrated ground.

His grandmother and her sons erected a simple wood headboard, and if the good father noticed, he said very little. The old lady died happy and I'm sure Willie lies happy. The policeman is also dead. He was a very hearty man with a lot of humour. I'm sure that if he and Willie ever met on some celestial river hunting spirit ducks, they'll have had a good laugh about the whole thing, and perhaps on St. Peter's book there will be a tiny reprimand for the father because he failed to keep his fences in order.

May we go back to the Qu'appelle? Because there is more I want to talk to you about. You see we went there to visit one of Muriel's aunts who is waiting out the end. She has cancer and I don't think there is much hope. She's in hospital and heavily sedated most of the time, but her mind is good and she asked us to go visit a relative who is in the old folks' home next door. The old lady we went to see was lying in a crib-like bed, with a strap around her and the high sides up. I last saw her many years ago when she was a healthy, busy, hospitable farm wife. She hadn't the slightest idea who we were and she offered her hand. It was soft like dough and it had no strength. She looked at me with no expression and I wondered how many days and nights she has passed, how many more she must endure. She didn't speak, she didn't answer when spoken to. Another old lady in a nearby bed kept up a continual whine and a third looked alert and rational and asked me if I would help her, so I went over and she said clearly, "Help me out of this hole, I have to go back to my mother now."

The fear is so present you can feel it. Why, Claudia, why? You wonder, what were their joys and sorrows, what have they known, what have they forgotten? They were teenagers once. They were adults, now they are old. Their triumphs, their disappointments, their ecstasy, their sorrows, all behind, all forgotten. The things they did, the things they did not do, their sacrifices, their selfishness, all their emotions, Claudia. We never get a second chance. All these old people say one thing, for god's sake, experience the life you are living, take what it offers, because one day we will all pay the piper.

Later, in the hall at the hospital, a tiny boy, a patient, climbed on my knees because he too needed comfort, and I held him and watched his fear and anxiety disappear because he felt affection, and he went to sleep, the first time since 4 a.m. the nurse said. And I held him for a couple of hours because he'd wake if he were put in his bed, and I know the feeling of that small, sick body was a help. It took away the bitterness and resentment that people must feel because life is unfair.

It wasn't a good trip to Saskatchewan, but I learned something, Claudia. I went where I had never been before and I saw things that I hated to see, but they are there. I knew they were there, and perhaps I ignored them. I can't ignore them now.

Back in Winnipeg:
Got a little Labrador magazine when I got here. *Them Days*, it's called, devoted to Labrador history. Who is on page 31? My dad, looking like I remember him, pipe in one hand, other hand deep in trouser pocket,[11] and his usual independent, be damned to you expression on his face. He was a very kind but considerate man but could project more pure Irish in the way he stood than anyone else I've ever seen.

Nice old guy too, with a bald head and a ring of snow around just above the ears, like a slightly slipped halo. A fierce opponent of Confederation, he was a Britisher all the way. He was always torn between love of Erin and the misty bogs of the Outer Isles where his mother came from. He sang both their songs and had a voice that perhaps he could have made his living by if he had wanted. He was a romantic too, and the feelings I have for the rocks and bogs and tundra and sea, the land, came from him, his songs and his stories. He was sentimental and loved kids. He was patient to a fault when he knew it was necessary and could go into a merciless wrath if there was careless-ness or inattention to boats, nets or equipment. He had a tongue that could make you laugh for hours and that could literally take the skin off your back if your faults deserved it. He taught me a lot, but I think, above all, he taught me to learn. He hunted and fished all his life and would have tears in his eyes watching an eagle soar.

My dad was a bit of a mystic. He would have taken you to all his favourite haunts because he'd have known you'd understand. He managed to preserve Rigolet as a lovely place to live in, and when he retired it was allowed to become a shabby dirty village and all the old HBC buildings are gone, and the pride is gone. Like Tara's harp, it is mute and only when "some heart indignant breaks" do you know that it still lives. Thank the spirits he didn't live to see what it is now.

You'd have loved him, he'd have understood and loved you. Some-times if I catch a sudden glimpse of myself in a mirror I see him and I feel good. People say that I look like him and it pleases me.

And on page 33, among a group of kids at Rigolet, is yours truly at age 9 or so, looking anywhere but at the camera. Shall I write you a profile? I guess not, but in a few things, it might not be different from my dad's.

And this is the last sheet of foolscap from a pad that has all gone to you in a couple of envelopes. Shocking isn't it? I wasn't repressed as a child; I was talkative then too. One of my teachers said my tongue was hinged in the middle and wagged on both ends. I haven't improved.

November 1982

Dear Claudia,

Wish you were here. We could talk for hours bout a very interesting thing that goes back to 1919 or possibly 1918, when an Anglican missionary at Moose Factory became depressed and committed suicide. That part is probably not too interesting, but the following events are. I got involved in 1959, and tonight an old ex-RCMP man called me from Vancouver to talk about it. Let's go back to 1919.

This was before the days of the railway to Moosonee. The HBC and Revillion mail packets went out to a point on the east-west CNR once a month, pretty well all year round except for freeze-up and break-up. So, though it has not been confirmed, an order must have gone out to have a suitable gravestone sent in from Montreal by the HBC ship *Nascopie* to arrive in Charlton Island in 1920. It would be brought in to Moose Factory in a small ship or perhaps the steam vessel *Irene*, which did that part of the service.

The stone never did arrive at Moose Factory and perhaps you will remember that Freddie Moore showed us the unmarked grave where Haythornethwaite lies when we went around the church yard with him last summer. It's nice that you have an involvement too.

Well back in 1920, W.E. Brown was a constable in the RCMP and stationed at Fullerton, NWT, about half way between Chesterfield Inlet and Repulse Bay. HBC had a post at Repulse Bay and the manager was an ex-whaler, Captain George Cleveland.

The HBC launch *Caribou* came down to Chesterfield Inlet to meet the *Nascopie* from Montreal to pick up the year's supplies. Cleveland was there with two unpowered coast boats loaded with supplies for Repulse Bay. The season was advanced and the prevailing winds were north and north-west, making it a very doubtful trip back up the coast under sail. Cleveland had three natives on each boat.

So with the welfare of the Repulse Bay natives in mind, the RCMP agreed to tow the two coast boats from Chesterfield Inlet to Repulse with the *Caribou*. In addition to W.E., there was Sgt. W.O. Douglas, who later joined HBC and built several successful mink and fox farms (one was at Birds Hill here in Manitoba). The *Caribou* engineer was a man named Pierce, and old John Ell, later quite famous in that area as a hunter and guide, was along as pilot.

Anyway, the tow didn't move very fast and they had little navigational equipment so they usually anchored for the night wherever they could find shelter. Cleveland was an excellent cook, so the three crews usually met aboard his boat for the evening meal.

One night, Douglas and Brown came on board to find Cleveland busy with a hammer and screwdriver opening a heavy flat crate. It had very indistinct markings and he thought it might be stove parts that he had ordered. Instead, it was Rev. Haythornethwaite's tombstone that he uncovered. It had been obviously overcarried from Charlton Island, landed at Chesterfield Inlet, and somehow gotten mixed in with the Repulse Bay cargo.

They nailed the crate up and planned to ship it back to Chesterfield Inlet, where it would be put on the *Nascopie* the following year to go back down to Charlton Island and Moose Factory. You see, in 1920 the ship went to Chesterfield Inlet first, then to Charlton Island.

The stone should have gone to its destination direct from Chesterfield but it has never been seen, as far as we can find out, since that night.

I'd more or less forgotten it again, but tonight W.E. Brown, now very old, but bright and with an excellent memory, called me. Someone had questioned his dates and he was concerned. He has kept a diary for many years (I hope the archives get it eventually) and is upset that someone questions the dates he has given.

Want to hear about a coincidence? Yesterday I went to see Miss Preston (at *The Beaver*) about W.E.'s little problem. As usual, she was behind a mountain of paper but I got her to come out from behind, gave her a few old sail needles I found in Moosonee, and asked her for anything she might be able to give me on the trip the *Caribou* made.

She got down the earliest file of *The Beaver*, 1919, put it on her desk and stopped to untie the lace that holds it together and the volume opened. In her dry way she said, "This may be interesting," and passed me the book. It had opened to an article called "What happened at Moose Factory in the Fall of 1920." The first item I read, from old Mr. Gaudet's journal of events, said: August 31, 1920:

"...Today we finally managed to put out the fire started by Rev. Hay-thornethwaite..."

A bush fire, I gather, but if Rev. H were alive and well and setting fires, accidentally even, in August of 1920, how could his tombstone be on George Cleveland's coast boat in the same year? W.E. has to be wrong, unless Mr. Gaudet and *The Beaver* and L.A. Learmonth are wrong and the very idea is too terrible to consider.

I have been reading *Them Days* and *Atlantic Insight*, and I think my roots are hurting. I am remembering November when I was little. All the fishermen came in and shipped their fish, and loaded their boats with the things they needed for the trapping season. Instead of nets and twine and jiggers and hooks, they had axes and tents and barrels of flour and great tubs of butter. They had dogs and harness, and instead of boots, moccasins beautifully sewn with water tight seams by their women, who were either part Eskimo, or had learned from the Eskimo women.

There was always a faint smell of wood smoke as people warmed their houses against the cold to come, a smell of wood bark as huge piles of wood were sawn for winter and, of course, the smell of saw dust.

Day after day things changed slowly. I knew that the fall was getting on when one day the old cooper put all his wood brine buckets in a dory and took them to the brook where he laid them out in a row with their tops just under water to "sweetin" them before he put them away for the winter. To keep them under water he placed a round stone in each one. When he was finished, he piled the stones on the shore where they were locally known as "James' Rocks." No one ever touched them year after year.

When I heard many years later that he had died, I wrote Gus Flowers and asked him to get James' Rocks and make a border around his grave. I hope he did, I never heard. I wish I could give you a picture of his hands, Claudia. They were big, calloused from years of holding heavy hammers, but gentle, incredibly gentle. I remember yet how it felt when he was teaching me to whet-stone a draw-knife, how gentle that big hand was, how mobile the long fingers, how they held my little paw and showed me the correct angle. Yes. I'll have to tell you about James, because his is a story that must be told.

The geese came back and the water of the inlet was alive with sea birds, auklets like little miniature penguins, only as big as a robin but paddling around miles from land, huge self-satisfied eider ducks and gaggles of harlequins (lovely name) and scooters and sea pigeons and great black-backed gulls with their screaming and greediness. And the loons, the solitary huge northern divers that swam purposefully on the surface like black and white ghosts, appearing with hardly a ripple to mark the spot and vanishing silently so that you could not believe that they had ever been there.

The sounds that carried so far in the clear air. I used to sit on the hill across from the post and watch someone chopping wood. He'd stop and the sound of his axe would continue for a few seconds. Once I saw a woman open a door, step outside for a moment, then return to the house and close the door. After she vanished, I heard in succession her voice call to a child, and the slam of the door, and there was no one visible to cause the sounds. And I saw a man with a wheelbarrow going down a bumpy board walk. First he moved along in silence, then the rumblety-rumble of the wheel reached me, then he stopped and the noise of the wheel came clearly to me. It was like another dimension.

I had a special place where I used to sit under a huge balsam fir. Its branches drooped almost to the ground, almost like a tent. I could sit there and see everything at the post laid out on the point that jutted out into the inlet. I could see into the inlet as far as Henrietta Island and out into the misty blue Atlantic. I could see the tide hurrying in to raise the water till you would fear our wharf had to be submerged and I'd watch the big gentle black whales move slowly against it, feeding on the shoals of fish that came and went with the tides.

I knew so many of those whales as individuals. No one ever hunted them, they came year after year. The great grandfather that was around before even the oldest man could remember, he had a crooked point to his fin. There was one with a curious white mark near his eye. There was a portly old lady nearly always attended by a youngster, but we never saw her with a baby. Apparently she always gave birth far to the south.

They were there day and night. Many the time I awoke in the midnight silence and lay waiting for the long "soough" that told me they were there, like me, resting, but allowing themselves to sink slowly till their air was exhausted, then coming to the surface to breathe in a somnambulistic fashion. In the clear early mornings they'd awaken and their breathing became brisk and business-like as they started feeding.

All summer they came and went, a mile or so apart, and if you put a paddle or a pole into the water and put your ear against it, you could hear them talking to one another. An American scientist came one year with a fantastic listening device and spent hours listening and recording on a primitive wire recorder. I was with him early and late and he told me a lot about whales, especially black whales. There was, he said, not one single instance where those huge peaceful creatures had ever shown the slightest hostility to man. I could understand because many times I had been fishing and would see the big black shadow pass under my boat. Many times I had been enveloped in stinging spray from their breath as they blew only feet away. There is a strange bitter smell to their breath, and it stings on your face. On the surface they are voiceless but under the water their voices chuckle and reverberate till you want to laugh too.

In November, they'd gather in pods and go through their mating routine, breathtaking in its simplicity and grace. Perhaps half a dozen beautiful black backs would show above the water in an unaccustomed display as normally they merely surface to breathe and immediately disappear. Now they swam with the whole back exposed and would approach one another swimming fast, and as they met would

turn half over on their sides and couple for seconds only, then separate and submerge only to surface again and go through the same
stately movements again. Unlike walrus and seals, there is no fight-
ing or bellowing. There doesn't seem to be any rivalry. I think they
must mate for life. Sometimes two pairs would mate at the same time,
more often one pair in the pod, then another pair and so on. I have
seen busy people just stop and watch the ritual that ensured that we
would always have our kindly friends with us.

In spring, the arrival of the geese, ducks and small birds was
eagerly anticipated. The arrival of the grampus was spring. I have
seen my mother come in with wet eyes and say, "The grampus are
here." When they came, there would be a new smell on the air in the
deep water coves. The smelt were running and we'd have fresh smelt
for a brief period, then they were gone, and some night in November
my dad and I would go down to the wharf, on a calm moonlight night
when the spring tides brought the cold salt water far up on the rocks,
and there would be that smell and the surface of the water would look
like it was raining. We'd catch a few dozen and they'd go into the big
iron fry pan and we'd eat them with fresh bread and lots of tea and go
to bed happy. From then until the ice formed I'd tend a smelt net, and
how my hands would ache, taking those small perverse fish out of the
icy water. But it was worth it.

Fat tasty smelt for breakfast, then a trip to see how all the summer
puppies were faring, a call to see how the goats, Belle and Reckless,
had survived the night and I could go to school, not happy perhaps,
but able to bear being shut in for a few hours in November, when
every thought in my head was to be outside.

I'd like you to see the fat partridge sitting in the trees so quietly
while their cousins, the ptarmigan, fly and celebrate the ripening of
the berries and their summer plumage changes from brown to white.
It would be nice to show you some of the things that are left, but so
much is gone to greed and carelessness.

Same day—only at night now.

I guess we all get into places and situations where our lives are in danger. Perhaps we had more opportunity than a lot of other folk. To say one never feared would be a lie. I have been deathly scared many times, but I can look back at those times now and not remember the fear, only the gladness that I survived.

Once Bill Metcalfe and I were crossing Hebron fiord on very thin ice. Salt water ice is elastic and it's possible to see a wave running ahead of a dog team. If there is open water nearby, the seas will run under the ice and it's almost like being in a boat. No one goes out on thin ice unless there is a good reason, and I guess we thought we had a good reason. But if those rollers get big enough, the ice will eventually split, especially over shoal water. Well it happened. Bill and his team were driving along parallel to me about a hundred feet away, when suddenly a huge roller passed under us. I was over deeper water and my ice held. I was shocked beyond words to see Bill and his team disappear, the whole works, in seconds.

I knew I shouldn't, but I stopped my team. When the next roller passed, the ice opened again and I could see Bill struggling among the broken ice. He could just reach the end of my long whip and with the help of a couple of natives who had seen what happened, we got him out. All in all we rescued all his gear and only two dogs drowned. The rest were pretty groggy but after a few minutes they were rolling in the snow on the shore to dry themselves and ready to go back on the ice again. I'll never forget the fear that gripped me when Bill and his team disappeared.

Winnipeg, December 4, 1982

Dear Claudia,

Another day… morning rather, of oral history with Mrs. McKillop;[15] from nine till noon, and we are only at Hebron. At this rate it will take all winter.

Do you know how long it takes to tell about sixty-five years? Well yes, I know it naturally takes me longer.

People wonder how we survived in those primitive days away up in that barren, isolated country. It wasn't that way at all. It was a special, wonderful experience, in no way a hardship. No shows, no radio, no TV, no restaurants, no people. "Whatever did you do?" I feel like saying don't ever feel sorry for people who have had what I have. Some lucky ones get, or got, to go north. I'm luckier than that. I was born there. I got to grow up among some of the finest people ever. Wish my kids could. I wish I could give it to Joshua, to you, to all my favourite people.

One day, before either of you were born, and I wasn't very old either, I went looking for a lost canoe with a little Naskapi boy who was lame. A birth injury, I imagine, and there can be no more terrible misfortune to a person who is born a nomad than lameness. But he was bright and cheerful, and we walked along the river picking the easiest route because of his disability and because he fiercely resented help.

He said he knew a place, "*kitchee midassin*," very fine, and offered to show me. So we left the river and scrambled through dense under-brush till we came to a brook that came straight from the hills and was clear and cold and very sweet. The bottom was white stones all the

---

15 Jocelyn McKillop, the HBC archivist, was interviewing Len for an oral history project for The Hudson's Bay Company.

way. The pattern the sun made on those stones through the trees was an incredible display of sun and shadow. The water was rapid and the whole effect was a continuous kaleidoscope of brilliance and shadow too beautiful to describe.

We followed the brook along to a little jewel of a lake, small, almost perfectly round. It was ringed right to the edge with huge balsam firs where branches almost dipped into the water. There was not a sign of man anywhere except, about halfway along, there was a small platform made of poles covered with dry branches. It had been there a long time.

The boy told me that it once held his baby brother's body, till the band could take it to North West River for burial by their priest. He wasn't sad about it. He seemed glad that the little boy had rested there where everything was so beautiful. I wish I could describe that place, the green of the trees, the clear water, the white stones, the absolute silence, the feeling of content, "*kitchee midassin*."

We sat there a long time and I was half asleep when I felt his hand on my knee, a small brown hand with slim fingers. A capable strong little hand that caused an intolerable ache when I remembered his twisted hip. But he was warning me to be quiet.

Two muskrats had surfaced right in front of us. One had a long water lily shoot in its mouth. It started to nibble on one end and the other started eating on the other. The result was inevitable. They met halfway down where they stopped, each holding on to his half inch, each staring into the other's face. Finally the boy could stand it no longer and he went into a delighted peal of laughter that caused the animals to splash violently and disappear while the boy's mirth echoed around and around the lake.

I know people of my age here who have never seen a death, much less assisted at the end, dug the grave, make the coffin and sometimes read the service. We expected that to happen pretty early in life. The worst was the lack of medical help, the lack of medicine. The waiting for the inevitable. I don't want that for my kids. In a way though I'm glad I did it. I know now some things were intolerably hard. To put the first shovelful of earth on a tiny casket. The first time I couldn't, and an understanding man took the shovel from me.

Not a cheerful subject. It's just that talking about it has opened a wound or two, even after all those years. Maybe wounds were inevitable too, but the good things are so much more vivid.

Once I knew a native woman who had had a number of children. Not one lived more than a few days. She was reconciled to it, and once when we were travelling and her time was very near, she said, almost casually, that when it came it wouldn't be long and we could go on as before. But her eyes told what she was going through.

The baby came in the night, and we moved to another igloo. In the morning I went in to see her, and she showed me a fat baby, already nursing like mad, and I will never see a happier face than she showed me as she said, "*Angoti*," a man. What a precious man, strong and healthy after so many that died.

I can't begin to tell you how I felt when we brought back Christine's only daughter to her when she feared the girl was dead. There's a native way of putting their hands gently on your face to express gratitude and it creates a certain emotion never to be forgotten. A tiny little woman did that to me at Repulse Bay when I gave her two bony fox carcasses to eat. Gratitude for what? One more day perhaps. She had one small fish later that she insisted on sharing with me. Then I knew gratitude because in comparison her gift was so much more than mine.

December is trotting along nicely. We have worn out our first moon. It was small and fragile looking this morning but will soon be growing big again. Perhaps the nicest way of telling time is the native way of sleeps, moons and summers. Who wants to be more accurate than that? You are right. The dusty little men who calculate interest due. Dickens knew them way back then.

Dickens must have moved around a lot. He seemed to have met a sample of just about every type of humanity. Of them all, I like David

Copperfield's Aunt Betsy best of all, and perhaps Miss Murdstone was the nastiest piece of work, though her brother never generated much affection either. Guess I was introduced to that book pretty early. I took it all literally and had no thought or conception of the social commentary. I was like David first time around. At that time, perhaps even now, I thought that living in an old ship, bottom up on the shore, was the greatest possible way to live. I used to get very solemn at Mr. Peggoty's "Drownded."

There was another book, called *Naomi*, about an orphan. It had to be the most read book in our house. I'd still read it if I could find it, and always have a sneaking hope it will turn up at some bookstore. Maybe better not, actually. The memory I have is so good. Perhaps in re-reading it fifty odd years later, it might lose something. It must have been very well written. I can still remember the descriptions of storms and a funeral. Heigh-ho.

Nice to be back at ten years old again but where would you be? Nope. Much better to stay here at senior citizen level. Be nice though, to visit back to, say 1930. That was a good sort of year and I was all of thirteen, about as shy as a kid could be. I was wrapped up in the HBC at Rigolet and filled with admiration for the men who made it the place it was: Will Shewak, the foreman carpenter, Eskimo heritage, one of the most handsome faces I ever saw, the darkest eyes and the straightest whitest teeth. When Will smiled he had the most expressive face and he smiled a lot.

And James Dickers, the cooper. He hardly ever smiled but had a sort of humour. He was a craftsman, and not a barrel or keg, or puncheon, tun, cask or butt, that he made was ever less than perfect.

And John Blake, the one-armed skipper of our little schooner. He could do what any other man could do, including go aloft in the masts. He could square a lot as true as any man using only his one hand, which handled that heavy broad axe like a chipping hammer.

They were so kind. They tolerated me and my questions and were never too busy to show me exactly how it was done, and made sure I could do it properly. John could splice rope using his one hand and a foot. I was very young when he showed me how and I can still hear his laugh when he found me practising using only one hand and my foot. I was getting quite adept too.

Yes, to visit back at thirteen would be nice, or at twenty three— even forty-six. Perhaps it would be possible to recapture the original thrills. The first time I looked into a valley filled with caribou in their hundreds, so many that a mere human meant nothing more to them than the wolves that hung around the edge of the herd. The day I lay on a rock overhanging a lake at Repulse Bay with an empty stomach, and all I had for a hook was a bent wire. How my heart stopped when a monster trout casually nipped at it but wouldn't open his mouth. The pain of holding my breath and guiding that piece of wire into his gill. The ecstatic moment when it slid in and I hauled him out of the water in one swift lunge. It was the only way, and how good he was to a stomach used to ground squirrels and overripe gulls eggs.

My first sturgeon too. I can't explain the feeling as you see the reeds moving in the muddy water and know your fish is there, unseen. You have to watch the reeds carefully and estimate where the head is, then drive the spear down, sight-unseen. The thrill comes when you score a hit. It might be a twenty-pounder who'll give you an awesome fright, or an eighty-pounder who will contemptuously smash your spear like a straw and go his way. Sounds cruel, but a person will fill his belly the way he can. Perhaps one of the greatest thrills was one night I was alone on watch in the Canadian Marconi station at Cartwright. There was nothing doing on the ship frequency and I was tuning a small ham receiver idly, just listening to the talk. There were no voice sets in those days, and suddenly a way off on a quiet land I heard a whisper of Morse, a faint, faint voice away out, it seemed beyond the stars. And it called C-Q which is a general call.

On impulse I answered on the little ham set the chief operator and I had built. I nearly stopped breathing when he replied. He was in Antarctica with a survey and exploration group. He wanted a ham contact to get a message home to England. So I called C-Q on the ship frequency and raised a British merchant ship in the Atlantic.

I heard him raise another and that ship had a ham operator who was in contact with an English station. I waited, not able to hear any more till an hour later the merchant ship called me back with a reply and I called the station away down near the South Pole and he answered even more faintly. But he acknowledged my message and the last I heard was his "Tks O-M" as his signal faded out. That means "Thanks, old man." I went off watch shortly after and to my bed, but I never slept a wink. I had the most glorious feeling of accomplishment. It was a once in a lifetime thrill.

I can't explain it, Claudia. Imagine that almost inaudible thread of sound coming from nowhere, and I could read it and re-transmit it and return the message to nowhere. There are so many things.

Once I was walrus hunting with a group of natives and Father Cartier. A boatload of walrus meat is not pretty—necessary for life, but unlovely and you cannot escape it. It's meat and blood wherever you look. There is no cabin, the boat is full, you put a tarpaulin on the meat and your sleeping robe on that and sleep there.

In time your nerves are stretched to breaking. The natives have no such emotions. That meat is life, light, heat and survival. They almost embrace it. The smell is horrible. I lay there one morning knowing that I'd have to endure another day because the weather was bad. The ice was moving in and we could not go anywhere.

Then Father Cartier carefully dressed himself in his robes, set up an altar, and celebrated his morning mass as though he was in a cathedral somewhere. In the midst of such massive uncleanliness, he said his prayer as unconcerned as he was at home.

Maybe that wasn't exactly a thrill but it was something I had never experienced, and it gave me another view of a very wonderful person. Perhaps he felt as I did, but he had a way of cleaning himself which I had not. I've never mentioned that before. I'm not sure why, but you'll understand. I'd like to see your face as you read, because somehow you'll know how I felt. Sometimes my letters to you become a sort of confessional of the things I have never talked about. Things I treasure, things I am not sure about. Thank you for understanding.

FOUR

Morning, December 9, 1982

Dear Claudia,

...The cold north wind assaults the Labrador coast for a goodly portion of the winter. True there are days when the south wind blows softly, the snow is moist and the air is mild and balmy in comparison, but sooner or later the north wind returns.

It follows that any valley facing into the north wind is gradually filled with snow during the winter. The first storm lays a scattering of white among the boulders, succeeding storms add to the accumulation till by spring there is no sign of the rocks and boulders, the valley is one smooth expanse from top to bottom. In some cases, gently curved up at the sides like a modern bobsleigh. What a place for a sled ride, and that brings me to my story.

The valley at Tikataw was one unobstructed slope for two miles, straight as an arrow from the sea beach to the top of the hills, two miles at a steep angle that would gladden the eye of any ski slope operator.

As soon as the spring days arrived, the village children could be seen on the lower part of the steep slope, sliding on every imaginable substance. Whole polar bear skins, hair side down, would carry a whooping, laughing crowd of youngsters lickety-split down to the shore ice in seconds, and, as mother well knew, remove some of the stains that might have been left on the hide while it was still worn by the bear, a double advantage perhaps.

There would be small *komatiks* made of scarce wood by an indulgent parent or a single hard-wood barrel stave on which a child perched on one knee and slid down while performing impossible balancing feats. Those equipped with sealskin trousers climbed up, sat down, and were whisked to the bottom on their rear, ignoring the inevitable bumps while attempting if possible to foul a climbing companion and bring him to the bottom long before he wanted. Groups of happy kids would end up at the foot of the hill in one glorious tangle, and many a parent would cluck disapproval at night over worn garments and ripped seams. There is no sweeter sound after the long winter silence than these youthful voices in the clear, still northern air.

There's a great gathering at Easter for the Moravian services. Hunters and their families come from all directions and in no time an igloo village springs up on the sea ice near the church. Usually it is not on the ice at the foot of the valley, but one builds where material is available and this particular year, good snow was found right at the foot of slope.

Magdalena was a widow. She was also a victim of the 1917 polio epidemic struck that the Labrador together with the Spanish influenza epidemic. Magdalena had been on crutches most of her life, homemade crutches that earned her the name of Kejuk or wood. She travelled and lived with her husband's family, who were good to her. She had a small government pension. In the thirties it was small indeed. It was paid in goods at the trader's store and helped to support her. When she could get around before the snow got too deep, she trapped the odd fox. The rest of the time she sat in her igloo or tent, sewed boots from the skins her relatives gave her, cleaned hides, and did the many things that fill an Eskimo woman's day.

For an Eskimo, she was a dour, independent type, asking little from anyone, accepting only what she must. She had never had any children. She did not pay much attention to the village youngsters, who expected it from their elders, and so they did not play or visit around Magdalena's as they did elsewhere. When she needed a pail of water from the river, she did not call the nearest child as the other women did. She would hang a pail on a peg set in the crutch and laboriously travel the quarter of a mile to the river and back. We hauled our water in hundred gallon lots by dog team and wagon in summer, and I finally persuaded Magdalena to call at our kitchen and get what she wanted at no inconvenience to us. She didn't speak a lot but occasionally I met her leaving with her little pail of water. The smile of thanks she gave transformed her worn, slightly bitter face into something of a Madonna of the snows.

This particular spring, her relatives built her usual tiny igloo near the beaten track to the church so that she could get to and from more easily. It just so happened it was directly in line with the middle of the valley.

Once everyone had assembled for the Easter festival and all the news had been passed around, there was not much to do, and the young men and some not so young became restless. Every year that smooth unbroken slope of snow in the valley proved to be irresistible. At first a crowd of teenaged boys, and perhaps the odd girl, would haul one of the massive travelling *komatiks* part way up the slope, and fifteen or twenty would climb on and down they would come and away out on the level sea ice.

Sooner or later the more adult men get the fever and suddenly you would see staid hunters busily hauling *komatiks* further and further up the valley to come roaring down, faster and faster and ending amid shouts of laughter far out on the ice. The women and the more timid girls stood in groups and cheer their favourites on. After a day or so, there seemed to be few timid girls.

The climax seemed to come a day or so before everyone was due to leave again for the outlying camps and the spring hunt. By this time, the trader, the policeman, their helpers and everyone except the missionaries were involved. Races were set up, and, of course, the more weight, the faster and further you went, so came down completely loaded with happy humanity.

In the spring I am speaking of, there were six white men at he village not counting the missionary. This was probably the largest number of whites that had ever wintered there. Early one morning, several young men invited us to be part of their team who would challenge the rest of the village to a race.

I had the longest, newest *komatik* and they carefully dressed its runners and got everything ready for the race. We decided to make a trial run and hauled the *komatiks* right up to the very top of the valley. It was a long way up and I remember a certain hollow feeling as I thought of the speed we would attain on the way down. There were seventeen of us, all fairly heavy types. The snow was hard and the surface good. We could not fail to make a record run.

Two of the stronger men were on the front as steersmen: Sam, the policemen's assistant, and a massively built young man named Millik. They would steer our juggernaut as well as they could but nothing on earth could stop us once we got moving.

We were seated roughly in order of weight, lightest in front behind the steersmen, heaviest on the back. This put me in the middle, a place where one could not bail out if panic took over. The course had been cleared, all children and dogs removed from our path. We would go straight down, then make a gradual swing to left or right to miss the igloos in our path, and so out on the ice. The course had already been run several times and there had been no difficulty.

I had been over many high hills with a dog team, always with a walrus hide or chain drag to slow me down if things got hectic. There would be no drag this time. We would go as fast as possible, leaning to right or left as the steersmen directed. I will confess that when I looked away down the valley at those tiny houses, tiny people, and thought of the trip down, my stomach settled itself uncomfortably near my Adam's apple.

Too late to repent now, we were away. The three men on the back started us off. Not that we needed that push, we were already pointed downwards at something close to forty-five degrees, at least it seemed that much. The first few moments were fairly quiet. Then as our speed increased, everyone announced the fact at the top of his lungs. I was sitting in front of Joseph, whose general build was that of a bear. He had his arms wrapped around me and I felt that if could hear above the uproar, I would be able to count my individual ribs by the sounds they made as they broke, one by one, under the pressure. However, I was probably exerting something of the same pressure on the unfortunate in front of me.

I could not see ahead because of the people in front and because of the constant stream of powdered snow sent up by the steersmen's feet as they fought to keep the *komatik* straight. I got a glimpse of the church as we flashed by. Then I heard Sam and Millik shout urgently for us all to shift our weight to the right. We had been going to turn left at the igloos but a small pup had managed to stray into our path followed by a child who was bent on catching the pup. Neither saw us hurtling down on them.

We all leaned to the right, but we were already too far the other way. We missed the child and the pup and roared out onto the ice out of control and in an instant we had smashed into one side of Magdalena's house and out the other. I saw the poor old lady cowering on her sleeping platform and we went shooting past and out on the ice.

There is not an unkind bone in the average Eskimo's body, but the whole gang were helpless with laughter long before we stopped. They knew the old lady was not hurt and they would speedily build her a new home, so they rolled on the snow and howled their mirth.

The policeman and I knew that as persons of some authority we must go back and put matters right with Magdalena. I shook some sense into my hysterical assistant and sent him at a fast run to the store for some peace making supplies, then I joined the policeman and headed for Magdalena's igloo.

When we got there, she was wrathfully gathering her belongings out of the welter of snow, and she greeted us with a black look and a sharp tongue. By this time, many of the other women were there and they were clustering around helping and offering sympathy. All the while they promised to wreak suitable punishment on their erring men folks. Our opposing team, who had not yet climbed the valley, were there and many witty and cutting remarks were make on our abilities, remarks that were belied by the twinkle in their eyes.

While I was humbly trying to explain to Magdalena what had caused us to suddenly erupt into her placid domicile, she suddenly threw both her crutches away and collapsed on the snow in gales of laughter. At first I couldn't conceive that she saw the funny side, but she did. She lay and gasped helplessly, probably as much at having brought the mighty white men to their knees as at the destruction of her igloo. There was nothing wrong with her sense of humour.

My assistant soon arrived with a pound of her favourite tea, a package of ship's biscuit which she dearly loved, a couple of plugs of black tobacco, which immediately vanished into her capacious boot leg, as Moravian ladies don't smoke, and last but by no means the least, a new pipe.

A competent crew soon built a new igloo and moved Magdalena's belongings in, lit her lamp and got her comfortably settled. She soon recovered from her lapse into laughter and her features resumed their usual expression, but I am not sure that the twinkle disappeared from her brown eyes.

It was some time before our express trip through Magdalena's igloo was forgotten, some time before I could drive my team through the village and not see broad smiles and a merry pretence of panic.

December 10, 1982

Dear Claudia,

Don't suppose I ever told you about when I first worked in a store. I wasn't even an employee, just filling in for someone else. My dad always allowed us lots of time for fishing and sailing and whatever, but he also believed boys should get learning early. So one day I was put into the store with all my shyness (he probably knew exactly what he was doing).

Anyway, I was scared to death of females, more especially strange ones, and this big, big, mannish American volunteer worker for the Grenfell Hospital strode in.

The other clerks became very busy. We had no girls and her breeziness sailed up to the little guy shrinking behind the long counter. No self-serve these days. We had to take things off the shelf and display them on the counter.

The large lady was going out to the coast and wanted warm clothing. Specifically, long johns.

We had a hideous garment, a one-piecer, neck to ankles a nasty grey colour mottled with a sort of purple fleece, lined with buttons and with a big hatch in the back. Probably the original hatchback. Anyway, this is what she demanded in a voice that could be heard up and down the Labrador and probably into Quebec.

Timidly I asked what size. She boomed, "How do I know. Bring 'em on boy, we'll see."

So in a short time she had small, medium, large and what was known as double-extra-large spread out all over. You gotta realize those days were one degree removed, at least on Labrador, from puritan times. Everything went on the clothes line but ladies' unmentionables. Honest, except for the limited stock we sold, I hadn't the faintest idea and here we were with acres of intimate things spread all over, and me at thirteen or fourteen, about to have an attack of apoplexy.

She held the infernal things against her and grinned at me over the top. I guess the item since known as a bra hadn't been invented, because our plum line double-extra-large had pockets fashioned right into the garment into which she shoved her fist and frowned dubiously, meantime asking me what I thought. I guess I thought about all sorts of things including smashing my way to freedom through a window.

When she made her selection and finally left, my troubles were only beginning because the clerks had seen my travail and were in a mood to enjoy it. If I hadn't been scared I think I'd have gone to my dad and resigned the position. Come to think of it I'd have resigned the human race, especially the part that wore plum line, double-extra-large. You can't imagine how desperately ugly a mottled grey undy in DXL can be. Nope, you have to see it.

I think I had nightmares that included Miss Whatever striding from iceberg to iceberg clad only in her longies which at least preserved decency in a repulsive manner. So much for shy people.

Winnipeg, December 16, 1982

Dear Claudia,

Today when I went outside early in the morning, it was very still, even in the city, that old insomniac.

There are times when you may think she is asleep and you are reluctant to touch her, but she isn't really. She's just lying there thinking about all the things a city must think about. At such a time you feel a bit strange standing in her bedroom and you wonder if she's not a bit of a fraud in her white bed gown of neat suburbs, the Tuxedo-Wildwood part showing as an embroidered bed jacket which covers the tattered nightgown the poor thing has worn for years. She's always afraid someone will see the Jarvis side of her.

And she's listening too, always listening. For what, I'm never sure, for an ambulance, or a fire call perhaps. She makes me a little afraid, apparently sleeping, but never quite concealing the massive human misery that must be when large numbers of people live cheek-by-jowl. The occasional picture in the paper showing ugly rooms with peeling paint and warped doors and broken windows make me scared too, because I don't know how much of it is my responsibility. Maybe she is just pretending to be asleep because she is scared too.

But it was still this morning. And I rested my face on my gloves on the roof of the car because I wanted to add one more morning to the mosaic of dawns that I have built in my memory. Not well said.

One can't remember that many mornings, but he does collect impressions. I guess I have faced morning with every emotion I am capable of, certainly with a huge amount of gratitude for the things that morning has brought. There's some regret that I may have, by neglect or inattention, soiled a part of the fabric, but looking back I am tolerably well pleased that at least a fair portion of the mornings given to me are of clean memory and unsullied. They form a tapestry, if you will, and the general effect of a tapestry is good, so you don't go poking around for little imperfections.

So while I stood there, remembering and listening, while the old lady city stirred in her sleep, the boy next door started his muffler-less wonder, shattering the fabric into a million pieces. The city woke and threw up her covers indignantly, and December 16th started to operate.

Now all of a sudden it's Sunday afternoon and the cats and I are alone. A friend called the other day and among other things, I told her how much my grandson talks. She said, "So much for heredity. What else is new?" Low blow, well, maybe not.

My dad always said I liked the sound of my own voice. He did pretty well too, except he had a good singing voice and knew dozens of old Irish and Scots songs. I listened to him many a night in camps where someone we met would ask him to "oblige." The most I ever heard him sing was once while we were travelling by motor boat when there was lots of ice in spring. He lost his pipe overboard and he dearly loved his smoke. Because of the ice it was a slow trip, and there was nowhere to replenish his loss, so he sang by the hour. Once he said, "You don't know how lucky you are not smoking," then he quietly added, "but I wish you did today."

All those old people smoked pipes. My dad and James Dickers used HBC Imperial mixture which might have tasted like tobacco but out in the open air it smelled wonderful. I think I'd remember that scent today. They got so much enjoyment out of their evening pipes. My dad would get his feet up and sit near the big box stove and light his pipe with a coal from the fire box. He said it tasted better. Then he'd sit and listen to the BBC news from Britain and look so comfortable.

There was a ceremony too. When someone sold a good lot of fur, my dad would offer his black tobacco pouch and the trapper would allow he wouldn't mind. Some of them would mischievously stuff as much as they could into their battered old pipes so they'd almost need a mustard plaster on the back of their neck to draw the smoke. The object, if there were two or three trappers, would be to extract every last crumb of tobacco out of the old man's pouch.

And if it were late in the evening, they'd put over their trading till the next day and sit around the office stove yarning, and I'd smell the wood smoke on their clothing and see the worn shoulders of their jackets, worn by the gun and packsack, and the white crosses on the toes of their moccasins from snow shoe straps, and envy them their lonely cold days, their cosy nights tucked away in some silent valley in their daily battle with nature to extract a living for their families from a bountiful but reluctant land. Quiet self-sufficient men, who in some cases hardly knew more than to read and write. But men to admire, men to listen to, men who left you with something new, some unforgettable word or experience. Trappers, hunters, fishermen, boat builders, carpenters, all those qualities packed into one man in many cases. Build a cabin, a house or a boat or coffin, and they'd easily walk twenty miles to help someone, comfort someone, or if time permitted, for a game of cards.

We had a sort of round robin card game going at the post once. No stakes, no one gambled. My brother had had a winter long streak of luck, and one night as we sat in to play in the "men's kitchen," two young men walked in from Doublemere. To trade? No, they wanted a game of cards and twenty miles wasn't a long walk. We played till midnight, and they broke my brother's streak. Then they put their snowshoes on and left again, twenty miles home to a normal day's work the next day. I don't think any of us raised an eyebrow. It wasn't anything special.

Can I tell you about Bill Suggaski, a Cree from Kirkness Lake? OK.

One winter, Angus Comber and I left Pikangikum for Red Lake in a wonderful Bombardier, a ten-passenger snowmobile. It had clutch problems, and we knew we only had a small chance of getting to the garage at Red Lake. However, every mile was one nearer help. We left long before daylight, and at six a.m. we met Bill and stopped to chat. He was starting out to visit part of his trap line and was already a dozen miles from home, on foot.

We continued on our way and when we were almost exactly half way to Red Lake, about forty miles behind us and the same before, the clutch gave up. So, since there was no trail broken in front and we had our track to travel on, we headed back to Pikangikum on snow shoes.

About dark, we met Bill again, heading home. He'd been on foot probably fourteen hours then. We had stopped to make tea and he joined us. Then he said he'd run home, a mere ten miles, get his dog team, and come back, and his dogs could haul our packs home. He took off in the darkness and we continued on our way. We had thirty miles to walk.

Before long Bill caught up again. He had two small dogs and a toboggan. He loaded our packsacks and gave Angus the team and he ran off ahead of us again. A few miles further on, we found him with a huge fire going, tea made and moose roasting. We ate, and as I was getting a bit impatient while Angus and Bill discussed yet another pot of tea, I took the little dogs and left them.

It was pleasant trotting along behind the toboggan alone. There was no moon but the stars were huge and bright and seemed only feet up in the air. It was cold, about minus 30 degrees F, but the motion kept me warm. On the lakes the wind was bitter but in the portages it was pure comfort. The trail was broken up into small lakes and long portages through the trees.

It wasn't very long before Bill caught up again. He gave me a grin and ran past with the tea pail and an axe in his hands. Ten or twelve miles along the way he had another fire going, more tea and moose, and a comfortable seat of spruce boughs to sit on. He and Angus were in no hurry and I'm sure they drank a gallon of tea each that night. It was a regular pattern. They'd sit there while I went on, Bill would catch up and go ahead, and every dozen miles there would be tea and a huge fire.

Long after midnight we reached Pikangikum and I was glad to turn in. I awoke in the morning in time to see Bill running across the lake with two dogs, heading back to another day on the trap line. Someone wrote, "Miles to go before I sleep." He couldn't know. Why must we try so hard to make doctors and lawyers out of people who are capable of so much? They'd probably make excellent doctors too, but think what they'd lose.

You mentioned the vapour on the lake. I always liked it. At Rigolet there is such a strong current, the inlet almost never freezes over. I only saw it happen once, my father twice, so all winter we had the vapour billowing up and the ice going in on the rising tide and out on the falling water.

At Rigolet, James Dickers' cooperage was on a little point that had water on both sides and the back. When it was cold and calm, the vapour did wonderful things to the clapboard on the building. It was hand-sawn lumber of course, and the frost crystals would hang on to all the little irregularities and the vapour would brush them, and seem to make them grow. They formed clusters of intricate beauty and were held to the building by the merest fraction. A puff of wind and they'd be gone in a burst of fragile delight, and a new cluster would form immediately. If it remained too long calm, they'd become too heavy for their fragile mounting and fall and become little mounds on the snow. Not even a crystal to show their original exquisite shape.

I used to look at them for what seemed to be hours, constantly changing, flying away and rebuilding. Even though they disappeared, some beauty is fragile and that's right and proper as long as it can reappear.

Just before the harbour froze there would be large clumps of crystals collected on the stringers under our dock. If someone trundled a wheel barrow over the planks, some crystals would fall into the water, and for seconds would retain their original shape spread out in the water. Then they'd dissolve, and slowly sink to join the millions of frost shapes already in the water, waiting to congeal the whole surface of the harbour the moment conditions were right. Once the salt water froze, the same crystals appeared on the surface, just as fragile and beautiful. It was a pleasure to skate through them and see them float away from every stroke of a skate.

A doctor once told me he couldn't bear Rigolet in winter. Too cold, too damp with all the open water, he thought it was ugly. He couldn't see the incredible patterns the drifting ice made as it went in out with the restless water. You would like it, I'm sure.

December 31, 1982

Dear Claudia,

Have a good New Year's Eve, and give my best wishes to friend Kathleen.[16] I am taking care of Josh[17] tonight. My Kathleen gives me these priceless gifts from time to time. Kathleen is a good name. I gave it to my daughter because she was, and is, special. When she was little and her mother was in the hospital, I had her whole care on me, and we sat every night and talked about nice things like fairies, and little fish, and baby birds, and sunbeams, and little grasses growing in the sidewalk. And we polished the big beams on the old fire irons and if you were little enough and stood on the sofa, you could see leprechauns, small grinning faces in the metal. No matter if they moved when you did or laughed when you did, it was only necessary to polish the ball and climb on the sofa to see magic. Magic is good for big people too, and it's there for you and for Kathleen too, because it comes from great affection. Kathleen, being young, will likely think I'm mad, but she's Irish, and fey, and she'll know.

Have a good New Year's Eve. It's a full moon. A full moon on New Year's Eve is the best of luck. You know what to do, of course. Near midnight stand near a mirror. Don't look directly into it but if you sort of sweep it with a casual glance and see yourself, it will tell you what next year will be like. In other words, if you catch an accidental look at yourself and you are looking happy, then 1983 will be happy. I am sure that the accidental glance will catch O'Halloran wishing you a happy New Year's from both of us. Should you be near a set of polished fire irons, look for his face. I wish you only good things in 1983, and Josh and I will toast you at midnight with orange juice.

16 Kathleen Dawson, my friend at Queen's University.
17 Len's grandson.

Winnipeg, January 4, 1983

Dear Claudia,

1982 slipped quietly away, hardly noticed it going. It so happened we were awake at midnight, but Josh had just awakened and needed changing.

I can remember a lot of New Years. Away back [at Rigolet] we used to gather at someone's house and it was a lot different because we'd play cards and there would be a big meal cooking. At the stroke of twelve, we'd all grab shotguns and salute the New Year. If it was nice and calm, we'd hear the guns at Burnt Wood Cove and they would have heard the Palliser's Head guns. We'd pass it along to Dram Brook and the Bight and they'd be heard in Mulliak. Carrawala would hear Mulliak and they'd be heard in English River and Back Bay and Flat Water and Fish Cove.

Once anyway, maybe often, the people at Fish Cove would alert Turners Bight, Mullins Cove, Cunningham's Tickle and perhaps an hour after we had heard our own echoes die away, we'd hear John's Paint. Hard to describe unless you know the geography, but it didn't seem to matter about the exact time. All the little communities followed one after the other.

On windy nights or when we couldn't hear the others, we fired our shots at twelve then went inside for a huge meal and the yarns that went with it. New Year's Day was always a hunting day and there were some pretty sleepy people leaving around daylight. There was a competition to see who made the best hunt. I remember how proud I was when I came home with the biggest tote. I won only by one partridge as I remember, but I was top man at least one New Year.

I also remember once, it was during a blizzard that Sam Lyall and I were returning to Hebron, travelling late to get there on New Year's Eve. It was long past dark in a storm of wind. We were within five miles of home when the lead dog stopped and refused to go on. He was a very special leader and I knew there had to be a reason so I got the trace in my hand and followed it out to where he was.

I couldn't see a thing between darkness and storm but when I reached the dog—he was on a trace perhaps sixty feet long—he was just standing there facing back towards the *komatik*. I could only feel him, and I knew the other dogs were clustered around him, but when I took my mitt off and touched him he was wet. Then I realized that the storm had taken the ice and we could easily have just driven out into open water but for the dog.

We turned back and eventually found the land. It was too dark and stormy to build an igloo so we turned the *komatik* up on its side, took the wrapper off, and called the dogs around. We lay on the snow, covered ourselves with the wrapper, and the dogs lay as close as they could. In a short time the snow covered us over and because we had warm caribou clothing, we slept till daylight. When we could see the next morning, there was nothing but open water between us and home which was across the fiord. To get there we had to go about thirty miles around. It was very cold and we hadn't had much food. It was a New Year's Day I'll remember for a long time. When we finally arrived at Hebron they had a big feast cooked and we ate and ate, then sat in the warmth of the huge old German tile stove and relaxed.

Is there anything better than to relax after a hard day outside in winter? Even if one can't get to a house, a tent is fine, or an igloo. You get warm and fed, and tomorrow is so far away, and every bone in your body lets go of the next one and you feel like Raggedy Anne.

There's always a little time to think before sleep comes. You think the strangest things. I remember looking at myself or as much as I could see, and wondering how it could take so much punishment. I would let my hands wander over a dog and think of the complex system of muscles and nerves that made the most efficient machine that hauled day by day, never complaining, asking only a meal a day and the affection generously shown that is vital for the animal's well being. Sleigh dogs are in some ways so remote and self-sufficient that it's hard to believe they need love, but they do.

I was fiercely proud of my dogs. I gave each individual the affection he needed in the way he needed it, and they responded. I'll give way to anyone in almost any matter but never about dog teams.

Once we were talking about, "if you wish long enough," etc., Mrs. Good, who recently became editor of the *Moccasin Telegraph*, came in and said, "Have you any ideas for something new in Moctel?"

Have I? Well, just slightly. For years I have been hitting bony skulls about the lack of historical articles in Moctel. We get long letters about people's holidays and weddings and that's right and proper in a staff publication, but we have never told people about their heritage and responsibility. Never once said, "Give the things you have to the archives and museum when you don't want them any more so that other people can enjoy them." We have never said, "Get out there and find things. People from all over are taking it away. Where are the HBC folks?" My heavens, Mrs. Good, we could put a biography in every issue till you are old and grey and not scratch the surface.

George Simpson and Simon Mc. And Donald S. are well documented, so for heaven's sake don't think they made HBC. They helped, and R. Parsons, J. Blackall, W. Wilson, J. Dickers, F. Geores, and George Budgell did the work in their time too. They helped.

Poor Mrs. Good! I hope she gets the ringing out of her ears soon. I hit her about our radio network, the only real private commercial one in Canada. Only the flying doctor thing in Australia resembles it and theirs was never so primitive or widespread as ours was. It died last year because satellite communications permit telephones everywhere, but no one thought to preserve the old equipment. No one said lock the building till we see what's what. Mrs. McKillop and I have been voices in the wilderness. Carol Preston too, and no one hears our crying.

The National Museum in Ottawa finally wrote me and said, "Where do we find samples of the equipment of this most unique network?" Where? In peoples' basements, in the junkyard. But I've got Mrs. Good fired up. She's going to print an appeal for people to come forward with what they can, not only radio stuff, anything. When you think what we had all over Canada and what we have left, it's maddening, and time is running out. Yesterday was the day. In ten years there will be no use crying; that's all we'll be able to do then.

I have delayed all I can. We are to have a foreign holiday. Bet I sound aggrieved. (There are two g's aren't there? If not, please give one to someone who would like it.) Let me say I get to pick the foreign place, and I say Portugal, specifically the Algarve, where the White Fleet used to sail from for the Grand Banks and Newfoundland. Alan Villiers wrote a book, *Cruise of the Argus*, and told the story of the lonely fishing villages of Portugal. I want very much to see it. As I am asking, the lines are becoming clearer. We will probably go in March.

I want the small fishing villages, and the sea. As a small boy, I used to get the odd orange off Spanish or White Fleet ships. They were big and really orange, and nothing produced in Florida, Anne Murray not withstanding, can compare. A salt ship would arrive direct from Cadiz, and you might not believe it, but above the lovely smells of steam and coal, there would be the scent of oranges piled in big crates on the bridge deck. We'd heave on the lines and get in the way of the crew tying up the ship and watch the men taking their mess cans to the galley for the mysterious looking mixture of salt fish and vegetables, "Soup of Sorrow," because the man who eats it will return to the banks, and they all had an orange or two on their plates. They'd grin and toss them to the kids on the wharf.

There is no way to describe the taste, especially to a palate that has not had fresh fruit for months. They were big and juicy and so easily peeled. The skins were thin and we saved them and put them in water with sugar and let them stand a while for a delicious drink when the ship was gone and the oranges a memory.

We had a neighbour who was old, arthritic and nearly blind. I took her an orange one day and she reached for it because she smelt it before I even said what it was. With her hooked, stiff hands, she slowly peeled it and separated it into sections. I watched her eat it and it was better than if I'd swallowed it myself. With all her afflictions, she was a merry soul in a crusty way, and she said I was growing up and one day I'd give oranges to some pretty girl who'd be able to twist me around her little finger. I was so shy I couldn't even think about it, but I liked to hear her say so.

Later:
A cold bright morning. Back in the thirties, forty-five years ago, I was a Hudson's Bay Company manager at their post at Hebron, Labrador. Many people associate Labrador with snow and icebergs, huge mountains and killing cold. The snow and ice are there in winter, icebergs drift down from the glaciers in their thousands. There are mountains, mountains of supreme grandeur.

There is beauty. So many times I have been frustrated by my inability to describe the loveliness of a stream that falls five hundred feet down the face of a black cliff into the ocean, what one feels as the huge Atlantic rollers rear their great sullen heads to crash against the timeless granite. The feeling that comes when one sees a half million tons of ice a thousand years old, sculptured into a fantasy of castles and grottos, a frozen fairyland with a clean ethereal beauty.

One is close to nature and one feels love for the creatures that exist in this land. Inevitably one's dogs become much more than mere draught animals. Each one has its own personality, distinct from the others. He or she may be wise or foolish, grave or playful, honest or lazy, but while the breed remained pure there was no hostility no resentment. They were happy to work and were not, as many people claim, wolfish and savage. My dogs had a very special place in my heart.

I guess I was what the local people called a teamster. I delighted in my dogs. I knew each one's moods and habits. I was instantly aware of any change in a dog's health or spirits and I thought of them as

Leonard Budgell, c. 1935. ANNE BUDGELL

Front and reverse of George Budgell's Victory Medal. BUDGELL FAMILY

Below left George Budgell with niece Phyllis. LEONARD BUDGELL

Below right Phyllis Budgell with niece Phyllis. PHYLLIS FAWCETT

North West River, Labrador (Leonard Budgell's birthplace) in the 1930s.
MUN

Inside the Hudson's Bay Company post at North West River.
THEM DAYS MAGAZINE ARCHIVES

Indians at North West River, c.1930. MUN

Dogsled at North West River. MUN

Left: Len with his brother Max, c.1922.

Right: Max Budgell was well known in Labrador
for his unique skills and experiences.
TERENCE BUDGELL

Rigolet, Labrador, in the 1930s. Len Budgell grew up here.
BUDGELL FAMILY

Inhabitants of Rigolet, c.1930, with members of the Budgell and Shewak families. Will Shewak stands at the far left, with Len next to him. George Budgell stands second from right, and his wife, Phyllis, beside him.
BUDGELL FAMILY

Halden Budgell, age 3, on the boardwalks at Rigolet.
ANNE BUDGELL

The Customs House at Rigolet, 1923

Above John Blake of Rigolet, trapper, skipper of HBC schooners.
THEM DAYS / MILLICENT BLAKE LODER

Opposite James Dickers, Hudson's Bay Company cooper at Rigolet.
THEM DAYS / CLARA VOISEY COLLECTION

Fogo Island, Newfoundland, c. 1926. MUN

The house at Fogo where Len's family stayed around 1927,
George Budgell's furlough year.

Ralph Parsons aboard the *Nascopie*, 1938. Son of William "Pappy" Parsons, customs officer at Rigolet, he was the HBC's last fur trade commissioner. He hired Len Budgell. Len always had great admiration for him.

Murdoch McLean, his wife, May, and daughters Merle and Ruby. Murdoch was one of the many Rigolet characters who populated Len Budgell's youth.

The Hebron settlement on the North Labrador coast.
Len Budgell was posted here from 1938 to 1941. HBCA

The Moravian Mission at Hebron, and panoramic view of Hebron. HBCA

The Hudson's Bay Company store at Hebron, c.1940. HBCA

An example of the heavy iron hardware at Hebron that the ghost unlocked.
CLAUDIA COUTU RADMORE

Cape Mugford, Torngat Mountains, south of Hebron. MUN

friends. If we made an exceptional day's journey, I petted each animal a little extra and I basked in the delight that comes from co-operation and success. Many, many times I lay awake at night to savour again every instant of a precious day.

Later:
Had to go downtown this afternoon. On Portage I walked with a youngster for a while. Running shoes, jacket open to mid-chest that wouldn't have been much better fully closed. Bare hands, bare head and he didn't seem to be cold. Made me feel pampered and not too hardy in my parka. Must be how little you wear all along as some of these kids are poorly dressed but don't seem to feel it.

I was pretty casual too once, till I got caught out and froze my face and hands. Old Christina Semigak thawed them out for me with her little gnarled paws and scolded me for a heedless white man. I had walked across the fiord on a nice sunny morning wearing only a windbreaker to look at a net. A storm came up and I had a rough time coming back. I met her and Gustav about a mile out, also on their way—home dragging a seal. She made Gustav strip on his outer kulitak and put it on me, and when we got to her igloo insisted I come in to be thawed. She and her young daughter did it very well too. I lost all the skin on my face of course but no flesh, and my hands were okay.

Couple days later she came in, inspected all my heavy clothing and decided I needed a new kulitak, which she made by measuring around my wrists. That apparently multiplies to give the rest of one's dimensions and since Eskimo clothing is loose fitting, it always works. When she came back, I had inner and outer kulitak, pants, knee length fur socks and winter boots. She scolded me for wanting to pay her because I had kept my boat in the water late in the fall to be sure she and her family got in for the winter. They had lost their only son and it wasn't safe for them to be away out on the land alone.

It was no sacrifice for me. We always kept a boat in late for the seal-ing. But I couldn't give her anything for her hours and hours of work cleaning and tanning the skins and sewing them. A cup of tea sitting on my office floor certainly, nothing else. So when the next festival for young women came along, her daughter, who at twelve sang like a bird, was one of the best dressed in the group. I could arrange that, for in those days they loved ribbons and pretty colours, and, if at all possible, a new *amaktuk*, which is the woman's garment's with the tail. At twelve, they can wear it, but the tail is pinned up, denoting that they are not of marriageable age. They make festival clothing out of HBC duffle and it is most intricately decorated.

On Easter morning at four in the morning the band and choir go to all the graveyards to sing and pray for the recent dead and celebrate Christ's rising. After that they come to the various houses and sing. I could always hear young Christina's beautiful voice above the rest. Rev. Grubb, a musician himself, said she had a perfect voice and made sounds about sending her out, but it couldn't be. Her parents would die, and she would wither away from them. That was very plain to see. Girls don't leave home even when they marry. The groom joins the family for as long as ten years. I've always felt that she lost nothing by never singing on a concert stage. She was appreciated where she was, and besides that, she was loved. She could never have had that in the south. I'm rambling again, must do a little work.

FIVE

Moosonee. Len had gone north early to do some preparation for the season's work with Moosonee Transport.

February 10, 1983

Dear Claudia,

I'm sitting on the second and top floor of the Polar Bear Lodge in Moosonee. It's exactly 8 a.m. and the sun has just come up over Moose Factory Island, and that's what I want to tell you about, but without an instant colour camera and a dictionary of superlative phrases, how can I?

To begin, it's a clear, cold, absolutely still morning. There is a light frost haze which lies just above the level of the snow. My window looks over the road across the ice and the vehicles duck in and out of the haze and the condensation trails left by other vehicles. In a way they look like ducks feeding in a pond. They are visible, disappear and become visible again. The air is so quiet. The haze and condensation hardly moves at all. The sun shines on the roofs of the cars and they are all nicely finished with burnished gold, and there is one lonely dog that came trotting along on his way to somewhere. He is now just a moving dot on the ice, half way to Charles Island.

But it's the sun I want you to see. It's a big red molten ball. It's finally shown its whole circumference above the trees and all the drifts on the river now have rosy tops, underlined in black on the side of the drift facing me, exactly as if mother nature were unsure I'd appreciate the picture she is creating and wants to draw my attention to some of the fine points. Little does she know, or perhaps she does, that I have seen many of her sunrise specials and never seen two which are alike.

So often we would like to freeze time, for me sunrise, whether across the snow, over the mountain, over the sea. If there is a moment of rebirth, that is it. One special moment, before "the cares that oppress the day," only that one moment, because it only takes that much to fill a heart that already has uncounted memories to overflowing.

The moon is different, she can create so many feelings of gladness, sorrow, love. She is a silver chamber of delight. She holds memories, messages. She rises, smiles gently, and passes on her unurgent way over and leaves only her cool breath behind. She has no mandate to create life and colour as she passes. She is there to calm and cool us after the impatient passage of the sun. Much as I love her, much as I would fail without her, much as I love her during long hours of serene sailing, or the storm tossed hours when she frantically rushes through the cloud strewn sky, I will always turn gratefully from her for that one moment in the morning when the first tiny ray of the sun shows, because then a person is renewed.

An old Naskapi Indian on Labrador, Pasteen Assini, was dying. He was very old and had two desires left. One was to see his priest again, the other to commence his spirit voyage at the right time. They brought him by canoe from away inland, just a frame of bones, covered with leathery skin. He couldn't move, he couldn't eat, he couldn't speak. He lay like a dead man in the canoe when my dad and I paddled across the river when the band arrived.

His son said he would not go to the hospital. There was no need. He was only waiting. Later I took two doctors to see him. One was

Dr. Paddon who spent many years at North West River, the other a famous surgeon from the States who gave several months of each year to Grenfell's work in the Labrador. My mother was there too. I'm sure Pasteen had not moved since I had last seen him. The doctors checked him and said if he lived another day it would be a miracle. Because he would need a coffin, they measured him so the hospital carpenter could start getting ready. His son smiled and said, "He will speak in the morning only. He will not die, he will see the priest first."

Claudia, it was several days, perhaps a week before the priest arrived. Pasteen's tent was set as close to the water as possible facing the rising sun, and every morning at sunrise he would rouse, ask for the priest and when he was told that Father O'Brien had not arrived he went, it seemed contentedly, back to sleep.

The doctors were interested and, when they could spare time, one or both would be there at sunrise. I took them to and fro, and several times my mother went along. There was no grief or any change in the routine at the camp. It was just as if the old man had finished preparing for another hunting trip and was resting before departure. The men lay in the grass talking as they always did after the long winter travelling and trapping, and the hard trip down the river to the coast. The women tended the tents, fished, made snowshoes and talked. The children played, that was all. He was sleeping.

Then, one day, Father O'Brien's little white St. Christopher puttered up the bay and into the river. He came at nightfall, saw the doctors, and acting on what they said, went to Pasteen's tent. Only he and Pasteen's wife and son were there inside the tent, but standing outside waiting, my brother and I could hear the old man's whispered responses, and when the priest came out he said that Pasteen had revived just for minutes, long enough to accept the priest's ministrations, that he had indeed recognized and spoken to him. The son said, "Perhaps he will die in the morning now, not before."

The next morning, Dr. Paddon was there. At sunrise, Pasteen roused, asked clearly how the weather was, and relapsed again when his son said simply, "Raining." And every morning for several days the same thing happened. Then one morning, I got up and it was clear and bright. The sun was just showing. My mother and I left immediately to cross the river, and when we were half way across, the sun was fully risen.

When we came to the tent, the old man's body was lying facing the sun which was pouring in through the tent door, full on his old weather beaten face. In that direct light the wrinkles and clefts were a written memorial of a life, a long life, lived under hard, and at times, impossible conditions. But the ravaged features had only dignity, even a sort of gladness. The eyes were not completely closed, as though he were looking his last at the sun which had helped guide him over so many trackless miles. There was not the faintest warmth in his bony hand, no moisture on his forehead.

His son said that he had roused as usual, and when they said the sun was coming up, he said, "Let me see." After seeing indeed that the sun was up, he smiled and drew no more breath. My mother was crying and I, all of twelve or thirteen, was in the same condition. The son smiled at the old wife and she smiled back, and the son said gently, "He is travelling."

I heard the doctors talking. They agreed that it had taken an incredible amount of will to accomplish, but that was all, no real miracle. I don't think it was a miracle either. The old man had to see his priest before leaving on a far journey, he needed a good day to start, and he rested in preparation. But it was the sun, the early morning sun. I wish you could be here to see what I can see. I wish I could tell you properly what I mean, what I know you'll understand about Pasteen, and why my cheeks are wet, why in spite of that, I am not sad.

Now the sun is well above the trees. The rose colour on the ice is fading, the black shadows underlining the drifts are gone. It's another day, one of the many that have dawned on the Moose River.

The land has changed so, the buildings, the roads, but one is impressed with the lack of change on the river. Really it is never the same, but never changes. It freezes in the fall and stills the water, and the snow comes and covers it and forms intricate drifts along the banks and furrows to show the direction of the wind. And man comes and scratches his tiny mark across, and no doubt congratulates himself on his fine road, but miles and miles of the river never see man or his tracks and it remains unchanged. Every fall it freezes, every spring it breaks and puny man must build around its desires, and when the time comes, it takes man's little road and hurls it downstream to melt on the shoals in the sun at low water. What are three hundred years of occupation to the river? A minor irritation perhaps, nothing more.

This afternoon I had to go to Moose Factory Hospital to see old Joe Grom who is there. He has been having breathing problems for some years and they take him in every so often for treatments. So, though the lodge manager offered to run me across, I decided to walk.

It takes about forty-five minutes each way but since the road is ploughed to the bare ice, walking is good. There was no wind. The sun was shining and while it was still about thirty below F, it didn't seem cold at all except when I stopped to take a picture of the old church in the snow. Then my fingers realized it was cold. It was a nice walk. No one else on foot and I kept away from the track of the cars and ski-doos.

I love to walk, if not with someone special, then alone. On a day like today, one can wrap himself in a cocoon of silence and thoughts inside his fur lined hood, and like Christopher Robin, "No one knows that I'm there at all." It is wonderful. You are aware of the snow, the ice, the bare poplars and the prim spruce, the tracks of the squirrels that jump boldly in twin imprints from tree to tree and result in neat little piles of dissected cones, and the nervous, timid little marks of the mice that scamper across the surface of the snow from one little hole to another, the least sound or motion sending them diving out of sight in the snow. The solitary independent right and left track of a fox, the blurry prints of a ptarmigan's feathered feet. Not much, and only a raven overhead, but one sees it all while his mind walks other trails in other days, or dares to leap ahead to walks that will be.

When it was Sunday School time and I was very small, it was not difficult for me to grasp the part about, "not one swallow falling," because I felt that way about things so much smaller. In spring there used to be a tiny-tiny, dark red flower that grew along the paths that followed the beach, and in due time they formed the small raspberry-like fruit that I showed you on Willow Island. We are strictly rationed. One never finds more than a dozen or so at any one place, and those flowers are so impossibly tiny and beautiful and even in their size have such a seductive scent. I would find them almost as soon as the snow had gone and I'd be in dread that some careless person would walk on them, and I'd put stones as big as I could carry near them so people wouldn't walk there.

I'd sit on the huge laundry box in my mother's back kitchen on wash day, when the steam hung heavily in the air from the big iron boiler bubbling slowly on the stove, and the windows were misted with condensation. It was important that the little droplets that formed from nowhere I could see would roll down the pane, leaving a little track to reach the sill to collect one by one, till the little gutter cut in the wood was full and they could all rush outside and go wherever raindrops go on a fine day.

There were so many small things that seemed to need our attention for reasons I would never be able to explain. The millions of transparent minnows in the water, all destined some day to be cod, trout, salmon, or whatever. I never knew, but I felt that they needed protection and I'd feel a little panic when a greedy sculpin would leave the bottom and swim clumsily up with its huge mouth open and engulf half a hundred of the little minute shreds of sea weed. I'd drop a stone or push a pole down and disturb the sluggish old sculpin and feel that I'd saved lives, that perhaps one day one of those almost liquid little fish would come back as a huge silver salmon and perhaps thrash furiously in old Bill's net so that he could come quietly into our kitchen with most deprecatory air and produce once again his "first fish," hanging by the gill on his scarred brown finger. And another of my fears was that someone else would be the first to bring a sea run salmon to my mother in the spring. It was terribly important that nothing change I guess, and if Bill wasn't "first fish," why, anything could happen to the world, my world.

So when spring came, I alternately dreaded and hoped till the wonderful day when Bill slipped in the back way, face expressionless, and eyes about to dance out of his head, to say, "I suppose you been ate a dozen salmon already, but this one do seem a mite better than some." And he'd carefully lay it on the huge metal tray my mother kept, I'm almost sure, for Bill's first offering, and he'd sit there and eat a huge pile of raisin cookies. "Missus, I likes all buns and biscuits, but them there raisin ones do seem better." And he'd drink his tea and regard the great fish which my mother would never take away. When he was finished and his stubby pipe was loaded with his "Light Beaver Plug." and reeking away, he'd say, "Well since I'm here anyway," and he'd take the fish with me and perhaps a younger brother following, and walk to the beach where, with his huge splitting knife, he'd reduce it to two bright red fillets and the fat back bone, which we thought the finest part of the fish.

Then, when he had brought it back, my mother would say, she always did, "You have to stay now and help eat it." Bill was shy, and he'd protest and mangle his sou'wester in his hands. Finally he'd agree, providing he could eat in the summer kitchen with the two girls and the overflow kids from the big dining table that sat fourteen. Yes, there were a lot of us including several clerks, the customs officer and tidewaiter. There was an overflow.

Bill was always the same age, at least I never saw him any different. He had white patches in his bushy hair, and half his moustache was brown, half white. He had pale blue eyes that watered copiously when the sun was bright on the water or snow. He was the kindest man on earth and used to supply the post with firewood.

He had a team of undisciplined fat dogs and never punished them. Many the time we'd see Bill pushing mightily on his load, while shouting the most monstrous oaths ever heard, and threatening each and every dog by name with all sorts of horrible punishments. "Soon as I gets this load to the bank," he would threaten he never did, and they took advantage of him, day by day, so that he was famous for his big lazy dogs. They were so used to his constant swearing that they plain ignored it.

One warm day in the spring when the dogs were lazier than ever and Bill worked harder than ever at getting them going, quiet Will Shewak, the post foreman, a man I always felt could easily give God a constructive hint or two, said, "Bill, I've not been in the wood path for so long. How about I take your team and get a load of dry wood for my house." The dry wood cutting was farthest away. I knew Will had a reason, he always did, and he was known as the best teamster in the bay, the best carpenter, engineer, you name it.

So when he started off, I grabbed the back horn and rode along. I don't remember, perhaps I accidentally missed school, but there was no way I was missing whatever Will planned. Looking back, I saw Bill strolling off to the net loft with his usual cloud of smoke around his head. I knew he and Peter would be having a long yarn. Will let the dogs take their own pace in through the wood path. They tried to turn off at the green wood, which was closest, but he firmly ordered them on, and sat quietly while they balked a bit, but he never changed the tone of his voice and they glanced back, no doubt missing Bill's frantic cursing.

Finally they went on, and Will whistled to himself and occasionally tipped me a grinning wink. We got to the big dry wood pile, turned the sled around and loaded it with a load much heavier than Bill would ever put on. When he was ready, he called the dogs and they went out slowly and when the tracer came tight, instead of breaking the load out, they stood there, expecting to hear Bill's oaths and threats while he strained to break it out himself. Will spoke sharply and most of them glanced back, a bit apprehensive, but not trying any harder. Then he roared and I wasn't expecting it either. He cracked the long whip right over their heads. It was a mighty unexpected crash, and it scared them half silly. Not one was hurt but they put their bellies close to the ground and they yanked that load out and took off down that path as if all the devils Bill had promised were there. We didn't push on any load. We sat on top and had a royal ride home. Will's commands were sharp and incisive and they obeyed to the letter.

When we reached the pile on the bank and stopped, they all lay in the snow and watched Will out of their slanting, calculating eyes, and I could see their minds working. Bill came strolling back. Said, "How did um do?" Will said, "Well enough, Bill, but any two are heavier than you, so don't push on the load any more, no good for you or the dogs."

Bill promised with mighty oaths that "them so and so's won't get away with nutten." And Will snapped at them to go. They sprang up and were away like a team of the best. When they were half way across the little cove, they realized Bill was back, and before they disappeared into the wood path on the other side, they were idling along and Bill was trudging between the runners pushing as usual. Will's perfect white teeth showed in a smile and he shrugged. No one was going to change Bill.

Yes, Claudia, Bill was something that could not change. All through my childhood he didn't, and if Bill, and James, the cooper, and Will didn't change, the world was always there, always right. I was so secure that perhaps I invented things to worry about just to prove my security and great fortune to myself. And I can walk across a lake to this day with Will or John, or James or Bill, as well as I could then. Onliest thing is, in the years between, I also met other special people who walked with me today.

Moosonee, March 4, 1983

Dear Claudia,

Last night I went to bed with O'Halloran's moon shining in the window, exactly as it was last summer. Don't sleep in the moon path, they say. You can have dreams that can change you from young to old. Where can my fear possibly be at that? The reverse I could hope for. Sleep in the moon's path, they say, and you'll dream the dream of your own going. They say a lot of things, but I like to sleep in the moon's light and I've never had cause to fault the dreams she's given.

And when I woke the world was wrapped in whitest cotton wool. Visibility was down to yards and every wire was ten times its normal diameter and the trees were like a kid's dream of Christmas. Maybe not a dream either but what he actually sees. When I was very little, my my dad took me into a little old wooden church and there were a lot of brass lamps and chains and wall plaques to honour the war dead and those lost at sea. There was a huge brass eagle with wings outstretched to hold the Book. Everything was old and polished by generations of loving, careful hands, and I thought it was the most beautiful place I would ever see.

When I was older and had seen other beautiful things, I realized that the beauty I saw was only partly the brass and the ornaments. The rest was the love of many people I would never know. I can still feel my dad's hand on my shoulder as I looked at the tiny church and I know now why he took me there. He did things like that.

Today we had planned to leave at 8:30 to fly up to Paint Hills but the fog held on until ten. The sun was out when we left and there was no wind.

We flew straight up the bay, over the frozen surface for the first twenty miles. This is the land of fast ice. It congeals in the fall and never moves until spring. It is snow-covered and smooth. The tide cracks show as lines, stitched seams almost, made by a demented tailor. And as we flew, the little cruciform shadow followed us on the snow, hurrying along neither gaining or losing. It would break into a hundred pieces when we flew over islands and trees, pieces that tore their mad way till we again flew over the snow-covered ice when they reassembled again, as if by magic, and the little shadow again paced us on the flat surface. I like that shadow, filled with one purpose, to be able to follow and arrive at our destination with us. How many little shadows have been covered by cloud and lost forever. Tireless little shadows.

Soon we were flying over the unstable flow ice. It is regulated by the tide and can close up and remain that way for days. Then for no apparent reason, it can break up into leads and lakes that freeze over until the next change pushes them together again and the glass-thin new ice is formed into improbable, unbelievable figures. Angular and geometrically correct, they run for miles like the shingles on a roof, so square, so correct you could not believe it was natural.

Then for no reason, the pattern changes, and the wily artist, *Kee-way-tin*, the North Wind, seizes his brushes and paints great circles and scrolls, and white mile after white mile of impossible designs. Year after year he paints, and each work is never the same. To fly over a hundred miles of sea ice is to see a hundred patterns every mile, and at the end of the flight your head swims with the mass of impressions which are rolled into one breath-taking panorama in your head, till you wonder where you can possibly store the impressions. But you do, and tomorrow's, and tomorrow's.

And you wonder as you fly ever farther north, what it must have looked like ages ago when fire was born, and the first spark seen in the velvet darkness where man and his new toy crouched and fed the flame with twigs, afraid he would lose that precious flame. It must have looked almost exactly as it does today.

Is it loneliness that one feels? I don't think so. It is something else, awe perhaps, envy that our time is never so long, that we change and that huge piece of real estate was there before a human voice was heard and may well be there when human voices are again stilled. I have had so much of the big and lonely land, but I never fail to be glad when I can go once more, never fail to be a little sad when I stay behind to let the boys or Jackie go. But it is their heritage, and my heart never stays behind. My whole being demands, just once more, even though I have had so much.

After a while we flew parallel with a huge lake of open water, black and menacing against the white ice. No summer whitecaps there. The water is thick with frost.

It is calm, and a little sheen of new ice shows in the sun, and there are tell-tale marks, tiny little blocks thrust up where a seal has put his head through to lie with only his eyes and whiskers above water while he slowly twirls his body to give him three hundred and sixty degree visibility. The floe edge is firm, but it is still March. A few more weeks must pass before he can haul out and bask in the sun, alert for his one natural enemy in this land, the solitary polar bear, who knows that an opening like this will result in a concentration of seals. Sure enough, we shortly see the line of massive footprints leaving Trodley Island and pointing toward the open water.

William has already banked the plane and the line of tracks flows smoothly under the nose. From where I sit, the ice is reflected in the shiny underside of the plane's wing and I can see an indistinct line of tracks. (Imagine seeing polar bear tracks from an airplane by looking up.) The tracks come to the edge of the heavy ice and follow it north.

In a very short time we have incarnadine proof that the king has dined. As we go into a slow circle over his table, two white bushy-tailed ghosts race madly away from their feast on the master's leavings, and in the way of arctic foxes, they stop a hundred yards away, watch the plane closely, then scamper back to their repast, hunger or greed getting the best of fear.

Of the bear there is no sign. The tracks suddenly cease to be. He has taken to the water, the water that will kill a human in three minutes, and is perhaps now going his moody way on the far side of the water. We fly over Trodley just in case he has left a mate there. On the bare rocks we lose his tracks, but as we pass over the north coast, there is a dandelion puff of white, and a couple dozen ptarmigan rocket away in as many directions, only to regroup under our plane and glide to a landing half a mile away, while the noisy creature with the frantic shadow passes overhead and away.

It is dark now back in Moosonee. The bear is miles away. The foxes are fed and curled up near the remains of the seal on the bare snow, bushy tails over noses and eyes, two silent white circles. They will sleep off their banquet and there will be miles of nearly open water till they again find their royal provider whom they will follow till his next kill. The ptarmigan have buried deep into the snow and sit quietly, perhaps watching the moon that is again shining on my bed.

And I glance in the mirror at my wind and sun-reddened face and I am satisfied with my day, which I enjoyed telling you about. I hope your day was good. May the silver moon shine on you so you feel its good vibrations. Tomorrow we go back to Paint Hills. I will enjoy that too, but today was like the first cold drink from a rushing stream after miles of travel over a dry land.

I am so sleepy I can barely see to write, but I had to tell someone about my day.

Winnipeg, April 20, 1983

Dear Claudia,

In a short while I'll be going downtown. I'll walk down, not because I have the time, or for any reason except nostalgia, to the HBC Raw Fur on Princess Street. I'll go talk to Eric Curnew who is a fellow Newfie, and look at beaver, otter and muskrat pelts, and yarn for hours. I know Greenpeace would be mad at me, but it would be good to be a lot younger and be up north again where the beaver and musk-rats are coming in and where the air is clear and the snow is going and the geese are back. The hurt that comes with remembrance is almost too much.

I wasted a perfectly good morning as I knew I would. We looked at fur and more fur and it was good to know that knowing fur can never be forgotten. There is a feeling to watch a prime pelt flow under you fingers. I couldn't trap any more, I know that. The time of my life that included hunting is behind me, but am I sorry I once did it? I'll be honest, no, and I won't be, because there were other things that were part of it, things that were so good, like the hours I could spend in a canoe.

Claudia, that first time you slide a canoe into the water and climb in and watch that black element that has been solidified for months swirl beautifully around the paddle is special. That first time can never again be duplicated, you think. But it can, again and again, and some people were never born to sit behind fences or ride in cars along narrow little paths.

Evenings alone at dusk on a lake that turns black when the sun drops, when hills against the sky becomes dark and full of mystery. The water disturbed by the paddle has a comforting sound. The whisper of the keel on the sand as you touch shore is a poignant little punctuation that ends a paragraph of a day's delight. Your muscles ache pleasantly, and your knees feel creaky from kneeling and the slat of the cross bar seems to be permanently engraved on your seat.

Just to step out of the canoe in the twilight and stand in the quiet, to hear the secret night sounds when everything is so still you can open your mouth and hear your blood in your veins. You know in an hour there will be fire, food and rest, but first the precious minutes before sleep that are devoted to thought of the day, the morrow and those that have been.

It's possible to leave your body and watch your own frame lie relaxed and content? There is no feeling like it. Why is it, when we have everything, we become unwise and want other things? But it's good that when we have the other things that turn out not to be so wonderful after all, that nature or providence, who may be one and the same, recognizes our need. That impetuosity that overcame reason is forgiven, we are provided with the people, the friends, who make the barely tolerable pleasant. Well, friend, spring is hard on the heart strings, especially when distance is involved.

April 24, 1983

Dear Claudia,

Word is that the ice is going out in Moosonee this morning. Not much of a spectacle though. Guess the water is low and it isn't crashing and roaring like it sometimes does. Some years it piles up so that we can't see out the office windows. Once it came to within three feet. Didn't touch the building but was away higher than the roof. Makes one feel pretty small too.

I was at Norman Wells one year when the Mackenzie went out. Old Herman Pipes and I were at the C.P. staff house that is right on the bank. It was a warm Sunday morning and we sat on the veranda and watched the ice move a few feet then stop, move a bit more and stop. It was being held back by Goose Island. Then there was a bigger nudge from the current and the whole mile wide sheet of ice started moving. It simply buckled a bit and rode completely over Goose Island. One minute the island was in sight, the next there were huge slabs of ice moving slowly across it.

There was a huge wooden barge on the island, abandoned there by the American army when they built the Canal pipeline. It was the highest thing on the low island. When the ice reached it, there was no hesitation. The barge started moving. It would have taken a dozen bulldozers to even start it, but such is the awful power of the ice that it came diagonally across the river to the shore on our side of the river and straight up the high steep river bank. There wasn't much noise and it didn't move all that fast, but there it was twenty feet from us and still moving. It finally stopped a mere span away from the lower part of the veranda that we were not sitting on any more.

The last time I saw Norman Wells the old barge was still there. No one had any idea how to move it without huge expense, and there it will sit till some spring, the ice will have a change of mood and casually pick it up and push it higher. Of course, that means it will push the staff house over, or it may just play with it for a while and put it ashore miles downstream. You are very helpless when Mother Nature cleans out her drains in the spring. After it's all over and you see ice five or six feet thick piled up fifty feet high, you realize how insignificant man is, a grain of sand on Nature's cuff. She could flick us away just that easily.

But I think one of the most spectacular things I've seen was at Hebron one spring. There is a lake high behind the settlement between two hills that form a very narrow channel for the lake to flow down about fifty feet to form the little river that gave us our drinking water. One year a huge snowdrift formed across the outlet and a sudden mild spell caused the lake to fill with melt water that couldn't get away because the outlet was closed. Bill and I walked up one day to look. The water was rising very quickly in the lake, and only that plug of snow was holding it back.

We couldn't do anything. The village was some distance away and there was no danger of flooding anyway because the ocean is right there. But we kept watching, and one day the snowdrift turned yellow showing that the water was coming through. Bill and I had been out on the harbour ice fishing through cracks, and had just turned facing the hill when the plug blew out. There was one huge gush of mixed water and snow that shot straight out, almost as if it were out a giant hose. It must have spurted a hundred feet or more, and then the sides caved in, and the moving water that was probably ten feet deeper than the lake ever was started coming out of the small valley. It brought thousands of tons of snow with it in one great avalanche. We were a good way out on flat ice and I had a momentary fear that that huge pile might reach us, but it fell almost perpendicularly and filled the riverbed with solid wet compressed snow and the water ran over the top.

By the time we reached the shore the sea ice was covered for a mile with yellow muskeg melt water. There were a couple of loose dogs that were in the path of the water. They had to swim a bit but no one else was affected, except the Moravian mission garden. They had built it with bits of soil from wherever they could find it, plus a few bags from home every year on the ship. The main part of the snow-plug sat on the garden, and it was covered till late summer and realized no crops that year. If you have never seen a few thousand tons of snow shoot straight out into the air by hydraulic pressure, you might find it hard to visualize what it looks like. Scary believe me, but something I'm glad I saw.

Friday morning: [*Len had just put me on the train in Toronto.*]
At the moment you are sweeping a wide path down the rails from Toronto. Ever imagine what the engineer sees at night as he sits way up there and follows his light along straightways and around curves as he blows his horn quietly because of the sleeping people.

I wondered too. Then one New Year's Eve, talk about the proper night for the job, Harry Winney, a WW II pilot and one of the greatest bush pilots, and I, were at Wabowden, away up on the Churchill Railway, waiting for daylight to fly north. Ray Bohay, the owner of the cleanest, nicest little hotel, was an engineer on the HB Railway. Wabowden wasn't exactly a city terminal, and one word led to a suggestion, and we arrived at the roundhouse about the time a brand new year, 1947, was born.

It was warm and dark inside, and Old 202 was sitting there. There is a smell about steam engines, Claudia, steam, coal, metal, brass polish, travel, distance, reliance, so many ingredients. And steam engines are warm, put your hand on them. They breathe and they know people who like them. 202 had a banked fire and the bright red coal looked a bit surprised when the rattle of the chain hoist that opened the door woke her. She shivered a little when the midwinter cold flowed in around her but the fireman that was dozing in the engineer's chair gently stirred the coals and she sniffed the air and was ready to go.

Ever been in a steam loco's cab? Everything is huge. Harry was so pleased. He was used to dinky throttles in a plane cabin; here the throttle was a massive iron bar. His gauges were tiny; here they were huge and polished. The searchlight came on and Bohay gently moved 202 out on the tracks, pointed her towards Churchill, and put the throttle in Harry's hand.

The surge of power in that huge machine was tremendous and we were away, out of Wabowden in seconds, with only the bright light ahead on the rails. Bright stars overhead pointed out the dark forest on each side. A steam whistle has a sound all of its own. Once away, Harry pulled the cord and we left a fairytale of heart-catching sound behind on a chiffon skein of white steam. The light raced down the track and 202 puffed and the big drivers on either side rose and fell and the polished faces glittered in the starlight and the reflection from the snow. It was magic as pure as if newly distilled by a hundred leprechauns. I stood there and was warm and safe, enclosed in a womb of such delight that I'm sure most people never experience.

There was none of the bellow of the diesel, no clattering pushrods, no vibration. Just the feel and smell of the release of steam, the sense of power, controlled power. None of the feeling that you get with the internal combustion engines that the whole thing might get wound up too fast and never stop or even fly apart. Not that, but a feeling that 202 was alive and pleased to be giving us an unforgettable experience.

We calculated our time to arrive back in Wabowden to celebrate the New Year. As we slowed down, the whistle on the roundhouse screamed its delight that a new year, free from war, had come, and 202 expanded her stupendous lung and roared her challenge and welcome to 1947. Her whole frame shook and I shook with her. The delight I felt was mirrored in Harry's eyes and in Bohay's smile. Those two men have never been simply humans since, and something came into my soul that will never be washed away.

We eased back into the roundhouse to the diminishing joy of the horn and 202 panted softly as we left her and the ruby eye in the grate winked its wish for us.

The guns were firing in the native village in the old fur trade welcome to a new year, and the frost was sharp and invigorating so that you felt you could walk all night. We went back to the hotel, our clothes smelling with the exquisite (yep, that's the right word for the right time...) mixture of coal and steam and intense joy.

There was a free trader (no HBC man could ever describe him differently) in the hotel. He had been looking down the neck of a bottle all evening. He shouted for us to join him but after our experience it was not possible to endure the smell of liquor and tobacco and the sour odour of discontent and the inability he had to relate to the precious surroundings and the magic of that particular night.

"Where were you," he said, and Harry said, "Riding a locomotive down the track." He turned away and said, "Big deal!" I felt pity for him because if that could not fire him, he was dead. As I went up the stairs to sleep and to such dreams that cannot be expressed, I wondered how and where he might have been conceived, and I felt an even sharper pity for his parents. I know what your engineer sees as he rumbles down the track. You love trains, I know why I am sitting here in the early morning while you run lightly along the shining steel ribbons with O'Halloran pacing you in the moonlight.

Winnipeg, May 16, 1983

Dear Claudia,

Well the poor old earth is still in pain. No one likes anyone else in the Middle East and the USA and Russia are hollering nasty things over a very shaky missile fence. You know, when I was little there wasn't a single radio on the Labrador coast, and news was weeks late when it got to us in summer and months old in winter. A lot came by word of mouth and arrived probably distorted anyway.

So once we heard about any ship losses we were caught up. Travellers by small boat or dog team brought local news. We probably didn't realize how lucky we were to go to bed at night knowing we'd wake up to the same world tomorrow.

Strange, now, we'd think. No medical help if something goes wrong. It just never entered our minds then. We couldn't have cared less about world conditions and what they might be when the first ship appeared in spring, and deliciously, she just appeared, we never knew when. The thing we wondered about was did she bring oranges and apples and, to us anyway, new potatoes.

Our big shed on the dock was generally unused in winter, a few salt fish and salmon stored there plus hundreds of barrels of flour. So over the winter all its smells disappeared and we weren't aware of it. Then the first boat came and the freight piled ashore and into the shed. To open that door on a warm spring or summer morning, to smell fruit, biscuits, rope, pitch, sugar, molasses, cloth, was all so tangy and wonderful.

I used to sit on a big beam just above the men's heads when I was too little to work, and watch and smell. It was a horrible imposition if school was still in, as one of the men would reach up, grab me, deposit me on the boardwalk outside in the warm sun, and point me toward school. Standing orders from my dad, because I'd get in the carpenter shop or cooperage and time would cease to exist. I'd arrive at school on a dead run at the last clang of the bell, or if they were painting boats or barking nets which I had to pass on the way, I'd be late.

I must have been a frustrating pupil because summer or winter there was always something happening outside that I must see or hear. One of my teachers told me later that I was a bright kid if I could only bring my brains in from outside. You know, Claudia, you would have likely been the same. I've forgotten a lot that I was taught, but I don't think I've lost one thing of the almost intolerable joy of being a small boy in that place, at that time and with those people.

I can feel old James' hand on my shoulder, willing me to have the strength I needed to force the heavy croise around the top of a barrel, but never a finger's weight would he give as I struggled. He knew that I must do it. I've seen Will bent at a comical angle, using the full force of his body English to help me plane fair and true, but all he'd ever do was put his straight-edge on and indicate where I was out of line. They must have had the saints' own patience with boats, dog teams, ropes, nets, gear, sails, but they taught me because I wanted so badly to learn. They were good teachers because what I learned is there still, much of it unused now, but it is my fortune in memory and satisfaction.

They were also artists, craftsmen if you wish, but creators, and they made the things that we needed. I could easily go back fifty years and fit in perfectly while there are many things in the life I lead now that I'll never be comfortable about. At least I know I can tell you about things and know you can see the little boy in his funny clothes and understand the things that entered his heart so long ago, wonderful enduring things. I think maybe you might have liked that funny, serious kid.

It's mild again, supposed to get up into the high teens today. We usually have four pretty well defined seasons here but this year we have more I'm sure, a sub-winter and spring. Winnipeg has lovely seasons but they come so quickly. It's fall, then, wham! Winter, then abruptly spring, and without a pause, summer again.

There are longer springs and falls in the east. We did so many things too, especially in spring with boats and nets and animals. I had so much fun when I was little. The days were so long, so filled. Two deadlines perhaps, school and bed. My mother was very understanding about meals. If I wasn't there because I was busy training a dozen pups to harness, or lying on the dock trying to get the biggest sea trout for supper, she'd shake her head and put my meal to warm and I'd get it later. As like as not, I'd be too excited and full of news to even notice it was hours old.

Winnie, the girl who helped my mother for a long time, used to bake a special cookie that I and the horses, and by gosh, Ira, who liked Winnie, liked. So, I'd eat what had been kept for me and fill my pockets with cookies and go out to where old Maggie, who had been in World War I and had scars to prove it, would be waiting for her cookies. Have you ever had a gently friendly old horse search your pockets? Well she doesn't always wipe her lips first, and that big wet tongue can leave stains, especially in new grass time in spring.

Maggie worked hard in winter hauling wood and water to all the hospital buildings on a sled, but somehow no one ever got a wagon, so summer was hers unless someone hooked her up to a stone boat for a while. She used to come to school with me, graze around close by until she heard that unmistakeable clatter that meant we had been released. Then she'd come galloping with her great feet throwing clumps of precious sod around, and investigate my pockets again in case more cookies had gotten in there during school.

She was a bit shell-shocked and would have her bad moments remembering, but she was a dear old animal and everyone loved her. I remember once a volunteer worker from the States got annoyed with her when she got in his way and he walloped her with a flat board. It probably made no impression on Maggie, but it did on a number of local workers who were nearly all trappers in winter. The poor WOP (worker of pleasure) was suddenly aware that he was in the most hostile crowd he'd ever likely see. Murdoch McLean, who had also been in WW1, told him to make sure he never did that again because that "reever out there was a little cold."

Murdoch always talked around a bent stem pipe and I sometimes wondered how he looked sleeping with that thing in his mouth. Found out one day when my dad and I were hunting in a canoe one warm fall morning. We found Murdoch sound asleep on a little beach, his canoe broadside on the beach, his two huge feet up on the side, his packsack under his head and the pipe squarely in the centre of his mouth.

Humorous old Murdoch was one of my dad's favourite people but he couldn't resist. So we took a line we had, slipped it through a tracking ring on Murdoch's canoe and fastened it to a huge boulder. Then we woke old 'Doch and had tea and a yarn, and in time the tide rose and we got into our canoes and started away. About three paddle strokes later, 'Doch's canoe came to an abrupt stop but he never turned a hair. Sat there calmly paddling and smoking his big pipe. I'm sure he got back at my dad, he always did.

With Murdoch, everything was a leetle…leetle cold, or warm or windy, leetle whatever. He was carrying a canoe up the river bank one day and the mission bull, a mean creature if there was ever one, got loose. Murdoch couldn't see it and in the soft sand couldn't hear it, and the bull impaled the canoe and relieved Murdoch of his burden. He said it was "leetle suddenly."

The bull couldn't see too well and ended up across the United church doorway, canoe and all. The parson and the congregation ladies were spring cleaning and there was no way out, and no one was particularly interested in squeezing past an irritated bull, so my mother sent me up. Rufus and I had a working agreement. I fed and watered him, he tolerated me as he did Ira because we were necessary.

I got in close and grabbed the rope attached to the ring in his nose. He hated that ring and was very docile when someone had the rope. So we released the church prisoners and I led Rufus back to his yard, where it took some doing to release Murdoch's canoe. We had three bull calves one spring, all Rufus's sons, and they grew up to be real Ferdinands, I guess because the boarding school kids played with them night and day. I'm sure Rufus must have been disgusted. When the kids went inside at night, the bulls would line up at the fence and bawl.

Rufus was a champion donated by the Morgan interest in the States. I heard he was worth thirty thousand dollars, which in the late twenties was a fantastic figure. His sons were all called after opera singers. One with a reedy voice was called Caruso and when he ended up as steak for the boarding school kids, at first they refused to dine, but "hunger is good sauce," and I guess everything came to a good conclusion. My dad always had a laugh about Murdoch and the bull, and 'Doch would grin and say, "leetle funny."

It's another lovely morning. Didn't freeze last night and the sun is high just after seven. My yard is drying up and soon Ellsworth will have Robbie and Jim up here to clean up the winter's debris. I can tell how good business at The Bay and at Willie's is by the amount of potato chip bags and pop cans in my yard. The yards around the stores don't bear mention. I know it's a ceaseless job, but they should have a truckload away once in a while. The old company image of neat paths and buildings has been lost here. Now, if someone could invent an edible chip bag...

Believe it or not, when I was at Hebron for instance, a scrap of paper blowing along would be picked up, not perhaps in the interest of tidiness, but who knows when it might be necessary to write a letter. No writing tablets, as the little magazine says, in "them days." The mission school had only slates. All the people knew syllabic writing and it was not unusual to get a piece of seal or caribou skin with someone's shopping list inscribed in soot from the igloo lamp. Once got a wolf head, ears and all, sorry that should be the skin off a wolf head, with five white fox pelts. On the skin inside the head was a message from a young man which said, in effect, give Elias Tuglavinia the foxes, and have him send Jararause a wife. In sort of a post-script, he added, "a fat one."

Elias had several daughters. He worked for the mission and his daughters had had the benefits of school and, due to mission influenza, were not married off young. I delivered the foxes, and a couple days later, demure little Susie, who had the roundest moon face and a constant grin, came to sell the foxes and was helped by her sisters, who were all roly-polies anyway, to choose her bridal gear. Not what you might expect. A new .22 rifle...who needs a bride who can't help fill the pot? Material for travelling clothes, and since one must be practical, a length of duffle for a married woman's atiki, with the long tail that acts as a seat for momma and enough left over to keep junior off the cold snow. Needles, thread, a few yards of ribbon so she could change her decorations from young woman to married, a plug or so of black tobacco for the pipe I knew was secure in her boot leg. The missionaries didn't like women to smoke, so they didn't in front of the parson. Then as a serious about-to-be-married woman, the greater part of her dowry went on ammunition and hunting gear for her prospective groom, who hadn't even specified which of the chubby girls he hoped for, though I feel that was likely well known. To be properly polite, I said, "I will see your son in the fall," and she said she'd likely be unlucky and have a girl, with a grin that indicated she'd be just as well pleased.

SIX

Moosonee, Friday, May 20, 1983

Dear Claudia, ·

Foggy sort of morning, may rain, not cold, comfortable sort of spring
day. Last night I went down to the dock where there is still a big pile
of ice right in front of the ramp. I was standing there just enjoying the
warm evening when a young bearded seal suddenly popped up and
looked me in the eye. It just lay there looking, and probable thought
I was just another part of the unnatural set up of buildings and so on.
He was casually scratching his stomach with his flipper and looked
so much like Colonel Blimp in the English funnies that it was hard
to remember he was a seal. Albert the watchman saw him and started
walking down and old Col. B. gave him the jaundiced eye and rolled
over in his watery recliner and sank, by jove. The odd seal comes in
and becomes the target of any jack-ass with a rifle. They never use
any part, just shoot and let them float away. Not only natives either.

While I was at Berens River in 1956, I met old Johnny Berens who
had more than ninety years under his hat then. He was as spry as a
goat. His memory for recent things was gone and he wasn't sure how

many wives he had married. I could tell him three. One was buried at Berens River and I took him to see her grave. He asked her name and I'm sure would have been content with any, but I got him talking about York boat days on Lake Winnipeg…he wouldn't know the year, probably, but could tell you that they left Selkirk on such and such a Monday, and he'd remember every detail of the trip, where they camped, who they met, moose they saw, everything. Complete recall, and it was wonderful to hear him. He'd change completely. His speech would be firm and he'd have a rapid answer for any question. A few hours later he'd be the same disoriented old man that wandered up and down the lake on the old Kenora for something to do.

To the Selkirk Navigators' everlasting credit, they sold him a ticket every spring which he never surrendered and he travelled up and down the lake on it all summer. Some scientists from Ottawa came up to look at the huge fossils on Governor Island and they met Johnny on the boat. They were inclined to dismiss his talking. But he would look at their charts and would put a finger on a spot where there was something interesting and it would be there when we checked. One place though, they found nothing, and I asked Johnny about it. He pointed out that he saw it when he was only a boy over seventy years ago. The sandstone would have weathered. Take a shovel he told them, peel the turf back. They did and found the continuation of the vein of fossils he had told them would be there. I guess I'm a bit like Johnny because I can go back to things I did when I was little and can remember minute details, while yesterday is faint and the day before gone because there aren't the same interesting things.

The news at six. Three bomb explosions and the return of a war criminal to answer for the deaths of eleven thousand Jews, something to have breakfast to. So I strangled the newscaster and have Mouskouri singing.

Later:
The best thing of all I've saved for now, just before I turn the lights out on a satisfactory day. At noon, while we were having lunch, an

osprey flew by, went down the river a way, came back, and just opposite the window he dropped like a stone, entered the water and came up with a fish. They are lovely birds Claudia, and my generation may not be able to pass them on to the next if we continue using DDT. I will have him to fly across my dreams tonight.

I wrote a bit about the Reveillon ships for Miss Preston last spring. I couldn't say to her what those ships meant to me, but you know. I used to go into the forecastle of a wooden ship and as far into the bow as I could get, right into the tiny triangle formed by the sides and stem posts. There is more movement there than anywhere else in the ship and I'd sleep there cradled in her strong arms, where I could hear the wash of the water as she cut through it, where I could feel the lift and fall as she drove silently along under her sails.

On a mild day, there would be a chuckle from the cutwater, on a stormy day the crash and slap of the waves as she met them, a language all its own, a mighty, inspiring tongue. How warm and secure I felt there, like a child in the womb of a creature that met earth's greatest powers, wind and water, and used them. A strange imaginative youngster, I never quite got away from the idea that ships were alive. I had so many things my kids never saw. I don't suppose they miss them, but I would not like to be someone who never stood on the deck of a sailing ship or followed a dog team through the passes in the Torngats or watched spring come to Labrador.

Speaking of Torngats, they are a mountain range in North Labrador. High, brooding, inaccessible from the ocean, where they rise straight up from the black fathomless water. They can only be reached from inland by way of several passes. Dark mysterious places in winter, when the jagged rocks almost meet over one's head at times, and bitterly cold, windy, because the passes are natural chimneys that pull draughts of icy wind down from the frigid flat-land on the top. But in spring it is a pleasant journey and the view from the top is unbelievable, a panorama of ice and blue water for as far as the eye can reach, a place of fantastic mirage when one can sit for hours in the hot midday sun and see the images of all sorts of things projected.

Last night Jackie and I went to Ash's, visited a while, then took Ash back to the trailers where he put out two sorts of pie, three kinds of cake and two lots of cold meat and pickles, three if you count the bit of turkey he had for himself. There were just the three of us and Ash started talking about the years he fished on the Labrador. One thing led to another and he and I were yarning away about the North part. Ash asked me if I'd seen various things like the Farmyards. Then Hens and Chickens, Anchor and chain, The Sisters, The Mad Moss, Tumble Down Dick and others, all islands or strings of islands, and he mentioned the Torngats and Port Manvers.

He wanted to be able to tell Jackie of the awesome magnificence of that place, and he scrunched up in his chair, knuckled his eyes and fought with all his being to tell her. I could feel for him because I have the same frustration myself, to hold such beauty in my heart and hands and not be able to express it properly, to want to share it so badly and only be able to give it in the range of my miserable expression. If Ash is nothing else he is dramatic. He got up went down on one knee beside Jackie and pulled her face down and said, "Maid, I can't tell you what I seen, but I felt like in the bigges' church God ever made."

Jackie smiled at me. Ash is a hunter and fisherman and he loves nature. I wonder how much is locked up inside of him, he tries so hard. The boys tease him, so for them he has crazy funny stories of his hunting experiences. But when we are alone, he tries to tell me of the feelings generated by the flight of an osprey. "Skipper, dat bird don't fly, the whole world moves in under of he." His little Punch face gets so intent and he wrestles with the few words he has. There is a treasure trove of beauty locked up there that we'll never know about. I'm certain that glorious silent pictures unfold as he dodges around his galley preparing meals that might not raise a gourmet's eyebrow, but are another product of the affection he has for people and especially "Dem byes, who you never know what they'll do."

Saturday, May 28, 1983

Dear Claudia,

This morning six white whales came into the river. I had to go down
early to arrange a shipment of welding rod for Nelson River repairs
and the watchman was standing there looking at them. They never
fail to excite me, those aloof, mysterious beings that suddenly appear,
breathe their distinctive sigh, and are gone. They curve gracefully
from the depths, complete the quarter circle, and are gone their
remote way. Voiceless as far as most humans are concerned—at least
those who have not heard their buzzes, clicks and chatterings under
water. They are not like the seals who, once surfaced, like to loll there
to see and hear, to relax. The white whale never rests. It is always on
the move, always seeming to have an urgency to move on.

    In spring in the Arctic, the other creatures seem to be able to take
a spell now and then. The big Arctic hare will be found sprawled
like a house cat on a rock in the sun. The foxes pick lookouts and sit
there somnolent, dreaming. The seals lie on their backs on the ice
and look like the cartoonist's idea of stuffy gentlemen in their inviolate clubs.

    But find yourself a cape at the end of the land and you'll soon be
rewarded by the sight of the white, lonely, wanderers passing purposefully by. From where? Bound wither? No one knows. Porpoises
play and splash and act like merry creatures. Their near cousins, the
beluga have no merriment. Young and old, they spend only seconds
in the air they must breathe to live and are gone.

    I have looked into the face of a porpoise, seen the mighty maw of a
black whale open like a cavern from twenty feet away while the gentle
giant scoops up a barrel or so of capelin from the same school that I
take from. I have seen, close up, the intelligent living eye of a nursing
whale while I could almost touch her baby which was longer than my
canoe. But I have never seen any other expression other than death

on the beluga's high forehead. What do they feel and see and think as they wander their darkened way under the sea at night. You can hear their ghostly breath and you know they are sleepless, moving.

The black whale will take a deep breath and submerge, allowing the current to take him, and when in fifteen or forty minutes he has exhausted the oxygen, he will come to the surface, exhale, sleepily inhale, and sink again, but you know he is sleeping. His very sighs are sleep inducing and when I was little I'd hear the whales somnambulistic breath and sink into sleep myself.

What a place to live, right beside the water of what we called Gros Water Bay. The tides swept in and out constantly, never still. They'd run inward like a millrace for four hours then reverse and go the other way. This brought a fantastic collection or marine life past our door every day, winter and summer, because the inlet never froze over. Well it did once, one cold year, and when I went outside the water was gone. For the first time in my life there was no movement, no water vapour like the boiling of an enormous kettle. It was a strange feeling. It happened on a calm night and the next morning the world was standing still, completely still. I could not remember seeing the world standing still before.

And the white backs we saw this morning are gone. Where? No way to tell, but somewhere, perhaps miles away, they are moving, regular as clockwork, breathing and moving and we can never go with them no matter how much we want. Perhaps we'll see more whales this summer, white strangers whose paths cross ours and who leave a remote strange beauty in our hearts.

Moosonee, June 3, 1983

Dear Claudia,

Perhaps I am like you. I love the byways, the tiny adventures, the faces that smile for an instant and are gone, a little boy with his face between the railings of a fence, watching the shoes go by. What is he thinking about? The people and their joys and sorrows? No way, he is seeing shoes, shoes that tramp, limp, scuffle along, and perhaps his greatest concern is the tiny bug they might step on.

It's probably the true meaning of compassionate, wondering about people's passions, their feelings. Passion, one of the loveliest words in the language, one of the most misunderstood. One can have a love for so many things, but novelists sometimes overwork the word. Perhaps one can have a passionate belief but not a passionate love for a car or asparagus. Passion is private, gentle, consuming, understanding and personal. It expresses so many things but does not belong to lipstick. It is in nature, pictures, people, always people. I suppose compassion begins when you watch the shoes and worry about the bug.

When I was little I had the ditch and the words locked up in my heart. My ditch was minnowy and it had a little bridge that had been there for years. It was made of poles laid about four inches apart. The bottom of the ditch was white sand and gravel. Grass and weeds grew all along, but under the bridge there was very little growth, a few long green weeds that wagged tirelessly with the miniature current, and just as it came out from under the bridge the water tumbled over a flat stone with a comfortable chuckle.

It was a little fairyland and I could lie face down with the hot sun on my back and peer between the poles. Little things would float down, grass, water, spiders, twigs, and one by one they'd enter that special place, and one by one go over the miniature falls and on to the sea. There were minnows, little transparent fish and stickle-backs, and once in a great while a small trout whose coming created panic among the lesser folk. The minnows would dart outside into the sunlight and at the quiver of a grass, flash back to their shadowy, secure and familiar world, where they would hold themselves in place in the current and agitatedly discuss the monster that nearly got them.

Tiny crabs who had fought in their laborious sideways way upstream would clutch grasses in their miniscule claws and rest, but crab-like, they are determined, and would soon let go to hobble a few more inches toward whatever goal they had in mind.

Roethke had a ditch with a bridge. It was a place to lie and drowse, dream of tall trees, mighty rivers, thunderous falls. It took very little to transform it into a real world where a young man ran a fleet canoe from the hinterland to the ocean, a place where an adult world of chores faded in the roar of the rapids.

But just for a small boy, there was once an impudent muskrat who swam directly under my nose, and who never heard my delighted breath as he stood like a little man on the lip of my falls, and dived in so that I could see his brown fur instantly smoothed by the pressure of the water and the comical pink soles of his feet as he swam away. Bathing birds came past frequently, fluttering like little wounded fairies but obviously having an immense time, and once I saw a black and white cock partridge floating lazily along, and actually diving to get water on its back.

I had to tell someone and gasped out to poor crippled old George Flowers and was amazed when he said, "Yis bye, partiges do go in water in summer, colds 'em down." That image is always with me. All I have to do is recall the day, and I can feel the warm rough wood against my forehead and see that elegant bird, like a duchess in her bath, indolently bathing breast and shoulders in the clear white water. There was something sensual about it that stirred emotions in me that I had no idea I had.

Now to work, rain threatening, clouds rushing across the sky, in so much of a hurry, like school kids rushing to the washroom. The wind tears them so. On sunny days they play and the breeze makes hide-and-seek patterns for us to see, but on stormy days they are grey with fear and cower before the uncaring wind. I don't like the way airplanes tear them. I like ships, even motor boats, because they don't roar and bluster; they venture into fog and cloud, hold their breath and slow down. It's lovely to be on a ship in dense fog. Something makes everyone be quieter, and the vessel ghosts along.

I had a special feeling about fog. I liked to see a sail ship's masts rake slowly back and forth, never seeming to disturb a droplet, and the moisture would accumulate on masts, port lights, decks and rails and when there was no more space for water to build up it would let go and stream down. I felt they were little hands holding on as long as they could, then letting go to run back into the ocean. I thought a lot of crazy things.

We took a contract to service the buoys in Moose River, and ever since we have been getting big official envelopes with directions and safety precautions, and today one came. Jackie put it on my desk as if it were an ordinary letter, but it wasn't. Inside was a diagram of the fairway buoy, showing the new colours decided on, in their wisdom by the M.O.T. in Ottawa, along with a caustic note. It shows clearly how to paint the buoy in two colours, red and white, follow me?

Simple this far; now it gets complicated. On the bottom of the paper are two little squares. One is red, one is white. Now for the blockbuster, Ottawa style: the red square is neatly labelled RED, and the other, hold your breath, is marked WHITE. No foolin', I'll show you what they do with their money in Ottawa. And we figure they can run the country. I told Ellsworth, and he said, "Naw…" Even Jackie, with her aching jaw, had to laugh. Poor Jimmy scratched his head when they carefully marked his paint cans white and beige. He said, "I can see…"

I've painted a lot of boats, mostly work boats, and once I watched a man paint one. There was only one brush so I couldn't help, and anyway he loved the job and was good at it. We were alone on an island, a rocky place, no trees. It was spring and warm and I fished till we had all the trout we could eat. Then I lay on the warm black rock and watched Willie paint.

Of course, I went to sleep. When I awoke, Willie was gone but there were little pictures on the rocks, a man running, a fox, seals, bears, gulls, all outlined in white in just a stroke or two, and a careful picture of my grub box with a hungry man standing over it. I followed the sketches one by one and found Willie cosily set up in a tiny cove with the clearest possible water to stare into. He had the pressure stove going and a big flat rock sitting over it and trout boiling. I'd have found him by the smell if there were no pictures. I never went back there. I suppose the sketches gradually weathered away and by now are gone. I feel a bit sad that things like that are so impermanent, but I'm glad in a way, because they were mine.

Sunday, June 12, 1983

Dear Claudia,

Soon time for you to leave for the exhibition. Are you one of those super efficient travellers with your luggage by the door, shoes pointed in the right direction, ready to go? In the Irish way, I get all ready the night before. That's not a virtue, that's a character flaw. I roar out at 5:30, attack the bathroom and kitchen, and at 6:30 I'm ready to go, but my plane leaves hours later. I've been careful to finish my latest book, so there's nothing to read. In winter the snow is shovelled. In summer, or as close as I ever get to that blessed state at home, my lawn is cut, the garage is okay, so the next few hours stretch endlessly on just because I can't stay in bed. Good job I'll be dead when they bury me or I'd be early for that too.

People who explode out of bed with a bare minimum of time never miss planes or trains, and when they do they don't pace the floor till the next one comes. No they go back to bed.

I love to go to bed. The feel of smooth sheets under my heels is heaven. But I tell you, those same infernal heels hunt for wrinkles, and if there is one, it has to be obliterated, but then it is exquisite. I'm addicted to sleep, so I can't stay awake to savour my comfort. I'm gone, usually in seconds, and when I awake, my heels and I are on the floor instantly. I have deadlines, like feeding the cat or getting to a dental appointment. I think I have a disease, a condition that no one else has and no one wants to cure. Someday I'll make medical history. They'll put me to bed to study it, and I'll go mad.

So you'd better be off. Eat a good breakfast, Mrs. Dwyer always said. Did I ever tell you about Mrs. Dwyer? I must have. She's responsible for the absolutely screwy ideas I have on things religious. She made lovely hot bread every day. She had arthritis and her hands felt good in the warm dough.

I never knew a grandmother. Mrs. Dwyer was mine. At one time she made every wedding dress by hand. Probably be considered crude now, but there were dozens of rosebuds to embroider, yards of seams to be stitched. She made little things for the church, and in pre-Kleenex days, she made handkerchiefs for the merchants, and lovely tablecloths. One fall she gave me a white shirt, every stitch made with love. She was Catholic and wanted me confirmed into the Catholic Church, which in those days of intolerance, would have killed my mother. So I was never confirmed and carry a double guilt because I failed them both. The shirt was never worn, and my mother kept it, as far as I know, while she lived. I have no idea where it is now.

My mother was an uncompromising Anglican until, in her late years, her own minister refused to go to an old Methodist lady who was dying and wanted a man of God, any man of God, and there wasn't another one around. She went to any church from then on and died happily in a melody of faiths. I'm the worst sort of unrepentant backslider, but I like churches. I think I don't see them in the conventional sense. I see them as places where the Mrs. Dwyers, tiny babies and my mother are.

Winnipeg, then Moosonee, June 16th, 1983

Dear Claudia,

Whoever started using the word "Dear" to start a letter? He must have
meant dear friend, not dear paint manufacturer or dear Mr. Black. I
never write the word without feeling it. Dear Claudia means just that.
Poor little word. It gets thrown around, Dear Sir, or Madame, Dear
whoever. I'll say it to you or to my family, but I won't say it to a meat
packer.

When my godson's mother typed for me, she knew I didn't like
using the word to everyone and she invented all sorts of ways around
it. Once the office manager asked me about it, saying, "You don't use
regular office procedure, do you." And I said, "No," and he looked
strange and went away.

Same man once reminded me that we didn't have staff in our offices
at coffee break, that staff were not really supposed to drop in and chat
even on their own time. So I said, "I never have staff in here. The people who come are all family or friends. All I ever see is people, nice
people. I'll be very glad to treat staff as staff a soon as someone shows
me who they are." He looked at me and gave up again. I'm one of his
crosses, I guess. Some day I'll obey all the rules.

June 23, 1983

Dear Claudia,

The sun shines but it's cool. The water is low and the bars are high,
not the old river you saw last year. Next year old Mom Nature will
come along, and with one swipe of her brown wrinkled old hand, she
will smooth the river's bed and it will all be as it was before, till she

decides she wants to change it again. Foxy old lady, she doesn't give a hint, just upsets our human ideas, and sits back and grins. A sense of humour, she has.

I'll have told you about my Aunt Bella. She wasn't even a relative but she couldn't be anyone but Aunt Bella. Brown, work-scarred hands, white hair, the world's sweetest smile, long black skirts with a snow-white apron and little black boots. So good, so gentle, so impulsive, so much Mother Nature.

She had one daughter, Rachel. She loved Aunt Bella too, but grew grim and frustrated when she'd find the needle idle, or the iron hot and forgotten while Aunt Bella's tiny boots had taken her to peer under the bridge with me to see the trout. She'd spread a handkerchief and kneel on it to save the white apron, and I know now those logs must have been hell to kneel on, but she'd listen to me and use two gentle fingers to smooth the tuft of hair that always stood up on my head, and smile that funny little smile that always said there is a laugh handy. Everyone should, by law, have an Aunt Bella. Right in Mr. Trudeau's book of rights it should read, "The right to have from childhood and forever after, one Aunt Bella, to be yours alone." She was the same to all of my brothers and sisters and I guess they thought of her as I did, but she was my Aunt Bella, and we played hooky from our chores many and many the time. All the love that little lady generated would stretch from heart to heart to the farthest reaches. The last time I saw her was years ago. I was home for a short visit and my mother and I went to Rachel's to see Aunt Bella.

She wasn't a whole lot different and maybe a bit tired, smaller. We sat on the couch and she held my hand and murmured about the time when I was little, when she'd go with me in my little boat, anywhere, so long as she could go. We'd stop at salmon fishing places and talk to men on the nets, to women and babies, to grown people that Aunt Bella had delivered years ago. It was a calm warm afternoon and we walked along the river. The little boots were slower and she held my arm more tightly, but she giggled about the time one of my pups bit me on the seat. She told me again about the shirt, dress, or whatever they had for me when I was born and my two fat hands wouldn't go through the cuffs. She had to take the scissors and chop them off. She said, "I still have the little cuffs in a box where I have something from all my babies."

When I left we both knew it was the last time, but she smiled at me as she always had, while my heart felt like it was being torn out. Many the time when I was very little, she'd come to say good night and always pat my head and smooth my hair. She reached up and did it for the last time and I held the fragile little form and perhaps I knew true anguish for the first time. There were a lot of us to get born so she stayed with us a lot. She'd come and always seem to be exactly where she was needed. She'd look after my mother and take care of the baby, then one day she'd say goodbye and be gone to another home, another baby. How much love and comfort flowed from that heart, how much kindness in those fingers.

I wonder how adaptable people are. Sometimes you think they are set in a mould as youngsters and never change, but they do. At ten I was secure, confident. I knew everyone around for miles. I was part of the closest possible group, all HBC people. I had no conflicts with people or family, anyone. I loved Rigolet and I knew every part of it. I was curious and the men showed me everything, the world could not offer me more.

I don't remember a single dull day. Rainy days were just wet fine days. I loved the rain anyway. I'd get dressed in the old-fashioned oilskins, and how I loved the linseed oil smell, and go check the nets. It wasn't what was considered a prime birth but there would be some big frisky salmon and the square bodied trout that I've never seen anywhere else. Their flesh was a rose colour between salmon and the vigorous char. There'd be smelt, and the shoal water net had sculpin and flounder and rock cod for the dogs.

Sculpin is ugly, brown with big polka dots, sharp spines, a dozen or more on the head which is twice the size of the body. A lazy fish well camouflaged, it sits near a rock on the bottom with its huge mouth agape. Small fish scared by trout or cod dash to the rock for shelter and seeing the dark opening, dart in and old sculpin gulps and that's it. He can grow pretty large, will take any bait, a nail or button is as good as bacon. The dogs loved them and would crunch them up spines, spots and all. They don't harbour any parasites so dogs get fat and healthy and have lovely coats.

An old English clergyman who used to employ my dad when he was a student came to visit once, and told me, "A sculpin is the sweetest fish in the sea." So I got a big one, skinned him and filleted it. They have very strong bones and there are no lateral bones as in pickerel or herring. I slipped a couple fillets in with the cod we were having for lunch and asked Beatrice to mark them for me. They were delicious. I never got my mother convinced and the rest of the kids wouldn't even try, but my dad and I ate them from then on. I started to say people don't ever change or something like that and ended up eating sculpin.

Yes, rainy days. I loved the long boardwalks polished like a dining room table by the passage of hundreds of pairs of soft sealskin boots that nearly everyone wore then, even for fishing. When the planks were wet, one could take a run and slide like on ice. There was a shoulder high hand rail, painted white, which we could hang on to if it looked as though we might go over the side and down on the rocks or beach. I saw a picture recently. The board walks and rails are gone and there is a miserable muddy road which must be grim on wet days. You know that place was a complete set up for a tourist village, ancient buildings, boardwalks, everything. And it was the last; it should have been preserved. As my mother used to say, "I could bite nails."

Guess what I started to say was when I was ten everything was serene, everyone was a friend or acquaintance. Then I wasn't ten any more and was away to school, only back to Rigolet in summer. A lot of things changed. I became shy and very solitary. My brothers and sisters never were shy and they were away every fine Sunday in the motorboat to visit around the inlet. My dad would let them have the boat provided I went along to look after it and the engine. I spent many a Sunday walking along the shore or in the boat reading. I don't think I ever felt bad about being the only one on the outside. I'd yarn with the older men who were taking Sunday off.

It wasn't long before I was grown up and working for HBC. Still desperately shy, I hated store work. I wanted to go to sea, but with masters going as third mates just to get a job, there didn't seem to be a hope. We didn't expect a war to come along and change everything all over. So after a couple of years I went farther north and I liked the Eskimos. They liked me, because I was a loner and because I could do the things they did. After all I'd grown up doing those things. They were wonderful solitary years.

Then the war, armed forces, and a new lifestyle, a type of people I'd never met before, young and just casting off the shadow of depression and hard times. It was conform, or go under, and I conformed.

I had hardly ever spoken to a girl. Most of the girls I met now were armed forces, in no way like any women I'd ever seen. They were noisy and boisterous. They were also getting out from under the depression. I remember seeing one kid, recently joined up, showing her meagre pay, her first, and she said, "I never had more than a whole dollar before. Now I got two tens and some ones." I think I was scared of them and I had to lose the shyness.

I remember too, leaving Kingston for Montreal on a crowded train, I had a window seat and two CWAC girls came and took the others. Those seats could accommodate three. I guess I froze by the window but there was no place to go. In a very short time, they decided I was no fun and ignored me. It was a long, hot ride to Montreal and after a bit, they relaxed and tried to sleep. The one nearest me dropped off, and her head fell over against me. I don't think I'd ever seen a sleeping white woman before and I think I thought it was most immodest of her. I know I didn't move a muscle and never even glanced her way.

As time went on she leaned more heavily against me and the other girl against her. Her face left a streak of white face powder on my tunic. At Montreal she woke and said, "I hope I wasn't too heavy," and went away. Somewhere down deep I felt that we should have been forced to marry. Not really, but it was a strange experience. I soon got used to people sleeping against me.

This letter was supposed to end on that last page, but your letter came and I spent a pleasant time reading it and the poetry. I liked the poetry, Roethke's "Night Journey" most of all. But first let me get home, take a shower and I'll tell you about my very first night train ride when I was twenty plus.

Moosonee, July 14, 1983. Midnight.

Dear Claudia,

I couldn't sleep tonight so drove out to the quarry, parked the truck and walked up to the end of the road. I walked out a road through the bush to some cabins owned by the RC mission. By daylight, they are odd-shaped little places. At night, there in the tall trees, they are brooding and mysterious. The lighting, a feeble moon, the shadows and the trees, the silent blank windows, the smokeless chimneys, the closed doors, the little bridge across the creek. It was all still. Some time there will be motion, wild clouds, a sailing moon. I'll go back then. Something like from "Loch Na Gar," "Rides on the night-rolling (I love those words) breath of the gale. Surely the soul of the hero rejoices, and rides on the wind o'er his own highland vale." Can't you see them? The vanquished but unconquered, the dead but living, fiercely sailing above the land they loved and lost, red-bearded tartaned heroes, swords drawn, riding the great roaring winds from the west. When I was little, my dad sang "Loch Na Gar," and the words, the lovely descriptive words created visions of men who had such a passionate love for their sail, such a hatred for slavery. Me of Irish and Papist descent, and I cried over "Scots Wha Hae." I still can, while I treasure and weep the bitter tears of my mother's race and hold Tara's Harp more dearly than I can express. I have English blood too, and I am a Royalist, but while I love the gentle English songs, I agree that "England, they beauties are tame and domestic / To one who has roved on the mountains afar / I sigh for the crag that is wild and majestic / The steep frowning glory of dark Loch Na Gar."

When I will die, where will they lay me? In a quiet cemetery with flowers and green grass? When my soul wants to be where the wildest winds can tear at my cover till it is gone and what is left is again mingled with the land. The mountain above Tororak will do. When I will die, Tororak will do.

July 30, 1983

Dear Claudia,

What makes people communicate? I'm a lone sort of person, always have been. I don't knock it; I like solitude, but I love people too. But I'm not a man's man, if I can use that term. I don't drink, I don't like parties, I hate smoke and liquor. I don't like to see people flushed and noisy. In the army, I saw many men who made a regular game out of the pursuit and conquest of women, all of them living in a never-never land they could only have found because of a war, and that's the worst reason.

I have a very few close male friends, and many women friends, most of them with small children, many who have worked with me and with whom I hate to lose touch.

I love small gentle things like babies. At twenty and thirty years old, and unmarried, people thought I was weird because I'd rather cuddle a baby than make an amorous chase after her beautiful aunt. The normal male instincts were not lacking, but lady, were they repressed. I was shy in a time when lots of girls were coming out of the Victorian age. My brothers, nearly all younger, quickly got in style. I never did. I heard about conquests and wondered how many real, how many fancied. I was too young to have a platonic friendship, too shy to follow the crowd. I didn't feel rejected, except once. I felt that I was inadequate, so I was alone, not from choice, not really unhappy about it, but always wondering why I was out of step.

I hated store work because it meant dealing with women and girls. Later when I was older and stationed in a much larger place, I had opportunities to see more people and I could have mingled more, but I didn't because that was the way I was. At that time I had the choice and realized who I was. Before I didn't know. My worst experience was being made fun of by a pretty girl when I was quite young. That one hurt and I don't think I have ever recovered. She tried to make it up later when she probably realized how much I'd been hurt, but I could never speak to her. I couldn't be in the same room. I'm not proud of that. She did try, I didn't.

I could take her kid sister fishing or berry picking. She was a cute little tyke and spent days in a motorboat with me collecting salmon from the fishermen. Once she said, "You like me and my little sister, but you don't like my big sister, do you. She's like us and you don't like her. Everyone else does." I felt very guilty. They often came to our house. My mother liked the girl and often insisted that she stay for meals. I'd go to the men's kitchen, or eat in the outside cookhouse, never at the table if she were there.

I don't know where she is now, but we are the same age and our youth is far behind us. I could meet her now and be polite because I've learned a lot. I wish now so very much that I could have met her half way. She was young and thoughtless and influenced by the others. I could have been generous but I wasn't. Regret is bitter when you know you could have done better.

I guess, too, when she made a lot of me just for fun, I fell for it, and in my blundering way I was, at least partly, in love, puppy love for sure, but I thought she was sincere and I thought that perhaps now I wouldn't be in the wrong lane any more.

You know, nothing could have been a greater disaster than that she was sincere. We were so completely different. I was, and would have been, completely in her power, and I don't take easily to domination, I have found. Even if it had been genuine, it couldn't have lasted, but it kept me in the slow lane for a long time.

That was a long time ago, but it still hurts. I was so completely deceived. I don't think I allowed myself to think about the physical implications. They were not as commonly discussed as they are today. I do remember having a boatload of youngsters one day, and we pulled into a lovely cove because they wanted to swim. The boys hiked up among the rocks to change and the girls crowded into the tiny cabin, and there were the usual giggles and squeaks. I was sitting on the engine casing, much too shy to dream of going swimming, and Matt Wolfrey suggested that we use the long boat hook to flip the girls' cabin door open. I can still remember my outrage that he'd even suggest such a thing. I'd still be angry because deliberately embarrassing a person is something I can't do, but then the girl that I cared about was there and she was still precious.

In the army, I found that I could get along with women. I met a few misfits like myself. One melancholy person and I visited every graveyard around Kingston. She collected grave markers. Interesting friendship? Well, it was someone I liked to talk to, and if anything got me down, it was the incessant barrack talk at meals, breaks, free time and when possible, during training hours. The subject never varied and can it be boring!

Every so often I'd have a new class to train in wireless procedure, and every time I'd hope, perhaps, there is one here whose mind is somewhere else. They'd start practising on the key, and as soon as they worked up a little knowledge, I'd put them two by two and have them work up to a little military style conversation. You know, like, "We are being outflanked," "Send rations," or "Send ammunition." And they'd send the messages to one another and substitute words. Who cared; they were learning the alphabet and it spells every word there is. But lordy, how boring some of the words are.

We usually trained only men, as there were no women combat people in those days. But I had one class of RCAF women who were connected to a very secret radar program in Vimy Barracks. They were a joy to work with: keen, interested and they had a different language too. I enjoyed them. Because of the secret nature of their work, they didn't get too much liberty, and time was long. However, if "properly escorted," and the army classed me as proper, they could go places. So on Sundays I'd borrow several canoes and we'd go up the Rideau for the day. Some couldn't paddle but they'd have fun splashing along. Or we'd borrow, using the term lightly, a vehicle from the army and run across to the USA for the day, Rochester mostly. They were nice and I grew to like them a lot.

They did a lot for me. I was ten years older than the youngest, and I guess about five older than the most venerable, in their terms, ready to be a grandfather. But they couldn't associate with their own age group, so I was a good substitute.

A lot of things happened after the war. I got engaged, and I still don't know how I ever got up enough nerve to do that. I went to Repulse Bay for a year and then we were married and I don't suppose anyone on earth was less prepared for that than I was. Two weeks later, I was sent north for six months as engineer on a ship operating out of Churchill. Then I was transferred inland and fitted in quite well there. I liked the bush, I liked the natives, and while no one would ever call me a better than average merchandiser, I was a hotshot cleaner-upper. Since I liked that kind of job, the Company generously saw I got them.

When I was transferred to Winnipeg, and we were settled there, I was transferred to the transport division. I've been away now in Moosonee every summer for twenty-five or six years. The family would come up fairly often but you wouldn't call me an average married man.

Yesterday Ash phoned as usual at ten as he does every Sunday and said, "I spose you're coming up for dinner?" And I went and had the usual huge meal, and afterwards we yarned. Ash may not be all that articulate, but he has seen a lot. He and Bill argued about fish and whales and it was quite a session listening to old names, "thresher" for killer whale, "shark fish" for pilot fish, "maiden ray" for common ray. Where "maiden" came from, I'll never know. When I was in Labrador, it was maiden ray. Less like a maiden you couldn't find, but there it is.

We yarned a long time about sculpin and smelt and capelin and whales, particularly whales. Ash cooked on a whaling station once. To him it was just a job. He couldn't see the horror of hundreds of those huge gentle creatures being killed. Death on a large scale is nothing new to Ash. A hundred thousand little lives gasp away when a boatload of capelin is dumped in a garden for fertilizer. A cod trap is so full of fish that it takes many hours to process them. One by one, they are thrown on a table, and one by one, each small heart ceases to beat. People must eat and people must find food. So you never think of a cod as a creature that may be able to feel the sharp knife at his throat. You can't allow yourself to, any more than the men I see in Winnipeg waiting to cross the street at Canada Packers can afford to think that the red stains on their white coats represent death on a massive scale. Ash couldn't feel anything for whales because he had to live and eat. So a whale was a big black thing that was processed where he worked.

But he is observant. He finds it hard to tell what he saw as a fisherman. He has seen the great whales suddenly appear beside him, and will have stopped work to look at them. Ash can't express it, neither can I, the feeling when you suddenly hear the breeching of the water, and there is that enormous creature silent before your eyes, and you know that, like you, it has a heart purposely beating away, teeth that could mangle you and your boat in seconds but never will. Ash worked so hard to express himself, face contorted, eyes closed tight. "My sonny byes, you never did see something so big an' midnight black, an' he don't hurt nothin'."

In a starvation camp I saw a whale killed. It was necessary, wasn't it. How else could people up in that desperately barren environment live. Nature allows one kind to kill another, it's part of the law, but put your hand on that huge black side, look at that small eye, know that the poetry of motion that moved that creature is forever stilled and you wonder if man may not be the most savage of all creatures. He's among the few that preys on nearly every other being, that constantly preys on his own species. His food chain embraces all, from a scallop to a whale, from frog to elephant.

As a type, man is often rapacious and cruel, as individuals, often kind, tender and generous. So let's forget types and concentrate on individuals. Hard to pick up a small squirming mite with a red angry face, screaming because it has just come into a harsh bright world from the security of its mother's body, and feel that this may someday be a captain of industry, a prime minister, or a general who'll have command and domination over thousands of lives. It's only a tiny squalling baby and you love it.

Moosonee, August 18, 1983

Dear Claudia,

Depends on what happens in the next few pages whether you get this one or not. It's one I'll have to read carefully because I'm very angry. I saw a TV thing, two TV things to be exact, and got so mad I waited until this morning to talk about it, hoping I'd calm down. I haven't. I still have a futile anger. The damage is so wilful and irreparable that I'm shaken.

Well, to start with, John and Janet Foster presented one of their "If you are a good kid I'll tell you a story" things. Their photography is good usually and this time the setting was right in my own Hebron, Saglek, Nachvak country. There were no native people, part of what created my anger.

But the big old hills are there, the ducks whales, seals, and caribou are there. The old Moravian building that housed and warmed us are slowly crumbling down, though stabilized. The caribou have taken over the village where old Christina used to stump along to the river with her bucket, where Magdalena swung dourly along on her crutches. The high grassy knoll where my dogs, Alikou, Pal and the rest used to lie in the summer sun and watch the village activity is still there. The harbour is empty but the water is crystal clear. Even the piles of stones that anchored tents are still in place. They missed Tororak and I'm glad. It shouldn't be desecrated by helicopters and the stink of diesel fuel. There should be a law that anyone may visit that bowl of beauty and contentment only if he comes in quiet, by paddle or sail, or with the small natural noises of a dog team: the whuffle of a dog's breath, the soft muffled sound of their feet, the whisper of the runners, the slap and rustle of the rawhide traces. No other sound.

And since Coonera's ancient rifle has long fired its last shot for the game that gave him and his family life, let there be no more shots fired. No more spears stabbed into the water until the rightful owners of the land return.

It was good to see the land, the hills, the water, the icebergs. Janet's commentary with its weight of platitude faded as I watched and I heard Rena's voice as he told me about the death of a man. I heard Albert's merry whisper as we walked miles on a beautiful night. I heard the soft murmur of stone age voices as I lay in an ancient house under the ground and watched a family that needed almost nothing I and my kind considered necessary, people who had never worked for a wage but who rarely lacked, who had all the things in their own coin that the constitution promises us and will never deliver because we will never know that the things we want and need are far behind, that the wonderful future is a mirage because we have destroyed our own birthright and in doing so have savagely rent and divided a people who have never harmed us.

I looked at the empty beautiful land and I heard the voices, saw the faces and yearned to go back again, to see it as it was, as it should be, with people who lived on it for thousands of years and left it as undisturbed as when they found it. The signs of the original peoples are few; a few graves, a few bones, an indistinct trail in the turf.

When the program was over, I thought of how I'd love to show that land to you. I went there a young man, incomplete. Now that I know who I am, and why I am, I know that the land and the people were for me a compensation for the things that are normally expressed in the strange urges and desires of youth, which I, in my time, failed to recognize and therefore lost.

I would like you to stand on the deck of a boat, offshore, with the sun behind you, with the clean smell of the sea all around you, with flocks of seabirds making magic abstracts of the smooth canvas of the sea, and look at that land. See the black boldness that is like the strong strokes of your brush on whitest paper. See the shapes, the contours, see the land swell away from the water, see the mountains fall away into hills and valleys, feel that the land is living.

And the next program was a brutal, honest, appalling documentary of what we have done to the original people. Herded them like pigs into dirty, disease-ridden hovels, in scandalous villages where the whites live in serviced, painted, even landscaped houses while the Indians and Eskimos grovel outside their doors. Liquor, promiscuity, squalor, because it was too much trouble to let them range their own land and survive as they have been conditioned to for centuries. Tell me, is an old woman better off crouched on a bare plywood floor smoking a cigarette, with a wine bottle at her feet? Is she better off in a filthy sty because there is a nurse and teacher in tidy clean houses with a fence, clean people in clean surroundings who change their underwear every day?

Would that old lady be worse off out on the land in a clean tent, with her family around her, where her daughter and grand daughter will be betrothed in the ancient manner and wander alone on the land with her mate to possibly conceive a child in beauty and love, a child that will be wanted and protected?

Ask the missionaries. They'll tell you that "The People" are promiscuous. They are promiscuous now in an ugly way. A girl's body will earn so much liquor, so many cigarettes, cheap ankle socks, tin jewellery. If the people were promiscuous, they were so in an open, loving, natural way. I wonder if some of their kids even knew just when they actually entered into a sex relationship. The nights are long and dark. Only a feeble glimmer from a *kudlik*, which has been carefully darkened to save precious oil. Kids were like a ball of puppies tumbling together under the sleeping skins. Touching, discovering, until nature, one day, finishes her plan. Perhaps they go hunting or fishing and the magic seizes them and when they return to the igloo and the communal sleeping bench, they may move a couple of skins to a corner, conveying a subtle hint that their status has changed. And horrors, she may go from boy to boy for a while, and the crones will watch and figure, till one day she is pregnant and there is a lot of talk and teasing, until one lucky swain is decided on by her and the family. And they spread their bed skins together and the child that has been conceived is wanted and will be theirs. Since "the people" are promiscuous, she will, at times of festival and good hunting, be intimate with other men, as he will be with other women, but never with people who have the same blood. I have seen a young couple slip away from the gathering to benevolent smiles, and return looking as though they had experienced a wonderful joy. That's a terrible way to live, the missionaries say. Perhaps, but it is not selling one's body for a loveless act, for a price, a price that is paid many fold by the child that often results. Is that enough of a tirade for this time?

Trying to be calm. Why? What is the reason those people were snatched from their land, to live in settlements, where the land cannot support a concentrated population, where it cannot absorb their waste?

Is it better to have near children drunk, women subject to the most frightful degradation? Think of all the clean uninhabited land. I've seen them on the land, and I've seen them in the settlements. The government says they needed health facilities; they could have had radios, wind-generated radios to ask for help. Is it better to have the chance an illness out on the land? To go to school in a settlement atmosphere than learn to be Inuit on the land? Didn't Joe Smallwood say, "Burn your fishing boats, move to the growth centres and become wealthy"? He did, and many moved, now what? The ones that stayed are the lucky ones.

I can't sleep, Claudia; I see those pictures of men slumped on the floor, no hope, boys drinking out of a bottle, girls hanging around in the back, wanting a share and only one currency to pay. The pictures were strong medicine. I was sickened. I've seen starvation, and it's hard to see the children get thinner and thinner, and to know that some will die. But it's harder to look at what we've done to these people and know that they are worse than dead.

In every "settlement," there are those who refuse to quit, who still struggle to maintain the old life, and they get fewer and fewer. Does no one realize or try to realize that it is as hard for one of the original people to adapt to our life as it would be for one of us to adapt to the harsh standard that they lived by for centuries before we appeared? Imagine Mr. Trudeau or Mr. Smallwood crouching over a fishing hole for hours and hours, patiently jiggling a small lure to entice a fish near enough for the spear, knowing that if he has no success, he will not eat that day. As well as to ask Okalook to tell you what can be seen from the public gallery in Parliament. Some place it says, "We took their birthright and gave them a mess of potage." To our everlasting guilt, we did. How many millions do we spend to preserve wilderness parks for our children; why can't someone see that we could preserve wilderness people for their children. I ranted in this fashion once, and someone said if they were indeed out on the land, what good would they be? So! They are off the land, in the settlement; what good are they? While miles and miles of their land waits empty.

I have read this over again. So where do I get off. I have not gone to Ottawa and protested. Who knows, perhaps I could have done something, perhaps gone to jail. I didn't. Screaming does no good. The people didn't scream, they believed, and they went meekly, even cheerfully. Davis Inlet, three hundred people, of whom two hundred are children without a future, not hunters, not labourers. Some will drown or freeze, victims of liquor from a government store, some will die of gastroenteritis before they are half grown, and some will kill themselves in despair, and some will live to conceive other children to increase the ratio. But the old folk will sink deeper into despair and rejection.

Many, many years ago, I read this in a dictionary: Maori, "a type of Indian of New Zealand who do not seem to be disappearing as many 'inferior' races do when they come in contact with civilization." I was very young and could not accept that Will and Wilfred and Peter and Big Joe and Little Joe were inferior. The blamed dictionary had to be wrong. And it was.

SEVEN

Moosonee, August 22, 1983

Good Morning Claudia,

When I was little I used to find surprises in my bed. We had huge old-fashioned goose feather mattresses in winter. You sank down and down and the feathers rose up around you and nearly covered you. No heat in bedrooms then. We'd undress in the icy rooms, run to the stove and get warm, and when our pyjamas were so hot we couldn't bear them on our flesh, we'd make a rush for the feather beds, every one, even if two in a bed, with his own warm nest. And because I like to find things, there used to be little things there. I'm sure I told you before, didn't I? Sometimes when I was asleep I'd feel Aunt Bella or someone sneak something in that I'd find in the morning. One late confession, I had my own small bed, never slept with anyone else, though my younger brothers doubled up.

And years later, many years, when I was a young man and lonely at times and wondering about life and the things I didn't have, I tried to imagine what it would be like to sleep two in a feather mattress. Laugh quietly, but we used to get the first *Life* magazines, and they specialized in long-legged American beauties. I used to wonder if they could possibly be so slim and smooth and elegant and tidy and clean. You see my only point of comparison was the skin-clad ladies of the local camp who slept in their clothes, and the clothes weren't particularly form fitting either.

This must be confession morning. Many white men made temporary wife arrangements up there. One thing I'm glad of was that I didn't. I know the policeman who had conjugal arrangements considered me a bit weak in the wrist. There were times when I was tempted, but not very often. I had a horror of leaving a child who was mine to exist in a native camp. Fine for those who belonged there, my daughter wouldn't. And because part-blood children can be heart-breakingly pretty, she'd be game for the first white man who arrived after she was twelve or fifteen.

But every issue of *Life* brought more lovely ladies and when you get a year's issues at once, that's a lot to wonder about. Can you see the contrast? Clean beautiful hair, no twigs and caribou hair? It wasn't possible to believe that women had legs and arms like that, and wore them uncovered. Easy to understand now.

I was happy and content, but after I left home, the feminine was lost to me. I didn't know it but a soft woman's voice on the radio set up a Life picture in my mind. The occasional white woman was finding her way into the Arctic in those days and they were strange exquisite creatures but I could barely speak to them.

There was one in particular, the photographer, Lorene Squire, who came up on *Nascopie* for HBC. *The Beaver* still has rolls and rolls of her underdeveloped film. Capt. Smellie sort of gave me to her, to run the ship's boat where she wanted to go. She was a lovely lady, not only in my confused mind, but she had a very easy, friendly, manner. She was also very a beautiful woman. She was all the pictures, all the radio voices. She treated me as though I had grown up in her environment. She gave me things to carry, cameras, and gear, she wore a kerchief on her head and if it got in the way, she's whip it off and stuff it into my pocket or toss it to me. I was almost scared, I was scared, to touch those personal things. I'd never seen, much less touched, such a glorious person. She was always in a hurry too. Guess it's a fact of life with photographers. She'd grab my hands and position them when I had to hold a reflector or something. She could never know what that touching meant. I was her devoted slave as you might have guessed. She ate her meals on board at the captain's table. I ate in the officers' mess room with my friends, the mates and engineers. The saloon ate before us and she'd come down the deck, peek into the mess room and when the radio operator left, (he never stayed more than a few minutes) she'd come in, squeeze next to me and smile at everyone. She'd grin at Marcel, our mess boy, and he'd bring her a plate and she'd snitch a bit from everyone, and every man there would have given her his whole dinner.

I suppose she was getting some atmosphere for her articles at the same time, but that glorious lady owned that old ship.

Capt Smellie was dour and unapproachable but she'd get hold of his arm and coax him into a position where she'd get the exact picture she wanted. One night there was a fantastic cloud and colour effect in Lancaster Sound. Passengers only allowed on the bridge by special invitation, and not often then. But early in the voyage the old man relaxed that rule for her completely. Only stipulation was she must not climb to the yard or the ice barrel without a crew member along. So she was in the darkened wheelhouse with us.

It was fall and the midnight sun long gone. She stood at the corner of the bridge wing with her cameras and suddenly said, "Get the captain, quick." No one, but no one, even thought to call the captain at that time except in regard to the ship. The third mate looked properly horrified, the watchman froze in his tracks. Poor mesmerized me, I took off like a racehorse, and as I rapped on his door, I knew for sure he'd slaughter me.

But I guess I didn't care, because I banged right heartily and when he appeared I just said, "Miss Squire wants you on the bridge quickly." He said never a word, reached for his uniform jacket and cap and walked out, leaving me to close his door and follow. She put him in the corner near the old pelorus,[18] unused these modern days, and I can still see her take his chin and turn his head to get the exact pose, and with that absolutely fantastic light behind him she shot several pictures.

She never called me the same name twice in succession; I was Shorty, Bill, anyone of a hundred. I knew by her voice that she was looking for me when I heard George or Henry from some obscure place on the ship. This time she said, "Len," and told me "We got a beauty here." I never saw that one. I suspect that if it were developed before she died, the old man got it. There was one of him and the pelorus in *The Beaver* and on the cover of a book about him. Those were daylight pictures.

One winter listening to a news broadcast I heard that the photographer, Lorene Squire, had been killed in a car accident. I was alone on Cape Wolstenholme and I couldn't cry, couldn't feel. There was no one to confide in. I couldn't believe that lovely person dead, mangled, and I had no person to talk to.

We had a large HBC radio net in those days, and when the Nottingham Island operator came on that night, he said, "If no one has emergency traffic, we'll close down because every man up here has had bad news today." That was the only sound on 1356 KCS that night. It was a calm moonless night. I dressed and I walked miles and miles up the valley. I was alone in every sense of the word. I was young, perhaps starved for some of the things I had never known. I heard her voice, felt her friendly touch, thought of the gentle heedless things she did like resting her arm on my shoulder to steady herself in the boat.

18 A navigational instrument.

Back in Winnipeg, August 24, 1983

Dear Claudia,

I'll go to Maureen's today. There are pickles to be made, head cheese, vegetables to be dug, corn to be picked. There will be berries and good things, but I'll probably be able to ignore the harvest and the pickles and go talk to the foal who is growing up and who has recently decided he has a temper. Maureen had a tussle with him a few days ago about a halter and he reared and stamped and misbehaved until his mother nipped him sharply when he reared at her. So he and I will have a session.

First I'll use guile and I'll caress his neck and shoulders. That he loves, and he will stand and arch his neck and make foolish Eleanor Roosevelt faces to show his pleasure. He is only two months old. Then we'll find a little fresh clover, put the halter on, and if he so decides, we'll stand just as long as he wants. But sooner or later he'll walk, and when he does, part of the battle will be over.

One of the boys said he needs his spirit broken, and he needs to be tamed. I could never do that. I've always been proud that I've trained many dogs without a blow or a harsh word. I am an amateur with horses, but there can be no excuse for breaking the spirit of a creature so wildly beautiful. So we'll do what we must, but no force.

When I was very young at boarding school, we had two horses, Maggie and Bill. They had been artillery horses from the Great War with bullet scars on their flanks. Both were shell-shocked. Bill never recovered. He was much too wild for a little kid like me to be near. The man who owned him was an old Scot, stern, upright and just. We tried and tried but Bill was not able to be helped. So Old Malcolm let him live out the fantasy of war that lived in his old brain.

He would race around, eyes wild with fear and excitement, rearing and plunging and shying away from the fearful things he saw. He only knew peace when Maggie was let in with him. She'd put her big old head across his neck and she'd calm down. One day Bill died quite suddenly. Malcolm said he sank to his knees and raised his head to the sky and never got up. Maggie stood quietly near him. She never went back to that end of the paddock again.

She was also shell-shocked and now and then would become unmanageable, but we usually knew when it would happen. She did it once when a brutal idiot was using her to haul wood. Malcolm would never say no to anyone who needed help but he liked one of us to go along to see that Maggie was treated gently. This time she bolted for no reason except memory and fear. She left the wood trail and plunged about fifty feet into deep snow. I had been walking beside her but had to jump aside when she bolted. In a short time she was up to her shoulders in snow and the sleigh and the wood was buried. She calmed down when I could get to her but she was lying on her side and I couldn't release her harness.

Harvey had the stupid idea that she could back out and should be made to do so. He doubled the reins and before I even guessed what he'd do, he slashed her across the head. Her eyes, Claudia. I hope never to see anything like it again. I screamed at him to stop and he hit her again. There was an axe driven into one of the logs on the sleigh and I grabbed it. It wasn't a cool resolution, just to scare him. I was white hot with anger and I remember the tears coming so fast I could hardly see but I could distinguish him in a blurred way and I went for him.

Doctor Paddon, who was in charge of the hospital, was walking with Mrs. Paddon and he came just in time. I heard his roar, and I put the axe down. He sent me on the run to the barn for men and shovels. It was quite close and he held Maggie's head until we got back. When she was free and standing trembling on the road, he lit into Harvey, every word in measured English public school scorn meant to pierce. I couldn't feel sorry for Harvey whose worse fault was probably that he was an ass, but I could see that he'd probably never change either.

Of course, I knew my time was coming. The doctor was kind. He told Joe to take Maggie away and get her dry and warm and then take her home. When they had gone, he spoke to me about the danger of letting my temper get out of hand, but there was a twinkle in his eye and a curve to his moustache that didn't quite fit in with his words.

I didn't talk much about it with anyone. I told Malcolm and he nodded without a word as I knew he would. Many years later my dad told me that Dr. Paddon had told him about it and had a good chuckle describing poor Harvey's face as he looked at that axe coming at him. I must have been eleven or twelve then I guess.

Shortly after, Harvey made a vicious slash at a misbehaving dog with a long dog whip, the most cruel weapon imaginable. As usual, I was in the way, trying to do something with one of the Company dogs, and I got the whip in the face. It wasn't the very tip, or I'd be blind now, but it wrapped around my head and took all the skin off my nose. Harvey must have been convinced his time had come but I couldn't react. I couldn't see.

When one suddenly loses the biggest part of the hide on his schnozz, his eyes go out in sympathy, I guess. I could hear Harvey babbling on, trying to say it was an accident, but I couldn't see him. Anyway, there was no big axe around. When I got home, old Aunt Bella was there, dear old Aunt Bella, and she took a look and scolded me because I'd be scaring my mother, and when I wouldn't go to the hospital, she went out to her brother Albert who was repairing the stairs, and got a big flat brown leaf of the old chewing tobacco and fitted it over my bugle. It hurt like fire for a second or so, then felt wonderful.

She fussed over me and I heard her tell Winnie, Malcolm's daughter, "That blessed boy won't have a head to his neck by the time he's twenty." Blessed wasn't what it sounded like; it was Aunt Bella's harshest cuss word.

Your letter was waiting for me when I got back to the office, such a nice fat one and so many things to study. Perhaps everyone can alter his vision to get double images and such like. When I was very young

I learned to do it and it gives quite a variety of views to any single thing.

It's amazing what I see in your art. I would like to see exactly what you see as you create. On the other hand I have a feeling it's also very private and I want to be sure that I'm not prying. Is there any sense to that statement? I like to hear of what people have done and seen and felt, especially what they have felt. I would like to ask, and I do ask, but always with care because a person's life is like his suitcase or bedroom.

In a way, a suitcase, to me anyway, resembles a life. Some are carefully packed, everything in order, no old or ragged things. Others are a joyous confusion of new and old garments, worn perhaps, old perhaps, not packed with the idea that someone might look, but packed with love and generosity showing the owner as he or she is.

A nice old lady I once knew had an expanding case of old heavy leather, and all that held it together was two big straps. It was like two boxes, one slightly smaller than the other. To get into it, you lifted the smaller one off. To pack, you put everything into the larger one and put the other over it, pressed them down and fastened the straps. The old lady used to pile it all up and slam the top one down. One of us would sit on it, perhaps two of us, and she'd tug the straps through the brass buckle. Once the straps were fastened everything would be secure.

She'd have all sorts of things in there and it was usually well expanded. The first Life-Saver candy I ever had came out of that case, peppermint. I had a toy sailboat someone made me and I carefully fastened white Life-Saver rings in the rigging. The bath water soon took care of them, but never mind, I had them for a while. Guess I was a dumb little kid not to eat them. Guess I did a lot of dumb things but they were fun.

Once there was a hot spring day when school seemed a positive imposition. Don't know how I ever learned anything because I seem to remember every season was too precious to be inside. Anyway, it was late in the afternoon. The sun was shattering itself against the big windows and the time was so long. I had a set of shiny steel geometrical instruments and I noticed how a square had reflected a bright spot on the ceiling. Of course I had to reflect that spot here and there.

I have to tell you I was deathly afraid of Mr. Russell, the teacher, but I knew he had weak eyes. I also knew he'd half kill me and I was torn between aye and nay, but I did it. I flashed that little spot squarely in his eyes. He let out a roar and I saw him coming. If ever a person or a dumb kid knew fear, I knew it at that moment. He always wore a black robe and it was flying out behind him as he came at me.

Talk about a doomed person's past flashing before his eyes. I hadn't had much of a past at that time, it wouldn't have been a long flash. But I never got a blink, too scared. He had the big pointer he always carried and I'd felt it before. He stopped about two feet away and just about when I expected to be struck dead before the whole class, the miserable girl behind me, Emily, rammed an old-fashioned pen nib through the crack in the seat and nailed me squarely in the back end.

If I thought of anything in that instant, I would have thought your sins fall on your head, and if so why is the pain in the opposite end? At that moment my small world was exploding in every direction. I half stood with shock, surprise, pain, heaven only knows what emotions, and I guess he thought I was about to attack or flee or whatever.

His second roar put me back on my throbbing backside, and my seatmate put his head down on the desk. I imagine he thought that nothing could save him from the holocaust that was inevitable.

Mr. Russell stopped, looked at me for a good minute, probably trying to decide if he would have my heart or some other palpitating organ first. Then he started to talk and I felt like he stripped every inch of skin from my frame. He was famous for his tongue and I got the full benefit. When all my bones were bare and all the kids were expecting me to drop, he laid out my punishment: four big loads of coal to be brought up from the cellar every morning, and he added that if I were of a vindictive turn of mind, I'd best not think of stabbing Emily with a pen nib, much as she deserved it.

I didn't dare turn around but I heard later that Emily turned a good many shades of red. I knew Russell told my dad because my dad grinned at me one day and asked if I was sitting comfortably these days. Those old seats were cruel instruments. There was a wide crack in the back and the desk drawers sloped down. To ream an unsuspecting neighbour, you only had to shove your hand, armed with a long penholder, deep into the drawer, and bingo.

Did I ever get even with Emily? Well, I plotted revenge for a long time. Then one day I saw her crying because a better-dressed girl had made a nasty remark about her clothes, and it wasn't important any more. I told my sister and she told my mother and she and Mrs. Payne created a dress for Emily's confirmation. They had an excuse because Emily's mother was always sick.

I saw her again when she was big and happy and productive. She must have had six or seven kids. My dad and I were staying overnight at a tiny hotel in Twillingate, and Emily happened to be there too. She told the story all over again in the best-natured way and I thought my dad would choke. Emily is a year older than me. I wonder what she's like now.

Moosonee, September 10, 1983

Dear Claudia,

Berry picking again this evening, back to Pilgrim. Saw where Mr. Bear had had his morning or afternoon nap. Guess it's pretty comfortable there in the sun especially when you carry a big black rug around to rest on. Willie Millik and I once spent a long time watching a black bear take a rest. He was just like a baby, got a hold of his back toes with his front ones and look puzzled about what to do next. He'd roll over and over like a kitten and seemed to want an audience, not knowing he had one.

I can still see Willie's merry round face with his perfect white teeth, black eyes and brown smile. He was a handsome man, tall for an Eskimo and so merry, he laughed about everything. I think of all the friends I had in the Arctic he had to be the greatest.

Nothing disturbed Willie. No change in weather, or whatever, bothered him. Once we walked a long, long, way over very rough country to get to where he had left a small boat. We intended to use the boat to cross the inlet and get home without having to climb a huge mountain that got in our way. Long after dark, in mixed rain and snow, we got to where he kept the boat on a little gravelly beach. I was dreaming of warm food and my comfortable bed just across the inlet, only half an hour's rowing away. But no boat. Another native had borrowed it to go to the village across the water. We could see the lights but no way to signal, as there is no wood in that country to make a fire.

First of all Willie had a good laugh, then we sat down and ate some dried fish, and in the dark I could just see him as he held up and imaginary tea pot and asked politely, «More Tea?» That type of person stores everything in his head. Soon he got up and said he knew where he had picked up a couple of pieces of wood, probably tossed off some passing ship. Not far he said, and peeled off his outer kulitak and took off. He could run like a deer and see like a cat, and it wasn't close. He was gone half and hour or more, but brought back two small pieces of wood with Moirs Confectionary on them. Also a fair-sized tin can. So if we couldn't have a big signal fire, we'd have a reflected one.

Our little fire was so small I had no hope anyone would see it across five miles of water, but we took the wood and the can up the hill and Willie grinned as he lit the shavings. He said Magdalena Kejuk saw everything and she'd soon have someone over for us. It seemed a long cold wet wait with the snow getting thicker, but after a while we heard the tonk-tonk of Joseph Tuglavina's old Hubbard engine, and the boat pulled in loaded to the gunwale with kids and adults who had come out in that miserable weather just for the ride, everyone laughing his head off. When we got on board, Willie's adopted son poked his head out of the tiny engine house to offer us tea that he had been keeping warm on the exhaust. Hardly room in there to change your mind, yet he crouched behind the noisy, smelly old engine for that five miles so we'd have the tea Willie's wife sent, nice and hot.

My assistant was at the dock to meet us. He said his wife had cooked a roast of venison. Willie's family was already there, so we went to the big old mission house where Bill and I lived and when we walked in, our wet outer clothing was taken off. They pulled off our boots and we sat down to eat. Such a meal! Bill's wife had learned from the German missionaries and they were experts. There were two huge coppers of water heating on the big black range, and after I had eaten, and our tale or tales were told, I got into a steaming tub and from there to bed. Sleep? Claudia, the sleep we got in that country would make old Rip Van Winkle jealous.

Just boiled a huge lot of cranberries and now have the juice straining through a linen bag. I'll be honest, if you won't tell. It's a new pillow case. Outrageous, no? But it makes lovely clear jelly and what's a pillow case every four or five years? It was lovely on the river this evening, beautiful on the Island. Now it's raining very gently and I'm sitting here listening to the rain on the roof.

There's nothing like being in a tent listening to the rain fall on the surface of the water while a candle makes shadows, and a little sheet metal stove gobbles gently, and the stove pipe turns red where it joins the stove. My dad used to say for pure comfort you had to have dry feet, a soft spot to lie, a favourite pipe to smoke and the stovepipe red. He loved these things and because he had to spend a lot of time in the office, he enjoyed the outside things that much more.

He had a big Michigan axe that he got from an American prospector. No one could use it but my dad. In the fall, when things were quiet, he'd take his axe and for a week or more he'd chop firewood in a special grove he had marked for his own. Actually, no one else wanted it because it was high on a hill and hard and dangerous to get.

The wood was red spruce, almost overgrown, and would soon fall anyway. So he cut for his soul's sake every fall and my brother and I risked life and limb to haul it home with a dog team.

One year we hauled a huge pile and stood it up, teepee fashion, as they do where there is a lot of snow. An owl built a nest away up where the sticks crossed, and never a stick of that wood was ever used. Mrs. Owl didn't migrate. She was a horned owl and she used the pile summer and winter. So the wood just stood there and rotted. My dad wouldn't permit one stick to be disturbed.

He was short, Irish, hot tempered, kind and generous. You'd have liked him. He's long gone but my memory of his face is as clear as when I was a little boy. I was a strange kid and he understood me. I guess he was a strange kid in his day too.

I am supposed to get, one of these days, an enamel and copper brooch, a figurine of Nelson's *Victory*. When my dad was a boy, the *Victory* was reconditioned, and at that time they took some of the copper off her bottom and cast it into brooches which were sent all over the Empire as prizes for "exceptional progress" at school. My dad won one, and at his death, my mother gave it to my sister. She suffered a break-in at her home in Salisbury, N.B., one year and the pin was stolen. Weeks and weeks later, she was visited by a couple of boys selling something or other, and one had her pin in his hat. She gave him his choice: deliver the pin immediately and replace the other things, or go to jail for housebreaking. She knew who he was and he couldn't get away. I only hope that whoever does end up with it will value it as much as I would.[19]

19 Obtained by subscription and often given as school prizes, these brooches were cast in the shape of HMS *Victory*. They bore the following words on their reverse: "Centenary memento of the Death of Nelson, 1805 Oct 21st 1905. Containing copper from HMS *Victory*. The Gift of the Lords of the Admiralty to British and Foreign Sailors Society. E.R. VII (Edward VII).

Moosonee, October 1983

Dear Claudia,

When I was a kid, and before I had to go out to school, October was the month that we barged home the firewood. All the summer work was over, the salmon fishery, the cod and trout were all done.

The only nets in the water were for smelt and whatever we could pick up for the table: now and then a big fat salmon, or a big sea run trout. It was a joy to get up early, find ice in the boat, row out to the nets, and with freezing fingers take dozens of fat smelt from the icy water, and throw them into little wooden pails that James made just for that purpose, a pail for each house, then deliver it from door to door from a wooden wheelbarrow with a squeaky, bumpitty wheel that would make a delicious rattle over the frozen board walk. It was actually Edgar's job, but I loved doing it and would arrive home with frozen hands but warm everywhere else.

In October, we put the rubber and leather footwear away and ran light-footed in soft silent Eskimo sealskin boots. And the wood haul: if the tide permitted an early run, we were allowed to go before school. We'd lie in the piles of dry bark in the bottom of the old wooden scow while the motorboat towed us up to what we called "The Bight." There we'd go alongside a big natural rock dock and everyone would start carrying back loads of long poles from the big teepee-shaped piles to the barge, till she was piled high above the gunwales. Then we'd lie on the wood and ride home.

The inlet there is beautiful, Claudia, high steep wooded hills, birch, balsam, juniper and aspen, together with fir and spruce. In fall it is a symphony of colour, and on a sunny day the inlet is molten fire. Maybe kids don't really appreciate beauty like that, but I remember how my chest constricted and my heart beat faster when I thought of leaving it.

Even now, when I have seen so much other beauty, I can still feel the warm rush of emotion that I felt so long ago on the top of a pile of sweet smelling wood in that old scow. I can remember the incredibly delicate patterns in the soft rose-coloured jelly fish that would pass the barge in a never-ending stream, little and big, eyeless, finless, almost liquid creatures, pulsing along at this slow pace, but in some sort of a perfectly regimented order, and in the centre of each a lovely pattern in pastel. Take one out of the water and it became drab and colourless in your hand and the pattern disappeared. Put it back and it would start pulsing away again, going wherever the current took it, but having a purpose, and there would be miles of them, on every side of the boat, from tiny things half an inch in diameter to huge thick creatures, six feet or more across.

They'd get left behind by the retreating tide and die on the beach by the thousands. Walking in the dark, you'd suddenly find yourself up to your knees in jelly where some big fellow lay unseen in your path. I wonder why they exist. Nothing eats them unless the baleen whales strain them with plankton. I used to get right up in the bow of the scow and watch her blunt stern divide the ranks of jellyfish, watch them roll helplessly over, then come back to their normal position and continue their contracting and expanding which might advance them a few inches in an hour. It's more likely the pulsing is breathing and they let themselves be carried wherever by the current, but somehow they manage so that there is space between each pair. Lots to think about for a small boy who loved the inlet with a fierce protective love.

I would love to show you the flat water of the inlet under a fall moon, as the moon tides rose and the silent water crept higher and higher. That moon affects people, and the restless reaching water. If you have never felt it there is something in store for you.

Babies are born easily on a rising tide. The midwives always hoped for a birth when the water came in. I would guess that they are easily conceived on a rising tide because there is a restlessness that goes with that flow of the water. It is known that the sick revive on the rising water and decline on a falling tide. A person who is dying will likewise rally on a rising tide and remain till the water falls, then he will die. The expression "Going out with the tide" has a lot of substance. I've seen it often.

This is the day our last trips should be going out but we still have two loaded barges at the dock, the Nelson is still at the mouth of the river, and the Churchill still at Paint Hills. It's not the end of the world but it was snowing heavily last night. It melts as it falls but it soon cools things so that it won't be long before it is solid on the ground.

Gotta go. I'll soon talk to you and let you know when I'll be leaving Moosonee. They'll forward letters but it means that much longer before I hear from you.

Winnipeg, December 18, 1983

Dear Claudia,

Good old King Winter is here in full force tonight, -30 F and calm and clear, with a bright, almost full, moon. Tell me, why is the city so cold at these temperatures?

Thirty below isn't considered much back in the deep wood. Once, just before Christmas, my brother and I were quite a way inland and we found a lake we had never seen before. I don't think many others had seen it either, as it was very hard to get to. We had climbed a high range of hills, hoping that there might be caribou there. About mid-afternoon, we came to a place where our range met another, and at the bottom was this jewel of a lake. There were trees right to the high rocky shores, no sign of people. We had two choices, go back to our previous camp or go down into the valley and camp there, knowing we'd have to climb out in the morning. But there never really was any choice, we were going down and we both knew it.

We went down an almost vertical slope on the wide, almost round snowshoes they use in heavy snow country. It was a breathtaking experience. Tons and tons of snow moving ahead of you, not the wicked power of a mountain avalanche, just the almost gentle movement of the top layer of snow. At times you don't move your feet, just stand and go down so smoothly and gently. Claudia, what I'd give to be young and in that country again.

We arrived at the bottom, right at the mouth of a little rapid brook, so rapid that most of it was unfrozen. The trees there were huge black spruces, sixty or seventy feet tall, with branches so close and heavy that there was almost no snow under them, while the trees themselves had feet and feet of snow all over each huge branch. A camping spot one might dream about and never find.

I guess the temperature was around thirty below but the air was so close and still that it seemed warm. It took only a few minutes to clear the snow away. The big tree trunk made half of our shelter, and a dozen small balsams created a back shelter and roof, as well as a thick carpet of very fragrant branches to sit on. Not twenty feet away was a big dry tamarack, the finest possible fire wood, and while I chopped it down and reduced it to fire lengths, my brother put a noose on a long willow and snared four or five of the trout that were in the "steady," that's a back eddy in a brook.

We built a fire of big logs and when there were lots of big hot embers, we raked some aside and put our frying pan and tea kettle on them while the bannock thawed. The trout were red and tasty, and we cooked them to a nice crusty brown colour. It was a memorable meal, and even at that temperature, the heat reflected into our shelter was intense enough that we could sit there minus parkas, take off our moccasins and toast our feet. We had no blankets but needed none. There was not a draft of wind, at least not there. Up on the ridge, in the open treeless expanse, it was probably bone chilling cold but down there we were warm and comfortable. We ate our meal and cut another few trees for the night.

My brother was by way of being an inventor, at least he could always see some way to save work. So he piled a big wall of logs up behind the fire and he supported them with a green stake or two. The idea was that after a time the green stakes would burn off and the logs would tumble into the fire and we'd continue sleeping. Matter of fact, it worked, but a little bit earlier than he had planned. While the fire was still roaring merrily, the stakes collapsed and the logs tumbled in where we wanted them. There were sparks and smoke everywhere for a minute or so, and the dry tamarack took fire instantly so that we had to move away back because it was too hot to be near the fire. But what a sleep we had. I remember waking early in the morning when it was still dark and the moon was low. The fire had burned down and it was getting chilly so I built it up again and lay back and waited for the light to come.

Outside our shelter, it was bitterly cold. The ice in the lake was booming as the frost bit deep and there was not another sound. The moon was a big round silver ball away up there. The world could be empty of all people. It was hard to imagine there was anyone besides us, that millions all over were still sleeping in warm houses under blankets was incredible. It was impossible to remember that there was sickness and sadness and poverty. That world was so perfect that everything else should also be perfect.

Have you ever been in a mood like that when your head fills with music. I still do and I associate various pieces of music with some special happening. I never hear "Plaisir d'Amour" but I think of that night and morning, and that's why I'm writing. I was going though some old papers, a tiresome job, and I got Liona Boyd to play me some of her music, and guess what she played? Correct. I went back in time and the impressions were so strong I wanted to tell you.

I remember the sweet smell of the balsam in the fire, the glitter of the flames on the snow and the deep red of the embers, the almost silent sound of the flame eating that almost smokeless wood that burns so fiercely, and behind it, momentarily obscured by the leaping fire, I could see the moon, the dark blue sky, the millions of stars, and the music mounting and mounting in my head. There is no reason for a person who has felt as I did then to ever think he has not known happiness. That music makes me see a perfect moon, a perfect night, a dancing flame and contentment, such contentment as I would give to the world if I could.

That was perhaps fifty years ago. There is no way there except on foot and in winter, well by helicopter I guess, but even then only in winter, but I could take you there to that very place. The ashes of our fire would likely still be visible and the stumps of the trees we cut for firewood will still be there. Things change very slowly in such a place and I would almost bet that no one has been there since. It is a wonderful feeling to know that that perfect place is still perfect and that it will remain so forever because no on will even be able to desecrate it with buildings or roads.

Recently I read a book about the Depression, and the author said, "Those were the days of great hardship and privation." He felt we had nothing, but he could not ever realize what some of us actually had. He could never know, because he had never been fortunate to have those things.

Yesterday Jocelyn McKillop finished my oral history. She ended by asking a few questions about things we had not discussed, and some were about living conditions and the things we didn't have, running water and electric light, no regular mail, no medical facilities. While I do appreciate them now, I'm glad we didn't have them then.

January 7, 1984

Dear Claudia

Our meeting in Montreal was sandwiched in between a board meeting in New York and an extraordinary meeting of presidents in Calgary. Montreal wept all the while. She was grey and foggy and her streets were dripping. She had nice white petticoats on Mount Royal, but her downtown linen was soiled and she hated it.

But Montreal is always Montreal, and the rain and the grime don't really change her. She's like a lovely woman cleaning an old-fashioned stove, and the soot gets on her face and in her hair and on her fingers. By April, she'll have washed her face and changed her dress and she'll be so radiant that all the people will smile and feel that winter can never come again.

Right under the boardroom window of our new office, twenty-six floors down, is a tiny church. I don't know who she is; I never saw her before. She sits there, and the big buildings crowd in on her and she draws her skirts back. I can see she's indignant, biting her lips to keep the tears back because they have taken her sunlight away and her view. And while someone droned on about our fantastic year and our superlative results, I watched her, and I wanted to run down those twenty-six storeys and tell her that I understood, and one day I will. Early some spring morning, I'll get up early and go and find her and sit there with her in the cool air and listen to the silence that comes even to Montreal at the right time of day. I can't say I'm too strong on some of the things she stands for, but that's her business. I admire her for staying there, for saying "...that's far enough. Please don't touch me..." and I can sit with her for a while and it will do us both some good.

I'll go when Montreal is still sleeping, when the trucks and cars and buses and people have their eyes closed, and all their noise and turbulence shut off, when the tiny new leaves rustle a bit self-consciously, and try to hide, when a shaft of sunlight finds all the holes in the raggedy fringe of buildings and lies warm on the cobblestones. I'll be there when the arrogant and resentful old Crown Life building sort of smiles under her British straight upper lip, when the birches on the slope of the mountain stroke McGill campus so that she's like a brown tabby cat in the sun.

I'll sit awhile there and listen to a city turn over, stretch and wake up on a Sunday morning, some spring time.

I should have been basking in the flow of adjectives that described the financial results of 1983, but I know all that, don't I. We made money, a lot of it, and it was good to hear a quiet voice say so. Our president and a prince, he is a big cheerful easy Englishman who can take a financial report and discuss it and indicate how pleased he is. I sat there listening, stealing glances at the little church and I wondered about people. I guess there were some who thought I was inattentive. I can always say, "Sorry, I'm a bit hard of hearing," with perfect truth.

We did have a good year, and our results at Moosonee were the greatest return, percentage-wise, that the boss had ever seen on such a small capital investment. They find it hard to believe we do so much with so little equipment, and that we don't ask for the moon to make more.

I asked for a reasonable wage for my people and good benefits, and I have never been refused. The boys and the tug crews work hard. One of the accountants pointed out that our people make so much more than, say, his office staff. Sure they do, but in a week they easily work double the time his staff works. They have to leave home to do it. They earn their extra money and that's the only point on which I am prepared to be difficult. I don't feel they are employees; they are partners. That's one of the things Jackie said to me once. I had gone back to the office to do some work after supper and she showed up. I told her she could stay at home and enjoy some free time and she looked at me and said, "We're partners, so when you work, I work, and I like it like that."

There are a lot of changes to talk over with her. The inevitable; it's about time someone else has a crack at the job of general manager of MTL. I'll be back in Moosonee this year but I'll make fewer decisions and do less of the routine work. I'll leave the decisions to Cal and Ellsworth, and let then handle problems from Montreal or Calgary. I'll be very happy to turn it all over to Jackie and the boys in 1985. I told you I sent Jackie a briefcase and she liked it. I had put in a few sheets of MTL paper, pencils and pens so she'd know we want her back. I hope she can go to Moosonee the same time I do.

When we go up, I'll send her to the mission about their oil for

'85, to the Hydro about theirs, to talk to the hospital board about the freight for Albany. I'll take her to talk with the Quebec people about the pipeline and all their cargo. She'll stand eye-to-eye with people and let them know she is the person to talk to at MTL. Perhaps it's pushing her a bit earlier than I had planned, but it will, I hope, give her an idea of her worth.

Winnipeg, February 10, 1984

Dear Claudia,

The most frightening monstrous thing was in the *Free Press* last night. A man abused his teenaged daughter sexually when she was twelve. He got charged, and his lawyer asked to have the charge dismissed because she was a "non person," born out of wedlock, and therefore outside the law. That the man had committed a crime meant nothing. She had no rights under the law. But she had a father, didn't she? Someone was responsible for her being here? That a judge would even take time to consider it gave me the horrors. How many children are there of common-law marriages? The single lady who is on TV's *Journal* took time off to have a baby. Is that baby a non person too? Can she be abused by anyone who decides to hide behind a law that is vicious and horrible? There is this man smiling confidently in court while the daughter listens to his lawyer claim she has no rights and is a non person.

Non-persons have thin skins. Yesterday I had to stop my car, get out and boot a big teen-aged bully who was beating up a tiny East Indian kid who knew he'd better not resist, who even when I'd disposed of the bully, sat with his hands over his face as he had while he was being beaten. All of eight or nine, he was scared, and he knew it was only temporary relief. He'll get it day by day because of his dark skin, and because he's small. I took him to the school, found a teacher who tried to get the other boy's name, but he pinched his lips together and wouldn't utter a sound. Already he knew that if you are a non person, you hold your tongue, you stay out of the way of your betters and if you happen to get caught, you cover your face and endure till the terror leaves.

Once at Gordon Bell,[20] I had to leave my car to help a boy on crutches who was being beaten by two other boys. Guess people on crutches are non-persons too. There was a teacher on the steps who made no move to interfere. One kid was striking the boy with his own crutch while the kid held the fence for support. My car blocked traffic and a strolling cop ticketed it for $25. I took it into court, not because of the ticket but because that policeman must have been able to see the assault, and when my time came, I was told to pay my fine, because the law says, right on a metal plate, "no stopping at any time." I was warned that teachers and policemen will protect the public and that I am neither. I guess I barely avoided being a non-person. I told the magistrate that I will never pay twenty-five dollars to anyone with more pride. He flushed right up to, and including, his varicosed nose, but he didn't say a word. The clerk later told me I missed "Contempt of Court" by a hair's breath. My daughter says some day I'm going to get it.

20 A high school in Winnipeg.

EIGHT

Winnipeg, February 25, 1984

Dear Claudia,

I want this letter to tell you things that perhaps I did not tell you last night. There are a million things running through my head, and I want you to have them because they are yours to have, and this morning they are mine to give.

After I hung up last night and was heading to bed, the clock said past one, and I'd been up since 4:30 in the morning. On the way to bed after our marathon talk, I thought that music, deep feeling music, would be what was needed to express how I felt, and I thought briefly of the pan flute. But no, it is lovely, but it is for days of sunshine and tranquillity.

So what should I play. I found a bouzouki tape, and because I am alone except for the cats, I turned it up high until the floors vibrated, and I filled the house with glorious sound, deep powerful sound. There was the poignant sound of "Beautiful Girl from Arcadia," "My Friend the Wind," "Zorba'a Dance," "The Star of Mykonos," and "Velvet Mornings." And I let those vibrant voices chanting wordless choruses drive into my being, and smash resentment, anger and despair into shimmering patterns of melody.

The girls in the Rideau were thirty-four years before I met you. I'd just come out of the Arctic. I was a stranger and the noise and the people overpowered me, so I would get a canoe and go to the silent places. Perhaps I came there unprepared. Laugh if you will, but I was a virgin, a strange bird in the army, believe me.

So I would paddle into a world of beauty and life and awareness. And I saw the young women playing, sunning, swimming on the Rideau. I was aware of a terrible gulf between such creatures and me. They were wealthy, sheltered, every need taken care of. They looked to me to have been perfect from birth, but I suppose good dentistry and other services contributed.

I had never seen an unclothed white woman. Natives, yes, many. There was a picture, I think in a Jules Verne book, of an Eskimo "Ice Palace," where lovely clean beings reclined on beds of fur in chambers off a main hall, clothed to the waist only. In that, the artist was partly right. The rest, the rings of bright lights in high vaulted ceilings, the huge fire burning in the centre hall with a smoke cone of ice to take the smoke away was ridiculously wrong. I was young when I saw it, and even then, I knew nothing was more unlike the truth.

Perhaps DePoncins has described the day-to-day life in an igloo more graphically than most. Maybe a bit more than the truth. But an igloo that has been occupied for some time is a maculate horror, stained and filthy, with the smell of urine and feces present at all times. Not all igloos were as I describe, some were beautifully clean. Millik of Hebron and his wife were among the cleanest people I have ever seen. But the average igloo was a nightmare.

Why sleep there, you say, when there is a mountain of snow to provide your own igloo. Because, you see, there are customs, that one observed. Past tense, because they do not apply today. A white man, a trader, was an important person. He stayed at the headman's igloo, and once he was installed, as many people as possible crowded in. And as many as could find a place to lie stayed the night, possibly to bask in reflected glory, surely to see and observe the white stranger who slept with clothes on.

The visit of such a stranger created a party atmosphere, and there was great joviality, increased by the white man's gift of tea and biscuits. No people on earth could be more kind. Their ways were different is all. Once one had found the cleanest spot he could, and spread his robe and composed himself to sleep, the fires on the *kudloe* [snow shelf] would be lowered and the people prepared for bed. Naked, with one small exception: the women never exposed their feet. The last thing before lying down, they put their feet into a sleeping robe or under a deerskin, and removed their footwear.

The angels on the Rideau bore no resemblance to the bodies one saw in the igloos, though with soap and water, and maybe diet, some young people could be quite handsome. But these clean young bodies on the Rideau were beyond my comprehension. I couldn't believe such creatures existed.

Why all this? Because I wanted to tell you something else. From the army I went straight back to the Arctic, to Repulse Bay. I think I mentioned going to see an old woman who was dying of cold and hunger but who wanted to shake the white man's hand, and I told you that the next morning she was dead.

Very shortly after, I was walking across the hills and was near the Eskimo cemetery place. There is no earth. The bodies are merely covered with stones. In winter, due to the difficulty of prying the stones out, a body can be left for quite some time before it is properly covered.

Claudia, I found the old woman. It was a bad year. Every scrap of clothing was needed to help keep a person warm, and the dead had no need of clothing. She had been stripped so that not one shred of cloth or hide remained on the body, and as I looked, the image of the water sprites on the Rideau came back. They had never known real hunger or fear of death as she had. This had been a bad year and she had not survived. How many bad years had she seen?

She lay frozen with elbows bent and hands lifted as though she had become conscious after she had been put there, eyes open, frozen milky white, every rib standing out like a curse. How old might she have been? She looked ninety but was probably not past forty. Her breasts, flattened and deformed from years of feeding children to preserve their lives, hung down on both sides of her body and the hard pale sky looked down on what was once a human being. And in my mind, the girls on the Rideau were there, silent in the presence of one of their own, and removed from her by about a million years.

I went back to the post, found a piece of canvas, and tried to wrap her in it, but she was frozen to the stones, so I covered her as decently as I could and I covered her with snow because that blank face, those starved limbs, that wizened body that had given the very fibre of life itself could not be left bare under that pitiless sky. I was young then. I had seen many bodies, handled them, buried them, but none had been so utterly destitute of the dignity one should have in death. Perhaps that sentence was wrong. She did have a dignity, a dignity that surpassed the lack of clothing.

Next day:
Did I ever tell you about Frank Reid and his broken ribs, and what happened one dark night in Minaki, Ontario? Can you stand a tale of pain and terror? Hold on.

Frank lived upstairs over the store in Minaki. To get home, he climbed a high series of cement steps, and one night, instead of climbing them, he fell and broke several ribs. His assistant was on holiday, and I was standing there when the boss looked. "Go help Frank," he said tersely. And being at the time young, biddable, and in need of my pay, I said, "Sir, your wish is my command." Don't quibble now, maybe those were not the exact words, but the sense was the same. Young clerks in them days bowed, and on occasions, scraped. Verily.

Further instructions indicated that I should go to the grave old doctor for instructions on the binding of wounds, the pouring in of wines and oils. No, sorry, that was the Samaritan. Only no Samaritan ever got the knocks that I did in doing his thing in the binding of wounds and the thereto's attached.

On with the tail, as the monkey said after he got through the swinging door. Anyway, the old grave doc gave me sundry linens, ointments and diverse pins, belts and toothed objects of strange manufacture, and I hied myself to Minaki. For the sake of the record, may I say the CNR hied me there. Nothing like accuracy.

Now what had happened in the interval was that adhesive tape had been applied liberally as a kind of splint around Frank's torso. The doc said that first the tape had to come off. What the old Doc didn't know was that Frank was, in manufacture, like unto a dog, an old English sheepdog. I have never known a dog with a hairier carcass.

So with the kitchen stove burbling merrily to ward off outer cold, and Frank burbling gently, having taken what he called a "pick-me-up" to ward off inner cold and fear, and possibly two or more pick-me-ups, the stage was set for the main feature, so to speak.

Ever try to take scotch tape off a cat? Tar of good viscosity might stick to a wool blanket as tenaciously, but very few other creations stick to a hairy man better than adhesive tape. Old Doc had said, "Don't fiddle around; grab and pull."

You know what was around that man's ribs? You've come this far, you've got a right to know. A huge, six-inch band of revolting sulphur-yellow adhesive tape. He got it from the CNR and I know for certain that it was used to bind broken boxcars together. It could have no other possible use. Just to worry a little end loose while dodging Frank's fists was all I could do, while his wife alternately dodged and laughed and provided me with no real help, comfort or moral support.

Fiddling around wasn't gonna get me nowhere, so after worrying a short end loose at imminent danger to life, limb, future family, and good looks, I cut a small slit in the end of the tape, and into this slit fitted two of my fingers. Giving Mrs. Reid a nod to distract old Frank's attention, I gave a might heave. Ha girl! You have only known me in my declining years; I was a husky coot in those days. You ever hear a train whistle going through a station? A low wail, a rising screech, and a poignant fading note? Well Frank sounded like that, only there was no fading note. The scream rose and rose ever higher. Lily Pons, Madame Melba never held a note half so long. The good burghers of Minaki (actually I don't think there were any burghers in Minaki, but it's a good word, deserves to be used…) these good burghers thought that CNR Number One had probably blown up in the station with fearful suffering and loss of life.

Windows shattered at White Dog reserve, but since windows shattering there was a common occurrence, no one realized that Number One had probably blown up. Communities as far east as Vermillion Bay reported strange sounds, signs and portents. I was concerned with the portents because I was where they were about to happen. To me.

In that rip I removed, by actual measurement, enough hair from Frank's chassis to make one hair shirt for a penitent, to stuff two horse-hide bar room chairs, and a small footstool for an elderly lady. There was enough left over to clothe a small bear. I also removed a quantity of flesh from the tender, another good word, loin area, and the flow of sanguine liquid was impressive. It must have hurt like hell, and Frank wanted to impress that fact upon me with the fire shovel, which was the nearest persuader to hand.

There comes a time when discretion was the better part of valour. Discretion had gone by the board. Valour was useless. A pair of clean heels struck me as my only chance to collect a pension some years down the road, though my chances of collecting disability seemed imminent.

I am never last to abandon my tools and flee when the chips are down, so flee I did, along with Mrs. Reid and a scared-stiff Doberman. I never had thought Dobermans were cowardly but I guess some sights and sounds can unnerve even the bravest watchdog. Anyway, she'd just come through a long war and her nationality may have caused her some embarrassment in an Allied nation. In any case, she bolted.

I said it was December. It was, and Minaki has a reputation for temperatures on the down side. Out the door we went, scantily clad, followed by a shower of soft coal, though the word "soft" is only relative, as you would have guessed.

We stood outside the door, which Frank had unkindly locked from the inside and the cruel frost began to gnaw at our respective frames. The Doberman was the most fortunate. I was in shirt and trousers and Mrs. Reid, well, ladies rarely wore slacks in the kitchen.

I had a key to the store so we tiptoed down the stairs, entered the store, and sat pensively on the sale furniture, 25 percent off, for Christmas only. We went back once to try to make peace through the unfeeling door, and were rewarded with several sharp raps on the other side of the door with the coal shovel.

A gander through the frosty window indicated that Frank had done considerable "picking-up." He was not the one, however, to fold up after a few drinks, and it was well into the night before we heard him stumble into his room, and heard his bed creak as it received Frank's form.

We stole upstairs and found him immersed in sleep. We spread Vaseline all over it, which made him look like a bear who'd found a hive. And we wrapped him up in clean linen and we bound him up tightly in old Doc's belts and buckles and toothed objects. Discretion still being the better part of valour, Mrs. Reid elected to spend the night in the spare room, discretion to the point where she found a key after a protracted search, and locked herself in. I had no lock, so I, as Robinson Crusoe did, commended myself to providence, and slept, with one eye on door and window.

Frank felt, except for his head perhaps, better the next day. He slept till noon and came down to the store. Stiffly, I might say, but you know, broken ribs are no joke. He healed, and we became friends.

March 7, 1984

Dear Claudia,

It has been a week of stress and I have been very busy. I was sitting there, reading a letter from Bill Dawe. Remember him? The big quiet fellow at the end of Ash's table. The letter was written only two days before, and he said he'd be back to Moosonee with us, and that he was interested in the pension plan I was working on. Then the phone rang and Ellsworth said, "I have bad news. Bill died suddenly this afternoon."

Do you think that it is possible for a piece of paper to change its composition in your hands and become something else? Entirely possible. The letter became something strange and mysterious, the voice of a man from the grave. It gives one a very vibrant sensation, as though all the dead are standing there, laughing at the joke. I cannot describe it, but it happened to me once before. My dad had died, and I had learned by telegram early that morning.

That day the mail plane came. We were at Île à la Crosse, and the clerk who handled the mail came into my office and put a letter on my desk. I have the letter yet. My dad was a beautiful penman, and there was the letter, only a few hours after he died.

I could see him: short, heavily built, enormously strong, dressed as always in an HBC blazer, a marine cap, blue serge trousers, almost a uniform with HBC people on Labrador. And he took his old stem pipe out of his mouth, blew a cloud, I'm sure I smelt it, of Imperial Mixture tobacco into the air and he laughed, showing his strong teeth that he kept all his life, and for that instant, he was truly alive. At that moment I knew that I would never see him again, but he was alive.

I didn't open the letter for some days. I didn't need to. My dad isn't in a place of continuous joy where they'd sing all day. He'd sicken and die there. He is some place where they are busy, where old James, and Will and Uncle Jesse and all the rest were waiting for him to start work. Oh, there will be singing. Old robust songs that my dad sang so well, shanties that Uncle Jesse would warble as we pulled on the great tackles that came dripping out of the water with the schooner following slowly behind. There will be laughter and earnest conversation and there will be long periods of silence as the old men stare into the sun on the water and each has his own thoughts.

Winnipeg, March 1984

Dear Claudia,

Jackie feels it's time to have some more mother-daughter talks with Gwenda. There was a book that was recommended to her but she couldn't find it. I managed to get it for her.

Eskimo society had it all figured out. Once a girl was childbearing age, she became active and parents and grandparents were happily indulgent. If she had a child, the baby was theirs. Two good things: every baby was wanted and loved, and a girl who'd had a baby was a good marriage prospect because she had proved she could bear a child. There was no fear on the part of the parents. They put on a show of disapproval for the missionary and were secretly glad when it happened.

I can remember Christina, my favourite wrinkled old lady, sitting gloomily on the floor of my office complaining that her last daughter was almost grown up. She'd discovered boys and was never in the tent. Christina was lonely. She smoked her short black pipe and thought and thought. Suddenly she brightened. If the girl was interested in boys, then perhaps soon there would be a new baby in the tent. Wonderful thought, and she snuck a look at my red-headed Scots clerk and said how good it would be to have a red-haired baby. The clerk didn't understand a word in her language so didn't get the point. In time, Christina got her baby and she kept it when her daughter married. That was no problem; the girl soon had more.

All those years I yearned for my dream girl I thought of the creation of a child. Might as well be truthful, I was young, my desires and needs were acute; the fact that they can't be satisfied gives nature no qualms. She provides them, you look after them, and if there is no one to fulfill them, she doesn't even notice. So a lot of my longings were, as the Book says, of the flesh. I'd be an awful liar if I denied that, but while my body yearned for the softness and love of a woman, I always felt that if she ever came to me, we would create a child that would be there for both of us, the expression of all our desires.

I saw in the villages, in the tents and igloos, the act performed almost publicly, that would result in the birth of a child. There was no privacy. It was mechanical, perhaps eight or ten people all sheltering in one space, because there wasn't heat or food enough for more. The intimate and deeply personal relationship I dreamed of, here seemed crude and matter of fact. How could one ignore it. It happened within a few feet, and while it was happening, the others feigned ignorance, and once it was over, there were broad comments and even laughter in the dark. By morning it was forgotten.

And I dreamed my dreams and held my dream person, and the relationship was perfect, and in all the world, there would only be us. Sometimes I let myself think what it would have been like if so many things could have been different.

Convention, that old harridan, has to begin some place. Once upon a time a man and a woman who were not married to each other could not have stayed even in the same hotel when travelling together. Later she said that separate though not adjoining rooms would be okay. Now she might even agree to adjoining rooms. Convention and human nature have run headlong into each other for many years. But it amuses me how much convention can change to meet unusual situations. Lemme tell you.

When I was young, there was a very lovely young nurse at North

West River where I was going to school. She worked for a very puritan mission, and the local lads were very interested in her, naturally. Mind your own business. I was too young, and yes, she was so pretty I would have died for her if she asked, but she never did.

There were several elderly schoolteachers and the doctor's wife. Anyone who came to visit the nurse had to run the gamut of these people. If the nurse went out, she had to be accompanied by one of the hospital staff. Reason? Supposedly the danger was from local dogs who were supposed to recognize a stranger and tear them limb from limb. Good excuse, which served to protect the nurse's morals and the young men from tampering with them. In those days, men had no morals, of course. They were simple ravening beasts ready to assault any luckless female on a moment's notice.

So it happened that the nurse had to make visits to the smaller settlements by boat in summer, by dog team in winter. Ha! Now you have it. Sleeping accommodation on the boat was limited to a very small cabin in the bow of the boat. Due to the shape of the boat, there was room usually for two small bunks, and again because of the shape, you either had your companion's head or feet close to your head or feet, whichever you chose.

By dog team there were tiny travellers' cabins or small tents to sleep in. No way you could get far apart. Now for young people, there wasn't great hardship in those trips, but elderly teachers and doctors' wives have bones that rebel, and so chaperonage wasn't something they competed for, especially in fall and winter.

But nurse must go and she must have a guide or boatman. A third person would add materially to the logistics in the way of extra food and all the other necessary things. So a girl who couldn't walk around a village except in daylight, and who couldn't receive a visitor alone, could go out on trips with a young, ravening I suppose, man, who couldn't be trusted with her on a dark pathway between the houses. Conventions and elderly bones could get quite adjusted if they had to. We lived in some stupid times.

How about me? Well, you do know how shy I was. At times, when

I was still going to school, I got to make emergency trips with one or the other of the mission dog teams, but I never did get to take the lovely nurse. Perhaps she had something to do with that. I got the older ones, who said I looked after their comfort better.

But once I got a great big, and I mean big, American college girl who was doing volunteer work. She was a good head taller than me and very jolly and active. She bounced all over and everyone liked her. She wasn't a nurse but she could do a lot of the things they did. Once there was an emergency call early one morning in spring to go about thirty miles. I was selected because it was Sunday, I was a kid, I didn't have to be paid, and the regular men needed their day off.

Off we went. It was soft going, deepish snow, mild, even foggy. She had skis and she rode part of the time, used her skis part of the time, and to be truthful, was a bit of a nuisance as the dogs kept looking for her to be on one side or the other, instead of behind where she belonged. I was on snowshoes ahead.

We got where we were going and it wasn't a real emergency. Some Indians who had been hungry got a lot of caribou and had overeaten. She gave them handfuls of pills, and since there was only one small tent, we decided to head back.

There was a big wide bay to cross and when we were miles from land, we got a sudden storm like you got over there in the spring. Hard pelting rain and then an abrupt freeze.

I had heavy duck trousers and a parka. The rain hardly got through. She had wool ski pants, the old heavy melton cloth that acts like a blotter, and some sort of ski jacket that was just as porous. I had noticed her gear in the morning but was too shy to tell her, and I probably figured that was the doctor's job anyway.

In a short time, she was drenched, and though my clothes were a bit small, I managed to get her to put on my pants and parka. I can only say she'd have been in style with the kids of today. There were no zippers in pants those days, and the only way she could do the buttons up was to lie on the sleigh and let her stomach sink up under her ribs. I don't think you should be laughing, but if you want to howl, listen to this. Even lying down her hands were too cold to fasten buttons she couldn't even see. And there was nothing else to do, so away out there on the ice miles from anywhere, I had to put my shyness away, and fasten the lady's (or my) pants.

And it wasn't a matter of a delicate touch and away, no Ma'am! I had to struggle with those damn buttons and you'd be surprised how intimate your poor hands seem to get with a poor lady's personal anatomy. But we got it done. I'll probably bear some scars to the end.

Then the parka. Our parkas were Eskimo style, no opening down the front. They went on over the head like pullovers. I told you I was a head shorter, and nature had built her somewhat bulkier in the chest, and that was in the days when ladies were armour-plated in that region.

So getting the parka over her head was okay, but once the arms were in, she couldn't pull the confounded thing down by herself. So I hadda do that too. Quit grinning! I learned more about anatomy in those few minutes than I'd dreamed possible. But I finally got it dragged down over her, ahem!, front and by golly it nearly met the trousers. She was a funny-looking object, believe me. The pants were so tight she could hardly walk, so I made her sit on a sled and headed for a hunting cabin I knew not too far away.

The rain changed to snow and it got really cold. By this time, the clothes I had on were nearly saturated. She was a bit drier but all her clothes were frozen too. We rattled like the tin man. I kept thinking that if no one had left wood at the cabin, we were in for a bad time because before I could cut some wood and get a fire going, she'd probably be frozen some place and I had no desire to have to hunt all over for frozen spots.

But there was wood, a huge lovely dry pile of birch with kindling, and bark galore and a small sheet metal stove. To keep her moving I made her carry up all the gear from the sled to the cabin while I unharnessed the dogs and fed them. I wish I had a movie of how she looked struggling up the bank in those pants and with the parka looking more like a collar. But finally I lit a roaring fire and in seconds the little cabin was worm.

Our clothes were too frozen to take off right away. She was shivering violently, and even when I brought her a mug of tea, she couldn't get her hands around it, so I had to hold it for her.

The cabin was low. You moved around on your knees, so try getting a too-small parka off a large woman in the back seat of a Volkswagen, that'll give you an idea. I finally made her lie on the brush floor while I tugged the parka off.

Then the pants. Anyone happening to come in would have thought they were looking at a particularly violent rape. Anyone looking at my face would have thought I had sunstroke. Because if the buttons were difficult out on the ice, they were doubly so this time, because the heavy duck was wet, and the buttonholes were shrunken, and I, poor me, had to really get in there and dig.

I don't think she was conscious of it at all. She was cold and she was desperately scared. And wouldn't you be, as I dragged the duck pants off, they were frozen to her ski pants which came along too, leaving her in all the glory of...her red, yes red, long-handled undies. Thank the gods who arrange such things that they were in one piece, otherwise I'd have probably taken to my heels.

They were wet too, so after we had gotten everything else out of the way, I said I'd step outside while she took them off and I unrolled my sleeping robe for her to get into afterwards. She hadn't brought one for such a short trip. I told her to get out of her passion suit (I didn't say that...) get in the sleeping robe and we'd dry her scanties. Would you believe it, she was so scared she wouldn't have it. So I said, get into the robe, underwear and all, yank it off and we'd dry it. The contortions that large woman went through. Couldn't even get an arm inside. If I hadn't been so shy, I would have died laughing, but at the time it wasn't a laughing matter.

Finally she said, "Close your damn eyes!" and I did, and when she told me to open them, she was back in the bag and the garment was in a red pile near the stove. I thanked the gods that she was able to get those buttons undone because I don't think I could have assisted.

Being young, not so smart, and tough anyway, I let my clothes dry on me. In any event, there was no way I was going to disrobe in front of that lady. By the time dark came (we had no candles) her clothes were dry and she was composed enough to let me leave while she dressed. Sleeping robes were just a tube in those days, and I made her get inside mine again. I could have pointed out she was safe from rape because it was tight enough on her to act as a chastity belt.

I had brought in the sleigh wrapper, and when it was dry, I wrapped myself in it for warmth, not to preserve my virtue. After the pants episode, I figured my virtue was down the tube anyway.

Poor nurse, I wonder if she really knew how close she'd been to being a frozen lady. Perhaps the doctor told her. He gave me a substantial raking because I had let her leave without proper clothing or a sleeping robe. I didn't argue. It was probably my responsibility, but a shy fifteen-year-old doesn't tell a woman of the world what to do. I can still see that poor woman in a skintight sleeping robe trying to get out of a pair of wet longjohns. Try it some day. You'll have a ball. Matter of fact, the way games are nowadays, you could invent a new party game and make a million. If Miss Beard is still alive, she'll probably sue you for patent infringement.

Me? Well if I'd gotten the small pretty nurse, she probably would have had the right clothing, or if not, she'd have fitted into mine easily and I'd have lost a chance to learn about the female form divine. Divine was hardly Miss Beard. She was hearty and jolly and probably told the tale to everyone. As far as I know, I never spoke to her again.

Laugh if you will, those were moments and hours of pure hell for me. I went in trembling and in fear for days of the other boys finding out how I'd dressed and undressed Miss Beard.

April 12, 1984

Dear Claudia,

Last night I went down to look for Christianne Ritter's *A Woman in the Polar Night* for Mrs. Lowe. Somehow the story of Karl Ritter and the secret Greenland radio stations came up. So she wanted to read the book, which is as good as any for a reaction to the Arctic.

There are several books written on Karl Ritter. He and his wife came from wealthy German families. He went to Spitzbergen with a university expedition and he never lost his love for that land. Christianne came out from luxury in Germany to a trapper's hut on Grey Cape, and spent the year there with Karl and a Norwegian trapper. They wanted to start a family, and succeeded perfectly. I saw them the next year, she wonderfully pregnant and happy. She was appalled at first when she saw Spitzbergen, but she soon loved it. They were in Greenland on their way home to Germany.

That was the era when nearly everyone was making airplane trips. Lindbergh and his wife had just been through, and then a big amphibian loaded with "The Flying Family" came in. They had picked up the Ritters from Spitzbergen and they dropped them off in Hebron to go back on a little sealing vessel that was coming over.

Karl is one of the most gentle persons I have ever known. He and Christianne were going to put up a tent while they waited in Hebron. It was cold and rainy and she was pregnant; I couldn't allow it. It was just before the war. The parson's wife, who was English, ignored Christianne, so I asked them to stay with me. That was one of the best impulses I ever had.

Christianne is an artist and a writer, deeply interested in history. The big old mission house we lived in fascinated her. There was a large old German library upstairs. I took her there and she cried because the books were priceless and were being wasted there. She would sit for hours among the rocks looking at the old building, now a historic site. She'd make a few sketches and later put her impressions on paper.

We had a huge German wall clock. It was nearly two hundred years old, accurate. The works were made of wood, single pieces of ebony, precisely carved and hard as iron. She sat nearly a whole day on the floor of the hall, watching the clock. She said she was feeling the ghosts of the many people who had had their time directed by it. She did a black-and-white impression for me, the calm white face with its angular numerals, and around it, half delineated, the shadowy hands and faces of people, the ghosts she had seen. And in the corner, the eyes of a child, quick happy eyes, like hers, looking at the clock. "My baby," she told me. She was like that, so full of being alive and happy that you felt it couldn't be true, that you'd close your eyes and she'd be gone.

The Ritters were so in tune with the environment, and thank God, with me, that we were almost like one person. We would eat together in complete silence and I believe we all knew the others' thoughts. We changed the place around so we could eat and look out the window and see the mountains on the other side of the fiord. We all sat on the same side of the table, she between us, and when we talked it was so calm and peaceful. The war clouds were gathering fast but we never spoke about them, we never listened to the news. One day we were at the table and without a word, she took Karl's hand and my hand and put them on her. For the first time in my life, I felt the movement of an unborn child. No one spoke. She did things like that. My hand still remembers that tiny movement.

Late at night we would walk up the valley, slowly because of her condition, and at the top of a ridge that separates two lovely fiords, we would sit and watch the sun go down, and once or twice we waited there in the polar twilight till the sun rose again. It was summer, the sun was not long gone. She would sit between us on a small polar bear rug that I'd taken along and listen to Karl and me try to tell one another what fascination the Arctic had for us. His English was fluent. Hers was accurate but she'd not used it greatly. She'd try to express what she thought, and because the English words couldn't say it, she'd use the German. I knew what was in her heart so I knew what those lovely sounding words meant. Times when Karl would interpret, I'd be amazed at how accurate my own translation had been.

Claudia, when I saw her book last night, all those things came back to me. I read and thought late into the night. I remembered and I thought of the things that have happened since. And I wanted so much to go back. How I want to go back and I never will.

The night was alive with the little faces, yours, O'Halloran's, Christianne's fairies, trolls and elves. If you had been there, you would have been incredibly happy, and would have found the same rapport with the Ritters that I did. The ending is sad; I will not tell you now. Someday, I will tell you, not to make you sad, but of another woman whose kindness and compassion were so warm and so human that the shy young man that I was then was made aware of the affection of another person.

I had a box of Christianne's sketches, and her letters that were a mixture of English and German, letters that were her, and I lost them when the *Nascopie* went down. That was a bitter loss to me. Those things could never be replaced, but the memories are still strong and vibrant. Claudia, that was forty-six year sago. I never saw that baby but love her as my own. I had felt that small person's movements, that little kicking on the palm of my hand.

The little ship came suddenly one morning about five o'clock. I went up the long hall to call them. They were asleep and the door into the little office was open. I knocked on the frame. Karl woke and sat up. Her eyes opened slowly. As she says in her book, she was a great sleeper. She looked at me and said, "It has come?" I said yes and her eyes filled, and of course, mine did, as they do now at the memory.

Every Eskimo at Hebron was at the wharf. She said goodbye to each one. I had a team of the loveliest dogs you ever saw. She knew all their names and they crowded around her. Alikou, my short-legged little mother dog, was a special favourite. She was hugged and hugged again.

Did I love her? Of course I did, I still do. She loved the country and her husband as I did. When she first came, she told me, "You see me now, fat and clumsy. I am glad to be so, but I have been and will be as good as a man on skis and on foot. And I know she was; it is just that she was infinitely more precious to me because she was pregnant.

Last night I thought of what it was like forty-six years ago, and knew I would tell you this morning. It is spring here, the crocus is up, the sun is just coming up. No one but me is awake.

And in Hebron, the same sun is high above the land now. It is also spring, but the ice fields stretch away into infinity. The snow still covers the land but nature is awakening. The snow buntings are back, the eiders are in the pools of water around the capes. The ptarmigan strut and croak and forcibly mate with the patient hens. The seals who have long ago mated stretch and luxuriate in the sun. The heavy pregnant does are in the valleys waiting for the day their fawns will be born. The sun is higher over there, the shadows are black on the white snow, and there is not a human footprint.

There are no humans. They are gone from the peace and plenty there, but the footprints of memory are there, the sun is warm in the valleys, there is no change in the land. And my whole being wants to be back. There is anguish in my heart because the sun will never throw my shadow there again.

Moosonee, July 20, 1984

Good morning, Claudia,

There's a cloudless blue, blue sky out there. If I'm lucky, I'll get to take someone's kids out to the island today, or go berry picking.

Back in Rigolet, on a day like this, I was about eighteen I guess, I was accused by a lovely young twelve-year-old of trying to drown her. Sylvia was lively and outgoing, and likely became a beautiful young woman. She was a tease and a good guy. She'd come in and kiss my dad on his bald spot, dance my mother around the kitchen and flop down near someone because she liked the closeness. She was just a kid, none of the disturbing curves and bumps of her older sister. She teased me unmercifully. If I growled at her, she say, "But I saved your life!" Damned near drowned me, she did.

A huge salmon hit our net one day. I could see that it was big and soon would wreck the net so I ran for a boat and she was on my heels. She got in my way and lost an oar overside but we finally got the salmon. She screamed and howled with laughter as we were drenched with spray and when it was over and we were on the way back to the dock, she hollered for my sister to bring a camera. At the dock, which was twelve feet or more high, Gus Flowers met us and came part way down the rough ladder to help me with the fish that must have been over fifty pounds. Syl wanted to be in the picture my sister was taking from the top of the dock, and the next thing I knew she was trying to climb around me. I had all I could do to hold the fish in one hand and keep myself on the ladder with the other. Gus was reaching down, Syl was trying to get past me, she reached for the rung above my head, missed it and grabbed Gus's long rubber boot by the top and he over-balanced and came down head-over-heels, sweeping Syl, the fish and me ahead of him.

We landed on the side of the little boat, which overturned. Gus got clear, I still had the fish, and I was all tangled up with Syl and we came up under the boat. I could see her face in the darkness and hear her laugh. She ducked out from under, put her feet on the ladder and lifted the boat so I could get out still holding the fish. My sister threw a line and I tied the fish on. Syl gave Gus a hand to the ladder, and we all climbed out. She always claimed with a wicked grin that she saved our lives and the biggest salmon any of us had ever seen.

If she'd been older, I probably would have fallen in love, but she was so much younger, a kid, and I'd known her since she was a baby. She stayed with us when her mother was away, and I used to carry her all over, feed her, bathe her, put her to bed. When she was eleven or twelve, my mother showed her some pictures of me giving her a bath when she was a few months old, and she howled. She said, "Did he see me like that?" and my mother admitted I did. "Now he's got to marry me soon's I'm old enough, unless I find someone prettier." And she'd come bouncing into the store and call me "husband."

She'd do the damnedest things. A new school teacher came, about my age. Syl told her, "This is Len. Don't get any ideas because likely he's going to have to marry me." Schoolmarm gave me a hard look, but I never got mad at Syl who wore my clothes, stole my shirts and socks, who'd spend hours helping me do disagreeable things, who always took my part when I was too shy to do it myself.

She was twelve I guess when I saw her last. She came running down to the dock as I was leaving to holler, "Come back and marry me, don't forget I saved your life." There seemed to be too many years between us for me ever to imagine her grown up. I never saw her after that, but I will always remember her as irrepressible little Syl with lovely brown eyes and a devilish grin. She gave me a lot of happiness. The man who married her was fortunate beyond all deserving, I'm sure of that.

August 12, 1984

Dear Claudia,

In your letter you saw right through me. You said outwardly I probably seemed to adjust to retirement, but inwardly, like you, not so wonderfully steady. Of course, you are right. Like you, I'd love to yell and stamp, and also like you, I don't. You want to talk about fear? I've had ideas about it all my life. Not fear of flying or sailing, or heights, or darkness or policemen or school or the doctor or bellyaches, but real fear, the kind that grips you when you lose something or someone you treasure.

It's curious, but recently I got hold of a book written by a Dutch sailor who escaped the Nazis and reached Britain. The refugee Dutch population had managed to get some of their deep-sea towing fleet to Britain, and it was working with the British navy, helping to save torpedoed ships that were still afloat. So the Dutchman went out day and night and towed crippled ships to port. They couldn't avoid submarines and they couldn't defend themselves.

How does one survive? Every instant there was a chance they could be blown out of the water. All the sailors agreed that when the fear came, what they most desired was the touch and companionship of a woman. It sent some of the men to search the alleys for prostitutes and some to drink themselves senseless. He said those who took to the alleys lasted longer. It seems to be part of man's makeup that when he is in peril, he tried to leave part of himself behind.

Once at Cape Wolstenholme we had a great sleet storm late in the fall. All the steep hills were coated with ice so badly it was impossible to climb them until the snow covered the ice. Then, in spring, we had a sudden mild spell. The natives warned me that the forty-mile-deep valley would be dangerous, as the snow would get wet and heavy and slide down off the hills. I took it with a grain of salt and kept on going around my trap line, till, one evening, I was heading home in the dark and suddenly came on a great pile of snow across the valley. There had been a snow slide. I was picking my way across when I heard another. It was too dark to see but I knew that even on a recent slide there could be another from higher up the valley and the only way was up the centre.

That was a bad night, believe me. I heard snow falling everywhere, behind me, before me. Small slides even hit me and the only way to prevent being buried was to turn and run upward staying on top of the moving snow. I don't know how many slides I was caught in. Once or twice I was carried along for quite a distance before I got clear or the snow stopped. Luckily, I wasn't hit by a big slide or it would have been the end of the road.

I can't remember being scared. The main thing that worried me was the store. I was alone at the store at Wolstenholme and the nearest camp was forty miles away. If I was killed, there would be no one to let the natives have the ammunition and other things they needed to keep themselves alive. That bothered me. I had a small sleigh that I was pulling with a packsack on it. I had no dog team. I abandoned the sleigh as the snow slides had brought down sand and rock, and some of the blocks of snow were half the size of a small house.

I zigzagged around, and around midnight I reached the post. The last mile or so had been free of slides, as the valley was wider. The house was close to the side of a tall hill and a small slide had come down, not heavy enough to damage anything but the building was buried to the eaves, both doors covered with tightly compressed wet snow. I sat on the roof in the dark and laughed. Then went to the store and crawled in between a couple of polar bearskins and went to sleep.

In the morning I started to dig out the doors, and by noon I could get into the house. It was dark and cold but I'd laid a fire before I left and it only needed a match to stove and lamp to get light and heat.

I had a meal but still hadn't felt any fear till I walked back up the valley to see what the place looked like in daylight. Claudia, it was one mass of huge lumps and blocks of snow. I could see my tracks coming out of the centre of it. In many places they were covered feet deep by new slides and snow was still coming down. I watched for a while and I couldn't see how I managed to get through all that in the dark. I started to feel real fear then and I went back to the post. I kept busy digging out windows etc., made my usual radio contact with Nottingham Island, and finally went to bed. As soon as I put the light out, I started to shake and I was honestly terrified, not just scared but petrified with fright. And as the Dutchman said, what I longed for was a body contact with the dream girl I had been carrying with me for so many years.

In a way it has bothered me a bit all these years, some sort of weakness I guess. The self-reliant person wasn't so self-reliant after all. There weren't too many alleys or pubs in Wolstenholme, so I got through the night with coffee and the BBC that was broadcasting beautiful symphony music, but I didn't sleep a wink, and while the music was soothing, it couldn't still those longings for someone else, someone tender and loving. It shook me up, and as I watched those horrible excrescences of snow and rock gradually reduced by the sun, I couldn't help feeling I had no right to be alive.

The first natives arrived a few days after the slides and they walked up the valley to see what I'd managed to come through. Old Enowalik came back, looked earnestly into my face and said, "*Wat kadlunga*," which is a way of expressing extreme awe. There was nothing I had done to preserve myself other than to try and keep on top of the snow, but it was incredible that I wasn't killed. They reacted as I expected them to. They walked up the heap of snow to sit on the roof in the warm sun and they laughed and laughed.

I've been scared since, but I don't think I have ever again experienced a situation like that. I wonder how many people have had the same experience with acute fear and the incongruous sexual demands that it releases. Probably has something to do with the wartime baby booms and the number of war brides of the time. The Dutchman is the first person who could express in print exactly how I felt. I had never forgotten the experience but it was quiet on my mind till now. I wonder, are women affected the same way? Maybe not.

NINE

Winnipeg, January 10, 1985

Dear Claudia,

There is no reason this letter has been in slings for so long, except I don't have the time to write that I used to have. I'm a bit sore in spirit these days, not being able to move very far, not to see my friends and acquaintances. Perhaps it's the disease but Muriel goes into a panic if I'm away five minutes longer than I said I'd be. Fear is a terrible thing. I've never felt it much for myself, a moment or two of terror occasionally when there was a sudden danger to someone or me, but I didn't have to look in to the future to see all the things that might happen. I try very hard to do all the things expected of me and there are times when I must go off and be alone if only for a little while. Boil it all down and I'm just not good company for anyone and I guess you'll find it comes out in my letters.

I'm especially glad that you have a chance to be out in the country. You can have the evening on a darkening river and the peace and contentment that comes in the lone quiet land when the velvet blankets fall.

Once Stan Blake and I paddled, portaged, and tracked upstream for days and we came to a large lake of fresh water. We pulled into a creek off the river just before the lake and camped. It was blowing hard, the stiff steady winds that came with the first frosts of fall. There was not a human being for miles. There was a bright high moon over the angry water, and I thought how wonderful it was to be there, to see this as it had been for centuries, and will remain for many more. We had to cross that lake because time and food would never permit us to go around. There was no way we could go on, no one to help us and no one would ever know where we had been if we didn't make it back. We were looking for three men who had disappeared, so we knew it could happen. But in the camp that night there was only contentment.

For three days it blew, and the waves got bigger and bigger and came crashing ashore on the steep rocky sides of the lake, but in our hollow, there was hardly a breath. We hunted for meat, and with a small net we hauled out the reddest trout you ever saw and roasted them in front of the fire. It was a sensuous pleasure to see the red flesh darken with the heat and see the clear oil flow out and leave the flesh dry and incredibly tasty.

Finally, one evening, there was a hush. The wind dropped and in the silence we could hear the crashing of the waves dwindle to a leisurely lapping against the stones. We took our tent down, slept a few hours fully dressed by the fire and in the morning there was almost absolute silence. There was the murmuring of the creek, and the sound of an early rising muskrat sounded almost harsh in the cool air. While we ate our breakfast we heard the wind come again from the opposite direction and we knew it was on our side.

Cutting a tripod, we mounted our tent for a sail and paddled the last half mile to the lake where the soft wind filled the blackened ragged square, and headed away from land. By mid morning we were miles away from shore, with a constant breeze behind us and nothing except that breeze and the sun to steer by. I slept and woke and slept again as the day passed. We took turns guiding the canoe, most of the time not even using the paddle, just adjusting the sail. We talked about the monster fish that are supposed to inhabit the lake but they didn't raise a fin above the surface. We saw a couple of the landlocked seals that have been reported since the first Indians came. They were tame and came close. I thought they were the same as the coastal rangers, especially when they humped their backs to dive.

We came to a little island, likely the top of an underwater mountain as the water was immensely deep right up to the water line. We let down a long line and felt no bottom, so we went ashore, climbed the steep side, and came to the top.

Distantly we could see the land that we were aiming for. There were three trees in a hollow, perhaps thirty feet tall, that inclined toward one another, and in the tops there was a huge eagle's nest. The materials must have come from one side or the other of the lake. The birds weren't there but the ground was covered with evidence of their hunting. Mice, rabbits, winisk, all captured miles away and brought out to the young.

There was no sign that humans had ever been there. I felt we had visited a kingdom, the land of a great monarch, and that, even if he was not there, that we had trespassed. We stretched our legs for an hour, then sailed through the evening and into the night.

As the moon rose and shed a path of liquid gold across the miles ahead of us, I thought of old wives' tales of men bewitched by the moon who sailed on and on and on forever, following the moon's path. When the moon went down, the bewitched sailors followed it to the bottom of the sea and travelled with it again till it shone again above the waters. In the late night, our canoe grounded gently on firm sand and we were across those miles of water.

We stumbled ashore, cold and hungry, but across. We made a hurried camp, ate briefly and slept. At some time in the night, I heard the dreaded north wind in the trees, hesitantly at first, but with increasing ferocity and I knew it had brought snow. By morning, the storm was at its height. From the tent door, we looked out into a fury of lashing waves and windspun snow. No canoe could have survived on the lake that day and the next, but we lay in camp enjoying the blissful sense of being windbound.

We were a long way from the coast. Winter was near but the spirits of the rivers, lakes and forests had allowed us passage. There was no real feeling of fortune, just a realization that perhaps we had given the gods their due over the weeks of our trip and that they had given us ours when the time came. It was not a religious feeling of thanksgiving, but more pagan perhaps.

Our venture across the lake was unusual. As far as I know, no other person had attempted it. It received some attention in a newspaper some time later as the foolhardy exploit of two crazy kids.

When, a couple of days later, we resumed our way along the shore of the lake, and found the river and the supplies left there long before, we stopped at the throwing-up rock. No, not in that sense. It is the place where the natives threw gifts to the top of a huge rock in the river, gifts to the spirits that gave safe conduct and good hunting. I threw my token to lie with the pieces and bits of tobacco, candles, cartridges and other precious things. It didn't feel ridiculous. I felt very happy and complete when I heard the ring of cartridges that I contributed as they fell into the depression of the stone.

Many years later, my brother, who saw much more of that particular area than I ever did, told me that a party that had lost their supplies when their canoe overturned in a rapid, came to the throwing-up rock. They had only an axe and a rifle that had been lashed to the canoe. With the axe they cut long poles and managed to scramble up the steep rock. In the basin they found, along with many other things, two rifle cartridges that would fit their gun. The single caribou they saw and the beaver that they managed to get accounted for the two cartridges, but since the 30–30 was a common rifle in those days, they could have been anyone's.

A lot of years later, I was in La Ronge, Saskatchewan, and one evening a group was talking about various native customs, when the subject of throwing-up places came up. Everyone, or almost everyone, had heard about them, and one or two had seen such places.

They were evidently pretty common before the missionaries banned the practice. When I say banned, I guess they thought they did, but the gifts got tossed up all the same.

I remarked that I had done it myself, and was amused at first when Mr. Fisher, the Anglican, gave me a talking to about the sin of such practices. I hadn't felt it was wrong. After all, what can a plug of tobacco or a candle do to harm anyone or anything? He finally got my goat, and I said, for my part, I'd rather see a man do something like that, rather than see him go to church regularly and see him pay lip service to something he could never understand. Mr. Fisher and I never did become friends and I bore the disappointment quite well. If the cartridges I put up on the rock were the ones that saved the lives of a party of men, well, all I can say is, I know people with worse traditions.

Jan. 30, 1985

Dear Claudia,

The last weeks have been busy. I have felt for a long time that W.E. Brown's contributions to transportation and communication in northern Canada have not been fully recognized. He's now eight-five, a recent widower. He, along with others, is being forgotten as the old timers move along. The young people pay less and less attention to the people who did the hard work by dog team, canoe and on foot to open up the country that the kids fly over in comfort. So I decided to try and get W.E. an Order of Canada, because it is recognition that would brighten his days.

It's a formidable procedure, but Andy [Andrew Anstett, Len's son-in-law, MPP, NDP, Winnipeg] got a lady in the protocol department at the legislature to get the details for me, and Carol Preston and Phyllis Lowe and others got all the information on W.E.'s career, and others of his friends got details of his RCMP days. I called a professor at Carleton University who knows W.E. to enlist his help. It's meant a mite of telephoning and letter writing but it begins to look good. I've stuck my nose into some holy places and gotten it smote once or twice, but I'm taking the attitude that John Doe, citizen, has a lot going for him if he only gets up there and hollers. There are times when I'm frustrated and angry, times when I'm hoarse as a crow, but there are times when I see real progress. Tonight I feel that there is a very good chance of W.E. going to Ottawa next fall to be invested. The professor has asked me to go to Ottawa, stay with him, and see the investiture if it comes off. I'd like that because he is an old Arctic hand, and he, W.E. and myself could burn the midnight oil for many long memory-filled evenings.

Some place I have pages of memories that involve a special dog team. If I have ever written something that I like myself, it's those pages. One needs to be with dogs for days and days alone, to appreciate what they mean. You talk to them and know by their alert ears and intelligent faces that they understand. More than that, I think they know that you are absolutely dependant on them when you are miles and miles inland over mountains, or far out on the sea ice.

Once I was away out on the frozen ocean hunting, and suddenly noticed that the wind had changed, and instead of holding the floating ice against the land, it was moving it off. We turned and headed for shore and never did dogs pull and run like they did. We barely made it to firm ice across a quickly opening gap, and when we stopped in safety, those dogs stood and looked at the wide lead between the land and the moving ice, and no one could tell me they didn't know.

We camped right there that night and by morning there was a fresh gale blowing offshore and every piece of ice had been swept far out to sea beyond our sight. I've travelled behind those dogs for miles and miles of howling blizzard in perfect confidence because they knew where they had to go even if the poor human on the sled didn't, and

I've had the leader walk up to me when we were at our destination and proudly rub the frozen snow off his face against my knee before looking at me, saying plainly, "We got here because you had the good sense to let me find the way."

Once a disturbed man came at me with a seal harpoon, and stopped in his tracks when he saw eleven big dogs behind me all staring at him out of their slant wolf eyes. Had he harmed me he'd have been torn to pieces. He was crazy and murderous but he knew dogs, and carefully laid the harpoon down and turned away. That was the only move that saved him

Many years later, when he was recovered, I asked him why he didn't strike as he had intended. He gave me a wide grin. Eskimos are not embarrassed about things that are past and done, and he told me he knew what those dogs would do if he lifted his arm to throw the harpoon. Perhaps another instance of, "I may be crazy but I'm not stupid."

Winnipeg, March 8, 1985

Dear Claudia,

One of my recent letters was an outburst against the government's treatment of the Norway House people, probably more boring than otherwise, and since then, Mr. Crombie has been up to Fort Alexander to look into things. He is concerned at the sub-standard housing, broken doors, peeling windows, and on and on. He'll never understand that if you give someone a free house, and heat it and light it and repair it for him, he'll probably always have poor housing. It's the continual give, give that erodes the people. If he and others could only see it, the people would be happier, cleaner and better housed if they were allowed to go back into the bush and build their own houses and look after them in their own way.

True they might never have Dick and Jane, or see *Three's Company*, or *Question Period*, and it wouldn't likely bother them one whit. The profit would be in the fat brown kids at the end of the trapping season. No acne, no bad teeth, no vandalism. Didn't a great man say, "What shall it profit a man if he gain the whole world and lose his soul?" They have given houses, TV, phones, flush toilets, pop, candy, and jammy buns, but they have taken the soul, and Mr. Crombie can build another hundred houses at Fort Alexander and be no better.

I wonder how Mr. Crombie or all those who have gone before him would feel if a native came to Ottawa to take them out of their rut and set them to live a native's life. It might be a shock to have someone from a different culture say, "This is where you will live, this is what you'll do, and you should be very, very grateful."

Once a man came from a British University on a grant to study the Labrador people. It was during the depression and things were tough. He went with my dad on a trip by dog team, and he was critical of the way some of the people lived. What the people took for comforts, he took for granted, and one day as they left a place where the people were poor but they had given what they had in the way of food and shelter, the gentleman was quite critical. Said he thought that they could manage better if they showed some initiative.

My dad wasn't the quietest man you ever saw, and he listened a while, then roared at the little man and said, "You slept in a warm feather bed last night because the husband and wife slept on the floor in another room. They offered you the best they had in food. You are correct, they don't have a lot, but everything they have they paid for, and the next time you get into an expensive sleeping robe that you didn't pay for or eat food you get from money handed to you, just remember that these people owe no one. You can't say the same, and you may never be able to either."

Only, my dad was likely much more blunt. He spent a lifetime among those people and he knew how hard they worked. So that's my bad temper for today.

Did I tell you about the Order of Canada we are trying to get for Buster Brown? I'm so pleased that nearly everyone I've contacted is coming through with commendations. An important one from St. John's, Newfoundland, one from a retired senior vice-president, HBC Winnipeg, and one from a retired general manager. They all speak very highly about W.E. Brown. I am encouraged. I hope Ottawa recognizes that here is a very remarkable man, one of the last of the big men who carried the old HBC flag into the North.

It's sixty years and more since he took it to the North Magnetic Pole, which was in the Committee Bay region then. He had hopes to establish a post there, but it wasn't to be then, and since then, the stupid thing has moved again and I believe is under water now. It was not far north of Repulse Bay when I was there, and a magnetic compass was about as much use as a bikini. Father Bazin and I tried to use one in heavy snow once, returning to Repulse from Dr. John Rae's old stone house at North Pole River. We gave up finally and built an igloo and slept. What we could see of our trail the next day looked like a cow path, wandering all over, and we had followed the compass needle faithfully. Just too close to the Pole.

Since that last part, your letter came and I am glad you got to work with the teenagers in trouble. I know how you feel about kids and drinking, that's always scary. But that's how this generation is. The generation before this and the one before that all had different ways, and the ones to come will have their ways. Are we really on the way to hell, or is it that this generation scares us as our generation may have scared our parents. I have three girls and a boy, and I've had many an hour of fear in my turn. Now they are all grown up and doing well, and Kathy and Pat at least, are already worried about the things their kids will have to face. Perhaps it's in the cards that all parents will have their times to worry. Just part of the cycle maybe.

I can remember when an unmarried mother was "ruined" and people didn't know how to behave. One girl in our school in Fogo was pregnant. Her people took her out of school. Her "shame" became their shame. They came to church late and left early. The girl we never saw. I used to think how unfair it was that the parents had to suffer for her "sins." Yes, I was one of the righteous who were entitled to judge.

Then one day a family came to live near us. They were close to middle age and had no children, and we heard that they were adopting. The husband was a sailor on one of the coastal mail boats and was away a lot. On wet or stormy days, my mother would send a couple of us to get water and coal for this woman and chase her sheep and goats in, if necessary.

One day, as I stood in her kitchen, she brought a baby to show me, about a year old, blue, blue eyes, and fair hair and several white teeth in front. She captivated me as all babies do, and I gladly hauled water and coal from then on just to see and play with the baby.

The gossips got busy, and in a short time put two and two together. This was my schoolmate's terrible "sin" that I was holding. This was the child that couldn't ever go to heaven, who must have that ugly "illegitimate" on her birth records. This little one, in her time, might also suffer because of an act that she had no part in. And it seemed to be the most monstrous thing I had ever heard of. The day I heard, I walked miles over the wet fall hills trying to sort it out.

Like all Newfie kids of the period, I got a lot of my ideas from the Church, and it said plainly that the child was sinful. It also said that every child is conceived and born in sin, original sin.

I used to work my allotted time for the parson. We all did, it was our contribution to the Church. One day I was helping paint the study in the parsonage and looked into the parlour and there he was after a big meal, sprawled on a sofa, sleeping it off, looking and sounding like a great pig. And I thought, where do you get the everlasting temerity to say what sin is, or who sins. I thought about it a lot, and the more I thought, the more I could see that the girl may have been unwise to risk the punishment that could happen, but I couldn't see the sin part.

One day, when only the school principal and I were left in school putting new grates in the big coal heater, I managed to voice some of my thoughts, and he listened. He was a wonderful man, a good teacher who loved trout fishing in the ponds. He knew his duty as a teacher, (our schools were administered by the various churches) and he said, "Should you talk to Mr. Noel?"

I said I couldn't, because it seemed to me that a man who could say those awful things, the things he said when the baby was baptized, was more of a sin than the child's or the mother's. The principal laughed and he laughed. I can see him now, sitting on an overturned coal pail, black smudges on his face, and his whole body and face laughing. Then he said, "What did you think when you first heard that the girl was 'in trouble'?"

I admitted that I was probably one of the gang that discussed it and wondered who and when, and condemned her. We couldn't condemn the boy because he didn't have the guts to stand up and take his share, even though he was officially asked in church, three Sundays in a row, to speak out and confess. Some chance, and I guess it was more for the gossips than to see justice done. Then he said, "You love the baby." I said I couldn't see how anyone could fail to do that. So he said, "Don't be too hard on the mother. You will never know how she has already suffered, how much more she will suffer."

Claudia, I sat many evenings when I was supposed to be doing homework, and finally I had a letter, the most ill-written thing you ever saw, and probably ill spelt too, as that's never been my strong point. But somehow I managed to say that I was sorry things had turned out the way they had, that I had been told that the child I saw every day was hers, and that I felt that she was entitled to be very proud that she was the mother of such a baby. There was more, every sentence a grammatical atrocity, but I meant them. And it took me weeks, but finally I put a stamp on it and dropped it into the mail.

I never received a reply, but years later, after the war, I was in Goose Bay waiting for a ride out to Montreal on a cargo plane. There was no regular passenger service in those days. People put their names in and sat and waited. If there was space, they'd call the name on the top of the list and warn the next man that he was now on top. So when Joe Blow, or whoever, was called, the dispatcher said, "Len Budgell, stand by. You will be next."

That could mean one or ten hours or a day or so. I wasn't really excited, but in a very short time a different voice said, "Len Budgell, please report to RCAF Overseas Transportation." So I galloped up, and was met by a wing commander. He said, "Are you Len Budgell, who used to go to school in Fogo?"

I confessed, and he said that they had just come over from England with a VIP and were going direct to Montreal, no stop off at Moncton as was usual. I could have a seat and we'd leave in a few minutes. I wasn't long in getting on that plane.

I was in the back compartment with a bunch of RCAF types and the VIP's people. I never saw him, and I never knew who he was. It was all very secret. He was never named, at least not to me, but I had a good seat and the box lunches were good and the coffee much too strong.

After we got in the air, the wing commander came back and talked to me. He was very English, and told me he was married to a New-foundland woman he had met overseas during the war. He'd been shot down and was taken to a hospital staffed by Canadians, except for one nurse who stoutly denied that she was Canadian. She was a Newfoundlander, and it was before Confederation. I nearly fell out of my seat when he told me who it was.

And she still had my letter and had showed it to him, and he said she frequently spoke about me. I said that it was one hell of a let-ter, but it was one I would always be glad I had written. I never saw him again and I don't remember his name now, but I have thought many times since that the war may have been a terrible thing but it was probably the thing that got her to stop hiding and go out, get her training and go overseas. All this to say how cruel we were, how we lacked any charity or understanding, because that was the way things were in those days.

And a few days ago, I went to see a girl who used to work at HB House, now a single mother, and she showed me her baby so proudly, and she was so happy, and she will keep and rear her child. She said she just happened to want a baby but not a permanent type husband, unless, and I think these are her exact words, "…unless I find a man who is good enough to be the father of this baby."

In my mind I compared the plight of the first girl with the position of the second. They were the "good old days" in many ways, but not in that respect. If I have a choice, I'd rather a world that doesn't crucify a child because of society's notions of behaviour. This is another fat and happy child and I'll go to see her while I can, and it will be a pleasure. So much for what's wrong with the world and why parents worry.

I find that I've been dreaming a lot, and it's always about places and happenings of years and years ago. I'm amazed when I wake up and remember how true to life the dreams are. My dad and Mother as they were when I was little, James Dickers, the cooper, Will Shewak,[21] the most incredible craftsman you ever saw, and his brother, and so many more. I guess it's a subconscious desire to go back to those days.

Not that I'm not happy here, but I can't do see or smell the things that were in those days. There is no smell like the scent you get from an oak barrel as it sits over the heater to be hooped, its wood scorching without smoke. James would test by holding his hand on the hot staves, so hot I couldn't bear it, but long practice had taught him the exact temperatures when the staves would bend and not break. Or the smell of cutch, the dark dye that fishermen used on nets. It came from South America in big boxes, in one great lump as it was poured. Once we found a photo in a box, a dozen dark-skinned people stand-

21 Originally recorded by George Budgell in the Rigolet post journal as Will Chickquack, the family was known as "Shewak."

ing beside a furnace, where they were cooking the resin that is cutch. It always had a strange, far-away smell, but after the photo it was more remote, more romantic, more mysterious.

And there was nothing like the smell of the kelp beds when the spring tides have lifted the ice away, the freshest most invigorating smell. It's probably the iodine in the kelp, but for the first few days after the ice went, I'd be conscious of low water and the smell of the kelp. My room was about twenty feet from high water mark, and in the spring I'd have my window open to smell the sea and the kelp and the schools of fish that went in and out with the tide. Smelt, capelin, salmon, trout and cod, they each have their own smell. It's not like the smell of dead fish. It's alive and pleasant.

And the birds too. All night I could hear them, the great loons and their lesser cousins, the ducks, the eiders, the mallards, harlequins and the lonely sounding hounds, as we called them because their call is so much like hounds far away. Out there were the falcons that flew high and remote, and killed only to eat, and struck like lightening, or the osprey whose fantastic sight allows him to fish at night. On a calm night, I could hear them crying their single note as they circled high above the harbour. Perhaps it warned their mates of their position. There was the quick double note as they prepared to dive for an unwary fish close to the surface, the silence till the sound of the osprey's body entering the water cleanly, and the strong flutter as he emerged, almost always with his prey.

I used to lie there night after night listening and wondering what right I had to be so happy, so lucky. I could go to work at six in the morning when the whole world was freshly colour washed, when there was dew on the long boardwalk, when the seats of the boats collected water in huge drops that looked as if it were impossible for them to be so big, when the quiet was so intense that the thud of oars in row locks sounded intrusive, but if it was far enough away, it was wonderful.

I could see Joe Pottle and his son Henry against the horizon as they shoved their boat into the water. Two measured miles away they were, but in the stillness, I could hear clearly the sound of their voices, the grating of the boat's keel as they launched it, and the slow thunk-thunk of Joe's oars as he pushed the boat out to the first net. I could hear the sharp note as Henry lifted the head of the net, and the floats rattled on the planks, hear the thrashing of water as a big salmon was lifted and the rapid thudding as the fish kicked around the boat banging against the chutes and loose gear. And I knew if they were listening they could hear the same sounds from me.

I'd hear the old robber seal that lived in our cove exhale as she broached some distance out in the bay. She'd dive out there, swim along one of our nets, select a tasty fish and surface out in the bay again, beyond any chance of gunshot, not that she was in any danger. She'd been around there when my dad first came, and he'd protected her all those years. Now and then she got tangled in a net but could cut herself free with her sharp teeth, and every spring she'd come right into the cove, climb out on a big smooth rock right in front of the office and lie there, sometimes for twenty-four hours, till her baby was born. When he was strong enough, she'd nudge him into the water and they'd leave.

She was a Ranger seal, the most beautiful of all hair seals. They don't have their young on the ice like the other seals, always on the rocks after the ice has gone. But once they had their young on the ice.

We know because the little seal is white inside the mother in March, and in June when it is born, it is black. Seals are very intelligent animals who must have realized many years ago that bears and killers can see the black mother on the ice, so decided to change things a bit. The rocks are black, the mother and baby are black. That's no old wives' tale. I've seen many unborn seals taken from seals that were netted or shot in March, and always they are pure white, in April and May they are spotted, in June they are black.

How many times on a calm morning have I seen that old rogue swimming along the net, and seen her take a nice fish by biting the head off and leaving it in the net while she absconded with her meal.

Many, many times I could have shot her, as could any other of the post staff, but no one would. She belonged to the HBC at Rigolet, and my father would have had the ears of anyone who tried to harm her. He always said, "When we can't spare a fish for a poor seal, then we'll give up fishing."[22]

He'd cuss a bit when she cut a hole in one of his new nets, but he loved to get out of his office and on the water, so he'd get into a small boat and row out and sit in the sun while he repaired the damage, and from there he could see all that went on at Rigolet, his beloved post. Sometimes I'm sure the repair job took a lot longer than necessary. He'd sit there and work the big wooden needle, and the big crooked stem pipe that he smoked would send its little cloud up. You'd go a long way to find a more content man.

I guess I admired my dad in a way I haven't been able to admire any other man. A while ago I was privileged to read some of Father O'Brien's letters about people and conditions on the Labrador Coast. He was talking about the extreme hardship the Naskapi Indians were suffering with the loss of a great portion of their hunting ground because of low level bombing practice by NATO air forces. He detailed many things, and at the end he said, "These are facts, and my friend, George Budgell, agrees with my view." It was like saying to the Newfoundland Government that what George Budgell thought about Labrador could not be contested. I felt good about it.

And today I got a letter from old Mr. Learmonth, a many years Company man, who probably knows more about the fate of the Frank-lin expedition than any person alive. And why not? He found many of the skeletons and was so careful in his investigation of every site that he found George IV florins and ivory buttons that had lain there

22 Where animals were concerned, this was no idle threat. In the post Jour-nal dated July 26, 1919, he himself recorded: "...The Customs Officer (Walter Crosbie) and the Company's Agent (George Budgell) had a fist fight this a.m. over the former's threatening to shoot the Company's dogs. Each received a black eye."

for a century. He said at the end of his letter that in the years between 1911 and 1914, while he worked for the HBC on Labrador, he met my father many times and he said that there was no more loyal servant of the HBC than my dad who was a man who gave completely of himself to his Company[23] and equally to his customers who made the Company what it was.

Houseful of kids again tonight. Josh has been down here for some time as Kathy's hurt her neck and needs a lot of treatment. He came to say that Kaleigh is awake and calling Grampa and I can hear her shaking the rails of the crib. There are at least ten other letters to be written but they'll have to wait. Sounds like the crib is being taken apart splinter by splinter. So I'll be away.

May 15, 1985

Dear Claudia,

Five-thirty is a lovely time of the morning when spring is breath-ing her sweetness. The person who portrayed spring as a passionate woman must have been up at five many times.

You know, spring comes much later in the Arctic, but when it comes and we have all that extra light, there is a magic time when people, birds, and animals rest, everyone and everything except for Eskimo kids. At Tuk, in the Western Arctic, I lived way out on a sand

23 The HBC Archives has a letter dated July 23, 1947, from George Budgell to the HBC. When the Goose Bay base was being built, George Budg-ell was asked to open a commissary for the workers. He had received a cheque for $175 from the Hudson's Bay Company. In the letter, he thanks the Company, but says that he "hardly expected anything for doing what was so obviously my duty, but I thank you very much for the cheque." At the time, he was retired from the HBC on a pension of $66 per month.

spit that once had dozens of tents and a few houses, but the sea on the one side and the harbour on the other were gradually eating away the spit. I was alone out there and pleased about it too. I'd get up and go out into the warm air, yes, warm because the mighty Mackenzie is pouring millions of gallons of warm water into the delta.

There is no way to describe the feel of the air or the clearness of the air and sky. It was like looking at a world of clear silent crystal, but if you listened carefully, you could hear the water running through the slowly rotting ice. A murmur, that was all, but it was quietly causing those miles and miles of Beaufort ice to disappear, not with a great crashing and rending as the rivers when they go out, just ice silently dropping into all the crevices. Sometimes there'd be a continuous gurgle as a larger opening drained the surface to let the sun work, sometimes a hesitant tinkle as a little basin filled, then quiet till it over-flowed into the next and into the next—a miracle that only spring brought. I'd sit there on a big wooden barge that we'd hauled up for the winter, and listen for the sound and movement from the ocean on the one side, and from the harbour on the other.

Some mornings I'd sit there for hours just looking and listening. Both our ships were tied up next to the spit, frozen-in for the win-ter. The crews would be on board, getting them ready for the sum-mer's work. I used to eat my meals on one or the other. As the sun climbed up after its low point for the night, it nearly set at one point just behind a low range of hills, but never quite. We always had our midnight sun. The birds would waken. First the small land birds, then the gulls and ravens and finally the ducks and geese. There was a reindeer herd over on Toker Point, and I could see the deer against the skyline as they got up and started to graze. Sound carried so well in the still air that I could hear whales blow away out among the ice. So far I couldn't see them, but the sound came clearly. The clatter of wings as a flock of old squaw ducks got up, and the swish of water as they landed again, sounded so close that it was hard to believe hey were miles away in the ponds around the pingos.

Then, after a while, I'd hear the galley doors on the ships open, see the smoke start straight up from the galley flue, and perhaps see Barney Sorenson, a massive figure in white, standing at the rail admiring the morning, and hear his Scandinavian bellow, "McDuff!" He always had an Eskimo mess boy and he always called him McDuff. I knew that by the time I got on board, there would be coffee and the world's best sourdough hotcakes, which I could have out on the hatch covers under the sun.

One by one, the crews would get up, and without fail, every man would walk out on deck first, just to get a look at the morning before going to breakfast. Captain Adey and Captain Shaw would come out on their respective bridges, look all around, and have a few words across the few feet that separated the two ships. Two Newfies.

"Wonnerful marnin', Frank bye."

"Sartin' is, Len bye. Get some paintin' done this day."

Len was master of the *Fort Hearne*, and Barney was his cook. I'd known Len since I was very young, and it's only by the grace of God, or perhaps a lot of hard work, that I didn't weigh two hundred pounds, because Barney was a cook among cooks. Like Ash Cutler, he could make anything taste good. He was a huge man, with a sunny disposition, and he never seemed to be busy, but every meal was perfectly prepared and dead on time. You could never surprise him without hot coffee, pie, or cake. Come when you like, it was instantly ready.

There was always a black iron pot on the back of the galley stove. Many a night around midnight, the two captains, anyone else around that was awake—usually Forrest, Shaw's engineer, and myself—would go into Barney's galley, and that pot would yield something tasty, a delicious soup, or meat in some sort of sauce, always something new, always warm, and good to go to sleep on, and there was always a huge new baked loaf waiting.

I wish those days could come again, but they can't, and since the oil exploration started, things aren't the same. The village has grown, there are big drill ships and titanic barges, there is a Dew Line station and an airport. Huge tractors and trucks and all the things that progress brings. There are murders, rapes, theft, liquor, and I can

always feel good that we had Tuk at its best, when there was friendship between the whites and the people, not the sour suspicion that
they are about to lose everything to the rapacious whites as they did
their whales and musk ox. I wonder what Tuk will be like when the
last trickle of oil goes down the pipeline and there is nothing left
except perhaps the Dew Line peering across the ice-filled miles of
the Arctic Ocean at their Russian counterparts like two bad-tempered
kids peeking at one another through a fence, no one wanting to be the
first to smile and both knowing that just one smile might make a whale
(excuse please) of a difference.

*Len writes this letter as he and Muriel travel to Victoria, and then back to
Winnipeg. With CUSO, I was about to leave for work in Vanuatu.*

June 17, 1985

Dear Claudia,

Mid-June, Claudia, the Western Arctic is stirring and the sun goes
round and round the horizon and shines in all the windows. Some
people have dark shades to close him out when the clock says sleep. I
never had as much as a blind, and when I was sleepy I slept, perhaps
to wake at two or three a.m. to hear native kids playing just outside
my window. Maybe I'd see the same kids later the same day curled
up in the sun sound asleep. No one ever seemed to worry about them
and they came to no harm. And in mid-June the ice is gone from
Moosonee and is in small bits and pieces out in the bay and it's time
to send the tugs away.

    On Labrador, the winter ice and snow is gone, the bays and fiords
are free under the sun, and life is everywhere. The great caribou
migration is heading for the coast, more than half a million animals
now. The does are heavy with fawn, and in days the valley at Tororak

will be full of patient animals waiting for the yearly miracle, the sudden appearance of thousands of tiny duplicates of their parents.

I've told you how inexpressibly beautiful it is there, with its green terraces of ancient sea beaches reaching upward one by one, level and smooth, covered with moss and ground willow, and in each level the long legged caribou are standing, looking into the sun.

There is no fear. Even the wolves aren't able to cause a panic as they can in winter. They pass through the herd intent on their own business of cleaning out the dens in the sand banks. All last year's debris is scraped out and buried or let fall to another level. Nothing must show that there is a den there and that there are newborn cubs. The parents go about their work with a visible sign of urgency. There is a sort of truce. The healthy caribou walk freely past the dens. The wolves kill on the fringes of the herd, old and sick animals fall. They have made their last migration and might never find the strength to go back in the fall so nature gives them back to the land, but there is none of the winter harrying of the herd. The chosen animals are taken down and the wolves feed heavily and return to the dens to regurgitate the life-giving meat for the cubs and their mates.

The geese swim in the swift river and watch this stream of regeneration, and only protest when an animal comes too close to the nesting birds, or a sly fox sneaks along hoping to find an unoccupied nest with four or five huge white eggs for his meal. More often he is met by an irate gander with murder in his eye and maiming in his terrible wings and beak. Renard is usually long gone by the time the gander gets ashore. Eggs may be nice but mice don't have a guardian that can tear the very fur off one's back.

There was a special place down close by the river where I used to put my little tent, and a sloping shoulder that ran down to the water on one side and tapered away into a side valley on the other. It was a perfect place to watch the activity. Dry, tinder dry moss over the thin soil, warm and soft. It was difficult to stay awake, and one could nap or watch as he chose.

I've been there on a hot calm day in June, when the valley shimmered in the heat and one's eyes played strange tricks. A caribou a few dozen feet away would seem to shrink while one against the sky a mile away would look gigantic. The spring otters as brown as dead grass would play and fish in the river like house cats. They'd dive into the water and bring out a fish, but at the edge of the water they'd let it go just for the fun of diving again to retrieve it. The fish was doomed but I guess he never knew. If the otters tired of live game, they'd play with bits of wood or whatever came down the river. An ordinary bottle tightly corked and released above them would cause the maddest free-for-all you ever saw when they spotted it drifting down. They couldn't get a grip on it with claws or teeth, and if one had put a few pebbles inside, they'd go crazy trying to find out what strange thing this might be.

A very old, tiny little man called Coonera had the same feeling that I did about Tororak. He would drop whatever he was doing to go there with me. He had never been a great hunter but always managed to feed himself and his equally tiny wife. He was ancient when I first knew him. He had a wrinkled face and solid brown teeth worn level after a lifetime of use. He was gentle, maybe a strange thing to say about a man who killed animals that he might live, but he was gentle. He'd fondle little pups for hours and the village kids adored him. When he laughed, all his wrinkles and his merry eyes would conspire to make one want to roar his own laughter to the sky. He was old but he could carry incredible loads and trot over those high steep hills all day and seem to be as fresh at nightfall as he had been at day's break.

He could remember many things. He could tell you how many polar bears he had killed, and the exact spot he got each one. He counted his game from New Year's Day of one year to the eve of the next. He'd come in from fishing with a boat full of cod and know exactly how many there were. He knew how many pipes he'd smoke between Hebron and Saglek, by boat or dog team. He was alive, interesting, perceptive and human.

His head came to my shoulder and with his short legs he would cover the ground at an amazing pace, but he never for a moment forgot that poor *kabloonak*, the white man, isn't born with the Inuit's stamina. We'd be toiling along, perhaps up a steep hill, and he'd touch my arm and show me his pipe. Time to stop for a breather. He never once asked me if I was tired, and he never failed to need a smoke about the time my lungs were about to cede from my body.

There are a lot of wonderful people in the world, but if I had to describe the most complete gentleman I know, I'd think of Coonera and his brother, Albert. There were so many acts of kindness that they stand out in a group where kindness was absolutely normal.

If Coonera and I established ourselves on a nice dry look-out, it would take an hour or so with his old brass three-draw telescope before he had seen what there was to see. In a brief scan with my more modern binoculars I'd have seen the hundreds of caribou, a wolf or two, the otters and a few other things. Coonera would settle behind a convenient stone, steady his telescope there, and study one section of countryside for as long as need be before moving to the next. He'd hardly move for minutes at a time but would keep up a jolly commentary on all that he saw. And it was fantastic what he would see that I had missed: a cunning old wolverine making his stealthy way toward a calf isolated from the herd perhaps, or a flock of ptarmigan so perfectly hidden in their summer plumage that one might look and look but never see a bird till one moved. He'd see fox pups tumbling together outside a burrow, an eagle high in a cliff in the shadow, like Coonera, searching every inch of territory from his airy perch.

An hour or two would pass quickly in the warm sun. I'd drowse, just glad to be there and so comfortable, listening with one ear to Coonera and just feeling very glad to be alive and in that particular place. Eventually Coonera would close his telescope, sit up and lean back with his legs under him in the most uncomfortable pose, but one so natural to him and his race that they can sleep just by dropping the chin on the breast.

He'd give me a reproving pat on the arm and tell me all over again what there was to be seen, and he'd light his old battered pipe and sit there on his heels gazing out over the valley, very much like a little ruffled eagle. I'm sure he was dreaming of days that were, and people who didn't walk the hills and valleys any more. Now and then he'd sing a little song, and I should be able to tell you that they were songs to the great giver of meat and light. But I have to be truthful. His songs were more likely to be humorous or scandalous stories about himself or his friends. One in particular about himself would never get a repeat performance in Albert Hall, but even after years had passed, it was riotously funny to him, and because he enjoyed it so much, to me too.

Coonera had many years before put aside his heathen beliefs. Well officially, at least, and his early indiscretions had been confessed and forgiven by the good Moravians. The songs were forbidden of course. Once I asked him if he had ever sung such a song to the missionary. You know, he was so startled that he just sat staring at me. Then he said with a broad grin, making his points on his stubby brown fingers: one, the days when he was bad were behind him; two, what the missionary didn't know wouldn't hurt; three, with his whole merry face just beaming, that he'd found it necessary to confess and ask forgiveness a number of times since his first conversion, and with a very sad face he said he was getting old and his bad days were gone. Perhaps one, perhaps two more confessions and it would be *tavalee*, all finished.

He never had any children by his wife and they both felt it keenly. One day, he and I were pulling a big seal up on the beach when a big husky young man with a cheeky smile stopped to help us and then went on his way. Coonera looked after him and I was surprised to see tears in his eyes.

Eskimos are fatalists. They don't often cry. I pretended not to notice, but he put his hand on my arm in the appealing way he had and said, "My son, my blood." Apparently one of his youthful indiscretions involved a young woman in Nain, many miles south. He had not known she was pregnant and went back to his own country. A hunter from Nain married her and of course, her child became his.

But there was no doubt of paternity. The grin, the walk, the cheerful manner, all were Coonera's.

Bill Metcalfe, who had lived in Hebron all his life, told me that that was Coonera's and his wife's greatest sorrow. They had lost their boy. Every time that young man came up from Nain, they'd have presents for him. When the government moved the Hebron people down to Nain, I hope that Coonera was still alive and could go down and see something of his son. When I finally left Hebron, I think Coonera was the last man to come up to shake my hand and grin in my face. Eskimos are not prone to long farewells and some white people are hurt at what seems to be an indifferent goodbye. It's not indifferent, far from it, but to demonstrate would be to let the spirits know that some one is going on a journey and it's as well if they don't know, obviously.

So I said, "*Autsunai*, my father," and was rewarded by the most heart-warming smile one human ever got from another, a smile that is as fresh this day as it was over forty years ago. I don't know where Coonera's old bones lie, but wherever that may be, there lie the remains of a man that I am very proud to call tlik, friend.

A few days later.

Soon I'll drive out to Sidney to visit Linda Moran, who used to be my steno in Winnipeg. She has two boys, nine and six. We went there yesterday and Muriel went with them to church while I just drove around. I had hoped to stop to see an old HBC man but he had gone to Ottawa. So I naturally headed for the water, and going down a hill, I saw a little old sailing ship tied up. Nothing could have said more plainly that the ship had been designed by Colin Archer who, in the late 1800s and early 1900s designed the *Fram*, Nansen's ship that drifted across the North Polar Basin exactly as Nansen predicted she would and came out at Spitzbergen two years after she entered the ice almost on the day he predicted, and who later took Amundsen to the South Polar regions to be the first to attain the South Pole. Archer designed the *Gjoa*, which sailed the North West Passage and an Archer design brought Commander Graham across the Atlantic solo. So many proud little ships, and I was seeing one, I thought, I'd never even heard of. She was *Providence*, designed and built in the 1890s as a sealer, survived the First World War. Between the wars, my friend Karl Ritter and his brother and a crew of Arctic men chartered her to hunt hooded seals off Greenland.

I think I told you about the book his wife wrote, *A Woman of the Polar Night*, her experiences with Karl and another trapper on Spitzbergen before the war, and read *Greenland Patrol*, which tells the story of Ritter's experience in Greenland when he, a pacifist, had to establish radio stations in Denmark territory because his wife and child were in the hands of the Nazis.

But here was *Providence*, and I went down. She is privately owned now, acted as a mini tender after Denmark was invaded, then sold and finally bought by a Canadian, refitted and sailed across the Atlantic for the last time perhaps, through the canal and away up here. She is all oak, copper clad and fastened, good for another hundred years. The people who own her live on board and are gradually going back through layers and layers of paint to the wood and bringing her back to life. The rigging won't be Archer's and the bow sprit sticks out at an unlovely angle to the firm sheer of her deck, her rigging is laced clumsily through the original dead eyes and not seized, rather the bitter end is looped back upward and fastened by round turns and a raw knot. But I don't think she minds. She is obviously loved, and her top sides are warm brown and varnished. He masts are dressed and glisten, a fat sleepy dog lies right under the cat head which is formed of a natural bent root and has seen many a wave come tumbling over the bulwark to wet the anchor and flood the deck. There are no ugly travellers to mar the sweep of her spars, the back stays loop the mastheads in the old style and they are served and parcelled neatly. There are a boy and a girl to go aloft to loose her one top sail.

TEN

Winnipeg, October 1985

Dear Claudia,

How does one talk to a dear friend who is half way around the world?
Same way as before, you say, but we are just melting out of the first
blizzard of the year while you are maybe forgetting what snow looks
like. Anyhow, your letter has been read by everyone and I think a lot
of thoughts are, "How does one get on with CUSO?" It sounds good
and strange and fascinating, but very far away.

 Your multitude of jobs sounds wonderful, the problems formidable,
and I hope they will soon seem less so.[24] What can I do from here?

---

24 With CUSO in Vanuatu, I trained pre-school teachers at the Port Vila
 campus of the University of the South Pacific (Univesiti Blong Saot Pasi-
 fik), main campus Fiji. The Vanuatu campus is on the main Island of
 Efate, one of over 80 islands. Thanks to the Canadian High Commission
 in Australia, I travelled by small planes, aluminum runabouts and dugout
 canoes to visit the students, their families, villages and schools on their
 own islands.

That isn't an idle question. Can I send something? Or go agitate with some department? Let me know please. What conditions are attached to sending things? Will you be liable for duties? You see, I don't know a thing. Perhaps I should ask at CUSO. That sounds like a practical idea. I'll do it.

I can see you in the warm sun, getting more and more tanned and loving every minute of it. It's a great adventure, and to be there doing what you love, what else is there to want?

So what's new? We went back to Victoria which was mild and sunny. Then coming back we hit snow at Neepawa and fought a full scale blizzard all the way here. The city was a mess, cars stalled everywhere, the buses running late. The snow has since melted and we are hiving normal sunny weather. Today I raked leaves and crab apples that have fallen during the blizzard. My neighbour hasn't put hand to rake and he hasn't a bag of leaves on his property. The wind has brought them all to me. The scripture says that rain falls on the just and unjust alike. Trust the leaves to find the sinners.

W.E. Brown was here in Winnipeg a while ago. Muriel and I saw quite a lot of him and one evening he invited us to a dinner at the Fort Garry. W.E. has no memory for yesterday, but 1920 is a different matter, except for names. I have worked with him a long time. I've heard all his tales, which are worth listening to, and I was supposed to sit next to him and furnish names as required. He was in great form at dinner and told Shirlee Smith some yarns about his early days with the RCMP. I kept up pretty well, but when he talked about people who were up north when I was about five, I lost out on a few. W.E. looked at me and said, "That's the first thing you'll notice as you get older, your memory fails."

There are times when he thinks I was up there in 1919. I was all of two at the time. He is right though. I find that my memory for recent events is not reliable, but I'm getting very sharp about things that happened fifty years ago. I forget school matters but remember day-to-day events in the little outport on the island where we went to school. The various steamers and schooners that came and went, I remember, and the names of kids I fished with and the ones that got into the same scrapes as I did.

Why I can remember W.E.'s names for him is because just after the war he and I and Harry Winney, one of Canada's first bush pilots, were stuck in Churchill for twenty-two days in winter, engine trouble and weather combined. We sat in the old hotel with parkas on, and told yarns because there was nothing else to do. I heard some fascinating yarns from two great men. I wonder, what does this sound like in Vanuatu, where the sun is probably going down in a great flare minutes before the velvet tropic darkness descends. The sun goes down so fast in the south. In the Arctic, especially in spring, sunset goes on for hours. What did the man say, "The moon is up and yet it is not night, sunset divides the sky with her..." [*Childe Harold*, Lord Byron].

It was very true in the Arctic. I liked those words. At Wolstenholme the sun would go down, rest a little while on the rim of the hills, then slip below. In half an hour it would appear again at the head of the long narrow valley that went inland from the post. Only place I've ever been where you get two sunsets. The valley would darken as the sun went down behind the high hills, and suddenly flash back, full of bright sun a bit later. The wild creatures knew it. The geese in fall would stand in the semi-dusk and wait. At the first flash they'd start talking and feeding again, but as the sun went down the second time, they would settle in for the night. The hills there are so high that to see the midnight sun, one had to climb way up, but it was worth the effort. The tops of the hills and the western slopes would be sunlit while the valleys and Hudson Straits would be in darkness, not black night of course, but darker.

And in winter it was an experience to go way up the valley, ten miles or so, and look back to see that one light, and to know that for miles and miles there was not another light and not one other person. I was there nine months once, and never saw a soul. I had radio and the reception was fantastic. Stations from all over the world from all over the world could be heard, and I could talk, not on voice, but with key, to Nottingham Island and to other HBC posts around the Straits and Baffin Island. Sometimes I wish I hadn't had radio. Then I could have gone up the valley and looked back at my one small light and really felt that I was alone. In these days, there are no isolated one-man posts any more, but there are still living, some of us who have had that experience.

I wish I knew a bit more about Vanuatu. Your letter opened the door a tiny bit, and I hope that you'll open the door further. I asked the local drugstore postmistress about postage to Vanuatu and she went into a flutter. I don't think she ever heard of it, so I'll go down-town to post this. Please write again soon. Never did have a corre-spondence with someone on the other side of the sun.

Winnipeg, December 14, 1985

Dear Claudia,

W.E. Brown has been trying to persuade me to get something pub-lished. One should know one's limitations, but he kept at it, and I finally sent something to a small historical magazine. They have agreed to publish it in March unless a more important article becomes available. W.E. is happy that I have done it, so I'm happy too. I know the editor and perhaps that had some bearing on her accepting my attempt. In any event, don't look for me on the best seller list yet. I enjoy the magazine it's going into, which is called *Them Days* because it deals with Labrador, and I frequently see people I know or read articles about them. In fact, in an issue several years ago, there was a picture of a school class at Rigolet and who should be there in the front row with crew cut skull but yours truly.

Which brings me to the film we saw at Pointe du Bois. On the beginning of a reel, there was a brief shot of Greg Furlong, then third mate RMS *Nascopie*, and again, yours truly. Gave me a little shock, as I didn't know it existed. Greg has since passed to his reward. When I think of those days just before the war, it doesn't seem that long ago, but it's shoving up for the half century.

Guess I got to thinking, and I went away back to see how I remembered the men working with their hands when I was little. I have pretty clear recollection of when I was four, the year before I was sent to boarding school. And I could see James, the cooper, making barrels, and Will, the carpenter, building a house or making a *komatik*, and John and Peter using huge broad axes squaring logs. And it's all still there.

James taught me to make barrels, so I know the drill, but what entrances me is that I can see his big hands, see the great knuckles and the deft way those hands worked. You know, a carpenter takes the plane to the wood usually. A cooper reverses the process; his huge jointer is permanently set bottom up, and he puts the wood on the plane. James would take a stave in his hands, one, two passes, and one end was tapered and bevelled. He'd flip it in the air to the great danger of his nose it seemed to me, catch it, and two more passes over the plane made a stave.

The big old plane was dark brown. Every so often it was oiled with a mixture of mineral oil and pine tar, a most aromatic product, in no way resembling the horrible stuff you see on the roads. After all it came from trees. Over the years, the wood of the jointer took on a polish that was as good as the ads for Mansion Floor Polish. Just thinking about it, I can smell the Stockholm tar, smell the sweet smoke of the barrels heating over the round stove before being cinched in by the Spanish windlass and having their hoops put on.

This was in Rigolet. The old buildings, their contents, and the work still went on in very much the same manner as it had been done when they were new, away back in the mid-1800s.

When I was young many things came in barrels: flour, salt, meat, fish, vegetables, apples. Chinaware, packed in straw, came from England in barrels. Soft drinks came one gross to a barrel. There is a story that Lord Nelson's body was transported from Trafalgar to Britain in a hogshead of rum. True or not, it is not outside the bounds of possibility. If the rum was equal to the task, I am sure the hogshead was. British coopers were second to none.

James Dickers was a Hudson's Bay Company cooper, perhaps the last. At least I haven't heard of one that survived him. He was born in 1867, near the Moravian village of 8 on the North Labrador shore. At the age of twelve he was apprenticed as a cooper at Rigolet where he learned his trade, and in 1885 he became cooper at Davis Inlet, and serving there till 1907 when he was transferred to Rigolet. He spent the rest of his life there with HBC.

I spent so many of my days with James, or Will, or John, that I learned every detail of the way they did things.

John had only one arm, but he used an axe or a saw or a plane as well as the next. When he needed a boat, he built it. So did Will Shewak. Will was a genius in many ways. Unable to read or write, he weighed every salmon or cod that HBC purchased. He invented his own system of records. He could build a house from a plan because he knew where things went. He didn't need to read.

He was a young man when the first simple gasoline engine arrived to go into one of the company boats. The first thing he did was to take it completely apart, and my dad, who was the manager, wondered if it would ever be put together again. It was, and Will installed it and ran it. Much later, when I was just apprenticed, we got a multi-cylinder complicated engine for the little schooner, as unlike the first simple machine as could be, but Will installed it and ran and maintained it.

He was never stumped. He always knew what to do. He was proud to be an Eskimo, and proud he could do things no white man would ever attempt. He made snowshoes, a thing few Eskimos ever needed. He got an old pair and dismantled them to find out how they were laced.

His memory was prodigious. When old Arthur Rich died, his son came to Rigolet to get Will to make a coffin, but he lost the measurements on the way, and it was a long way to go back. My dad said, "Make it good and big." Will smiled and said he'd seen Arthur many times, and went ahead and made the coffin. I heard my dad say to the clerks that he hoped it would fit but it looked a mite tight. Young Arthur took the coffin, and next day my dad went to do the honours at old Arthur's funeral. There was no minister or priest; the HBC man did it all. When he came back, he said that the coffin fit old Arthur like a tailored suit. Will smiled and said nothing. He knew.

The first airplane that ever landed on Labrador came to Rigolet and damaged an undercarriage on landing. The pilot, the famous Major Cotton, was in despair. No parts, no radio, no way in those days to get word out except by a long slow trip south by dog team which might take months.

Will, like the rest had never seen an airplane before, but my dad asked him to take a look. He was gone only a short time, lighted his forge and went to work. Cotton sat in the office, smoked cigars, cursed the weather and about drove my dad nuts. Will worked into the night and the next morning he brought the piece to the office. Not only was it the exact size and shape and the boltholes all in the right places, but it was painted the exact same colour as the broken piece. Cotton was completely amazed. They jacked up the plane, put the piece on, and it was exactly right. Cotton started his engines, taxied around and around, came back, shook hands with Will and the rest.

Before he left he said to my dad, "You should get that fellow an airplane. I'm sure he could fly it," and my dad said, "He'd soon learn how."

Will go mail this now. May 1986 give you, as the Newfies say, a fine time along, Maid.

Winnipeg, March 19, 1986

Dear Claudia,

You know, one of my most precious memories is of spring days when March has rained and snowed,[25] and blowed, sorry... blown just doesn't sound right for March, and the wind has been from the east, every draft laden with cold and everything is wet. The sheep, horses and cattle stand in corners. They like to be outside but there is no green grass. Even the goats are quiet. The chickens come out into their run then go back and cluster in the stable window just waiting.

No one is working outside. The men go down the road in oilskins and sou'westers to the net lofts and boat sheds. In there, it's busy and warm and cheerful, but every eye goes to the window, every ear is listening for the sound of the west wind. Then one morning, it always seemed to be one morning, after milking a damp, disconsolate goat, after eating an egg laid by a bored hen, with a pale yolk because of the lack of green feed, there is a change on the way to school. At that age, you don't connect your feelings with what you hear; the sea-booted men on the road shout to men going the other way: "Glass rising, bye." Nothing more. Everyone knows a rising barometer will bring the west or south-west wind.

The change is instantaneous. It's a known fact that people who live on islands do get that odd faculty to react to a change in pressure. Instead of rounders with a sodden ball on a saturated field, the boys stray to the corner of the hill to spy out the leaden gray Atlantic heaving against the shore but almost as languid as the weary cattle straggling along the lanes. Even the schoolmaster, who hardly ever comes outside at recess, strolls up the hill after the boys, stands talking to the older lads, making plans to take an afternoon off soon to clean

25 This is a memory from one year on Fogo Island, during his father's furlough. He was about ten or eleven.

the untidy schoolyard, mend the broken palings on the fence, maybe even paint the building some good Saturday.

The afternoon is unbearably long, but at last you are on the way home. The rain has stopped, the sky is still sullen, but the air is appreciably warmer. Along the lane, stable doors are open, boat sheds are busy, small craft are being hauled out to where the sun will reach them. They must be dry for painting. Men are saying, "The glass still up, bye, perhaps we'll get the big voyage this year," in the eternal human hope that comes after the long dark winter.

The goat bleats a more cheerful welcome and the muddy and frisky kids put more into their battles to beat you and your pail to more than their fair share of milk. Mathew's placid cow, Rose, will be standing quietly outside the barn, content to wait in the warm, humid late afternoon.

No games in the lane after supper. Everyone is restless, and again we head for the hills where we can see the western skyline. Minutes before sunset, the huge red eye shows briefly on the horizon. Yes, there is a clearing, a thin band of clear sky. At dusk, on the way home, there will be men leaning on gates, smoking a last pipe, reluctant to go inside. Those who haven't been up the hill say, "What's she look like, bye!" You say, "A bit of clear sky wester," and he nods his head and says around his pipe, "Aye, she'll be here be marnin'."

You feel you'll never sleep this night, but boys being boys, you are no longer "stritched," then you are asleep. Morning is here in an instant, and your first look out the window shows the sky neatly divided between laggardly cloud and clear blue sky. The sun is still behind the cloud, but seaward, long fingers of exquisite colour are probing the sides of the hills, brightening the water, making a fantastic floating castle of crystal and emerald of the lonely iceberg or two.

God help all schoolboys if this isn't Saturday. No one could stand the books this day. The goats are milked and released. They trot briskly away followed by the kids. There are dozens of mock battles between animals that have never seen one another before. Calves bawl because for once mother does not return to a sheltered corner to stand all day patiently staring out at the rain. No, she purposely plods down the land and perforce the calf must follow the muddy road that leads to an unimagined new world.

Among the men, tweed caps and overalls are the order of the day. The sou'wester is relegated to a back pocket where it may droop, half in, half out, for a few days before being tossed to a shelf in the boat shed to languish till fall. It's a high glass; it won't fail, and by mid-morning the sky is clear from horizon to horizon. The air is like clear water, and the western water has a pebbled appearance, half mirage, half the distortion of the approaching wind.

Soon the first gusts arrive. Clothes that have hung forlorn on dozens of lines yawn and stretch and flap briskly. The wind swoops across the neck connecting the two islands and beats up a froth of ripples growing into frisky whitecaps. Boats and dories that have hung to their moorings, facing eastward for so long, swing around to the west and pull their tether the other way and begin nodding in the bright sunlight.

For the first hour, no one wants to go inside. Women stand in the lane holding babies, chatting in the warm sun, watching the youngsters instinctively head for the muddiest spot. The men bring their mid-morning cups of tea out into the road and collect in groups, all facing the west and the warming, drying wind.

Soon there is a burst of activity. I remember it as immediate, but it must have been days. There are nets and gear hung out to dry, sweet wood smoke from a dozen fires under bark pots full of nets, the strange mysterious smell of cutch boiling in the pots, cutch from the forests of South America. Paint brushes, hammers, saws, oars, bait pots, lobster traps, all the thousand and one things necessary for the fishery are everywhere. A clang as a dozen trawl grap-nets are flung outside to dry in the sun like so many rusty octopus, punt sails standing by the sheds flapping madly, peeled poles ready to repair the flakes. Smells of oakum, tar, the bitter coal tar odour and the fragrant scent of pine tar, paint, linseed oil, rope and spun yarn. Sounds of saws and hammers, coughs and sulky barks of motors long idle being tested. Men and boys everywhere with pieces of engines, batteries, coils, switches. Shouts and chatter as boat after boat slides down the rollers, immaculate in new paint, clean and dry, ready for the new season.

In no time, there is grass to be seen around fence posts and the cattle prospect the lanes finding the fresh green shoots. Soon they ignore the dry hay in the stables and come home to be milked and are immediately gone again. The calves and kids grow apace, become shy of people and more independent, the chickens luxuriate in the dry dust, and one after the other, "steal their nests" in some dry corner and try to incubate a clutch of eggs, protesting long and vigorously when they are discovered and moved to a safer spot where the weasel or half-wild cat won't find their brood.

And we bedlammer boys spent all our hours around the boats and schooners that were outfitting for the Labrador fishery. All the time, that is, that we could beg or steal from our regular chores, fetching wood and coal, feeding the animals and chickens, errands to the store a mile away, in addition to school. The big piles of manure had to be carried to the meadows and spread, not a job anyone looked forward to. Some of us were smart enough to spread it regularly all winter, and the reward was sweet when we only had a load or two to wheel, while those who spent their time otherwise in winter had to slave in the warm spring sun while the more prudent or fortunate were away almost with the dawn to the trout pools.

And as spring drew on and school was a positive imposition, the mornings became sweeter and more delightful. The sun would come bursting out of the ocean before five. One would awake and hear the cattle moving around, the robins and blackbirds bickering over nesting sites. The screams from the ever hungry herring gulls on the reefs in the harbour, the dignified call of the great saddleback gull, and the limpid double note of the raven that never ceased to charm with its clear bell-like sound.

I couldn't stay in bed after the sun was up. The fishermen of course, would have been long up, preparing for another day at the trawls, nets or traps. Our house was practically over the water. It stood on long stilts, shores we called them. A medium height person could walk in under the front and follow the slope of the shore almost to the back. In the fall, when the great orange moon was full, the tides would silently run under our living room floor and we could hear the water chuckling among the stones. I could look out of my window on the second floor and see water all around and up to the second and third step of the front door. I used to tie my boat up at the front steps, not on the neap tides, but on the full moon. The fact that water ran under the house gave me a wonderful feeling, one that has never left me.

There was a big unused wharf in front of our house, built many years before, when the house was owned by a schooner captain who tied his vessel there, right under my eye. It was a great place to observe the goings on all around the harbour. I'd get up early, tend to my chores, and long before anyone in the house was awake, I'd be sitting on the edge of the wharf watching the sculpins and flounders, rock cod and capelin going about their business. Once or twice I saw a seal ghosting along underwater, looking strangely snake-like compared to his chunky appearance on land. There were always a few ducks and guillemots swimming around, and in the clear water, I could see them using their wings to fly underwater while their ridiculous red feet paddled frantically to keep up.

The wharf was a great place to see and hear the harbour wake up. I'd see a man leave his house across the harbour and make several steps before the slam of the door came to me. He'd walk to the head of his wharf and stop to enjoy the morning and the clump of his sea boots would reach me after he had stopped. I'd hear chains rattling as trap boats were freed from their moorings, the thump of bait tubs on gang boards, the splash of water being bailed out of a boat, the rattle of oars, voices, all the magic noises of preparation.

Then the first motor would start. These were not multi-cylindered machines. They were one-lung, two-cycle workhorses, make-and-break ignition, fuel efficient, heavy, dependable. They lasted forever. It was common for a man to own and operate his grandfather's old Meanus or Lalthrope.

It seemed that the first bark was the signal for engines to start up in every corner. They all headed down the harbour past our dock and took one of three entrances, tickles, they were called, because the bottom tickled the bottom of a boat perhaps. In an instant, from dead silence, the amphitheatre of the harbour would be a cacophony of sound.

No two engines made the same noise. We knew them all in the dark as well as in the daylight. Mr. Ackroyd away up in the upper harbour had a big old Meanus, and it would go bellowing ill-temperedly out the Wester tickle. Caves' eight Acadia, with its slow tiny bark, would go straight out the middle tickle; Taylor's Hubbard had a wheezy note. It seemed that the man and his engine bore one another a resemblance. Cheerful Mr. Walbourne and his chuckling Adams were nearly always first away.

Coffin had a quiet little Perfection, perfectly matched to its owner. He fished alone. He didn't talk much, but every morning he'd cut close to the wharf, standing up with the tiller between his knees. He'd take the pipe out of his mouth and give me a wink. If my mother wanted a fish for supper, I'd stand on the wharf in the afternoon and Coffin would throw a fat cod or a small salmon deftly at my feet. The little Perfection seemed to glide that boat along by magic. There was almost no bow wave, no wake, but it was one of the fastest boats in the harbour.

Sheppherd was nearly always last to get going. He had a compulsion to be one of the first out past the harbour islands but he hardly ever made it. He had one of the most modern engines on the whole island. Maybe too modern, it was a six-H.P. Acadia. Unlike all the other dependable old Acadia make-and-breaks, Sheppherd's was a jump-start affair. Though faster than the other types, it was affected by dampness. The trembler coil and sparkplug would be wet with condensation every morning and the high tension spark would short out in all directions.

I'd hear Sheppherd cranking his engine. He lived only a few doors down the harbour. Crank, prime, crank, prime, curse, crank, until finally it would emit one sulky bang and die. By now Sheppherd was frantic. Half the boats had already started, more priming and more cranking and much swearing. It would catch, run a few revolutions, and relapse into silence, but each time it got a bit warmer, a bit drier, until finally it would keep going. Belching out smoke and misfiring, it would go out the harbour making a prodigious fuss until the plug and wiring would dry from the heat and Sheppherd's six would settle down to an even beat and behave all day.

At one time or another, every hotshot engineer in the bay would try his hand on Sheppherd's six. They all failed. There was only one way to start it. Sheppherd's way. As the sound of the six died away down the Easter tickle, I could fancy that I heard an exhalation of breath all around the harbour from those fortunates who didn't have to get up just yet, but who held their breath till Sheppherd got going. He could easily have changed his engine for a make-and-break. He never did. It was his conversation piece and many were the wondrous tales he had to tell about its performance.

They were great old machines, all gone now in favour of the querulous outboard with its whine, and discontented ways. Fishermen have to carry specialized tools to fix them. The old two-cycles needed little in the way of equipment. Long, gloomy John Payne was asked what tools he had to keep his Atlantic in such perfect condition. He said, "My son, all's I got is a zaw voile (saw file) and a haxe (axe) and I hardly ever uses the voile neider." Not all that far fetched.

When, after years of service, one of the engines required journal bearings, it would be hoisted on the wharf, turned over and the base detached. Then with a bar of hard soap, a lump of babbit and a round wooden dowel that came with the engine, the owner would run a new set of bearings and be away on time the next morning. There wasn't much to know about them. We kids knew it all by the time we were as tall as the flywheel.

And so it went, delicious morning after delicious morning. We were bathed in sensations. Yes, there were rainy days but who minds a rainy day in summer? The fishing went on just the same, warm water never hurt anyone. I only remember the odd rainy day when something out of the ordinary happened. Nothing much ever did. Only one experience so vivid I still feel almost the same fear as the day it happened half a century ago.

The bishop[26] had arrived in a nice little cabin boat, a beautiful thing, built especially to transport his Lordship. It had nice cabins, a galley, chart room, all the best, and the dining area was right under a large skylight. One could look down if the skylight were open and see the prelate at his meal. We were all interested in the lovely craft, and it happened one day we were around the wharf at noon and the smells coming up though the skylight indicated that the bishop was about to have a fine meal. Of course, we wouldn't have dared peek under the skylight. Bishops have a way of turning bad kids into buck goats. But an unbeliever from the other end of the island decided to worm his way along the deckhouse just to get a good look into the cabin, and he did just that. Edgar Oake, who is now probably a senior citizen and a pillar of the community, was seized with an impulse, and he grabbed poor Tom by the ankles and elevated them as high as he could. Tom, not expecting such treachery, was taken unawares and his head and shoulders slipped under the skylight. Edgar saw the danger and hove back right heartily, too heartily, because Tom's loose-fitting rubber boots came off in Edgar's hands, and Tom went crashing down onto the bishop's table.

Has your heart ever stopped in mid-beat? Have you ever suddenly become absolutely unable to move? As if it were only days ago, I can still feel the taste of blood in my mouth. Fear, absolute terror. There was a dead silence, and as far as we were concerned, in all probability a dead Tom. Edgar was the guilty one, but we knew that our various punishments would equal or surpass his. The local doctor happened

26 This was most likely William Charles White (August 31, 1865–June 14, 1943) who was the fifth Anglican bishop of Newfoundland, 1918–1942. He was the first native-born Newfoundlander to become bishop.

to be dining with the bishop. He knew us all; there was no escape. Every second we expected to see the bishop's head come out of the companionway and hear the awful words of the prayer for turning kids into goats.

Edgar was standing over the skylight with Tom's boots in his hands. We expected to see him blasted into a human torch and he expected worse. He recovered first. With a howl, a scream that could have been heard ten miles offshore, an unforgettable expression of a monstrous terror, he flung the boots into the cabin after their owner, and tore up the gangway headed literally for the hills, and we tore after him.

There was a place, way up on the North side hill, almost a cave. Some instinct, perhaps that of a hunted animal, directed our feet there. I know it was no conscious effort of mine. My feet weighed a ton each, and while my breath was coming short and my heart was bursting, I was moving at a turtle's pace. After agonizing ages, we got to the cave. There we could look down and see the yacht.

There wasn't a soul to be seen. Tom's headless body didn't hang in the rigging, fire and brimstone weren't pouring along the wharf. In fact, it was a very pleasant scene in all. We waited and we watched. Nothing happened. Nothing at all. We came to the inescapable conclusion that our human bullet had killed the bishop and his guest, and a final ricochet had killed the cook. What other explanation could there be?

One by one, we took our ways home, expecting dire retribution the moment we opened the door, but there was nothing. No one said a word. We knew the blow would fall, that we were living on borrowed time. Suppertime came and we were fed as usual, no bread and water.

The blow fell after supper. Everyone was to get ready to go to the church to witness a confirmation service. Everyone meant every one. There was no avoiding it, not crippling illness, nothing short of death, so we made our last toilet, and started out. Edgar came out of his gate with his parents as we passed. We joined forces. He had no more information than we did. The church was more than a mile away, but never did a road slip under my feet faster. We were there before my heart beat more than twice; in fact, I don't think it had made two normal beats since Tom disappeared.

At the church, the usual crowd, the usual greetings and finally the bell started to ring. Toll, I should say. Permission to go inside with Edgar was sternly refused. Too many times we had been caught skylarking during the sermon.

The church was quiet and serene. No candles, no gold and purple, lots of pure white. The minister was standing in his usual place, looking preoccupied. I guess the bishop weighed him down a little. No sign of the latter, no bank of flowers, no coffin. All those to be confirmed sitting quietly and a bit smugly up front.

The bell stopped ringing, the organ started, and through the vestry door came the bishop, alive, very much so, not even damaged as far as we could see. We felt relief of course, but a horrible frustration too. The service passed in a daze. When it was over and we walked with all decorum to the door where the minister and the bishop waited, we expected to be struck dead or turned into pillars of salt. All we got was an absentminded pat on the head and an admonition to be good and study the catechism, and we were free, free to race home to discuss these things that had come to pass.

By the little corner store, who should we meet but Tom, in his ill-fitting boots, alive and hearty, with his jaw bulging with the largest bulls-eyes that the store boasted. Tom, the ever-broke, feeding on the fat, sugar anyway, of the land!

The story came out. As he started his slide into eternal damnation, he managed to grab a heavy curtain rigged off of the table to protect the bishop from the draft down the companionway. He came upright and hung there like a monkey while his boots clattered down, landing on the table, which fortunately, hadn't been set. Poor Tom, he thought the end of the world had come. He was speechless as the doctor lifted him down and detached his frozen fingers from the curtain.

He was from the other religious camp across the island, a fact that was apparent to the bishop the minute he opened his mouth. That kindly man had no intention of scaring the child any further, and with the help of the doctor, succeeding in convincing him that Protestant bishops don't eat Catholic kids, nor even turn them into goats. The story came out, probably complete with names, and the bishop realized that Tom was more sinned against than sinning. The cook was called, a plate set out, and Tom, the renegade from the opposite parish, sat with the doctor and the bishop and made his meal. As he left, he was presented with a whole dollar, an unheard of sum to us all, even more so to Tom, who was one of a large family where dollars were rare indeed.

Nothing more happened. The bishop soon sailed away to visit the rest of his mission. I'll confess that I felt relief when that little ship left. I never did end up in front of that or any other bishop for confirmation. Maybe my experiences had something to do with that, I don't know. All I do know is I've never been comfortable with bishops, any sort.

Bishops or no, I wish there was a way to go back to the place as it was, to the boy that I was. It won't be, can't be, but if I had to give a precious gift to a child, I'd give a springtime in an outport exactly as we had them sixty years ago.

I am writing something up about outports, but it made me want to tell you about it first. It's about when I was ten and in awe of ships, and anything to do with the sea. Once I was on the deck of a little schooner and her owner wanted to replace a flag halliard. He threw one end to me and said, "You'm big enough, go aloft now and reeve he in the main pole for me."

I took the end and, hardly breathing, fear and pride mixed, I climbed into the backstays. There were no ratlines, just two wires angling toward the masthead. I twisted one leg into each stay and started to pull myself aloft. I had been at the cross-trees before, just gone up, stayed a while and slid back down, but never with a flag line tied to my overalls.

I had to scramble up to the masthead, climb over the cross-trees, which I had never tried before, stand on the narrow strips, shimmy up the topmast and reeve the flagline. I was scared, but I wanted to go.

Reaching the cross-trees was easy. As long as I didn't look down, I was okay. Standing there with shaking knees on the cross-trees I embraced the topmast, and if ever I prayed, and I never did, I prayed that I could climb the twenty feet of smooth pole. I was standing on twenty feet of thin air with twenty feet to go. I wrapped arms and legs around the spar and started up. The small gold-painted ball at the top looked miles away. I did look down, and saw that the captain seemed unconcerned, chatting away to another man.

As I reached the top, I was conscious of a bursting feeling in my head and lungs. I must have still been holding my breath. I had a bad moment when I saw that the line had been caught around a ring bolt in the deck, and when the captain shouted, "You gonna come down boy, or we goin' to have to paint you up thar?" I tried to say casually as possible that I'd be down as soon as he cleared out his end of the line. Back down on the deck, he sent me back up, but only to the cross-trees, to do something else. He simply gave me orders as he would to any other seaman. I thought that day that I had taken the first step to becoming a fisherman, and was highly proud of that, and proud later to tell someone when asked where I had been, that I had rove a couple of halliards for Skipper Doyle. He knew how scared I'd been though, had seen that I needed a bit more confidence, and had let me build it up.

Some years later he and I suffered through a brutal day that saw one boat wrecked and several others saved by our united efforts, and I treasure the memory of him saying to me, "Damn good man in a boat." I can only give credit to him and to my father, both good men in a boat, and both very patient.

In Fogo, the schooners would be brought in close to the wharves and were hove down by the mast heads (turned on their sides), in pirate fashion, to have their bottoms scraped of barnacles and their seams recaulked. There it would be, the great ship lying on her beams end, her masts parallel to the water while the men swarmed over the exposed part of the bottom. How it felt to walk up to a set of cross-trees about a foot off the wharf that had formerly been sixty feet over my head. To remember the thrill of touching the same cross-trees after a heart-constricting climb from the deck just last fall. To stand there and remember the feeling of looking from that height to the deck, to see the actual shape of the vessel that was not possible from anywhere else. And to walk along a keel that had travelled trackless miles of the deep Atlantic. There is no way to express the way a boy will feel standing on the side of a ship's keel, a heart swelling experience.

And all I can do is put it all on paper, and try as I will, the words can't express the sights, sounds and smells of that time on Fogo.

Moosonee, June 12, 1986

Dear Claudia,

How does one respond to thirty-one pages of adventures written with a magic touch that makes them real and reminds one of the days when Peter Pan and his alligators and pirates were so easy to comprehend and envy. Well, I am in that position. I have read your letter over and over, and of course, it is always new, and only you could have written it. I told Carol Preston about it and said pretty soon I'd have a book, and she said, "Why not? Call it Letters From Vanuatu." Or maybe when you come back, you will write your own book. And on that point, when are you coming back?

I sense your commitment and I know it will be a wrench to come away. I wish we could have a face-to-face talk. That may not be easy. I'd love to go and there is little in the way except Muriel's health. Right now she could never do it. Travelling and eating strange foods and drinking different water would be impossible for her. If she improves, we may visit her family in BC. I'd love to go on from Vancouver to Vanuatu myself, but I know she'd feel badly as she'd love to go. So unless there is a change, the project will have to go on hold.

At night now, just lying here, little windows open, I am back watching a happening that has not been in my mind for years. Suddenly it's there, bright and clear. A clear warm spring day. Kutjucak and I were sitting in the bright sun just looking at the hundreds of birds sitting on and hovering above a large open water area. We had all the game we needed and we were not hunting. Suddenly twenty or thirty feet away, an old monster of a walrus broke the surface of the water. Somewhere he had lost one tusk and he had a queer lopsided look, but the expression on his wrinkled face and in his red eyes was so astonished to see us there, that we shouted with laughter, whereupon he spit out a mouthful of clams that he had intended to eat and floundered away, apparently indignant.

But what I remember isn't the walrus so much. It's the warm sun on my face, the wonderful clear light over the land and the ice, and the good feeling of just being alive at that time and place. One memory among hundreds. I am lucky that I did and saw those things, so many and so varied.

You know I could have worked as an accountant or something just as dull. Thank God I didn't. People who work indoors all their life should get extra pension benefits to compensate for the things they never enjoy. And I feel that every kid who reaches eighteen should be sent into the North for a period, every one, just so they get to see what we have up there and how precious it is, feel the peace that is there. You know parts of it aren't that far away,

I recently found an old book, published in 1907, written by a priest that describes Labrador more fully than anything I have ever seen, particularly the scenery. The fiords north of Hamilton Inlet, the wild life, the ice, yes the ice, the bergs are always fantastic, but the drift ice too has incredible shapes and colours.

The original J.B. Williams, the shaving soap man, visited North Labrador for thirty seasons, because, as he said, it wasn't tamed. There were serene days of sailing along the coast in his little yacht, *Nimrod*. There were blustery days when perhaps the survival of his ship and crew were in doubt, but there was always a cove or a harbour where he could shelter. For thirty years he came, and he never tired of it. Best of all he told my dad, no one knew or cared if he was Williams or just another person. He paid for what he could and accepted the kindness and friendship of the people because there was no way he could pay for that.

Their complete indifference to who he was amused him. He called to see one old settler year after year and picked up a few smoked salmon. Austen never knew, never asked, his name, couldn't read so didn't know the name of the yacht. He always referred to Williams as "that old man with the black yacht, wi' two topmasts." Williams was a very old man when I last saw him in Hebron. He said that nine months of city life was only bearable because he could look forward to three on Labrador. Said he'd looked the world over for a place to spend his quiet weeks and Labrador had what he needed. He used a tiny portion of what we have.

No, I don't want to see huge money-making resorts. I'd like to see little coves where people can come to rest and feel the warmth of the spring sun, experience the absolute serenity and perhaps know the bite of the fall gales and see the Atlantic on the rampage in fall. They would see the great seas assault the land as they have done for centuries, and perhaps know the insignificance of man as frost overcomes the sea and the ice forms a highway across the fiords. The snow mantles the land so that the hills stand out clean and white against the incredible blue of the sky. If a person's soul cannot be healed there, then there is no hope.

Once I stood on the top of Cape Mugford at midnight, bathed in and surrounded by the aurora. I and my dogs had climbed a mountain, entered a valley through a pass at the very top. The aurora flashed like a silent explosion right into the valley. For a moment there were no separate colours. The light was white, much like a modern florescent, and there was a clearly visible corona above. The dogs stopped and we stood transfixed.

In a few seconds, a lovely warm rose tone spread through the white, almost a blush, incredibly delicate. The light seemed to be about fifty feet up and concentrated between the rocky sides of the pass. Suddenly the corona appeared to oscillate and all the normal tones of the aurora were visible. They seemed to interweave. A beautiful green would shimmer in and its vertical or lateral movement would be matched by a rose or purple and the colours would coruscate together, then blend into one another.

Then I noticed that the light body was dropping, almost imperceptibly. Where, at first I could see a clear horizon all around under the lights, I could now see colours between me and the surrounding cliffs. The dogs became quite uneasy. Normally during a stop after a climb, they would attend to various personal matters, then lie in the snow and rest. Now, against all training, they came back to me and clustered around. They were not afraid, but they seemed to realize this was something far out of the ordinary. They stood, heads erect, and tails, in the Eskimo dog fashion, tightly curled over their backs.

The lights continued to drop and the intensity of their colours increased. The little valley became a bowl of shimmering skeins of fragile light rapidly changing in a bewildering kaleidoscope of coloured motion.

Then I noticed they were touching the dogs' fur. Now the dogs' hackles were raised and their manes erect. The lights played along their backs delicately, not touching the heavy underfur at all, just fingering the raised guard hairs. Each dog was outlined in colour, haloed. The dogs were not aware of it. The colours would fade to one colour or to nothing, then ignite again.

I was wearing a caribou fur *kuletak* and I saw that the lights were playing along the sleeves. I had caribou mittens, and if I touched them, fingertip to fingertip, the lights would pass from one mitten to the other, continuously changing in colour and position. I removed the mittens and the colour would not touch my bare flesh. I could see them around the fur on my hood.

There was no sound. I've heard of the whispering of the northern lights, but they were silent. I could hear the breathing of the dogs and my own, and the little crunchings of the snow as the dogs moved, but no other sound.

The dogs were becoming physically agitated, so I stood up and gave them the word to go. They started down the valley toward the sea, and for a while, I was too busy with the *komatik* to look back. At the first level place, I stopped the team and turned to look. I could see the pass we had come through hung with iridescent curtains and that the sky for miles was brilliant with the aurora. Even the Bishop's Mitre on the top of Cape Mugford was crested with a more beautiful crown than any pope ever wore, at least on earth.

There wasn't a soul for heaven knows how many miles. The only visible living creatures the dogs and myself. It was a moving experience that I'll never forget.

That land is empty now, abandoned, and the original people have been moved south where they live in settlements with the whites and travel by snarling ski-doos across the snow that is torn and disfigured by more and more mechanical toys, and where the dog team is only a memory. These days the kids have never experienced a day behind a team over a pure surface where the track of a fox or ptarmigan is the only sign that other life exists. They grow up not knowing that the quest for meat to survive is a contest, not butchery from a fast-moving and tireless motor toboggan.

Am I saying that I'd like to be thirteen again? Well, those years were so good. There was nothing in the world that one wanted outside of what we had. Who knows, memory being what it is, perhaps I enjoy it more now, but at least I had the sense at the time to hope that things would never change, and they didn't really. I grew up, went North to a different land, but the things I'd learnt were still valid and I was supremely happy. People talk about the terrible loneliness of the Arctic. I never experienced it. I didn't know how to be lonely. Nine months absolutely alone at Wolstenholme is still a wonderful memory.

ELEVEN

Winnipeg, July 23, 1986

Dear Claudia,

Out to Maureen's to babysit Stephen. When I go out there, all the horses crowd around because they know I grind the oats for the cattle, so I give them all a handful. You can give a cow a bushel of oats or feed and she won't likely remember you unless you do it regularly. Not so a horse or goat, they never forget.

A horse will sometimes forgive an injury but a goat never. Hurt him and he'll get back, sometime, somehow. I talk too much about goats, but did I ever tell you about old Father Dubeau, the priest at Sandy Lake? He had all sorts of animals around and was good at training them. There was a boardwalk from his house to the church, and the father would walk up and down reading his breviary. He'd be followed, honest, by a big brown cat, a huge black dog, and a billy-goat, up and down. As long as the father walked, his animals would follow. He tried hard to get a big white rooster to join the procession, but with no luck. He said the rooster was likely a Protestant.

The black dog, Mackush, was a bit of a marvel. Father would give her a note and tell her to take it to the brother or the teacher, and she'd go to the right place. She'd bring notes over to me on the other side of the bay. She could open and close doors. Brother had made latches she could operate. In winter, she'd go to the fish shed, pick out a fish, take it to the rectory, go in the kitchen put her fish in a pan that they kept under the stove for her, wait till it thawed, then take it outside to eat. She'd open and close every door on the way. The father had a bad heart and would have problems at night. The dog would immediately go fetch the brother if the father appeared to be in difficulty.

She was an Indian sleigh dog, no special breed, but quite a dog. The father used to tell me how he noticed that he was losing a lot of turnips out of his garden. The native women used to come and go that way from the camp, but no one ever saw them with turnips. But one day a woman came to visit with a baby in a tikinagan. The dog was very interested in the baby, so much so that Father Dubeau decided to take a look himself. He hefted the tikinagan and it was very heavy. Inside he found not only the baby but a few of his turnips. He told us about it and said with a twinkle, "That woman was a Protestant too."

Sunday, July 27, 1986

Dear Claudia,

It's nice to be able to get out and do the things I used to do so many years ago. Then, tracking animals was a skill every kid learned at an early age. How to hunt was important. There were no butcher shops, and while there was salt meat for sale in the store, fresh meat had to come as a result of someone's lucky or careful hunting.

There was a little Eskimo man, his business name was Joseph Palliser, the surname given to his grandfather by Governor Palliser many years before. His native name was Kejuk, meaning wood, because he was small and neat like the wooden dolls they used to make. I once went caribou hunting with Joe. It was mid-winter. The caribou were high in the mountains where the wind kept the snow blown off the moss. There were a lot of wolves, and the caribou knew it. They were very shy.

It was cold, bitterly cold, and the snow was dry, and crunched under our feet. Getting close to an animal would be difficult. There was constant drifting, visibility was nil. Not a day to be out, and we were way up in the Mealy mountains. The wind was so strong that it was difficult to walk against it and if one ventured to put his back to it, he was immediately forced into taking short stumbling steps. We came out on a large open place between two higher hills. The wind was worse there, compressed and funnelled between the cliffs. No place to hunt, no place to camp, but Joe said a good place to find caribou. We got the dogs and *komatik* in behind a pile of rock and we went against the wind on foot.

The only sign to be seen of caribou was the odd frozen dropping, and they could be an hour or a month old. Caribou don't have the best of sight and always graze into the wind to take advantage of their 20/20 nose power. Joe wasn't very tall. His nickname was Little Joe to distinguish him from Big Joe, who was not a giant, about my height perhaps. Little Joe said being short just put his eyes that much nearer the ground, the better to see any game signs. It wasn't long before he said we were behind several caribou. One big stag, the rest were does or young stags.

The ground was frozen like iron. There was almost no snow. He pointed out a scrape in the lichen on a rock. I'd never have noticed it, a bit like a fingerprint on an iron rail, could be anything, but on we went. After about half an hour, in which I followed Joe with my rifle ready and my mind in a cosy camp in some sheltered valley and very little conviction that we'd ever catch up with Joe's phantom caribou, he pointed out a little patch of snow that had accumulated in the lee of a small boulder, and there, sure enough, was the print of one caribou hoof. We must have come a mile in that blizzard and all that could be seen with the wind and drift tearing at our eyes was the odd depressed place in the moss, a scrape on a rock, a few crushed Arctic willows, but we had come surely to that one foot print.

The wind was so savage that it was impossible to look ahead. Our hoods protected our faces, though I suppose my *kabloonak* nose stuck out a bit more than Joe's arctic modified beak. I wondered how the heck we'd ever see the animals and how it would be possible to sight along the barrel of a rifle with those ice spicules coming like shot.

Joe gave me to understand that we were close. I guess I looked unconvinced and he turned his head so that instead of blowing straight into his face, it blew past the front of his hood. He motioned me to do the same and touched his nose with his finger. In a second or so I realized that I could smell the strong caribou smell, almost like farm animals. They were upwind and invisible in the drift but close, very close.

Joe headed off to the right and motioned me to go left, walking almost sideways. I watched him doing the same for a few seconds before he vanished in the blowing snow. In another moment or so, I thought I saw him coming back so I stopped, and then realized that what I was seeing was a caribou facing down wind, listening. Somehow he had sensed our presence. I brought up my rifle and was about to shoot when I heard a muffled report and my caribou went down. I knew the rest would have gone. Since I'd never seen them, I had no idea where, but caribou are strange animals. They'll dash off madly when scared, and just as likely double back in a short while to see what had scared them.

So I stood waiting, and after what seemed to be hours but was likely only five minutes or so, I saw shadows in the snow racing back and coming to a stop almost in front of me. By now, the little light that we'd had was failing into the night. I picked out what looked to be the largest animal and fired. I had the satisfaction of seeing it go down. The others were gone by the time I'd reloaded.

So there I was. I had my deer, but where was Joe and his animal?

I needn't have wondered. Out of the dusk and the storm came Little Joe, grinning from ear to ear. He knew he'd probably see the first caribou and it was a great joke to him to shoot it under my nose.

We were talking about tracking, weren't we? Well I'll tell you, we skinned and cut up those two caribou, took enough for a meal and one for the dogs. By that time it was pitch dark. Joe said, "Go home for supper," and started off. I followed his shadow and never walked a longer mile in my life. Dark? It was absolute blackness and there were rocks and things to be wary of. It's no joke walking in the dark over rough country. You lift a foot and expect to put it down on the same level as its mate, but you find it brings up much sooner than you had anticipated. You are standing with one foot on a boulder, what do you do now. Put the other foot up there too, or bring the first one back? Decisions, decisions. But that was nothing to the fact that I wondered if Joe had even the slightest idea where we were. Again, not to worry. The first thing I knew I was stumbling among the dog traces. They, sensible animals, had gone to sleep, hardly expecting to see us until better weather and more light.

In a short time we'd built up a snow wall, since there was no hard snow to make an igloo, and put our *komatik* wrapper over the top, fed the hungry dogs, and were sitting in our makeshift shelter with a primus stove going, watching the meat cook by the light of a candle.

We needed six caribou, and in the next day or so we got them, all except for the last day in blizzard conditions, but Joe acted as if he could see for miles. He'd pick up tracks, decide that they were fresh enough to follow and we'd be away. The last day the weather improved, and it was possible to see where we'd been hunting. To me it was a wonder that we hadn't been killed by falling over a cliff and said so to Joe. He just laughed and said, "When you follow caribou in drift you not got to worry. He don't fall over cliff, so you don't too." Well and good for someone who could not only see in the dark, he could see tracks where none existed.

We picked up all our meat and headed back. On the way out the valley, in the first trees that we saw, we found a party of white hunters who'd been there for days waiting for the weather to improve. They were experienced men who knew that there was no chance for them until they could see. They weren't a bit surprised to see that we had got caribou. Joe never came home empty handed. On one of our last camps I said something to that effect. He said, "Most times I do good enough, but once old black bear he beat me." Seems that Joe had a net some distance from where he was camped. It was late fall and there were not many salmon, but he'd get two or three every day. He was salting them lightly in preparation for smoking for his winter breakfasts. So he had a barrel full of weak brine near the net.

Several times he put salmon in the barrel and as regularly the bear would come at night and help himself. Joe tried everything, deadfalls, traps, but as he said the bear was too cute. That being a Labrador expression meaning smart.

Well he was getting no place and the sealing was good so he couldn't stay there and wait for the bear. Also I figure he was too stubborn to just take the fish home. So he said, "I got big old double barrel must loader (muzzle loading musket). He set it up and attached a line to the triggers and arranged it so that the bear would pick up a salmon, pull on the line and shoot himself. So Joe said he was sitting at home smoking his pipe, when bang went the old blunderbuss. He waited for the second barrel but not a sound, and he figured he'd gotten his bear. It was a bright moonlight night, so he decided to paddle across to see his victim. He said, "I paddle very quiet, big moon, I can see good. Then I see that bear, he standing up, and I see he got the gun. You know what that bear do? He find the gun, shoot one barrel so I come running to see him dead, and he ready for me with second barrel. If I walk over, not paddle, he shoot me sure."

I said, "Joe, if old Uncle Joe Michelin hadn't told me that story I'd believe it happened to you." Joe looked at me very solemnly and said, "That old Joe Michelin he steal my story. Never mind, he old man, not live long, then I tell my bear story some more." But by a lot of different camp fires in very different places, Joe told me many yarns that were true, perhaps not exciting to a lot of people, but stories that were impressive when one remembered the amount of knowledge and ability that little man had stored up in his head.

I remember once on a trip stopping at Joe's house. There was a travelling minister who happened to arrive at the same time. He was telling us about an accident up the coast where a girl out hunting ptarmigan had slipped on the ice, dropped her little .22 rifle, which had discharged and the bullet had gone through her skull and lodged between the skull and brain. The parson and a doctor happened to arrive shortly after the girl's father had found her. He told us how, by the light of a flashlight, the doctor was able to remove the bullet and move her to a hospital by dog team where she was recovering. Joe thought a while and said, "Pretty cute, that doctor." The parson said, "Yes, but he spent nearly ten years of his life learning to do that sort of thing." Joe said, "When I'm small boy, my father started teaching me things. All the time I learn some more every day. I getting old man now, sometimes I think I don't know very much." I guess his life was one long learning process.

Like all his race, there was genius in his hands. He could make and fix. He could handle a boat or dog team so that he was noted in a country where these things were an indication of a man's worth. He could watch a clerk add up a long counter slip in the store, and even though it was upside down, he'd have the answer, and correctly, before the clerk, and he never had a day of formal education. He learned somehow to read and could write a letter in English or his own language.

There were several Joe Pallisers. He always signed his name Jos. Palliser of John. Last summer, when Doris Saunders of the magazine *Them Days* was here, and she and I were talking about many of the people that were around when I was young, Kejuk's name came up. She'd never heard of him, but when I said Jos. Palliser of John she knew immediately. He died only a few years ago, and before he went she recorded a lot of his memories. I asked about the bear and the musk-loader. She hadn't heard it, not from him or Joe Michelin, who I believe was the original liar, so I gave it to her as I remember it. It should go in Joe's dossier.

More characters from Len Budgell's youth.

Top left Joe Michelin, Rigolet, former lumberman, teller of yarns.
LAC/FRED C. SEARS/INTERNATIONAL GRENFELL ASSN.

Bottom left Gilbert "Bert" Blake, trapper, North West River, c.1930.
LAC/FRED C. SEARS

Right Joe Palliser, Rigolet, an Inuit man with whom a young Len Budgell
hunted caribou in the Mealy Mountains. VAL HEARDER/THEM DAYS

The Hudson's Bay Company supply ship *Nascopie* held up in ice in Eastern Arctic waters, 1934. HBCA/HARVEY R. BASSETT

Captain Thomas F. Smellie aboard the *Nascopie*, 1938. This is the photo Len speaks about. HBCA/LORENE SQUIRE

Photographer Lorene Squire at Chesterfield Inlet, August 11, 1938.
Len Budgell, aboard the *Nascopie*, was assigned to assist her.

The captain's table on the *Nascopie*, 1938. From left: J.W. Anderson, R.C. Bishop Clabait, Ralph Parsons, Captain Smellie, Major D.L. McKeand, Superintendent T.B. Caulkin, W.E. Brown. HBCA/LORENE SQUIRE

Bow of the *Nascopie*. HBCA

Henry Voisey operating a HBC radio system. Henry, once Len's
schoolmate, was a life-long friend. CLARA VOISEY

Chief radio operator S.G.L Horner aboard the *Nascopie*, 1938. He developed
the HBC northern radio communications system. HBCA/LORENE SQUIRE

P.A.C. Nichols and his wife aboard the *Nascopie*, 1940.
Nichols was HBC post manager at several northern locations, eventually
Section Manager, Western Arctic, and Manager, Transport Division.

Art Atkinson, HBC bush pilot. HBCA

H.J. Winney, bush pilot, 1947. HBCA/J.W. ANDERSON

"Wolstenholme Post—Trading into Hudson Bay"
Hudson's Bay Company 1935 calendar, from an original painting by Adam
Sherriff Scott. Len Budgell was HBC manager at Wolstenholme in 1942–3.

Father Pierre Henri meeting Pope John Paul, c.1965.
Photo given by Father Henri to Gerald Coutu (Claudia's Coutu Radmore's father) on Baffin Island, 1969. Len Budgell met Father Henri while stationed at Repulse Bay, 1945–6.

Leonard Budgell and Muriel Watson on their wedding day, 1947.
BUDGELL FAMILY

Len and Muriel with Pat and Maureen, Christmas 1954. BUDGELL FAMILY

Len and Muriel with Pat (age 4) and Maureen, 1952. BUDGELL FAMILY

Captain Frank Melvin Shaw, a captain on HBC ships when Len Budgell was based in Tuktoyaktuk. HBCA MOCCASIN TELEGRAPH, SUMMER 1976

Captain Len Adey (right) greeting L.A. Learmonth, HBC post manager at Cambridge Bay, aboard the *Fort Hearne*, August 1954. HBCA/DON BLAIR

W.E. Brown at Pekangekum. He was instrumental in developing the HBC's
northern radio communications system. HBCA/D.D. MCLAREN

Acrial view of Pekangekum, November 5, 1965. Len Budgell was HBC
manager at the northwestern Ontario settlement 1951–5. HBCA

Leonard Budgell at Cartwright, Labrador, 1935.

Speaking of Joe Michelin and lies, he once told my dad that when he first came to Labrador the curlew were so numerous that a man could fire one shot and get enough to give him a curlew every Sunday for a year. He said, as a matter of fact, that once he had fired one shot and picked up ninety-nine birds. My dad said, "Might as well say you got a hundred." The old man looked shocked. "What, tell a lie for one lousy curlew?" So there was Uncle Joe Michelin, who wouldn't tell a lie but could spin yarns of his days in the lumber woods in Quebec that rivalled Paul Bunyan. In fact, they were so close to the Bunyan yarns that you'd think they were the same. They couldn't have been, Uncle Joe didn't tell lies.

You guessed it, yarn spinning was a favourite evening entertainment where there was no radio or TV and only a limited number of records for the few old wind-up gramophones. Old Uncle Jesse Flowers, one of our principal yarn spinners at Rigolet, used to say, "Now I can't guarantee this is true, but a man who never in his life told a lie, told me."

Was to the market this morning. Have to admit the market does have lovely blueberries. They should, at the prices they charge. One of my favourites too. Rigolet was a great place for berries of all kinds, and the late fall blueberries were a great target for the fall geese. We'd try to get what we needed before the hungry young geese came to the coast from inland. They soon scoffed the blueberries and went after the low bush cranberries, marshberries and bake apples too.

Greed did get the best of them though and a good few ended up in the oven because they were too busy eating to watch for hunters. We always kept the biggest fattest goose for Christmas. We had a special airtight box to keep fall meat in. Using a mixture of ice and salt we could freeze a bird early in the fall and have it in perfect condition for Christmas. My dad insisted on goose for Christmas and salted salmon for Good Friday. The other holidays got what we happened to have.

I wasn't very old when a lucky shot got me a big Canada goose.

Can I really remember it? Not only can I remember the actual stalk and shooting, I can remember how my breath hurt in my chest, how my hands shook with excitement. I knew I could never hold the gun steady, but at the last moment I found that I could. As I've said so many times, we were brought up to hunt. We had to, and because it was a necessary part of living, there was a wonderful joy in bringing home a Sunday dinner.

I can still taste that first goose. My dad carved at the table and he served the meat from the platter. My mother served the vegetables. I can see him now as he laid that crusty gold slice on a plate and passed it to my mother. "First cut to the hunter." There were several clerks and employees and my dad at the table, all adults, all hunters, but it was my goose, my first one. I was alone when I got him and he was a heavy lug back home over the hills and through the marshes.

I put a good many more on the table later on, but that is the one that I remember. I got home late, after dark. My mother always worried. They had just about finished supper when I turned up. Mother heard the door and came out, relieved that I was back alive, and in her relief inclined to scold me for being late. "What kept you?" I can't tell you the pride that was in my heart and in my voice when I said, "This old fellow, I think he weighs twenty pounds," and I dropped him on the floor as if I'd brought a hundred others home. I got a wash and went in to the dining room and got seated.

My dad started serving whatever there was and old Mr. Parsons, the customs officer, who ate all his meals at the house said, "Any luck, boy?" I said as modestly as a ten-year-old who has just got his first wild goose can, "Oh, I got a goose." The old man, a retired ship master said, "You did, well I'll be damned," then quickly to my mother who wouldn't have swearing in the house, "Saving your presence my dear," and he had to know where I got him, how, and all the details. He said to my dad, "We got a coming hunter here. Remember that when you have no further use for the rifle."

That almost brought tears, because the rifle in question was one

Scenes in the Torngat Mountains, Labrador, a region that greatly impressed Len Budgell.

Above Cape White Handkerchief. MUN

Opposite, top Cape Mugford. MUN

Opposite, bottom Bishop's Mitre. MUN

his son, Ralph Parsons, the last fur trade commissioner of the HBC, and my hero, had given his Dad years before. When Uncle Bill's eyes gave out, he gave the rifle to my dad. It was a beautiful gun, and if I'd ever been asked what the thing I most wanted would be, I'd have said a .22 high-power savage. And now it was going to be mine, not right away perhaps, but I would own it one day.

Sure enough, when I was in Hebron my dad decided the time had come and he sent it to me. It travelled with me a number of years. I left it at home when I went into the army, and after the war I was going to Igloolik from Churchill so my folks sent all my things from Labrador on *Nascopie* and she was lost on the way in. I grieved for that firearm, but some how it was appropriate. Ralph Parsons, the *Nascopie* and that gun opened up the Eastern Arctic. I don't mean that the gun played any significant part, but it was there, and since R.P. was long dead, what better place for the gun to rest than on board *Nascopie*, my favourite ship, on her last voyage.

I wish I had some new or exciting news, but things don't change much. One more month of summer and we'll be looking at frosty nights again. Used to be that was just another joy, especially with the fur trade. The trappers would be getting restless and one by one they'd disappear, nothing left in the summer campsite except bare poles and floors of wilting spruce boughs. An abandoned Indian camp is a lonely thing, mostly because they leave the poles behind. Even in summer, to suddenly come across an empty muskrat trapping camp is an odd sensation. There will be weeds and new poplar half way up the tent poles, but the signs of life are still there. A broken toboggan board, a pile of shavings where some one made a paddle, a few tin cans strung together and hanging in a tree, saves Mom calling the kids back before they wander too far. A jangle of the tin ware means get back here—quick.

Eskimo camps aren't lonely. There are no tent poles, nothing is left, a ring of stones that marked the tent, that's all. Eskimo country is so big and open that there is no place for loneliness I guess. For me it's possible to feel quite alone in the bush, never in the barrens or the Arctic, but I can't tell you why. The loneliness of the bush is a good loneliness though, especially at night, when all the trees crowd a bit closer and gossip under the stars.

They watch you too, you can feel it. Marjorie MacDonald, "The Egg and I," said mountains watch you too. I've felt it. It's an impression you get. If you come at a mountain across a wide valley, it seems to stare at you, and as you get closer and closer it seems to bend over to look at this strange little thing that's crawling around its ankles. Okay, so it's the changing angle that convinces you that the mountain bends over. If you are alone, it's kind of nice to have a friendly mountain watching your progress, just the same as it's nice when you are all nicely bedded down in the bush to have the huge spruces move a bit closer and stand with their heads together watching the tiny spark of your candle. And when you put the candle out and the fire dies, you can hear them whispering together, with maybe a big old horned owl chuckling to himself at his own jokes.

You know a horned owl can make more strange noises. His hoot is quiet and mournful, but the rest of his tricks can amaze you. He can make a noise like running water in the middle of winter, imitating a creaking tree in child's play, and once in a great while a mad person's laugh that can scare the boots off you. Poor old Mr. Bunny will be quietly ambling across a moonlit clearing, minding his own business, when this mad woman screams right beside him. He isn't wise enough to streak for the nearest cover. No, he sits upright and his black shadow on the snow tells Mr. Owl what he wants to know and bang, midnight supper.

I once spent a night in a tent with crazy John Michelin, a man who'd do anything on a dare, who was one of the best woodsmen in the Height of Land trappers. He could walk further and faster, carry heavier loads than anyone else and laughed and joked the whole day long. Well, John put a candle low on the ground inside the white tent and he made rabbit shadows with his hands on the canvas. After a while, we could hear two owls talking together about the funny goings on. After a while, they decided to investigate and they came over low, almost touching the tent. We could see them by the light of the moon, and their shadows made breath-catching cruciforms on the canvas. You'd have loved them. Great outstretched wings, and in the clear moonlight, the taut wing feathers were faithfully reproduced for a second on the tent roof. A second of intense beauty and motion.

They never came back, but that second is frozen forever in a special chamber in my memory. Not a sound, just a sudden flash of black shadow, one just slightly ahead of the other. Flat images one would say, no indication of the fierce eyes and claws or of the big soft bodies in perfect soundless flight. In my memory I see them as two black cut-outs in the sky, giving for one moment a glimpse into a world of mystery and motion. I don't suppose there is a camera made that could record that moment, or an operator so skilled that he could catch it. I'm glad too, because it's mine and I wouldn't want to see it reproduced in Life over some silly caption.

From the sublime to the ridiculous. I was once, in my Easter holiday, given the job of taking the travelling doctor from Rigolet to West Bay, where he'd be picked up for the next relay along the coast. I had our travelling team, twelve or fifteen big dogs and an excellent leader, with a light *komatik*. The middle-aged doctor and I sat aboard and the dogs romped along in great style. As we had a light load, the first fifteen miles was along the shore with pretty well perpendicular cliffs on one side, and a few feet away on the other the open water of the inlet which, due to strong tides, seldom freezes.

I had been brought up on the ballicaters, as the narrow ice foot along the shore is called. The doctor had seen little of the same on the playing fields of Eton. He hung on for dear life and cringed when we made a sharp turn to go around a corner and the back end of the *komatik* and his long legs hung over deep freezing water. Almost no one ever actually fell in, so, though he knew it not, he was in no danger.

When we got to fast ice, deep, firm and with no water to be seen in any direction, he confided to me that the terror mark of all his winter travelling was reached when he left Rigolet "bound up the bay," and again in summer, when his little ship was buffeted by the tides and whirlpools that kept the "infernal" place open in winter. I rode a long mile or two digesting this, as I'd always been of the opinion that we at Rigolet had the best of possible worlds. Winter and its delights on one hand, and on the other, open water that brought us our share of seals and eider ducks all winter as well as some of the more cold resistant fish like smelt and trout.

Anyhow, that's not what I started to tell you. The second day out, as we were spanking down the back way, we caught up with Israel Williams. He deserves a little description.

The grandson of an old HBC seaman who decided one fall to remain on Labrador and marry an Eskimo woman, Israel was one of the hairiest people I ever knew. He was also not quite the average model. He was short, very broad, with exceptionally long arms and a bent spine. Standing fully erect, Israel could touch his knees with his palms. All you could see of his face was the tip of a red nose and two black eyes. The hair and beard looked like an enormous black mop.

Shy as a mouse and timid, he lived in a place called Flatwater with his brother Tom and his family. It was an out of the way place so they saw very few people. Their women and children were even more shy. They were good trappers and fishermen, but even though they had a good income, due to their odd shapes, clothes purchased or even made at home never fitted very well.

So, away out on the ice of the back way, we fell in with Israel. He'd been to Rigolet to stock up on grub to last them over the break-up season. He had a small team of small dogs. He lived too far from salt water to get many seals, which meant his dogs ate mostly fish, not the best diet for working dogs, who thrive on the meat and fat of seals. He was poking along at a snail's pace, using a pole to push on the back of his *komatik* to help his dogs a little. It was a warm day, the sun was bright, the snow soft, and his heavily loaded *komatik* wasn't long enough to "bear up" as we used to say and it was ploughing along half-buried in snow.

Israel's place was of course one of the doctor's calls. He visited every house and camp along the coast. As a matter of fact, we had expected that our second night out would be spent at Flatwater. So we pulled up alongside Israel, and I loaded all his freight on my *komatik*, which was twice as long as his and had ten times the dog power. He said the river at the end of the Back Way was bad and that we should wait for him there as he knew where all the good ice was.

We went on ahead, and when we got to the river, Israel was nowhere in sight behind. Both the doctor and I had previously spent nights in Israel's tiny crowded cabin, which was dark and airless. It seemed to be just too much when we had a beautiful evening coming on and a most inviting campsite right at hand. So we decided to camp there, wait till the night frost had dried the water off the ice and frozen the deep snow on the long portage across the land to Israel's. The sky was clear, so we made an open camp. No tent, just the shelter of a huge spruce and a big fire of dry wood. We were all set up when Israel and his exhausted dogs showed up. We were well supplied with man and dog food so we gave Israel and his team a good supper. He was a bit amazed that we intended to sleep in "them old bushies," rather than go on for a couple of hours to his house, but he was tired and very happy to be there with all his goods instead of being miles up the bay struggling with a heavy load. Now you say, we were talking about owls, where are the owls in all this? Well hang on, girl, we'll get to that. Terrible thought, I may well have told you all this before, if so, "I 'umbly begs your pardin."

Labrador is a pretty country. Hamilton Inlet, or as it was once called, Esquimaux Bay, is prettier than most other places. We had an ideal place to camp, by the side of a little river that was already half open, and the water rioted madly down between the banks in the first rush of the spring thaw. We could look from where we sat straight up the Back Way to where the hills come down to the Narrows, forty miles away, and above the Narrows there are sixty miles of level ice to the far western end where North West River is situated.

We were blessed with a calm, clear evening, and it was still warm as we sat after our supper watching the sun head for the notch of the Narrows and fit right neatly in, then expire in a blaze of red glory beyond the rim of ice that was our horizon.

The doctor, who was a literary sort of bloke, quoted from a long comfortable sort of poem ending with "and seldom have I seen such a setting of the sun." I don't think he got through to Israel, who could neither read, write or figure, but who had an extraordinary pleasant voice and who could sing long painful ballads about sickness, death and jails for hours at a time if you managed to get him started. I tried but he was too shy. Too bad, because he sang them in a dialect long out of normal use. They were brought over from the old country many years before and passed from father to son. The doctor was hoping to hear them too but Israel said maybe his son, Garge, would oblige when we got to his house. George, or Garge, was as short, hairy and ill-shaped as the rest but had a lovely tenor voice.

Once the sun had gone, we built up the fire and sat around in complete comfort drinking a last cup of tea. There is nothing that tastes better than a trapper's tea. You boil the water, put in the tea, leave the lid off, and hold your pail over the fire for a second or two till the tea boils up once. Only once remember. Tea made like that will taste different and all the leaves will settle to the bottom. That's only a hint in passing and has nothing to do with owls, what gave you that idea?

We yarned a couple hours away and Israel smoked a short black pipe that was so close to his nose and whiskers that it was a wonder his whole head didn't go up in flames. He'd take a flaming brand out of the fire and apply it to the pipe and I'd think, this is it, he'll go this time. How can you tell a man's wife that his whiskers caught fire and he went out in a blaze of glory. Well he didn't, I'm glad to relate, and because of the extreme purity of the air, the smoke from Israel's black plug tobacco was in no way offensive, just a pleasant counterpoint to the smell of the brush (brushies) we sat on, and the tea and the wild marshy smell of the running water. The doctor said it all as he got into his sleeping bag. He said, "May my best friend, sometime in his life, have one evening like this. There could never be two."

Israel wasn't too well supplied with bedding. His plan was not to camp outside but to reach someone's house every night, mostly for the visiting, the gossip and singing that went on. But he had a couple of blankets and he built up the fire and lay close, again awakening in me a fear that I should see Israel immolated before this trip was ended. He wasn't and I didn't. We were all asleep in a short time.

Once the sun went down, the frost went to work, the melting stopped. The fire burnt low and sometime in the night Israel's blankets started to admit more of the night air than he wanted and he got up to replenish the blaze. It had nearly gone out but he raked a few glowing coals together and laid some small pieces of wood thereon, and in order to make it catch more quickly, he got down on his hands and knees and started to blow on the coals.

Now I've mentioned that Israel lacked a number of things. One was the services of a barber. I guess his wife caught him occasionally and chopped off a few locks, Sampson and Delilah fashion, but he always had a veritable tuckamore of a head. Well that head was silhouetted against the coals and probably looked like an early rising partridge or something of the sort. A horned owl sitting in a tree saw it and figured, "Well here's breakfast," and he struck.

Israel's mop probably saved him severe scalp lacerations but the bird had dug its claws in, expecting to lift whatever it was that it struck. It just couldn't let Israel go either, and it couldn't lift him. It beat the air with its powerful wings and threw ashes and fire all over the place.

The doctor and I woke in a hurry, and my first thought was, He's gone and done it after all. All I could see was Israel in the centre of a tornado or something. I couldn't see very well at that. Our fire had produced a lot of fine ash in the hours it had been burning, and most of that ash was presently being agitated by a pretty hefty pair of wings. I wasn't long in getting out of my sleeping bag, and did the first thing I thought of. I flung one of Israel's blankets over what seemed to be his head and the turmoil ceased somewhat.

The doctor had a powerful flashlight and by it we could see part of Israel's head and face and part of the south end of a pretty big bird. The doc was a Britisher, and they like to be brisk, so he said, "What's the trouble Israel," and Israel who was about dead with terror anyway said weakly, "A 'orrible big devil bin got me by de 'eed yeer, I be dead for sure!"

Well, by carefully keeping the owl's head covered, and by shifting the blanket around, we finally found the huge claws still clutching at Israel's hair which was about the texture and strength of small steel wire. Holding the bird by the leg, I tried to loosen its claw. I might as well have tried to break a steel shackle with my fingers. He had one claw on each side of Israel's head and was holding on like grim death. He wasn't moving but now and then he'd make a fierce burping sound that boded us no good if he ever got his eyes uncovered.

Israel was crouching like he was carved in stone. I wondered how long his heart would stand. But doctors are equipped, and this one dived into his medicine box and came up with a big pair of shears. He worked the points in between the bird's foot, which I held at the ankle, if owls have ankles, if not, at whatever joint they have instead, and after a lot of huffing and puffing, he liberated one claw which still gripped a big ball of pure William's hair. Then he moved around to the other side and cut the other foot clear.

The rest was simple. I carried the owl a little away from the fire and Israel, set him on a dead tree that had fallen, and whipped the blanket off his head. It was too dark to see the expression on his face. I have an idea that he was displeased. He sat there a couple of seconds balancing on his claws that still clutched a part of Israel, then he took off. I have a picture in my mind of a sadly frustrated owl sitting high in a tree looking at two claws full of a black kinky substance, and wondering what sort of an animal he'd almost got.

There were ashes everywhere, in our own hair, our bedding, even in our grub box. The kettle had been flung into outer darkness and we decided that it was no use in going back to sleep. The doctor checked to see that Israel hadn't been cut, and Israel put on his big fur hat but had no intention of going any place near the fire.

It wasn't till daylight came that we saw the damage the doctor's shears had done. Two great areas just above Israel's ears had been sheared to the skin. Probably that part of Israel hadn't been exposed to the sun since he was five or six. The doctor was a kind-hearted man, and he went for a hasty walk out on the ice. He seemed to be having a bit of a problem keeping his composure. Have you ever seen the two pouches on the head of a prairie chicken doing its mating dance? Well Israel was by no means a sleek dancing bird, but he did have two huge white spots on the sides of his head.

There had been a good frost, and with full light, Israel pointed out the safest route across the river and we took off leaving Israel to follow. We made a brief stop at his house to leave his groceries and to advise his wife that he'd soon be along. No one needed a doctor and we went on. The doctor, usually a very sober man, cracked up half a dozen times that morning. He'd say, "I wonder what Israel's wife thought when he took off his hat?" Knowing Israel and his ways that might not have been for a while, say a year or so. But I bet it made a good yarn over many cups of tea and pipes of tobacco.

Israel finally came to a sad end. He lived close to Tramore, the Wonderstrand of the Viking Sagas, forty miles of pure white sand which rises from the sea to two hundred feet in height. During the war, the US navy, lying ten miles at sea, decided to use it for target practice and they shelled it for several hours. Israel and his family were not in line of fire, but of course they didn't know that. They crouched in their house till the shooting stopped and found that terror had killed poor old Israel. I guess the Yanks sailed away never knowing they had killed a harmless old man.

August 29, 1986

Dear Leisale,

I like the name they have given you, and the meaning. Of course, you aren't the "woman from across the water" to me, but it has a lovely sound.

You mentioned Little Joe. Only a few days ago I was hunting for a book on the RCMP ship *St. Roche* for my niece's young son, who's crazy about "old things." Here now, the *St. Roche* and I are from the same generation! Well, we'll let that pass. Anyhow, when I was looking, and making a tour of various books on the way, I picked up a copy of *Them Days*, and there was Little Joe, at a much more advanced age than I knew him, but not all that much changed. Joe had heartbreaking luck with his first four children, who only lived a very short time. Then his last son was born and he lived and was Joe's whole world. What Joe knew, he taught the boy. You'd expect a spoiled child, but no way. The child would sit shivering with excitement and anticipation while they drifted in a small boat waiting for a seal.

And when they were lucky, he'd hardly contain himself. He took his part in the hauling out and cutting up. His mother, a very quiet woman, would stand beaming at her two men and their catch, but Joe was the boss. A word from him, and the boy obeyed. I never knew him when he grew up, but if he was like his dad, he was a good man.

There is something in me that desperately wants to go back to see the sun on the green hills, to see the snow-capped mountains that Joe and I hunted on. I want to go back to the things that cannot change, like old Father Henri, who passed most of his life in the Arctic. I would like my last sight to be across a frozen sea or of an Arctic mountain, but also like good Father Henri, I will not be there at the end. He tried so hard to get his bishop to send him back to the tiny stone house that he built at Pelley Bay. But it wasn't possible, and a man that gave his

life to a cause was denied his last wish. He had never disputed anything his Superiors wanted so he died in a clean hospital bed, with
attentive doctors and nurses to care for him, with only one desire,
as he told me, to see "my old land." Not the warm fields of Brittany
where he was born, but the rocks and crags of almost the utmost end
of northern Canada.

Remember I told you about Mrs. Oldenburg landing and leaving
me the bread and tomatoes and Father Henri was having a "fast day"?
Did I tell you that later that spring I managed to get a goose, though
geese are not common around Repulse. By then, we were getting a
few seals and had a little fuel. The only way to cook my gander was to
boil him over a fire of seal fat outside the house. I told the father that
if this was another fast day I'd feel obliged to write to the pope and
complain about his management. He said it wasn't a fast day so we sat
outside on the rocks and fished bits of boiled goose out of the pot till
there was none left. Don't know why I thought of that just now.

I like thinking of Father Henri. When I was at Repulse we had no
fuel so we could get barely enough to drink. As a matter of fact, I
used to fill a big pickle jar with ice and take it into the sleeping robe
with me. Eventually it would turn to slush and I'd get a drink. It was
an experience to have that cold glass next against my back during the
night. There are easier ways to waken. Then spring came. Repulse is
right on the Arctic Circle so spring arrives slowly. But one day Father
Henri and I were hunting up in the hills and found a shallow lake
that was about half ice, half water. It was a sunny day, fairly warm
by Repulse standards and that water was so inviting. We took off our
boots and put our feet in. It was bearable for a few seconds at a time.
We had not been able to bathe for many months, so I said we should
try. Father Henri's modesty would not allow him to strip in my presence so he went a little further along and I stripped and tried walking
out over the smooth rock that formed the bottom of the lake, but it
was impossible. The line of water around my ankles was pure liquid
fire. I knew I could never walk in far enough to splash the rest of me,

so I went back out and when the agony had gone, at least partly, out of my feet, I found a place where the water was about shoulder deep and I gathered my courage together and plunged in.

I don't think there was any sensation for a few second; then I was conscious of the most rending pain I had ever felt. I've been in icy water many times, fully clothed, and by accident. The clothing helps and the fact that it is accidental helps. One is only interested in getting out, the pain comes later. This time I was unclothed and it was deliberate. The pain seemed to shoot down from the centre of my body to my legs and feet, into my arms. If I could have, I would have screamed but my breath had stopped. To save my feet on the rocks I had jumped in crouched and I went completely under.

The reaction was immediate, and I lost all my strength. I knew I wasn't breathing and I forced myself to swim maybe four or five strokes, then I shoved my feet against the bottom and shot straight up and managed to get on the shore. Naked as a baby jay, I shot off across the rocks. I couldn't have stood still and as soon as I got my breath, I let out a yell that could have been heard for miles, I'm sure. I ran around in the sun but I was shivering so uncontrollably that I couldn't get into my clothes. The only thing to do was run. When I finally began to get some feeling back, I looked around for the father and a quarter of a mile away I could see a white figure with a long beard doing the same dervish dance that I was.

There is no way to describe the searing agony that strikes with the water. It took a long time to regain circulation and when we were finally dressed and warm again, the sensation was glorious. How much accumulated grime came off in that brief plunge I can't say but we felt wonderful. On the way home Father Henri smiled thoughtfully at me and said, "We are not of very wise mind, Len." I would find it hard to believe that I would do it again, but many times that spring I went into water that was nearly as cold. I avoided pools with any ice in them. It's not something you get used to, that's certain, but such is the power of open water that one does such irresponsible things. I will say that nothing will change a white skin into a scarlet one any faster. I remember looking at my feet and legs and thinking only a tern has feet that red. On the way home we met an elderly Eskimo, and he listened to what we had done and said gravely, "*Wah kad lunga*," which can be translated as "How terrible!" but can mean so much more when spoken by a short stocky person who knows every way to survive in the world's most severe climate, and jumping naked into pools of ice water isn't one of them. He possibly thought, "…whom the gods will destroy, they first make mad." If, as I suspect, he saw us running over the tundra in our birthday suits, bright red and gasping strange words in English and French, he probably had a mirthful audience when he told his day's experiences in the tupik that evening. I can stand under a soothing shower now and remember, even with a little longing, those plunges into that water of fire, and I'll never forget how I felt after. Mad dogs and Englishmen go out in the midday sun. Only Newfies jump into ice water, though what excuse Father Henri had, I can't say.[27]

Winnipeg, October 16, 1986

Dear Claudia,

I shall have to see how this goes. Perhaps you'll turn out to be my wailing wall. Let me say now that nothing is wrong, at least nothing that I can do anything about. Briefly I have just returned from a visit to W.E. Brown in Vancouver. He is eighty-six now.

He is suffering from Alzheimer's disease. I found it hard. We have been friends and co-workers for years. I admire him very much and he is failing fast, not in a physical sense, but his memory is going. He

27 Father Henri was known to the Netsilik as Kai i o (The Red One), because of his red beard, and perhaps for other reasons.

recognized me and knew Muriel. We talked about old days in the
Arctic and in Transport. Then suddenly he stared at me a long time
and finally asked my name. I told him and he said, "Not Len Budgell, my best friend?" I had to say yes and that seemed to lift the veil.
He was very agitated and said that he was going crazy. I managed to
change the subject, and in a few minutes he seemed to have forgotten
it. I have just finished a long letter to another of his friends, Professor
Rowley of Carleton University, telling him how I found W.E. That
wasn't easy either so I looked around for someone compassionate
and understanding and thought of you and how long it's been since I
wrote. I feel better already.

Our trip to BC and back was a mundane sort of adventure but we
enjoyed it. Not one leaf had fallen, not one had escaped nature's
paintbrush. Breathe it not to a soul, but there were times when the
Rockies were almost as pulsing with colour as Labrador can be. Not
quite, but almost.

   You would not believe Labrador in fall. Rigolet, where I spent my
thoughtless youth, was on a straight stretch of the narrows that con-
nects the outer bay with Hamilton Inlet. Leading straight west is the
Double Mere, and almost straight east, the Backway. These are bays
fifty miles deep. The hills are high and steep, forested from the water's
edge to the summits, which are bare, but not obviously so. The forest growing almost to the top provides them with a frieze of green,
and when the first snow falls, it melts near the water but stays on the
higher hills, providing a contrast of white and green. The trees are
largely spruce and fir, but there are expanses of birch, larch, aspen
and dogwood, as well as the various berry trees. In some places there
will be a bold swath of lighter green from the top of a hill to the water.
These are the birches. The colour is quite noticeable in summer, but
with the first frost they become swaths of gold and red, painted in one
stroke by a gigantic brush. The only way to experience it is by boat.
You can sail far enough away from land so that you can see every col-

our, yet near enough to appreciate detail. Even when I was young, I knew I was seeing beauty that could not be matched.

I once caught a ride with an old Eskimo, Mark Palliser. He had a whaleboat with no engine. His power was the wind, or in a calm, the efforts of his old wife and her two sisters on the oars. There was very little wind, but it was with us. We soaked along at a couple miles an hour, vastly content in the warm fall sun. We stopped on convenient little islands to boil a kettle for tea, eat a few of the millions of ripe berries, and check for any sign of bear or caribou. Mark was on a hunting trip but not working very hard at it. The wind was cool, the planks of the boat comfortable in the warm sun.

It was a day when work and hurry were out of mind, the clock forgotten. The three old ladies sat together and muttered away to one another, their eyes missing nothing. Mark sat in the stern, the tiller under his arm, and his black pipe in his mouth. Me? I lay on a pile of nets just out of the wind but well in the sun. I slept, and when I awoke, I watched the hills as we slowly passed them. The colours in the hills were somehow remote and unreachable. Those on the slopes were brilliant and friendly. Every shade of red and yellow you can imagine.

Late in the afternoon, we passed the last of the islands and picked up a breeze from the sea. As we left the narrows, old Mark stood up and stared back at the calm water and glowing colour behind. He said, "Me, I live here all my time, summer and winter. I think the old bay, he more pretty as anything." Amen, Mark.

TWELVE

Winnipeg, December 12, 1986

Dear Leisale,

You know I'm very fortunate to have you as a correspondent. The letters flow along so. Do you know the word "swent"? Well that's a Newfie way of saying extra smooth, extra delightful. Once a man showed me his baby son, his first boy, the one he'd hoped for for years and years. The baby lay on his stomach, bare nekkid, kicking his feet, and was obviously the greatest thing in his dad's world. The father ran his hand over the little boy's head, down his back to his heels, and he said to me, "Swent, oh so swent." I don't know where the word came from or what it should be, but the look on the man's face gave it all the meaning any word on the breath of a man could have. So your letters are swent. They flow, and things come in from the edges toward the centre, like a huge gentle whirlpool that goes dreamily round and round on a calm, warm summer day.

What do I know about whirlpools? I grew up among them, short fierce ones that split away from the eddy formed by the last of the ebb like tide in the inlet, and joined the faster flow into the inlet. Most were too small to be of much danger, though they could give you a feeling of their power when they grabbed the keel of your boat and shook it, and you suddenly knew that they, not you, were in control for the moment. It didn't last long, but there is always an underlying feeling of panic when you cannot influence the direction you want to go. They'd soon pass and hurry along. On a calm day, there would be a huge dimple in the water, perhaps ten feet across, with steep black glass sides and right at the bottom a collection of flotsam, bits of sticks, sea weed, and perhaps jellyfish.

That sort went by our dock all day long and around the point, not easy to see on windy days, but perfect to watch on a calm quiet Sunday when you were warned that the Sunday clothes must be preserved. I'd lie on the wharf and watch them pass between the big ballast cribs and drop a few bits and pieces in the centre just to help out. Lying on the dock wasn't so good for Sunday clothes either.

But we had the big fellows too. We were never allowed near them till we had reached the age of some sort of reason. By then we'd heard so many yarns of boats, whales, and men that had been sucked down and never seen again, that we approached with great caution. They formed in the Backway, where there is a big island almost directly across the inlet. The tide comes in from the Atlantic and hits the island, where it splits—one arm going west and usually behaving itself very well, the other arm goes east and is in conflict with the enormous amount of water that is still trying to get back to the ocean from the last tide. The Backway is wide and deep and fifty miles long, so there is quite a conflict. The outgoing water and the inflow don't really mix. They race past one another going in their opposite directions. Large deep whirlpools form at the place where the two waters slide past one another.

No one goes near between half tide up and half down. They can be fifty feet or more across and their steep sides ten feet deep. But as the outgoing water loses its force and the incoming flow is about spent, huge lazy whirlpools form, much larger but not violent, maybe only a couple feet deep at the centre. Then you can safely steer your little sailboat along the rim till you feel it take hold. You go in a huge slow circle around the circumference, gradually working your way down toward the flotsam in the centre, and all the while travelling along the shore as the whirlpools doesn't remain in one place. You get lower and lower, and soon you are looking up at the water which doesn't seem to move at all and maybe wondering what would happen to you if those sides decided to tumble in. The bottom of the pool comes up like a fountain and you catch a quick elevator back to sea level. It is only possible at certain stages of the tides and only on calm days. But if you are lucky you can get a couple of roundabouts in an afternoon. It's so slow, but the strength of the water is magnificent.

You know, rapids and falls, rivers, brooks, almost any running water roars, chuckles or makes its own particular sound. Whirlpools are silent, even the little quick ones. That water just goes around and around and makes no sound. You go sweeping around with it and all you hear is the flutter of your sails as they lose the wind. Well, on your first ride around, you hear your own breath as you draw it in, but that's only the first time. They used to say that when the pool reaches half across from Back Point to the Island, that it's safe to go. Maybe it's a bit like taking a ride on a huge kindly old whale. Not Jonah's style though.

Doris Saunders from *Them Days* magazine is here. One evening we took her to Cotters' as his parents had spent a lot of time on Labrador. George has an old photo album that one of his aunts made up of pictures she inherited from her folks and Cotter's folks. Many of them were taken on a pinhole camera that old Cotter made himself. Most of them are really good and go well back into the 1800s. Some company made slides of the whole album for George and he has loaned the slides to Doris to take back to Labrador. There will be a lot of interested people. One good shot was of a little sailing ship called the *Milda*, built by my great-grandfather and named after his wife. Some of the native pictures are priceless as it shows the Eskimos and Naska-pis as they were nearly a hundred years ago, maybe more.

The *Milda* was gone when I came along but HBC at Rigolet had the *Thistle*, built by my grandfather. He built several schooners, the *Rose*, the *Shamrock* and the *Sharon*. In a time when people named ships after relatives with names like *Hannah* and *Harriet*, he refused to follow the mode and picked names that he thought fitted his ships.

The *Thistle* was a spirited little ship. She did things on her own. Once, on a lovely calm Sunday, she swept around her anchors. I guess the current helped her. She picked them up in her chains and when the water rose, she started off out the inlet with no one aboard. My dad and most of the men were away with another schooner, and there was only the old cooper, James Dickers, and a couple of boys left on the post. My mother saw the *Thistle* go, and she went and told James, but since he was a cooper and took little interest in the motorboats etc., she had little hope that James and the boys could do much.

James was always surprising people with what he knew and what he could do, and my mother was amazed when he called the two boys, went aboard one of the motorboats with an ancient two-cycle Palmer engine, actually the first gasoline engine that ever came to Rigolet. He started it, chased the *Thistle*, hauled in her anchors, towed her back and anchored her again. When my dad came back, he couldn't believe that James, who was quite elderly and who never seemed to even notice what went on outside his cooperage, actually knew how to run an engine. But James made light of it. He'd seen from the wharf what was done and just filed it away for future reference.

When the *Thistle* was very old and beyond repair, orders came that she'd have to be broken up. My dad didn't want to do it and my mother was quite emotional about it. The *Thistle* solved it in her own way. Doctor Paddon, the Grenfell doctor, had a load of hay sent in to go to the mission farm at North West River. All the ships going in the inlet were fully loaded and the season was well advanced. Paddon hired the *Thistle*, loaded her and started to tow her to North West River, about ninety miles further in the inlet. They got to St. John's Island, a good harbour when a storm broke. They anchored the *Thistle* and moved *Yale*, the towboat, into a cove to wait out the storm.

Thistle, somehow, shook both stocks out of her anchors. The fact that they were very old may have had a bearing, and she sailed herself in and out among a maze of shoals and reefs and into Peace Cove where she went ashore on a lovely sand beach and leaned over on her bilge. When they found her most of the hay was still dry, but she never came out of Peace Cove. My dad said if that was where she wanted to be it was up to her. And there she remained, all alone in her comfortable harbour. After a while her masts fell down when her standing rigging decayed, and her top works were damaged by ice and exposure. Then, one spring, an extra high tide and some help from moving ice pushed her into deep water where I expect she still is.

There is a place on Labrador called Run by Guess. The story is that one stormy night in spring, a fishing schooner was caught in a terrible storm, and with visibility reduced to zero in snow, and no way of telling where they were as there were no charts of the area, the skipper gave his wheelman a course, which he picked haphazard, and told him to steer it. After a while the wind dropped, the waves were much quieter and they found soundings, but still couldn't see a thing. So they took sail off and anchored. They were there a day or so in thick fog and calm water when the wind shifted and the fog lifted. To their amazement they were in a completely landlocked harbour, and had to put a small boat overside and row around to find the way they had gotten in there, and it took a while. So the place was called Run by Guess ever after.

So when *Thistle* had a similar experience, no one gave it much thought. However, one dark night coming down the inlet with a gale behind her, the crew lost contact with the land and got everything ready to leave her when she struck, as she would have to, not having enough sea room to wear around, and nowhere in particular to go if they could. So when one bare rock after another showed up and she missed them by inches, they took to the boats and *Thistle* went on her own. They got ashore and found by daylight that they were on Pelter Island.

When the storm died out, they started for Rigolet in their small boats, but when they got out where they could see down the bay, there was *Thistle* tacking back toward them. Her sails were all every which way but she was unhurt, and after a bit of a chase they managed to board her and sailed her home. Old Uncle Jesse Flowers, who was cook, said they'd have been a lot more comfortable if they'd trusted *Thistle* to know where she was going. Tall tale? Well I was pretty small, but I remember them talking about it, and when I grew up I never could figure out how a ship could ever make all those twists and turns on her own, but *Thistle* did it then and later when she made her final run.

Then again of course, it's a matter of history that *Fort Chesterfield* drifted out of Churchill harbour in a storm and out into Hudson's Bay. Given up for lost, she was found two years later, unhurt in a safe little harbour way in among the Belcher Islands. Taken out and put into service again from Moose Factory, she sailed for a number of years until finally she was stranded in a huge storm near Fort Severn, sorry, York Factory. She went in on a very high tide caused by the violent wind. Again she wasn't hurt, but was so far from deep water and in an area of the deepest mud you ever saw that there was no way to get her out. The first time I went to York Factory, there she was among fairly well-grown trees sitting bolt upright on the sand.

And how about *Neptune*, a three-masted bark, built in Aban, Scotland. She was sold to Newfoundland and one fall drifted across the Atlantic and back to Aban. There an engine was put in her and she came back to Newfoundland, only to drift away again unmanned back to Aban. The first time she had a crew on board. They were longshore navigators, and lost out of sight of land. There is a book called *Forty-eight Days Adrift* that records their experiences. The second trip she was not manned, but she was brought back from Aban to

Fortune, Newfoundland. The last time she went away on her own she was again unmanned and no one ever heard of her again.

Then there was the famous case of *Marie Celeste*, found at sea with sail set, fire in the galley stove, the captain's wife's sewing things on the cabin table, everything in order, and no sign of the crew or the one boat that was missing. They could only have been gone a very short time when she was found, but no trace of them has ever been seen. So who would question the things *Thistle* did on her own? Good thing cars don't have souls like sailing ships. Just think if your car took off on its own someday.

Winnipeg, January 25, 1987

Dear Claudia,

So what's new? Well the big thing is the award of an Order of Canada to my friend and long time co-worker, W.E. (Buster) Brown. Remember I put in a nomination for him in March '85, and have spent the time in between getting people to write to Ottawa to second my nomination. It took a long time, but a week ago he got a letter to tell him he'd been selected. He's been depressed, as he knows his faculties are not what they were, and he's been lonely over there in Burnaby. He has his younger sister with him. She's in her seventies and very active, but none of his old workmates are close by. There are some in Victoria, but they seem to be happy and comfortable there. There are quite a lot of them and they see one another, while Buster is alone across the water.

He phoned his son when he got the letter, and I guess Ross told him that I had nominated him, so he phoned me. He was like a youngster, even though he is eighty-seven. He'll be going to Ottawa in April to receive his decoration from the Governor General. I'm hoping he can stop here coming back, and I have approached the Company about a dinner for him. His friends could arrange it but it would make him so happy to have the HBC put it on. So far they seem to be pleased to consider it. It will depend on his health at the time, but Ross, who is a doctor, feels that it will be quite possible and will be good for him.

W.E. is an old Arctic hand. At first he was a Mountie, actually one of the first to be sent to Ottawa from training in Regina for the original musical ride. He did a lot of exploration in the Keewatin, both while in the RCMP and later for the HBC. He experimented with short wave radio in the Arctic and it was on his suggestion that Ralph Parsons, the last fur trade commissioner of HBC, hired George Horner, a radio engineer, to develop what became one of the most unique communications systems on earth, more than two hundred radio stations at HBC posts that brought two-way communication to the northern part of Canada. It was in fact, the only system until the Dew Line and the introduction of microwave. W.E. certainly earned his Order of Canada. That makes a lot of people beside me very happy as so many politicians and friends of the same get the order every year and many others deserve it more.

Buster is the first real HBC fur trader to get the order. You know, I'm quite pleased with myself, not only in a very deserving man getting his due, but I had a small part in making it happen. Beside that, what else?

You are going to laugh when I tell you that a young friend of ours told me the strangest stories today. I'd always wondered why one of my friends and her family moved out of their nice place in a lovely suburb, and went to a new place where there is mud and no trees and everything is bare and raw. Because, honest, they wanted a place where no one had ever lived before on ground where there had never been a house.

Glad you asked why…Because after seven years in their other house, which was only three years old when they bought it, they had to get out because of visitations. Nope, not the Avon lady, not the vacuum salesman, not any of the hundred other pests that come to the door. Because of the kind that you don't see, that set a rocking chair moving, that moves dished around in the kitchen, that put a hand on the dog's back, so that you can see the hair flatten, and that push the dog flat on the floor while he looks with eyes that say, "What the heck's happening to me?" People that open doors and close them, that cause floors to squeak, that step on the rug till their tracks are visible but no one stands in them. People that dance in the bedrooms at night. They don't talk or laugh or make any sound except when they move dishes or things around. People that the dog avoids in the hall as though he could see or feel them coming. In short, people who aren't there.

She and her husband are both chartered accountants, both, till now, not likely people to pay attention to ghost stuff, very solid dependable people who have worked hard for their degrees and who have excellent jobs and prospects. She said to me today, "You are laughing at me." I said half of me was and half wasn't, because it's a well known fact in HBC that an old fur trader who spent years at Arctic Bay alone went back there after he died here in Winnipeg. We heard stories coming out how Jimmy would be heard in the post dwelling, muttering and putting things where he always kept them, opening doors and cupboards, leafing through books, all sorts of things. Reaction was, "Was this about the time they got their yearly supply of rum?"

But one of our pilots, Art Atkinson, stayed there overnight and said "no more" for him. He accidentally put his sleeping bag on the sofa where Jimmy used to sit and listen to the BBC every night. Art was tumbled out on the floor and had to put up with Jimmy muttering and bumping around all night.

Now Art was a different kettle of fish. So the divisional manager, the son of a bishop and a very straight-laced man, went up, spent a couple of nights in the house, came back and sent a complete new house in. Left the other place as it was, furniture and everything just as Jimmy kept it. No one bothers the staff in the new house. Now, while I've not been there since Jimmy died, I have talked to both Art and P.A.C. Nichols, and others. The clincher, though, is the fact that a hard-boiled outfit like HBC sent in a new house. Sure it could have been mass hysteria, but at least once since then they have invited some person passing through to spend the night and he reported badly disturbed sleep.

Now you are laughing. I would like to, but at this moment I just don't know. Maybe I've told you about a great heavy door in an old Moravian mission house on Labrador that opens. Never a sound, but it does open, and it isn't that it doesn't catch properly. The lock is a massive iron thing with a great bolt that falls into a deep socket.[28] The house is huge. It used to shelter the whole mission and their families in separate apartments. I have been alone in that house, carefully closing the door when I went to bed, and just in case, putting a heavy chair against it. I didn't hear a sound but in the morning the door was open and the chair moved. In this case, there are old Moravian journals that go back to the early 1800s and they mention this wayward door. It never closes on its own, only opens. Go ahead, laugh, but it's true. I saw Bill Cobb last fall. He lived in that house in 1931 or 1932 and he told me about the weird door.

Later:

Was supposed to take Muriel to a funeral today. I don't mind going to funerals to pay my last respects, but I hate that ghastly reception afterward. I didn't know the fellow who died. He was one of the people on a tour to Churchill that Muriel and my sister went on last summer. Shelagh wasn't working and she offered to go so I stayed at home. Did grocery shopping, and spent a lot of time reading a photocopy of a book written by an Anglican minister on Labrador, the exact same one who put cold water on my head when I was a day or so old.

As far as I know there was no great disturbance at my personal christening, but did I ever tell you about our goat, Reck (from reckless), who hated dogs and who broke up my youngest brother's cer-

28 I have been to the Moravian mission house where this happened. The locks are truly immense.

emony by chasing a poodle up the hall of our house where everyone was gathered for the event. Reck had been set upon by two dogs the year we were in Fogo, on my dad's furlough. He was a couple of years old, and had formed an attachment to my mother I think, for she was the one who took care of him at the time. We'd brought him back to Rigolet.

The Company house we lived in was a large building, with a long central hall with a door at each end. During the service, the poodle went to the open back door and barked when he saw the goat. When Reck started to attack, the poodle turned and raced up the hall and out the front door, followed by the goat. The congregation was split down the middle, my brother and I after him.

We found the little dog on top of the wire chicken run and the goat rampaging below. A hundred-and-fifty-pound goat is not easy to handle, but fortunately one of Reck's habits was an addiction to tobacco, and a large handful of fine cut got him to the stable. It was harder to get the dog down from the centre of the wire roof.

My dad used to say he was never sure if my brother should be legally called Halden Earl, or "Oh my God." I must have told you about Reck. I've told everybody who would listen. If not, remind me, unless of course you aren't particularly enthused about goat stories. Lots of people aren't. I think, much as I like dogs, that if I had a choice of an animal to evolve from, I'd pick a goat.

When I was a youngster, sheep and goats, sometimes pigs even, were allowed to wander around the roads and crop whatever they could find. Many fences were made of round pickets, which, when they dried, tended to crack and loosen the nails so that an animal could get its head through, and by a bit of extra work get its body through. This, of course, was to the detriment of the garden or meadow inside, because if you remember, sheep in particular are good at following the leader. If you don't believe me, just see how neatly they jump over a fence or go through a gate some sleepless night when you are counting sheep.

Well people used to put little triangular yokes around goats and sheep's necks so that they couldn't get a nose or a head through the fences. It worked on sheep. They'd give it a bang or so then go on. Not so goats. They would try every possible combination of body and head movement, and in many cases, succeed.

Sheep will get into a garden and, like a crazy lawn mower, chop off everything in sight. What they don't eat they trample. A goat will only take things he likes. In a row of carrots he'll pick out the nice juicy ones, here and there. He'll have a good feed if he isn't caught and most likely leave by the way he got in, with a map in his head for future reference. A sheep or a chicken for that matter seldom knows how he got in, and if caught he'll try to butt his way out the hardest possible path.

People in some parts of Newfoundland used to use goats as draft animals. They had dinky little carts and could haul a fair load. Willie Warren used to tell me about a goat he had. He'd take it into the woods, load the cart with split firewood and send the goat home alone while he got the next load ready. His wife and kids would unload the wood, give the goat a slice of bread and molasses and send him back. He'd trot back and forth all day as long as he got that "lassy bread." No bread, he'd back the cart into a corner and put his head down. He had big horns. Nothing could get him to move except his earned and expected ration. The labourer is worthy of his hire.

There were goats everywhere when I was young. You could watch them for hours. They were all different, independent, brave, resourceful, and if you treated them right, good friends. If a goat likes you, you can get the milk. If she doesn't, save yourself the bother, you won't get a drop. Mrs. John Walbourne had two shaggy nannies. Coming home from school, I'd see them standing by the stable door waiting to be let in and, always on their backs, several very contented looking chickens also waiting for supper. You guessed! I like goats.

January 27, 1987

Dear Claudia,

The big news came all of a sudden, yesterday. Friday evening just about closing time, it was announced that HBC Northern Stores had been sold to Mutual Trust and a group of HBC management. Guess it won't make prime time news in the South Pacific but it sure got phones ringing around town. There are so many things involved: pensions, discounts, even our little monthly meetings. So we've arranged to go down next Tuesday Feb. 3, and Mr. Tiller will answer any questions that may come up. Nothing will happen for presently employed personnel, the usual day-to-day routine will not be changed. The HBC name will be used for the next two years. It's after that time that things might change and people want to know now.

My chief reaction is a very great sadness, because this is the final end of the old fur trade that's been in existence since 1670. It hasn't been a real fur trade for many years of course, but in two years, Moose Factory, Norway House and a host of others won't be HBC posts any longer. The chain will be broken; the HBC flag won't fly any more.

At one time, a stranger or visitor arriving at the posts would look for the HBC flag. If he were missionary, policeman, game warden, yes, even competitor, he'd be given a place to stay. Many the fur buyer stayed at my dad's house. Very few ever bought much fur, not that they wouldn't. It was just that the trappers knew my dad would give every penny the fur was worth so there wasn't much fur left to be bought. He actually got a kick out of seeing some hotshot buyer try to get his hands on the fur. I won't say he didn't, at times, see to it that these fellows got a parcel or two that on closer inspection, didn't measure up.

Once I remember a trapper[29] who badly needed the money, came in with a choice silver fox when the price was a thousand dollars or more, before the fox ranches. Looking at the skin, my dad discovered that the ears were tainted. The fox had been buried in snow and so preserved, but the ears had projected above the snow and it was a bad case of fur slip. My dad told the trapper that the damage would discount the pelt quality, and advised him to hang on to the skin till one of the travelling fur buyers came by.

One did, quite soon, and as usual he came to our house. At supper he spent a lot of his time telling my dad that HBC traders were too conservative, scared to risk exceeding their tariff. He said, "I can buy any HBC man under the table."

So my dad sent a note to the trapper, told him to bring his fox to the house and ask for the travelling buyer. When the trapper came, my dad pretended to be surprised and demanded a chance to value the skin.

The usual method when two buyers were on hand, was for each to write his bid on a slip of paper. My dad handed John his slip with his original price. John took it and smiled. The travelling man saw the smile and put his bid at quite a bit over the best possible price. John said, "Your fox, sir," and took a bank draft for over a thousand dollars. The buyer was very happy. He razzed my dad all night about buying fur from under his nose, in his own house even.

The next morning he came out of his room for breakfast with the rest of us. My dad took the fellow's plate and put it on the floor under the table. At first the buyer didn't get it, then he almost panicked. He ran back into his room, was gone a while and came out smiling. He said, "You almost got me scared."

My dad said, "Take a look at the ears." The poor fellow almost expired. He wanted to know what caused my dad to look especially at the ears, and my dad said, "Nearly three hundred years experience."

The fellow was a good sport. He ducked under the table. Later though, another hot-shotter arrived and the buyer got him in a poor

29 John Blake

light and sold him the fox. I wonder how many travelling buyers owned that fox briefly until someone was caught at the end.

John's thousand dollars really came in handy, as he had recently lost one of his hands and at the time was having a hard time making out in a country where two good hands are none too many at times. He made it though, and I lived to see him become one of the best trappers in the area and captain of a schooner. You'd guess we called him Captain Hook. He was a carpenter, boat builder, salmon fisherman. He could climb a mast, row a boat, set traps, do anything the rest of us could do except, as he said, scratch his remaining elbow, or simplest of all, he really couldn't really wash his hand. He could shave, do anything else, but working with paint, tar, grease or the like, he'd have to get his daughter to scrub his hand with a big scrub brush. He had many a quick laugh over his thousand dollar fox. He used the proceeds to buy a boat so that his sons could fish for salmon while he worked with HBC.

Away back in the thirties when the depression was at its worst, I had just started working for HBC. The London office sent a crew of nuts out to show us how to do things. They were called the Development Department. They invented new traps and harpoons for the natives, whose own gear had evolved over the centuries. They made huge iron things that were supposed to soften seal leather better than the human teeth. Only thing was they were so heavy the people had no way of moving them around. They decided that the Eskimos, a meat-eating people, should have milk. So the store manager had to get up early every morning to mix powdered milk and deliver it to every igloo he could reach.

You guessed! They wouldn't drink it, and anyway, in winter, it was frozen solid by the time the post manager got to igloo three. They built small frame cottages at Hebron to give the natives a place to live. These were completely nomadic people at the time. There is no fuel near Hebron, so the agreeable natives accepted the cottages.

In winter, they built igloos nearby to live in as they were so much warmer. In summer, they pitched tents as they were so much cooler, and in the little cottages they kept their spare gear, meat, fish and such like, nicely out of the way of the dogs and weather.

Anyway, one of these fellows was an efficiency expert, guess they all were. He came to Rigolet where we were packing salt salmon for export to Holland. John was always in the thick of the salmon packing, or anything else for that matter. He supervised the washing and particularly the salting which is very important.

Mr. Binney[30] watched awhile, then took my dad aside. By this time, father, who was no shrinking violet, was almost trembling with frustration at the way these people were interfering with the post work. Mr. Binney told him that it wasn't efficient to have a one-armed man do the salting. The way it was usually done was to have a man take a fish from the culler and place it in the tierce, a large barrel. He had to turn the fish just so, so that it would conform to the shape of the barrel. While he reached for the next fish, the salter, John, would sprinkle the exact amount of salt on the fish in the barrel and so on. The salt was brought from the store in a wheelbarrow in small lots because both sun and rain could deteriorate it. Binney pointed out hot a one handed man would tire earlier than a man who could switch over, and, big point, how could a one-armed man go for more salt with a wheelbarrow?

I've heard my dad tell the story many times. At the moment, the crew was finishing up for the day. He controlled an impulse to chuck Binney into a barrel and have John salt him, but he said in effect, "Fair's fair. Tomorrow morning, you follow John and do everything

---

30 George Binney was in the Company's employ 1926–1931, hired as personal assistant to Charles V. Sales, Governor of the Company. He was involved in the selection and preliminary training of apprentices for the Company's fur trade posts. In 1931, he brought out *The Eskimo Book of Knowledge* (London: Hudson's Bay Company); he was knighted by HM George V for services in World War II.

he does. If by night you can prove there is inefficiency, then we'll talk about changing things."

We went to work at six o'clock. Binney was more the nine o'clock type, but my dad had him out at quarter to six with the first bell, and out following John at six sharp.

John's first job was to top up all the barrels previously packed with brine, as the fish absorb a lot of liquid during the first days. He used two heavy wooden buckets. Brine would corrode metal in days. So with one bucket on the stump of his arm, another on his hand and a big funnel tied to his overalls with a string, he started off, followed by Binney, similarly laden. At least Binney was, like the usual English-man of higher status, a good sport, but he just couldn't handle those two huge buckets with a big funnel clanking along between his feet.

By seven o'clock and breakfast, he had handled maybe a couple of barrels or so, was liberally spattered with 80 percent of the brine, which was turning his clothes white and burning his hands. Half an hour for breakfast, then back with John. Somehow the poor man struggled along till the pickling, as we called it, was done. By then a load of salmon was at the dock.

He was given a great oilskin apron and a soft brush. Each salmon had to be carefully washed, front and back, better tell you. They were split when caught all the way down the back, not the belly as with most other fish. They lie flatter in the barrel that way. Some are pretty large, twenty to thirty pounds. You hold them by the tail over a slop-ing board over a tank of water and make sure they are absolutely clean. The least speck of blood or foreign matter and the culler will slap them back to you. It is traditional that the culler never says why. You just wash it again and hope it passes.

John took pity on Binney after an hour or so. He was probably as kind-hearted a man as ever lived. He had grown up working hard. He had trained his sons to work hard, and he was visibly concerned that this strapping fellow made such heavy weather over the easier jobs. So he put him to try packing. But Binney's wrists couldn't take the strain of twisting the fish. He took so long that the irate culler quit passing salmon to him and just piled them at his feet. It all came to a head when his first tierce was taken to the cooper, old James Dickers, who was a perfectionist plus. He took one look at the unsightly hump in the barrel and roared a plain refusal to put a head in that tierce until the salmon was properly packed.

So Binney tried salting, not bad at first. John directed him, but salt is heavy, the fish come thick and fast. There are only a few seconds to sprinkle salt before the packer is ready to slam another big fish down. Binney's arm tired. He used two hands, they tired, and he was again being barked at by the culler, who had fish piling up, and the cooper who was standing idle waiting for the next barrel.

He had one hope, I guess, that the salt in the wheel barrow would run out and at last he would have his big moment when one of the two-handed people would have to break off and go for more salt.

Wrong again. While he was struggling to keep up with the packer, John slipped a rope sling over his arm, or the stump, picked up the barrow with the sling and one hand, trundled it into the salt store, used a shovel to load it by grasping it well down the handle, and was back with more salt while there still was lots on the barrow Binney was trying so hard to empty.

That got him. He threw down the big wooden scoop, said something about "you chaps aren't even human," and tottered up to the office where my dad was working with a grim eye on events on the wharf. It was very early in the day of course. When poor Binney arrived, the old man said, "It's not time for lunch." We never got coffee or any sort of morning break in those days.

Binney said, "I know," then went into a long apology for being so unutterably stupid as to think he could keep up with those tireless machines for even a moment. My dad sad, "Now, since you're an expert, how about efficiency?"

Binney had to admit that someone might be able to follow John around, but definitely not he. Binney was around for a while and my dad would see John high on a ladder painting the eave on one of the tall old buildings, or in the rigging of the schooner doing some job, or using a heavy broad axe to square a timber, all with one hand and possibly a bit of rope. He'd say to Binney, "Care to give it a try?" The expression, "no way" hadn't been invented then, but Binney had his own very correct English to explain that he wasn't about to be that sort of a damn fool all over again. To him, the most appalling thing was that these fellows cheerfully rolled out before six a.m., worked a full hour before breakfast, were back in half an hour to work steadily till noon. All people worked that way, not only the HBC.

Binney came from a wealthy English family, used to what I guess you'd call gracious living. The depression didn't bother them. He thought living conditions on the *Nascopie* were primitive, with linen on the tables and a steward to serve him. He talked about the crossing from England on such a ship as if it were an ordeal. Later he was given a ride, if you could call it that, on an Eskimo boat from Port Burwell to Fort Chimo. There was no galley, no toilet. He shared the hold with twenty women and kids, uncounted dogs, and six or eight walrus and seal carcasses. Poor man. He told my dad about it in the fall when he came back. My dad said, "Bad as following John?" and Binney answered, "There is nothing on earth that ever will be as bad as that trip."

The development department didn't really develop. Ralph Parsons, a tough Newfoundlander and Arctic man, became fur trade commissioner. He threw out all the crazy ideas and set about steering the fur trade through the terrible depression. He did it, and because the fur trade survived, the rest of the Company did also.

I heard that Binney and his group went to Africa to show the natives there how to do their thing. But for years, the natives in the Eastern Arctic used to laugh about the time the Company tried to turn them all into babies by trying to make them drink milk.

John Blake, Will the culler, and James the cooper were lucky. The old ways didn't change much in their time. They had a distrust of power tools, liking the feel of a block or jointer plane. They liked to saw with a properly set and sharpened saw. They accepted modest progress such as gasoline engines to drive motorboats or to saw lumber and fire wood. They didn't see the final end of sail or dog teams, of salmon and cod fishing.

Things I never think about come up in the pages of *Them Days*. The name of a ship will start a train of memory you'd not believe. Poking into an old book the other day the name of one of Grenfell's ships struck me. "*WOP.*" Nasty word now. In those days it meant "Worker of Pleasure" and indicated the young people from British and American universities who came to the coast at their own expense and worked for Dr. Grenfell for free.

The WOPs did any sort of work: cutting and hauling fire wood, digging wells or graves, painting, caring for cattle, all with the greatest will and good humour. As Rev. Burry said, to read down the list was like reading the social register. One of the Vanderbilts came year after year under an assumed name. Semi-royalty wasn't unknown.

When I saw the name WOP, I remembered mostly the ugly little steamship. Old as the hills she was, of wood. People said it was only the paint that held her together. She had a regular captain and engineer, but the crew was all WOPs. They hauled freight from station to station, and they had a ball every hour of the day. No one ever figured out why Grenfell didn't lose a half dozen every year. It must prove that a special providence looks after fools and sailors. Those boys were a combination of both I suppose. In a way more fools than sailors. They'd do things that we, more cautious, would never dream of. They got into many a scrape but always seemed to survive. One thing was that when a Grenfell boat was around, everyone looked out for them and sort of shepherded them along.

I made one trip on *WOP*. My dad loaned me to the engineer to help tear down and rebuild an ancient steam generator. There were about ten of those students aboard. They worked hard, but in their spare time, they engaged in some horrible pranks. Once we were anchored in a calm little harbour. They tied one of their number hand and foot and heaved him overside to see if he could free himself as he said he could. The engineer and I were the only others on board. One student armed with a knife was standing by in case the fellow under water wasn't able to free himself, but the water was deep and the bottom black so there wasn't much visibility.

They waited awhile but there was no sign of the man and believe me I was some worried. There was one fellow with a little more sense than the others who had agreed with the engineer that, at least, they should put a line on the poor fellow before chucking him overside. Well at last the man with the knife went down and soon was back in panic. Couldn't find him. We grabbed the flag line and gave the end to the more sensible fellow. *WOP* had been swinging at her anchor and the bound fellow could be anywhere but his would-be saviour dived and swam away from the ship and by pure luck he got the man. We got a tug on the rope and hauled him up, the rope around one ankle. He was just about gone but there were several medical students there. They got busy and revived him, but he was in his bunk a couple of days, and very groggy when he did get out.

The skipper, who'd been ashore, was livid when he came back. Someone had told him. He gave the poor old engineer a rough time, but how could he stop a crowd of great big kids who thought they were just having fun? The doctor who was ultimately responsible for the safety of the Wops heard about it. He'd just gone through an incident where his own two older sons had just about strangled his younger son in some stupid prank involving a rope around his neck. He was wild. The engineer and I stayed quietly in the engine room while he raged around topside. It was soon forgotten. Them days the Americans were all hyped up about "natural high spirits." My dad and others had different words for it.

A week later, when I'd gone back to Rigolet, they had a shooting contest, trying to put out a match held by someone else. I never heard how many matches got put out but it ended when one fellow lost the top joint of his thumb. The head of the mission happened to arrive. He himself had once dived overboard from a ship in mid-Atlantic after a tennis ball, but the local people and his own staff were fed up. So he loaded the WOPs on his yacht, and took them and their silly activities home to the States. They were all wealthy and I suppose later became professional men and captains of industry. They were all older than I was, but in the week or so I spent aboard *WOP* I figured that one thing money can't buy is brain.

Those days seem far away now. One of the things that gave stability to us was of course the HBC. It had been in Rigolet long, long before anyone could remember.[31] To me it was security in days when jobs were not to be had. I'd have liked to go to sea, on a Company ship of course, but fully qualified masters were glad to get jobs as second and third mates. What chance for a new kid? So Mr. Parsons told me that the Company would hire me. I never had to go out and hunt for a job. All my life the Company was there. During the war, when I was in the army, I always knew that once the unpleasantness was over, I'd be going back to Labrador or the Eastern Arctic.

Even now, when I'm retired, no longer an active part of the Company, I feel a great sense of loss that my department, the old fur trade, will disappear as a historical unit in two years. The retail stores will remain, there will still be an HBC, but the retail are latecomers. It's the fur trade that gave birth to it, it's the fur trade that I was born into; the fur trade that occupied my working life. I was in fur trade transportation at the last, but I have bought fur, I trapped fur (don't tell Greenpeace), I managed a fur trade post, several of them in fact. I went hungry and cold for the fur trade and I lived in some less than comfortable places, but I was never unhappy, and never once did I gave any thought to other employment.

I grew up and lived under the old flag with the Union Jack in the corner and the white HBC on the fly. In those days, the Company was

31 Louis Fornel claimed Rigolet for the French in 1743. Marcoux built a French post at Rigolet in 1788. In 1836, The Hudson's Bay Company established a post to oppose David R. Stewart at Rigolet and in 1837 bought out Stewart.

proud of its English origin. We were all royalists, and it was comforting to have the Jack on our flag. One thing, the people who will still manage the new company are all HBC men, fur trade men, most with long service to the NSD.[32] They will carry on in the old tradition. One of the things that was stressed at the meeting the pensioners had with Mr. Filler yesterday was the fact that there will be little or no change in the appearance of the stores or in the management.

Over time, of course, there will be the inevitable changes that have been going on for over three hundred years, but the bones of the Company lie in the fur trade in the small isolated communities. We have been assured that the Company's dedication to the North and the native people will remain. The incubus that was Toronto has been removed; the NSD is here, as it used to be: in the North, Toronto and its foolish expansion ideas, its huge debt, its poor policies, no longer burdens the fur trade. Already there is talk of a revived fur trade. In later years, Toronto sold off the fur auction houses in Montreal, New York and London. Mr. Filler said yesterday that we handle 25 percent of all the fur sold in Canada through our stores in the North. He said in time we may set up our own auction house. That got a cheer from all present. Perhaps the sores will heal. The loss of the name, the end of a history, can never be forgotten, but there will be stores in the North, there will be people, fur traders there too. We can't go back to my time, but we will be there. In time, there will be a group as loyal to the new company as we were to ours. I hope they will feel the same security and sense of belonging that we did.

But as though it were yesterday I can see in my mind, the tidy post at Rigolet. Everything there was HBC. The white buildings with their red roofs, the inlet in front, the thickly wooded green hills framing it all, and the tall white flag staff in the shape of a ship's mast and top mast with the HBC flag at the peak. I can never forget that. That

32 The Hudson Bay Company's Northern Stores Department.

place, those people, were the essence of HBC. They are gone and they can never be replaced.[33]

In April 1987, the chain will break. The post will become part of a new company, and perhaps on that day, very quietly, my heart will break. The grass will grow, the sun will shine and the streams will flow. Nothing outwardly will have changed. The break with the past will be silent, and we of the old days will be the only ones to feel it.

Winnipeg, February 6, 1987

Dear Claudia,

Away back, so many years I don't really want to count them, there was a book in a travelling library, written in the early 1900s I guess, about a girl named Anne. It wasn't much, but in those days a book was reading material and there wasn't that much available. I won't inflict Anne on you. You'll have guessed that she eventually proved herself to be the missing heiress, got back into the manor with full honours, and of course got her man. But in that book there were letters from a school friend who was lucky. When Anne was slaving in a laundry, the friend was travelling in exotic countries with Mom and Dad.

She wrote Anne about being on an island in the midst of a hurricane, and my mind said to me, "Would anyone write letters during a hurricane?" Well after all those years, I find that at least one person will, and that her letters are away above Anne's friend in interest and description. Fantastic is the word. Now all we've got to is find out which huge fortune you are the heiress of, and we are in the way of proving that 1900 novels had something.

33 On January 26, 2006, The Hudson's Bay Company was sold to Jerry Zucker of South Carolina, a longtime minority HBC shareholder.

Your letter is so absorbing that I read it first, then Muriel read it, while dinner waited cold in the kitchen and Fitz went into a sulk waiting for his ration of Tender Vittles. Kathy came and she read it. I've read it several times, each time I'm more firmly convinced that here is a person who can paint, who can teach, who can climb volcanoes, do all manner of unusual things, and write. Boy can she write. You are with the people, you see things and talk about things that we are completely unaware of. We have our puffs of wind here, not enough to take my hat off usually, but you are where roofs come off, people are hurt, property is destroyed, gardens that feed people are torn up.

I've had some experience with wind in the Arctic but there is a difference. We went in there knowing how it could blow. One of my first posts was at Hebron. The German missionaries built the house I lived in, built it to withstand gales of heavy brick and huge timbers. The roof was like an old fashioned tent. It came close to the ground and acted like a great knife to split the wind. We were always safe, though smaller and lighter buildings were blown away, but while we could feel the wind it couldn't get to us. Perhaps we couldn't get outside but we had everything we needed inside.

Travelling, we used snow houses, built where we knew the wind could only cover them with drifts and we'd still be safe. We never saw what you describe. We had no trees to blow down. If a person went out on foot any distance, he carried a snow knife and if caught, he either built a house or dug himself in. Either way he survived. Those who didn't usually forgot some rule or panicked. But one hears of the Cruel Arctic and the Golden South Seas Paradise. You have had an experience that none of us in the Arctic could ever have had. Sort of changes my way of thinking about different parts of the earth.

Once when I was in Wolstenholme, which had the reputation of being one of the windiest places in the Arctic, there was quite a large native camp near the post. Probably five snow houses, not really a great town, but you'd not get enough people in five hundred miles to fill a small apartment building. Anyway, it was stormy and we had rigged ropes from building to building so that we could find our way around in the drift.

An old lady had a fox skin she wanted to trade for tea and tobacco and she left the snow house to come over to the post to do her trading. Somehow she missed the ropes and got out on the harbour where the wind was pretty fierce. She was blown along like a bundle of tumbleweed and finally ended up near a small iceberg that had been frozen in. She had a snow knife and built herself a shelter, and there she sat for two days and nights, she and her fox. The people were all relatives, and those in one snow house thought she was in the other. The storm got really bad and no one ventured out. When it was all over she was missed, so the search was on. Then someone saw her coming in across the ice.

She'd been warm and comfortable enough but no tea, nothing to smoke, and she was cranky. Took a good few mugs of strong tea in my kitchen and a plug of black tobacco to restore her good nature. Then she traded her fox and went off to her family. Once she got there, she had a tale to tell and it was hilarious. Ever after, she brought a big dog along so she could follow him home, and if worst came to worst, she'd have him to help keep her warm if she had to dig in again.

She liked to visit, and by a strange chance she nearly always came when I was cooking a meal. She couldn't tell time so it had to be by chance, wouldn't it? Anyway, she wasn't used to heat, (you don't really get much in a snow palace) and when I got the big coal burning kitchen range going, there would be quite some heat all over the house. The old lady would sit on the floor near the door and drip with perspiration but she'd hang on till I got a share of the meal for her. She'd eat in a hurry and drink a couple cups of tea and escape, but she always came back. She liked my cooking.

Once I asked her how old she was, she used up all her fingers then took lumps of coal out and lined them up on the floor, each one for a year, she nearly got out of the kitchen into the little office before she was through. How she figured I'll never know but I got her age at something over sixty. She looked a hundred and one. Even at that age her eyes were fabulous. She could sew watertight seams in kayaks and boots stitches so small you could hardly see them. She could take a stained greasy white fox skin and bring it back shimmering white and soft. Quite an old lady she was.

THIRTEEN

March 17, 1987

Dear Claudia,

St. Pat's day, or as Al Snyder used to say, the 17th of Ireland. Al was one of the great bush pilots. I don't know how many miles he and I flew together. All put together in a straight line they'd sure reach to Vanuatu and probably back.

He was a natural happy non-worrier. If the weather was bad we sat it out. He knew someone every place we landed. If the conditions were good, we flew.

He could fix anything, and when we were at HBC posts, he repaired generators, washers, typewriters, sewing machines, ski-doos, dolls, you name it. No wonder he was popular. There haven't been too many men like Al in my life. I don't think anyone has likely met more than one, if he's been very lucky, that is.

Seals are pretty sharp people. Over the years they learned how to have their young born in a white jacket so that they would be almost invisible. Then as the sun melted the ice and the rocks, pebbles, sea weed and various flotsam thawed out, brother seal changed his coat for a ragged jacket and could still be relatively unobserved. Then man caught on I guess. Some seals didn't figure he was that smart so they didn't change their habits and got clobbered. But the Ranger, or dotard as the old ones are called, figured it out and in a couple centuries or so they decided to abandon the ice and have their youngsters ashore on the rocks.

But there a white jacket was no use, so a little more figuring and junior was born on the rocks in a black jacket, and whereas his white cousin couldn't swim till he'd managed to go through his white and ragged jacket phase, your Ranger could swim as soon as he was born.

Wily man still could find him on his rock though and did, because the pelt of a newly born Ranger is as beautiful and soft as a pussy willow bud. So Mrs. Ranger gave it more thought, and she decided to go up the rivers at a time when man was about immobilized by melting snow, deep mushy drifts and raging downhill water. That stopped him, cold and wet. And in the beginning all it meant was a change of mating dates. I wonder how grouchy old Pop felt about it all. I wouldn't be surprised if he tried to stay on schedule and got a sharp mouthful of teeth across his nose for his trouble.

Ha! You said, how do I know? Well it all falls into line when you know that the little seal inside the mother is white as snow in January, February and March. That's when white coats are born, March. They can't go in the water with their mothers because they can't swim, so they lie there and the wind howls around them, their fur freezes to the ice and they cry. They are so fat they probably don't feel the cold, but it's miserable out there alone with your eyes and whiskers full of drift.

And I guess little rangers were born in March too once. But in late June when they are born now they are black. Somehow the mother manages to be impregnated three months later than other seals, and she manages to have her youngster change colour before he's born.

Mom Ranger has her baby in the nice warm sun on a rock when the ice is gone. He can swim and he can live in fresh water so if it should rain he likes it all that much more, lucky kid. He won't be crying in the cold. Wouldn't Mr. Darwin have been pleased?

There was a mother seal who lived in our harbour at Rigolet. She stole fish from our nets but no one ever saw her do it. You'd see her head away out in the Inlet. She'd dive in that distinctive way Rangers have. They hump their backs while most other seals just draw their head straight down. Then perhaps you might, on a calm day, see the net floats bob up and down, nothing more, and later again you might see her out in the Inlet floating there enjoying a fish.

There were a dozen men with rifles on the post who'd have loved to get that seal and she knew it too. Perhaps she also knew who shot at her. The fact remains that when it was time to give birth, she'd come boldly ashore in front of the store and stay there while the youngster was born, and leave with him later that day. The wharf was a hundred yards away with boats coming and going, engines running, people talking, hammering, all the usual things that went on day by day and she'd still come.

So many people coveted the shiny black skin of her baby and she knew it. When the tide was high away they'd leave together, and we'd never, as far as we know, ever see the baby again, for sure not with its mother. She'd be back with her usual caution, to steal fish. She'd be seen daily in the Inlet. But no boat, no hunter ever got near. Her skin after the first year was worthless anyway and her flesh so rank that not even a sleigh dog would eat it. She was pretty safe herself and no trigger-happy character would try a long shot at her from the post because of my dad. But she'd hide that baby some place somehow, and treat us all with extreme caution until it was time for her next baby and she'd be back to that same rock as bold as brass.

I wasn't there when the war came. There was an army camp built right at Rigolet, where the HBC had been supreme for nearly two hundred years and my dad for most of his life. They cut his trees that he allowed no one to touch. He loved that grove spreading up the hill behind the post. Every fall he'd go in there with his big axe and clear-cut small stuff that might one day strangle the big old fellows that were there when HBC came and many years before.

There were no roads of course, only a long boardwalk around the rocky shore between the buildings for wheelbarrows and hand-barrows in summer, dog sleighs in winter. The army brought a tractor and they built immediately behind the post. No way would they spare the big trees. Down they came, up went the ugly huts. Hundreds of years of beauty were destroyed, hundreds of years of quiet gone in a month. Guns were set up to stop submarines from going up the inlet to attack the airbase at Goose Bay. What better target for the guns but the slow moving black whales that had been there every summer for years, some so well known to us that they had names.

No one had ever harmed them. We'd lived in peace together. They'd swim right up to our wharf when we were processing salt salmon, and feed on the capelin that swarmed around because of the brine that was dumped in the water out of the boats that brought the salmon in. The whales would open their big mouths and scoop up a half barrel of tiny capelin and swim slowly away, never touching a boat. They'd surface so close to us youngsters that the warm steam from their breath would blow across our boat and remind us that whales don't use Scope or Listerine.

And the army gunners would shoot at them. Soldiers would range all over with rifles and shoot at the huge black-backed gulls that had nested on the top of the wooded hill across from the post for years. An osprey nest that was there when my dad first saw Rigolet was as big as a small house and perfectly visible across the inlet. Excellent target for the army.

Then one day two off-duty soldiers strolled out on the HBC wharf and started taking pot shots at the seal that visited our harbour. That finished it, my dad declared war on the army. He raged into their camp and he roared as only he could do. He saved what was left of his trees, and he insisted that no soldier carried a rifle any place on Company property. He got lots of things changed, but they broke his heart anyway.

The tractor tore up the caribou moss that made a walk up to the top of Sunday Hill an exquisite delight. They put an observation post on the hill opposite and shoved the gulls out of the way. They used the great symmetrical sand hills across the inlet, the only ones of their type, except the "Wonderstrand" of the Vikings at the mouth of the inlet, in all of Eastern Canada, for target practice and blew huge craters in them which will take forever to fill again. They spoiled a place of beauty that had been since time began. They banished the big harmless whales and the submarines came and went anyway. Only after the war did they find photos of Hamilton Inlet in German archives that could only have been taken during the war. Well, you know it was what you'd call a legitimate casualty of the "War to End All Wars." As I said, I wasn't there to see it happen, and I'm glad I wasn't. I think they broke my heart a little too, because, even though we moved around a bit, Rigolet was my home, not my birthplace, my home.

And about seals, you tired of seals? Well just this one bit more. One summer my brother was coming back from somewhere when he saw a female Ranger seal dead on a rock with her tiny baby alive beside her. The baby was pretty lonely and the only thing to do was bring him home. Our big old Newfoundland dog had just had a litter of pups and the young seal fitted right in, except that Kit, who was real good natured, seemed to be a bit surprised that this big clumsy pup had sharp teeth while the rest had none. Well, you win a few, lose a couple, so unless he bit too hard, she put up with him. Now and then she'd get up and move away and he'd take a while to find her again.

He grew like a seal, apt description, but he didn't know he was a seal. We didn't give it much thought. He had a big wooden tub that he shared with the pups who also loved water of course. As time went on, the pups went to other homes, and Kit was quite resigned when she was left with her ugly duckling. Fall came, then winter. Brother seal lived in the house, perfectly content under the big wood stove. He'd

hump himself over to the door a couple of times a day for a brief visit
to the great outdoors. He must have had a bladder as large as himself.
The rest of the time he lay around the house. Kit worried a bit because
he never romped around like the average pup but she wasn't as young
herself any more. He made up for the loss of her pups and she'd play
with him, mostly rolling him over and over till he got peevish and
snapped at her. They spent the nights sleeping near the stove.

Came spring and the ice went, so what do we do about Ranger who
was getting to be a big boy, and who soon, after the nature of his family, would be getting a bit objectionable and probably a bit more than
slightly irritable. So the male seal rookery, (why rookery? they ain't
birds, but the experts say it's rookery) was across the inlet. Let him
into the water and he'll soon find his way over and all will be well.

Like heck it would. We took him down to the beach, shoved him in
and he commenced to scream and flounder back toward the land. Kit
jumped in true to her life saving heritage, and after all, wasn't he her
kid? And she hauled him out. So now, what do we have? A seal who
can't swim, and one who had no intention of learning. He thought he
was a dog. We tried him in salt water, we tried him in fresh. If it was
shallow so he could sit on the bottom, he liked it. But get out in that
deep stuff, a fellow could drown out there. No way man! It was a silly
predicament. Sunny days our dog-seal lay out in the grass and the
goats grazed around him and wondered what he was. Rainy days he
hauled indoors and slept the day away. He ate anything, he minded
his own business, and he barked hoarsely at some people. Others he
ignored. As far as he was concerned life was pretty good.

My mother started putting her foot down. She liked him as well as
anyone, but a seal grows. A male dotard can get to be six feet long or
more. Like all male seals, he can have an aroma that the Avon Lady
doesn't supply, so where do we turn. Well, a chap in the charity business used to make regular trips along the coast in his boat all the way
from Boston. Once my mother had given him an orphan caribou and
he'd picked up various animals for zoos in the States.

Would he care for a seal? One that couldn't swim but who belonged to a relatively rare species up our way and one that was unknown in the States. Honest. The Carnegie people didn't even admit that such a seal existed until 1938, when one of their people got a piece of a skin from a native of Richmond Gulf. Then they sent an expedition in to check on it and got two specimens from Seal Lake. Freddie Moore's brother was one of the guides on the expedition. Read all about it in a book called *Needle to the North*. Strange thing is, these seals ascend the rivers on the Labrador Coast, find their way all across the Quebec Peninsula, and are seen inland from Richmond Gulf in Hudson's Bay, but no one has ever seen one on the Hudson's Bay or James Bay coast.

Anyway, the man would like such a seal, and we crated Ranger, who travelled far and wide and ended up in a pool in Seattle with a gang of sea lions, who accepted him as a slightly nutty relative I guess. He found that his roommates got tasty fish for dunking themselves in that cold wet stuff, and a guy has to do what a fellow must, so he finally learned to swim, half a world away from his home and with different companions. Perhaps it just goes to show what I tried to say pages back. Ranger seals are smarter and more adaptable than anyone.

Now what I want to know is, if Ranger and his offspring, always providing he could have found a mate with his personal limitation, had been kept on dry land, how long would it have taken for them to grow legs? What sort of fellow would he have become? Except for a different shaped head and his short arms and legs, his skeleton is very similar to a human's. Be something if they should come out of the water and shove us back in. No more than we deserve I guess, but uncomfortable with no car, no TV. Oh well, it would take a long time. I can sleep easy, especially way back here on the prairie.

The HBC pensioners met last week at the Museum of Man and Nature. Someone thought we should know about whales. The only people there, including the lecturer, that had ever seen a whale were Henry

Voisey and I. We had a long tour looking at the exhibits, mostly small stuff, beluga and narwhals, listened to a recording of whales singing and saw a film, mostly on California grey whales, which I've never seen or heard. The noises they make are similar to the Atlantic whales but they had the tape speeded up fourteen times to show the similarity to humans singing, so I don't know.

We used to listen, especially at Hebron, to the Greenland whales talking, but it was slower and seemed to be deeper in sound. Another language I suppose. One thing for sure, they can hear and communicate over great distances.

At Rigolet we used to hear the little black porpoises. They sound like a gang of teenaged girls giggling about boys. They are the most pleasant intelligent little fellows. They get themselves tangled up in salmon nets sometimes. If you handle them roughly, they get scared, and fight like all get out. If you are gentle and talk or whistle to them, they'll allow you to untangle them, even open their mouths so you can get the twine from around their teeth.

An old fisherman, Sam Wolfrey, could speak to them, at least he could whistle, chuckle and make spitting sounds so they'd stand up in the water and reply. I've had them reply to a whistle and swim round and round the boat, but that's all. They'll do it in fall on a calm snowy day. For some reason they are exceptionally tame then.

People are very superstitious about porpoises over there. They are the souls of drowned seamen. No one would hurt them then. I wonder how it is now. Everyone had or had heard a yarn about porpoises bringing a drowning man ashore. How many places are there in Eastern Canada that have a porpoise who always escorts a newcomer into the harbour but ignores local boats? Quit a few. Why, I dunno. No one does, but every here and there is a local pilot. You can believe anything after you have been in a small boat on a quiet dark night watching a lighted ship pass, and have seen a group of porpoises standing on their tails in the water watching her, and talking in their bubble and squeak language. You can feel very happy that you have been so close to the friendly little fellows.

You know the difference between our letters is that yours are written today about things that are happening now, leaving room for things that may happen tomorrow, while mine are memories about things that have happened, some of which can never happen again. I only hope you get some interest out of mine to return a little of the immense joy yours give me.

Last letter got me a quick look from the lady in the post office. Vanuatu? Where is that? It shows on the list as so much per ounce, but no one knows where it is. She wasn't busy and leaned across the counter asking questions.

She doesn't forget either, and when I go in to get rid of my Hydro bill, she wants to know what's new in Vanuatu. I told her about the letter written in the midst of a hurricane and she was so interested in how you must have felt not knowing when the roof might go, sitting there in the candle light, you, the man, the boy, the parrot, the dog and the guitar.

The Crees say "*nis-ko-mitten*," the Eskimo "*nak-o-mak*," but English can only say "I am grateful." You have to have an old native lady hold your hands and for some trifling thing, say, "*nis-ko-mitten*" or "*nak-o-mak*," and it's something else indeed. That's how I want you to know I appreciate your letters.

Gratitude is a big thing among some people. I think I once got much more than was coming to me. It was at Repulse Bay, and a starvation year. Everyone was hungry. The father and I had given all we had; we hunted daily for our next meal too.

One day I shot two foxes; they were thin too, but they were meat. I was on my way home when I met a tiny little woman, old Pealak's wife. She was out on the barren hills where the snow had blown away picking twigs of tiny arctic willow to make a tiny fire and perhaps boil a cup or two of water to drink; no tea, but when you had nothing, a cup of warm water can be a treat.

She was small, old, her face wrinkled and lines from a lifetime in Arctic wind and cold. Her eyes, black as ebony, sparkled and she was always smiling. She was so kind and so generous and very precious. When she saw me, she came running. She had a bundle of twigs smaller than a bride's bouquet for part of a day's work. She exclaimed over the two foxes and immediately said she'd skin them and dress the skins for me if she could have a little of the meat.

I said that I had been lucky the day before too; I had meat and she could have both foxes. I knew full well that a fair share of what was there would go to every igloo in the camp.

You never saw anyone so delighted. She abandoned her hunt for willows and skipped ahead of me, laughing and encouraging me to go faster. "Hurry, white man, you are slow. You will let my meat freeze." Two starveling foxes, not much to make a person happy perhaps. But she held my hands when she got to her igloo and she told me how happy she was. She said, "One day I will work for you."

The year ground down. There was hardship, there was death, but spring eventually came and the snow started to melt. Long before we could expect to see any seals on the ice, between the post and John Rae's North Pole River was a wicked morass of water and snow fourteen miles wide. Pealak and his wife walked all that way to see if any fish were to be had in the river. Fourteen miles knee deep in water and slush, and they were not young by any standard, old by Eskimo figures.

The river wasn't out, but after hours of trying, they caught one small char in a crack in the ice. That gallant little couple walked that fourteen miles back to their family at Repulse.

I saw them coming and walked down to meet them and to see how they had done. Laughing, they told me the river wasn't out yet, no fish. The worse things are, the more an Eskimo will laugh. She pulled the little fish out of the bag to show me, and from some place under her shawl, she brought out her ulu, her woman's knife. She cut a piece of the tail of that fish and insisted that I take it. Twenty-eight miles knee deep in water on an empty stomach and she'd give away part of the only fish she had. I shall never receive anything that I appreciate more.

And she did work for me. When the ship finally came, when things were better and no one was hungry, she came one day and scolded me about my ragged parka, and dragged me to the store to get duffle and thread and what not, and she made me a fancy new parka.

When I left Repulse, she came one day with her little granddaughter, and they gave me a bowl made of amber coloured musk-ox horn. I never see it but I see Mrs. Pealak's happy face and hear her chuckling, "Hurry, white man ..."

Winnipeg, April 23, 1987

Dear Claudia,

I suppose nature is busy covering up the scars of the hurricanes. One thing about the warm countries, they heal so quickly. Not so in our climate and less so the further north you go. When I was quite young, let's say about sixty years ago, almost three quarters of an everlasting century, but no matter, well my dad had an ice chisel he used to punch holes through the harbour ice to keep a record of how much ice grew each month of the winter. Like his special axe and other tools, no one, but no one, ever used that ice chisel, and one year the wooden handle just plain wore out, as Don Learmonth said about the engine in the old tug the *Watson Lake*.

Anyway, my dad needed a new six-foot handle for that special chisel and one day he must have caught me looking bored, though I never ever was, and told me to get into a pair of snowshoes and go up the valley about three miles to where there was a stand of the most lovely white birch trees you ever did see. I was to find a nice new handle there. I was all for the idea. It would take me out in the bush for a long spring afternoon, so away I went.

That birch grove was one of my most favourite spots, summer or winter. In summer, the side of the hill was ankle deep in caribou moss, and the trees, which would be in full leaf, could take your breath away. There was always the chance of seeing a fox or a lynx. They liked the place too, and families of willow grouse would nest there, one reason for the fox and lynx, and now and then a grumpy porcupine passing through. He liked balsam and spruce and never chewed the bark on the birches, though he would eat the new green shoots now and then.

In winter, you would love the place. There was a high steep hill going up from the bottom of the valley and the snow would cover it like a great sheet of paper. I never see a blank movie screen but I think of the backdrop formed by the hill. Standing in the valley looking up in winter, the bare black branches against the white snow looked like delicate tracery on purest white paper, not stark and cold-looking, but somehow warm, as if one had placed his hand on a paper after the artist had finished work and felt the warmth still there. You see many Christmas cards showing bare branches against white sky. In that valley, you saw the most beautiful Christmas card ever painted.

In spring, there would be that lovely green tinge that birches have against the remaining snow or the newly exposed reindeer moss, which has a colour all its own. Always reminds me of a pail of creamy milk, foaming and warm from the cow. In passing, did you know that if you sprinkle deer moss with molasses, cows will eat it and produce milk that is heavy and yellow with cream?

And in fall, when the birches turned colour and the tall larches behind put on their fall dresses, you could get light-headed with the colour and the absolute vitality of the place. We would get a light snowfall before all the leaves were down and there would be another dimension to the picture. The white background would have an embossed design of partridge tracks, almost invisible till you got them at the exact angle of sight, and there they were, printed right into the paper. Willow partridge have feathery feet and they leave feathery tracks. They go winding around all over looking for low bush cranberries that grow all along the hill, and where they stop to eat there are often little red circles in the snow beside their tracks. White snow, perforated with delicate tracks and red, red marks for contrast, all so beautifully worked in with the pencilling of the bare branches, the bold yellows of the remaining leaves and the bordering of the tall russet larch. Russet sounds dull, like Maid Marian's dress in the forest, but the larch colour is never dull. It's only that I have no word on my tongue to describe it.

What I started to tell you was once I got in there with my sharp axe on my shoulder per directions, I couldn't find my tree. Trees of the right size aplenty, the right length, lots, but how could I axe a lovely creation that, in that cold climate, had probably taken a hundred years to grow. I couldn't put my axe to any one of them. Sixty years may be a while, but I can remember exactly how I felt, that each and every tree of the hundreds was watching me, each one holding its branches tightly in fear of me. I patterned the snow with snowshoe tracks up and down, and not a tree could I cut. Ha! Geo. Washington had nil on me. He only had to say why he cut a tree. I'd have to explain why I didn't, and my dad, who was outwardly stern and inwardly as conscious of lovely growing things as anyone could be, would most likely have understood completely. I have wondered if he sent me because he wouldn't have wanted to harm one of those trees either.

But a handle the chisel must have and I must get in. Well, there was one last chance: our carpenter, net maker, engineer, talented master of a dozen trades, Will Shewak, an Eskimo, a man so capable that highly trained people not only listened to what he said, but came long distances just to ask his advice. A medium-sized brown man with black eyes and the most perfect teeth you ever saw. Prince Andrew, eat your heart out.

Well, Will had never failed me. No matter what the problem was, he'd drop his work and fix it. From the time when I was four or five and would go into his work shop with a shapeless chunk of wood to be made into a toy boat, till I was old enough to own my own sailboat. Will was always there to help, and not only me. Everyone on the post depended on Will. He could join wood together like no one else but Mother Nature could. When he died, I hope they gave him a nice work shop in that far, far off country and a supply of nice straight grained wood and sharp tools to shape it. He would not have asked for anything more.

So, sitting there on the tails of my snowshoes, I figured I'd better get back to Will, post haste. He was working in the net loft looking over dozens of huge salmon nets and figuring out what repairs were needed. I told him my problem and he just smiled. He said, "Remember last summer, when the mail boat bringing the mail ashore from the steamer broke a paddle when it got caught in the wharf?" Well, that paddle was seasoned ash. He'd fished it out of the water and put it away to make hammer and chisel handles, but the best part was still there and needed only a little dressing to fit perfectly. Well my dad got a handle for his special ice chisel, which became just that much more special, the only one around with a lovely grain in the varnished handle. He never did ask me how come I didn't get birch. I have never told anyone till now, it all comes out on account of a birch tree standing on my lawn and showing the first shimmer of green and a desire to tell someone about a very special place that is in my life and in my heart. There is an airstrip in that valley now I'm told. My birches? Oh they are safe and well, every one of them, in my memory. They can't be cut, they can never fall. They'll stand always and hold their branches just so, to make a design that is never the same and never changes. See? If I ever go back, my valley will never change. I just wanted you to see it.

April 29, 1987

Dear Claudia,

A friend of mine started talking about when he was in the Red Lake area in 1955, working with Lands and Forests on a survey. He said he always remembered the two Indian packers that were on the party and the amount they could carry over any sort of surface, the way they could pack all day and never seem tired at night. So I asked what were their names. He said he had forgotten, but knew they had the same first name. So I said, "Were they Moses Turtle and Moses Pascal?" and they were. How did I know? I was at Pikangikum, and Forestry asked me to hire two extra special packers for them, as they would be operating in dry country and couldn't fly their gear from lake to lake as usual. They needed packers.

They got packers, the very best. It's hard to believe but when we had a load of flour flown in to Pikangikum, it came in eighteen-sack loads, one hundred pounds per sack. We had a very steep hill from the dock to the warehouse. Angus and I found a hundred pounds quite enough to hike up that hill and across to the store. If either of the Moses was around he'd take it up in six trips, three sacks per trip, only because of the hill. On the level or going down, they'd handle four every trip. They never entered a packing contest when you only have to go ten yards or so. I'd bet on either of them taking seven or eight hundred on a short deal like that.

They were tall rangy men, but once in Lac La Ronge, a little shrivelled-up man, Thompson Venn, conned me out of a good deal of cigarette tobacco by carrying sacks of flour down the hill and putting them in a canoe. We were wheeling them down a couple at a time, when he came wandering along looking like the next gust of wind would blow him away. Bill Sanderson, who knew better, asked me why I didn't give the poor old fellow my wheelbarrow and let him earn a dollar or so.

I agreed, but Thompson said he'd only come by for a tin of cigarette tobacco. Would I give him a tin for every sack he could carry down at one time. I figured he might make it with one, seeing it was downhill all the way, so I said fine, let's see how many you can handle at one time. When he whipped out a well used pack strap from his pocket I figured that I might have been had. He straightened it out on the platform and Bill piled first sack, then, looking very doubtful, the sneak, he put on the second one.

Thompson stood like an ox, so Bill, with a glance at me, put on number three. Thompson still stood fast. I was about to tell Bill to quit when I thought, if this is a game, let it be played. Bill said, "*Keeabity*," and Thompson nodded, so on went numbers four to seven. There was a pile of flour about as high as the packer. Seeing he was on the ground and the flour on the platform, it towered away above Thompson's head. Bill said, as if he didn't know, "*Keeabity*." Thompson shook his head regretfully, no, the tumpline wasn't long enough for more.

I sat there expecting the big laugh that was bound to come from the gang that had gathered. No way could that wee undernourished looking little man carry that amount, but I had told myself that I'd give him his tin of tobacco. The joke was worth it.

Thompson put the tumpline around his head, and squared his feet for the mighty lift. Suddenly, he slipped out of the line and went over to the onlookers where he cadged a tailor-made cigarette and a light, and stood there smoking, looking mildly at the formidable heap of flour.

Then he suddenly went back, slipped into the tumpline, leaned forward, lifted the seven sacks and walked steadily and quietly down to the canoe with the cigarette sticking out the corner of his mouth.

Yes, the big laugh came, but at me, at the look on my face. That small powerhouse came back and he wasn't breathing heavily. He said, "Seven sack, seven cans," and I was dazed enough to say, "How many were going to St. Ives?"

He didn't understand or react. He just stood there, and I sent Bill for seven tins of tobacco. With a blank face, he put them on the platform, put his tumpline around them, backed up, and put his head in the sling. After two or three mighty efforts, he lifted the three and a half pounds of tobacco, and staggered away down the path with no change of expression, and everybody laughing at me.

The old rogue never bought a tin of tobacco while there was an ignorant white man to impose on. He had all his cronies, who'd let him know about a victim and he'd be there, so timid and weak looking to pick another bone. Yes, I helped him too. A planeload of Great Big American Sportsmen landed, and behind them another planeload of baggage. They wanted a packer to take it to the lake. I suggested Thompson.

They were doubtful but had the time, so agreed to give him ten dollars a man. There were nine and the pilot. Then one kindly fellow said, "Look at him, he'll be hours, but he needs the money. Come on fellows, let's make it fifteen a man." So pathetic Thompson accepted his fee, and hiked the gear across so fast that the Yanks hardly had the time to pick up the souvenirs all big hunters need to take home. Like me, I think some of them felt that they'd been had, especially the good-hearted fellow. Where the strength came in that little fellow I'll never know, but it was there, as my seven tins of tobacco will prove.

You may or may not have noticed Jim Linklater at Moosonee. Not much to look at for sure, and he lived on a pretty steady diet of potato chips and soft drinks. He never had breakfast. Ellsworth used to stop the truck outside his house and honk till Jim woke and came running out. Something to be said for sleeping in your clothes I guess.

Jim never changed. He wore a garment till it wore out and if he could afford it he put on new. If not, well a piece of string or a couple of nails can repair quite a rent. Just before noon Jim's wife would show up with a bag of chips and a soft drink. That was his lunch. At quitting time he'd jump off the truck at the store to restock on chips and pup and head for the movie show in the church basement. But Jim could work like a machine, he'd unload box cars all day and he was fast. He never seemed tired.

One year I had a big young kid from Winnipeg. His dad had pull with our manager, so this fellow got a job. He rode to Moosonee with me in a new truck I was taking in. In case you think there was a road that you never noticed, have no fears about your eyes. We rode to Cochrane and put the truck on the train. On the way along, Neil explained to me that he was an athlete, that he wouldn't expect any of us to have the same degree of fitness that he had. Very decent of him, and to reward him I decided long before we got to Moosonee, that I'd let him work with Jim, especially as he had been kind enough to offer to show the natives how to get fit by exercise and jogging.

Poor Neil, he had a lot to learn. Before he got around to his usual early morning job, he spent a day in a box car with Jim in charge. Frank had made it clear that there were to be no exceptions on race or colour. Neil leapt into the car and fell out at noon, exhausted. At one he asked me to assign him to some task more suited to his brain, but I explained that he came to work, and that he was double the size of any Indian in the car, which was a car of canned goods. When Frank and I looked in at mid-afternoon, the Indians were handling three or four cases at a time. Neil, poor innocent, was picking out the little ones and staggering to the door with one per trip, and his trips were about one to the natives' three. That evening I asked him if he wanted to talk about a training session for the natives and he didn't answer me. He forgot all about his regular morning jog, and lay in his bunk reading body-building magazines after supper.

Neil is now an executive in a bank in New York, doing well I'm told. I saw him last fall at a party on the occasion of his parents' for-tieth anniversary. He said that he'd never before seen people with stamina like those Indians. He also said, to his credit, that he wouldn't have dreamed of going jogging at Moosonee because he was sure the little kids would get out to deliberately show him up. He said as a learning experience it was fantastic. As a carefree summer in the bush it was a bummer.

And he might not have been wrong. One of the young policemen used to run every morning and evening. Then one day he was over-taken and passed by old Joe Koostachin's fat wife heading for the liquor store with two cases of empty bottles on her back. He used to laugh about it but he was a bit shaken when it happened. It's a pity we have to collect natives on reserves and settlements when hundreds of years of training has put them so far ahead of us as long as they are in their own country.

I could go on, and I usually do, but enough is enough. Some day when we can sit nice and quiet and not have to move I'll tell you about

Johnnie Turtle, whose name didn't fit. Doctor McCammon told me the story even though he said he could hardly believe it after seeing it. I could. You see I knew Johnnie Turtle and Isaac Guill,[34] and Roderick Keeper, and Bill Suggaski, all of whom could leave me miles behind at what they'd call a slow walk.

Then there was D'Moose Kakegumik, who'd run forty miles to sell a couple of weasels for candy for his adored son, and yarn for a few minutes in the store and run back again. There are many tales about D'Moose, all told to me by old Father Dubeau, who wouldn't lie just to make a good story better. In fact, he used to say one couldn't lie about these people. The truth was often less believable. And he was right. That's why it hurts so much to see them hanging around the beer parlours in the city—with all the big clean country that they can live in up north, they don't need what they find here. The white man has a lot on his conscience.

I am always thankful that I have a halfway good memory. I can bring back the wonderful and precious things. I can lie in my bed before I go to sleep and bring back a special day, almost hour by hour. I can remember conversations with special people word for word and see the expressions on their faces, but I can never remember what days the refuse is picked up, or what store hours are, or TV programs, or airline flights. I can sit down and write you a list of every man who had an account at Hebron fifty years ago. I know because I tried it and check in the archives. The ceremony of handing over The Bay's Northern Stores was on May 2nd. It was the same day as our fortieth anniversary dinner, so neither Carol nor I was there. I would like to have seen it. It took place on the deck of the Nonsuch. They hauled down the corporate flag and gave it back to the HBC Governor after 318 years. I have asked that the actual last flag flown on HB House be sent to the Archives, tattered and not as clean as it might be, but a very significant item in history.

---

34 It is difficult to discern the spelling of this name in the original letter.

None of us quite know how we feel about the Northern Stores being sold. Me in particular. They had been going 247 years when I was born; they were always there when I was young, when I grew up and when I retired. Hard to describe. No one else except the army ever paid me a cent of wages. They provided security all my life and even more, they provided people. People who were completely loyal HBC servants. You have to live in that sort of atmosphere, you must feel it to understand it. The Company was our life, what was good for it was good for us.

Today is the pensioners' meeting. Debbie Stutski at Hudson's Bay House, who arranges it with help from Miss Harris and yours truly, will be leaving in June to have her second child. She's the only young-ster among all us greyheads and everyone is so concerned about her. She laughs; it's her second time, she's young and healthy and very happy. I've known her since she came to HBH seven years ago. We became friends, in short, and I have enjoyed knowing her. She works in what I think of as personnel, but these days is known as human resources. I suppose I was a human resource when I was working, but I would rather be called an employee or even, as in the old days, a Servant. My dad and his staff put in their time proud of being HBC Servants; he'd have had a sour word for anyone who called him a human resource. I get old and crabby. I can't reconcile to gallons being litres now, and pounds being kilograms. I saw a kid of ten who couldn't tell the time on my wall clock. He said at home he only had digital clocks.

Anyway, with a new company, I suggested to Debbie that the female part of the staff should agitate for several female executives and since wholesale and *The Beaver* are moving out, there should be room for a day-care centre. She thinks it's a great idea. I've been trying to get them interested in a day care centre for years. So many good people leave because they have no place to leave babies and they spend time training replacements who will likely have babies in their turn. I'll keep pushing.

Winnipeg, November 9, 1987

Dear Claudia,

Out to Pointe du Bois on Sunday last with Carol Preston to see an HBC widow, Mrs. Anderson. She and her husband were in the Arctic many years and the little house is full of all sorts of things. Since Geordie's mother lived in Africa most of their later years, you have flavour of Arctic, Canadian, Scottish and African to enjoy. Her ivory collection, Arctic, is wonderful. I hope it will get to a museum intact one day, but there are Boer War and WWI medals side-by-side with Canadian Indian bead work.

She has a lot of 8-mm film that she and Geordie took at their various HBC postings. One which the Arts and Culture people in Ottawa want is of the last great whale killed by the Eskimos at Pangnirtung. The HBC helped them to tow the great animal in to Pangnirtung and gave them the old whaling plant to process their catch. For them it represented a winter of security as far as food and fuel went. No threat of hunger if hunting was poor. But, and it was a huge but, the poor HBC hit the papers and the International Whaling Commission got up and howled. Greenpeace, or whatever stood for Greenpeace in those days, wrote to Ottawa and Geneva and anywhere else you could think of. The people at Pangnirtung, white and native, were confused. They were a native group doing what they'd done for centuries, and the HBC lending them a helping hand, and all hell broke loose.

So Geordie did the sensible thing. It was fall. No ships could get in and he was the only radio operator, so he ignored anything about whales and whaling. At times the demands for an immediate answer to "ours of the umpty first" were pretty threatening, and he must have wondered how many years of a jail sentence he was accumulating, but he persevered. Messages in plain language and in code were filed and forgotten. His district manager in Winnipeg was an old Scot, very set on his own way, and he grew more and more furious that regular messages about business etc. were acted upon as usual, but no reply to any of his or Ottawa's demands for the why and wherefore of the whale.

I remember listening to one. I was at Wolstenholme at the time, and the message informed him that, "You seriously imperil your standing with the Company by refusing to act on certain messages which we know you have received." The Eastern Arctic had an almost daily situation comedy to listen in on. We all had the same code so we had no problems in keeping up with our own soap opera. Many the midnight the air would be busy with people contacting one another or Geordie to discuss the latest.

Meanwhile, a few dozen busy jaws and a multitude of dog teams were reducing the whale to its basic components and the flame on a hundred *kudloos* kept many an igloo warmed and lit that winter. In fact, that turned out to be one of the poorest hunting years ever experienced. We all envied Geordie and his happy gang at Pangnirtung.

Then came spring. The annual supply ship was on her way north. In those days, she went direct to Arctic Bay or Fort Ross from Churchill, and serviced all the other posts on her return. The RCMP, of course, had no alternative but to reply to the messages directed to them at Pangnirtung during the winter, just as Geordie had no alternative but deliver the messages to the police. However, at the time of the whale hunt, the RCMP were on the south coast of Baffin Island hunting walrus for the needs of their own dog teams and were not around to see or hear of the great whale.

So the corporal, a man of a lot of good sense, replied to all his messages and always referred to "the alleged killing of one Greenland whale." He also reported that while he had visited many scattered camps, he had been unable to interview any of the natives who had participated in the alleged killing, and that he had seen no materials that he could identify as part of a whale, Greenland or otherwise. I was picked up at Wolstenholme and went to Churchill to go from there on holiday and another posting. However, as one of the motormen had been injured, Captain Smellie asked me to make the round trip on the ship to replace the injured man. This would allow me to get off on Labrador where my parents were, so I gladly went along.

Excitement built up as we went from post to post, and finally, one bright fall day, we entered Pangnirtung fiord and anchored off the post. The spic and span post boat came alongside and Geordie, who was no shy violet, came bustling up the ladder to be met by the district manager, who warmly shook his hand and inquired what sort of a winter he'd had. "Well enough," said Geordie, "but whit was a' that senseless havering I had from you about some dammed whale?" There was a short difficult pause and the DM recovered enough to invite Geordie to his cabin for a touch of Nelson's blood and a conversation. The police inspector smiled at the corporal and they went off to the inspector's cabin to discuss this, and perhaps that, and a little of the blood, and we who'd come for that purpose went about the business of landing the supplies.

But a bit later, when most of the passengers had gone ashore, and the police and district manager were either sleeping or about their lawful concerns, Geordie slipped into the officer's mess room for a meal with us and told us the story of "the dammed whale." A year had passed. The International Whaling Commission was screaming about Russian and Japanese excesses, and one solitary whale that had probably prevented much hardship among the natives at Pangnirtung were forgotten.

Why the great love and loyalty to a commercial company? That I don't know, but I think the affection and loyalty had always been more to one another than to the firm. The company was only the mortar that bonded us. We were special people. We lived where few would want to live, almost in complete isolation, months for some of us without hearing another human voice, white or native. My longest was nearly ten months but none of us would have it otherwise. We dealt and lived with one of the world's most adaptable people, people who could live in comfort in one of the world's most barren environments, people who did not need us but who, with all the grace and good breeding in the world, allowed us to enter their world and taught us how to live there.

The Arctic people of HBC and the people who worked in the bush were two different types, each as important in his own area as the other, but there were many fewer of us in the Arctic, and we were, perhaps for that reason, closer. I know that today I can meet a person who served in the Western Arctic, or one from the Central or Eastern, and we are friends and companions. We are Arctic people. Not so with the Indian trader from Hazelton and one from Mistassinni. There is too much difference. They are Company people and respect one another as such. We were Company people and Arctic people and that is what makes us special to one another. When I see Ches Russel or Scottie Fall who worked a whole Arctic apart, I feel no difference. One day perhaps, there will be only one old time Arctic "man" left, maybe not too long in the future. He/she will be the loneliest man/woman in all Canada. I hope that I am not that man.

So, Guy Fawkes Day is not long past. When I was a kid in Fogo, there was a certain amount of religious difference. There were Catholic, Anglican, United and Salvation Army schools, and to each his own. People coming from Lion's Den had to pass three schools to get their own, people from Back Cove ditto in the other direction. Everyone in Lion's Den was Anglican and every one in Back Cove was RC. So as Nov. 5 approached, the Protestant kids started collecting anything burnable for the bonfires, which were always lit on the highest hills to celebrate the failure of the Gunpowder Plot.

And how about the RC kids? Well, forbidden by parent and priest to have any hand in such ungodly doings, they couldn't leave school and go with the happy gangs that begged, borrowed and stole anything burnable for a month before the great night. Just being seen would be cause for penance, but God is merciful, and October evenings in Newfoundland close in early, so humping a huge load of starrigans. Gotcha didn't I? A starrigan is a little tree that grows on or near the cliffs and never comes to any size, but is sappy and makes a most crackling fire and the smoke is aromatic bliss. Well, humping your back load of starrigans to the fire, you might chance to fall in with a shadowy figure similarly laden and find it was your friend Ben from the other school who, under friendly darkness, had joined the sworn enemies of Catholicism. If you stood fifty of us up in a line, and under pain of instant death, you demanded an explanation of the Guy Fawkes celebrations of November fires, you'd better be prepared to nail the whole hundred Protestant or Catholic. I'd be prepared to swear that most would only know that it was bonfire night. Anyway, while, or when, kids here in Canada were overturning outhouses on October 31st, we were carrying them away bodily to the burning.

Which brings to mind a tale. Seems that one cantankerous old fellow had shut off a portion of his fence that had been more or less a right of way for kids for years. So his outhouse was one of the first to go. Well, some adults inevitably arrived at the fires and the old man's next door neighbour had himself a wonderful laugh when old Enoch's one holer was heaved into the flames. In fact, he laughed right heartily till he recognized his own seat of state as it went sailing into the fire. From then on it wasn't so funny.

Appearances are everything. There was no way the parents of Catholic kids could be ignorant of where their kids were, but, like Nelson, they turned the blind eye. One night I went home with Ben after the fires had died down. We went into the kitchen of his house innocently. His father was there knitting a herring net.

"Where you been?" "Just out on the road." "You smell of smoke, you do." Quick thinking by Ben. "Everybody does. The roads are thick with smoke from all the fires." Then, to me, "You're a Protestant boy. How come you're here wi' Ben?" "Oh I dunno, we just met up." Then to Ben, "You got the excuse for the smoke, tell me about all that "vaar" (balsam sap) on your clothes. You been to the fires, boy." So we admitted, yes, we were at the fires, and it was fun.

A warning, while his eyes twinkled over the net: "Me, I don't care, but God help you if your grandmother finds out." "Yes Sir," and silence while we watch the busy needle and card from the meshes of the net one by one, silence that was broken by the old grandmother's voice from the next room. "Don't let Gran know, shore nuff! Why I washed more vaar out his clothes when he was a boy. More'n fifty years he is. Listen to him tell the byes, don't let Gran know. Gran knows plenty and one day she might tell." And in she comes with his tea and a grin of delight on the Irish face of her. It wasn't our generation that broke the rules by a long shot.

Gran, you'd have loved. She was little and neat, in a long black skirt and a brilliant white apron that never seemed to get soiled, no matter what she did. She was old, very old, and she had a leprechaun's face and smile. She feared no one because she had no reason, as she said. She "borned" half the Catholic kids around the harbour and many of the Protestants too. Old Mrs. Fury once said to her that she should let "the others" look after themselves. She said a Protestant woman borned three of my boys and I'll born a child for any woman that needs me, even you, my girl, but you're a mite past it now, but blessed miracles do happen, so I'll watch for you. From there on, as you might guess, "blessed miracle" covered many a case.

But Gran was someone to go to with any problem. She always had a reasonable solution. Bob Scott used to tell a story about a conflict between two men as to which owned a big drift log that both claimed. Bob said the magistrate said for heavens sake go see Gran Walbourne, I haven't the time to fool around with sticks of wood. Bob said Gran's decision was short and sweet, shake hands like sensible people, then saw up the log and give the wood for chobies (kindling) to the poor widows around the harbour. "Not me, I got sons to bring my wood and they don't fight about it." It could be true; Bob was a good sort.

Gran was near a hundred when I last saw her. I went to her house. She had been bedridden for a year, but she knew what I'd been up to, and her eyes were as keen as ever. She said, "Boy, are you feared of sickness?" I said I didn't think so. She said, "Are you feared of dying," and I said not now, maybe later. She said, "I'm dying. I won't be here when you get back in the fall." I didn't know what to say. She looked so small there and yet she was the same mighty Gran that I'd always known. My eyes filled and I felt terrible. She said, "Come here," and I went over and took her small, ancient hand, and on impulse, I leaned over and kissed her forehead. I said, "Fine time along, Gran," which is what one says to a traveller. She smiled and said, "Mind the rocks bye, and hail for a deep vessel every fall." She was gone when I got back, and when I was in her empty house, I wept harder than I'd ever done.

She was no relation, but she was Gran, and men from all over the island came when she died, to carry her to her rest, and the casket never touched the ground the whole five miles to the grave. Men and boys stood in line for the honour of carrying her to the place she would rest, overlooking the village that she loved and served and probably never went more than a few miles from for all of her hundred years, and every religion on the island had its place in her funeral.

I couldn't be there, but people enough told me that as the little casket was passed from one set of shoulders to another, men who had never been known to show any emotion wept bitterly. Her family put up her headstone and the community fenced and tended her grave. Even many years later, the word Gran meant only one person. The rest, and there were many wonderful old ladies, were Gran Piercey or Strickland or whoever.

There were few doctors in the outports, and midwives or "Granny people" borned all the babies, no charge. They would go for miles overland or by boat and in the cold of winter or during the busy summer. It was only necessary to knock on a door and in minutes the Granny was on her way. Some were younger women with families of their own. No matter, she left, and a neighbour came in for as long as was necessary. One pretty custom: the new baby's first gown usually went to the Granny who borned her or him. It was carefully kept, and a bit later might go to another baby and back to the Granny again. Many a child went into a well-worn gown at birth while its mother had a drawer full of new things. No matter, it was Gran's perquisite. The older and more worn the gown, the more credibility for the midwife, though I don't think any one looked at it like that. I wander a lot, sure sign of old age. If I were on my own home island now I'd probably be "Old Uncle Len." You only need a few grey hairs to qualify. Sort of nice to be everyone's uncle.

FOURTEEN

Winnipeg, December 11, 1987

Dear Claudia,

I shall not be around when you are an old lady, but you will someday be a wonderful old person. Perhaps like Aunt Bella, who was never a relative but whom I loved deeply and who made old age something you could never be afraid of.

When travelling I sometimes stayed at Aunt Bella's overnight and I always spread my sleeping robe on a pile of nets in the storage area and slept marvellously. Aunt Bella always clucked at me when I refused the "comfortable room," with its great big feather bed in winter. Where there are lots of geese, there are feather beds, and no one was ever cold in one. But I liked to sleep on the nets and Aunt Bella knew why.

What did she look like? She was small, and must have been very strong, because she could row or sail or handle a dog team with anyone. Even as an old lady, she had smooth pink cheeks and dark eyes, almost black, showing her Eskimo heritage. She had black hair with very little grey in it, even when she was very old. Her hands and feet were small. She always wore a long black dress with a white blouse with a high collar, and her hair was always braided and formed into a bun at the back. Over her dress, she wore a rougher barbell, or apron, to protect the rest of her clothes.

`She looked merry and she was merry. She loved to yarn about old days, old people, and she loved to tell funny stories about them. One of them was Moll Sawney. Moll Sawney was, to me, an old woman not quite right in the head, who was a menace to children and not someone you wanted to remember. I must have said something once, because Aunt Bella took me out one fine fall evening when I was young. We went to the wharf which was quiet after the men had gone for the day. And we sat with our feet dangling over the side watching the fish while she told me rib-tickling stories of Moll Sawney that I'd never heard before. Perhaps she invented some of them. I'll never know because I realized that Moll wasn't always a repugnant, dangerous hag. She had been a happy bighearted woman in her day, until disease, that she had no protection against, took over and changed her. I don't think anyone but Aunt Bella could have made me see that.

Another time, I was in a towering rage about some unimportant thing once and my brothers were not making things any better by laughing at me. Aunt Bella asked me if I'd to up the valley to a place where huge silver birches and alder grew to cut her some switches (light rods for cleaning algae off salmon nets). It's a lovely place to be, and when I got there, I just sat for a long time just letting the foolish anger leak away. I knew very clearly why she'd done it, just to let me find out on my own how useless anger actually is. I won't say it cured me, but it did tell me how being a jackass is no help at all.

I have been thinking about Aunt Bella a lot lately, perhaps because I've been trying to recall as much as I can about the old people I knew as a youngster for Doris Saunders' little magazine *Them Days*, a verbal history of Labrador. And when I think about others, Aunt Bella inevitably comes to my mind, because among outstanding and competent people, she always stood out.

Last week there was an article in the *Free Press* about a seal seen at Pine Falls. Most people said pish and tosh and other pertinent expressions, but Henry Voisey and I know it can easily be. Only one seal would do it and that seal does exist in Hudson's Bay and on the Labrador. In fact, they inhabit several lakes in Labrador and Arctic Quebec, lakes which are at least a thousand feet above sea level. So it's not so much pish and tosh either, always providing that it was a seal that was seen. The wildlife people tell me it was a seal and they felt that it was a tame one that someone lost or liberated, because, as one fellow told me importantly, there does not exist a freshwater seal in North America. So I asked how he'd feel if I told him that they already occur in Nueltin Lake and have been seen away up the Seal River, and where did that river get such a name?

He backtracked a bit. Said, well, I'm not a seal expert, I'm a whale expert. No whales have been reported at Pine Falls so I had to let him go. Where is the Arctic seal expert? Thought you might ask, so I did. He's where any respectable Arctic seal expert should be, in Florida, attending s conference on the sea cow or some similar thing that doesn't happen here. I talked to a lot of people and I must say I never saw so many who knew less about the job they get paid to do.

Who am I to holler. In 1937, the Carnegie Museum had a field party working around the Belcher Islands and Great Whale River on the old people who used to live there. They met an Indian who had a bag made out of a type of sealskin unknown to them. He said he'd shot the seal in, believe it or not, Seal Lake, away inland from Richmond Gulf. Well the museum said there were no seals in fresh water. This a hundred and fifty years or more after HBC had been shipping Ranger skins to London from Labrador and the Eastern Arctic.

However, the museum, in its wisdom, realized that this Indian did have a bag made from an unknown seal, so they sent Dr. Twomey and Dr. Doutt to Moosonee in the winter of 1938, and said to them, go forth and bring back that which we believe does not exist. So they went forth, and Freddie Moore's brother went third (That's new math) with them, and they went to Seal Lake after some trials and tribulations, and they got two specimens of the unknown non-existent seals, and took them back to Pittsburgh. Years later the museum still thought they had the only skins in existence.

So I asked one of the Manitoba experts why a seal couldn't go up the Hayes River into Lake Winnipeg. He said because there is no water route, so I asked where did the York Boats go? Easy, they ran from Winnipeg, then known as Fort Garry, to Grand Rapids and Norway House. I said why were they called York Boats? Took him only a second and they were built at York to save the expense of bringing nails and fittings all the way to Lake Winnipeg. Being a reasonable person I said they probably sent the finished boats to Lake Winnipeg parcel post, since there was no water route. He said, you raise a point, I shall investigate it. I was about to ask him to find out why Manitoba pays him a salary, but I remembered Aunt Bella and refrained.

However, the director told me that I had messed up their theory of a pet seal pretty seriously, and now they have to do some more thinking. I could have said, with what, but I didn't; you see, I am becoming quite civilized. If I were just a bit more stupid, I could work for Wildlife. Henry and I still feel that a seal could easily be at Pine Falls. After all, tourists go down the Hayes River. Granted they only go the easy way... down. But seals are wiser and much smarter than tourists I suspect.

Winnipeg, February 5, 1988

Dear Claudia, Leisale,

You see, I like your new name, but to me you are still Claudia. When I was first in the Arctic, some places had native names like Amajauk or Ivuyivik and others were called Wolstenholme or Southampton Island. Then of course, Ottawa got in on it, and they changed some of the names in the NWT back to a version of what the original native name might have been. Some weird spellings evolved, according to which Civil Servants (you see, I use capitals too!) did the altering and spelling. It ended up with the whites saying this used to be Frobisher, it is now Iqaluit, and the natives scratched their heads and wondered what new word this might be. Sounds Inuit, but doesn't mean Inuit. Oh well, these white people, you know. God be thanked, the average native is smarter than the average Civil Servant, so among themselves they use the old names which they always did, and dusted off the new ones for official use.

Don't mind me. I'm all riled up with Civil Servants, some not so civil either.

The other day in my mailbox was an official-looking letter which said briefly, you must appear in traffic court to answer charges that on day one, first century BC or thereabouts, (they love that word thereabouts) you did cause an accident at the intersection of Doom and Desolation, and that if you don't appear it will be at your peril. Well, maybe not those exact words, but you get my meaning. They were kind enough to furnish me with a licence number, not mine, of course, and details of an accident I never knew about, all nicely wrapped up under the name of Badge, but addressed to my home.

So I called the number conveniently displayed. I heard you. Right! I was stupid. But I have this belief that some day, somehow, officialdom can be rational, if only in answer to the laws of average, or if you insist, below average. So after the required number of rings, a voice, unutterably bored, said, "Mumble, mumble." I asked politely. Yes, I'm always polite first, it's later that I erupt. She was so amazed that I answered in English, and I felt like Oliver Twist asking for more. Emboldened by my luck in reaching a Civil Servant who was apparently alive or awake, or what passes for those conditions, I read to her the notice number and pertinent details, and she said, "Wait." Just that. So I waited in sure and certain knowledge that she had gone to get the beadle.

But she came back, said, "You are L. Badge." I said no. She said you live at 46 Conifer Crescent. That I admitted, so she said, "Mr. Badge, you will appear as ordered, etc. etc." I told her that was not my name, it was not my licence number, and I didn't know what to do with this ticket as it did not apply to me, that a mistake had been made.

She said, "You don't know nothing," and hung up.

Resisting an impulse to tear the phone off the wall, as I was sure someone would need it when I was in prison, I dialled again, and the bell rang and rang, and finally a man's voice, a little out of breath answered. I said, "Are you the sergeant?" and he said, "No, I hope to be one day, but this phone was ringing off the hook and was driving me round the bend."

You know how the first astronaut felt when he landed on the moon and saw the sign which said #1 Highway to St. John's, Newfoundland. Well, I too felt there was life in this here wilderness, so I poured out all my woe to this nice man, and in seconds he found that there is indeed an L. Badge, but he lives nowhere near me, and he said, "All's well, tear up the ticket." I thanked him and asked him to tell his opposite number that, except for her public relations and perhaps her grammar, she was my idea of a complete civil servant, my ideals not being that high anyway. I was delighted to hear a second receiver banged down rather briskly.

Now may God help me if my name ever comes before some lady on a traffic ticket. You will hear from me from solitary confinement written on bathroom stationery with a pen plucked from my thin feather mattress and done in blood for lack of ink.

By the way, they are little better higher up the scale. Several of my friends have decided to sponsor P.A.C. Nichols, retired from the HBC, for an Order of Canada. Having gone through the exercise for W.E. Brown, I was considered, with no justification, to be the resident expert. So since I find it hard to say no, and P.A.C. being the fine gentleman that he is, I contacted the Chief of Protocol in the Manitoba Government to obtain the forms.

"Why certainly sir, your name and address please. The forms will be in the mail immediately." Now I find that when someone says it's in the mail, don't hold your breath. I didn't and I would have been mighty blue in the face if I had. So after a decent interval, I don't like using the word decent when referring to protocol officers, but one must be polite, especially when he wants something.

After said interval, I asked my son-in-law Andy, now chairman of the Municipal Board, to drop a hint into the shell-pink of someone, that a form, official number OC-1 would suit my purposes to a tee. As a result, I got a call saying the forms were in the mail. The Kiss of Death withal. Well, more than one road leads to Rome, and/or Bally Clare, so I contacted the office of the Lieutenant Governor of Manitoba and was told, "But certainly, Mr. Budgell, we will put these forms in the mail this very day."

What could I do but wait another decent interval. You know, that's what they used to say about a widow who had buried number one and who waited a decent interval before admitting husband number two to all honours and privileges thereto pertaining.

Anyway, the interval becoming more and more decent and no forms appearing, and my date to enjoy a meal at Grapes downtown to deliver the forms and my expert opinions on how to proceed further becoming more imminent, I was returning home from taking Muriel to the University of Winnipeg when I suddenly saw in front of me, shining in the frost mist, the Parliament Buildings. Where there are Parliament Buildings, there are, by the laws of average, Lieutenant Governors, and where he is, there shall be forms also.

Everyone knows that parking space is never, never available within a day's walk of the Parliament Building, so it was with little hope that I took the circular drive, fortunately bare of protesters, environment cranks, and the fellow that's been picketing for four years because he wants workman's compensation. And as I pulled near the great steps where there are four, count them, four parking spots, always permanently filled, a Zipper Courier pulled out of one and I slid into that space.

If there was ever a sign from heaven…There must have been twenty cars orbiting the building looking for space, and the waters had opened like the Red Sea for Moses and let my Rabbit in. One trembles in the presence of supernatural things, but like Alice, I dared enter Wonderland. I avoided the Queen of Hearts, though I confess there was a lady whose resemblance chilled my blood. Feeling more like Oliver than ever, I approached the throne. Turned out to be a reception desk, but who could blame me? I said, "Please Sir, where might I find the Lieutenant Governor's office?"

Without looking up he said, "Room 235," and added, "That's second floor." How could he tell without looking that I was Oliver or stupid or both. Some things are never revealed, not even to those who seek.

So, hat in hand, mostly because it was a ski cap of a not particularly handsome green that clashed with my blue parka but kept my partially naked head warm withal, I mounted the great steps between the two buffalo, who, if the artist was correct, would have been most uncomfortable outside on the prairie on that cold and windy day. However, we are not here to discuss artistic detail, which in truth might bring a blush to the cheek. At the top of the stairs, for lack of indication where 235 might be, I turned left, since it is well known that while properly oriented creatures turn right, mules, lobsters and Newfies go left. It's hereditary.

But let me tell you. There is a Room 235, with two handsome doors. The right one opens. The left is bolted permanently, so I naturally chose the left, and in any case, a sprained wrist is no great thing when one is engaged in Adventure. The room was occupied by one, yes one, lady. I, with my usual tact and organizational skill, hit the place at precisely midday and everyone had gone to lunch in the palace, sorry, I forgot I wasn't Alice… the Parliament Lunch Room where rumour says they enjoy great meals at low prices, courtesy of the ever patient tax payer.

A more disinterested lady I never did see, but probably she was just sad that her fellow employees already had their feet in the trough while she remained to be pestered by uncouth people with unmatched parkas and hats. Ever wonder why people who sell parkas and those who sell ski hats never have the matching numbers? Well maybe we can get a protest going someday when it's warmer. One remembers the buffalo.

So I asked, hat in hand, how much more humble can one be…, "Do you have form OC-1, Nomination for the Order of Canada?" She said severely that OC-1 had been discontinued, as it is unilingual. I said, "Do you have the replacement?" She said, "I will look," while every fibre in me was screaming, "You have to have it. You already said it was in the mail!" But I prudently held my tongue. The woman is magic. The first file she put her hand on was full of forms for Nomination for the Order of Canada. And she gave me two.

Like Uriah Heep, I bowed myself out the door, returned to my Rabbit, which contrary to all expectations, had not been hit by lightning hurled by the Golden Boy.[35] Speaking of cold, how about him? Away up there in the wind chill in what looks to be pretty short shorts. Oh well. You know, when I got home I checked the form. It is completely in English, the only difference being that the little number OC-1 has been deleted. Yes sir, we are mighty proud to be a bilingual country.

Winnipeg, May 17, 1988

Dear Claudia,

This is the time of year when the Newfies who are away want to go home, and those who have been at home want to leave. Those, like me, who are bogged down on the prairie, and who have no reason to leave, and who would also face the grave displeasure of grandkids if they even considered it must needs find some distraction. In my case,

35 There is a golden statue of Mercury at the top of the Provincial Parliament Buildings in Winnipeg.

I can always turn to the books. And that's what I've been up to early and late recently.

Who'd write books about Labrador? Well a number of people, and over the years I've collected some. Early in the century there was a lot of interest in the Labrador. L. Hubbard and D. Wallace, with George Elson, a half-native from Moosonee whom I once met when he was very old, tried to cross from North West River to George River. It was a failure, notably because Hubbard took the wrong provisions and because he wouldn't listen to Elson or the trappers he met and insisted on going up the Susan instead of the Nascopie. They ran into trouble. George said turn back, Hubbard said no, and finally starved.

Elson, with no supplies but a fantastic memory, went back for help in deep snow with no snowshoes, living off bones and bits and pieces of food they had discarded at various camps. Even the Labrador trappers couldn't figure out how he could find these things in a foot or more of snow. He finally sent help back by some trappers he met. Wallace was still alive, Hubbard, they knew, was dead.

Much later, Elson went back directly to the tent, which was now buried in snow, and got Hubbard's body. Then he went to another spot where they had left all the film that had been exposed on the trip. Bert Blake, a trapper who was just a young boy at the time, was along. He told me that they were walking along the river and everything was deep in snow. Elson just walked ashore at a certain place, and dug straight down, and there was a bag of film.

The only other person I ever knew who could do that was my brother Max.[36] Even the Indians leave some sort of mark to identify a cache. We left Davis Inlet when Max was six. Twenty years later he was back there with HBC and could go to dozens of places where my dad had had rabbit snares, just as if he had been there only yesterday.

Anyway, Wallace wrote a book and two years later went back with better equipment, and made the trip that, of course, involved another book. Mrs. Hubbard, who wanted to finish her husband's work, also went back the second year after Hubbard starved. She had George Elson, Job Chapies, Joe Iserhoff, all of Moosonee, and Bert Blake from North West River. Not only did she finish the trip, but did it so fast that she and her group were able to come back from Ungava on the HBC's annual supply ship. She wrote a remarkable book on her trip. The man who helped her at North West River was George Cotter's father.

Later:

At *The Beaver*, Carol Preston's desk is always piled high. I'd like to go in to chat more but she is always so busy that I hesitate. *The Beaver* takes on more and more a new tone. The old HBC and the Arctic and the great men of the past don't appear very regularly and while the more modern look probably goes over well with the public, the old fellows like me and the rest of the retired, don't find the magazine nearly so interesting. Selfish? Of course, we want to see and read about the people and times we knew best, but we are few in number and the public is probably tired of our tales and experiences. So up the new, and may God remind us all to renew our subscriptions. Otherwise *The Beaver* could go the way of other things that don't meet Mr. Thomson's[37] standards, like our flag on all our envelopes and letterheads.

See, we don't change. Like all the Irish, we'd rather be mad than right. When I was young, people used to say that if you dug up an Irishman after he was buried, you'd find that he had managed to turn

---

36 Hubert Maxwell, Len's older brother. Len spoke highly of Max's tracking and survival skills. Max Budgell later walked from Voisey's Bay to Seven Islands across the Labrador peninsula with a group of Montagnais Indians to enlist in the army, a distance of about 700 miles. "He was put in jail for entering Canada illegally before Confederation. Went to the army and they turned him down for flat feet after he'd walked across Labrador. Then they found out where he had come from and they changed their minds." From the HBC tapes. Max served overseas with the 1st. Bn. Royal Highland Regiment of Canada (Black Watch).

37 Ken Thomson, a Canadian billionaire, acquired The Hudson's Bay Company in the 1970s. He sold the last of his shares in the company in 1997.

himself around so that his feet were where anyone else's head would be. The truth of the matter was that ages ago there were very few recognized cemeteries, and to sort of keep people sorted out, the Protestants who, at least then, were in the majority, were planted with their feet pointing east while the Romans were planted the other way. So, perhaps not to obstruct the view, the gravestones of the latter would be actually at their feet, preserving the look of the cemetery and allowing the Irish to be contrary to the end.

Capt. Dennis Hynes, who worked with us at Moosonee, was Romish, and he swore that sometime before he had worked on a road gang and it became necessary to move an old cemetery to make room so that the living could go straight to hell without having to go round the bend. He said that, not me. Anyway, when they got around to the move, they did find some people pointing east and some west. There were no stones. I guess the original markers were wood and had perished. Dennis said it proved that the Irish turned around after they went down. Who am I to dispute him?

Kaleigh's been here. Volcanoes are her pet interest at the moment. I have a book on the aerial mapping of northern Labrador before the war. There are some magnificent pictures of mountains that I knew. In one, there is even a far-away view of the house I lived in at Hebron. She'll pore over that book, looking for evidence of volcanic activity and there isn't any.

Near Natchvak, the Torngats are a particularly beautiful range. It means "the place where the spirits live." For sure no one will disturb them there. Kaleigh will look at that picture for long periods and finally pick a place on the shoreline because she knows no one has ever penetrated the hidden valleys. And when she has the exact spot pinpointed, she'll ask, "Grampa, were you ever right there? What is it exactly like?" I've been in Natchvak Fiord, and have felt that in its grandeur and absolute natural state, it is nature's cathedral, because while men have been there now and again, they cannot stay, and their futile works soon disappear. I've been right there.

I can tell her what a beautiful place it is. The sun shines into the fiord from the easy for a few hours everyday, then it is blocked by the hills at certain times of the year. In spring and early summer, when the sun is at its highest, it can shine directly down the great chasm. The rest of the time there is little sun, but because of the great crags covered with snow, there is lots of light. All manner of animals congregate there: seals, whales, walrus, arctic fox and polar bear. Once I saw a lonely and puzzled looking black bear. The great brown bear, now extinct as far as anybody knows, that used to haunt the barrens inland from Natchvak, had been seen in the fiord by the early HBC and Moravian mission people. The natives, whose legends over the years are surprisingly accurate, say that he was larger than a polar bear, much stronger, and would attack men on sight when the polar bear has never been known to do that.

I have seen the surface of the fiord alive with huge flocks of eider ducks feeding on the millions of shrimp and beds and beds of mussels. Lesser ducks and gulls, terns, shearwaters, sea pigeons, puffins and murres are there in the millions. Arctic char, salmon and cod are there for the taking, and in the days of the sailing schooners, Natchvak was known as a good place to "bring up" for a season's fishing, but so far away and lonely that only a few ever took advantage of the plenty there.

It was a place of security for a native culture, and so recognized by the HBC and Moravians who built there. They tried to entice the natives to settle also because there they would never go hungry. Neither trade nor religion would entice the natives to dare the spirits and all efforts to settle them there failed. There was another practical consideration; the shores of the fiord are so steep that land animals are necessarily restricted to the shoreline. How long the wildlife would survive if a number of hunters were to wander there is doubtful. The sea life is also concentrated in the narrow fiord and greater activity from the fishing boats and hunters might well deter the animals from using the fiord. There is a route westward to the barren caribou birthing area inland. Greater pressure on the does and calves could have an adverse effect on the herd. So perhaps the natives knew that not only the spirits were against a large population there. Perhaps they recognized how fragile the environment there was. Anyway, they restricted themselves to an occasional foray for seals, walrus and whales, and left the place in peace most of the time.

And what of the whites? Why didn't they wait it out? Well the lack of sun in the winter got to them. The HBC was staffed by Labrador people who were able to handle the situation. Sam Ford had his wife there with him for several years. He told me that even for them, born and brought up on Labrador, it was a tough place in winter, but had the trade been there, he would have stayed.

There wasn't a constant supply of Labrador people. Sam was needed to open up new areas much farther north, and so he was transferred. The next man, a young Scot, pulled out by dog team for southern Labrador in his first winter. The missionaries and their wives, from a much gentler climate in Germany, could handle places like Nain or Hopedale for a lifetime, and did, but couldn't take Natchvak, so they left it to the birds, animals and nature. And while efforts have been made to establish a tourist trip there in summer, they have not been successful, thanks be to God. Who'd want to see empty Kodak film boxes and soft drink cans on the shore? If there is a place on earth for a nature preserve, it is there.

Winnipeg, July 3, 1988

Dear Claudia,

I got a letter the other day from Bert Swaffield who now lives in Prince Albert, Saskatchewan. Bert was born in Labrador, son of an HBC man, what else. And was a clerk with my dad at Rigolet for a short while before being transferred north. He spent the rest of his active life in the Eastern Arctic, and has a place named after him called Swaffield Harbour. That's in direct contradiction of a federal ruling that says you have to be dead before they officially name a geographical feature after you.

Buster Brown (W.E. Brown) also beat that rap. Brown's Lake and River were named for him when he was very much alive. On the other hand, I was once asked to make absolutely certain that Old Cyril Wingnik, an Eskimo of the Western Arctic, famous as one of the last of the whalers and a marine pilot for years and years, was dead, because Ottawa wanted to name a point of land for him. I explained it to old Bertram Pokiak, one of the ancients of Tuktoyaktuk, and he caught on very quickly. He said in English, "Just like dead." He didn't say, "*Iukoyuk*," which means dead, dead, if you take my meaning. Since the Governor General was to announce the new name at Inuvik some time later that year, and knowing how governments tend to forget things that are postponed or delayed, I said that, to the best of my knowledge and belief, Wingnik was dead.

So, the Governor General added that to his little discourse at Inuvik and everyone was happy. In the fall, on my way back to Winnipeg, I was overnight at Inuvik and went to the hospital to see Mrs. John Roses of Tuktoyaktuk who had just had her first baby. While I was there, one of the sisters asked me if I would like to see Wingnik. Not much went on that the sisters missed, so I was taken to a part of the new hospital set aside for permanent patients and there was old Cyril large as life, but missing his legs, which meant he was "just like dead" as far as being a hunter and trapper went.

The sister smiled at me and said thanks for telling a little white lie because they had had the same request and had not known how to answer, and also knowing how old Cyril would enjoy having some rocks named after him, they were pleased when Ottawa announced that all was well. After the Governor General's speech, and while he toured the hospital, he of course, met Wingnik, but he was of good stuff and never changed a hair. He shook the old man's hand and passed on. I was never asked to explain how I came to believe that he was dead. Had I been, I'd have passed the buck to Pokiak, likeable old sleeveen that he was, who had had a good many moments staying ahead of the whites, and who could easily smile his way through another.

Winnipeg, September 3, 1988

Dear Claudia,

I've been putting my collection of books on the Arctic, which were in boxes and cupboards, into regular bookcases, and was agreeably surprised to find how many I actually do have. A lot are second hand from a shop in Alliston, Ontario, run by Helen and John Wray, a very special couple of people who seem to find a lot of things that are out of print, like a weird thing put out, yes I have to confess, by HBC in the 1920s called *The Eskimo's Book of Knowledge*. In the Company's defence, I have to tell you that it was composed by two chaps from an English university, who were hired to find ways of improving the lot of the natives.[38] Can you bear any more? I had one before but it was lost when our famous old ship *Nascopie* found a rock that was a bit harder than she was.

Poor old ship. She'd made more than a quarter century's worth of Arctic voyages before she found that rock. Many of her voyages were under the command of Capt. T.T. Smellie, a pint-sized bundle of what the old time English master mariner should be. He had a few expressions he used when tourists bothered him. They'd say, perhaps when we were in thick fog, "Do you know where we are?" And he'd

38 They worked as part of the HBC Development Department.

say, "We are so many fathoms from the bottom of the sea, so many miles from the nearest land, and if you want to know how close to Heaven, we have two bishops aboard, that is their department."

Once we were crossing Hudson's Bay on a beautiful day but there was heavy flat floe ice in all directions. We were temporarily stuck. I was on the bridge where the Old Man only allowed crew or the occasional special visitor. We had a reporter from a Toronto newspaper aboard. He was pretty thick-skinned and more than a bit ignorant. He came bursting up on the bridge all loaded with cameras as if he owned the ship. He didn't see that the captain was instantly more glacial than the ocean, and that he hated to be called Skipper. That title was for some joker in a little sailboat. But our friend shouted, "Skipper, I've been reading up on this ship. I find that she can break flat unrafted ice up to five feet thick."

Capt. Smellie looked at him over the big pipe he smoked much of the time, and said, "This must be a couple of inches over five feet then," and walked away. The poor fellow said to the second mate, "Did I say something wrong?" Len Adey said, "Son, you are all wrong. Wrong place, wrong question, wrong man." The reporter went quietly down the ladder and the Old Man smiled and said, "Thank you, Mr. Adey."

Captain Smellie grew up in square-rigged ships, an apprentice at twelve years old. His first voyage to China was around Good Hope, home via the Horn. I have a picture in a book, a little fellow, about swallowed up in his old fashioned heavy serge uniform. Boys became men very quickly on those ships. He never grew very big, perhaps five foot five, but he was a big man. He called all his seamen by their last names, he called his officers Mr. I never heard him call anyone by a first name, not even his chief steward, who was with him many years on different ships. Better stop, I'll be writing about him all night.

You guessed. He was a very important person in my life. He was asked once by HBC to look at a place near Lake Harbour, where there is a vicious reversing current that becomes an actual overfall at certain stages of the tide. A Company post manager had been drowned there a few days before our arrival. The Company wanted a report on the safety of the place for an official report and, of course, to warn future staff to avoid the place. Capt. Smellie asked me to go with him to run the ship's boat, which was much smaller than the one that had overturned. He said to really get a view, we'd have to go through the same way the other boat had. He said that he was satisfied we could do it, but to be certain, he would not take any of the ship's regular officers, as they would be needed to continue the voyage if things went wrong. Only one local native was willing to go, but he admitted that while he knew the way and where the deep channel was, he wasn't able to handle our boat. It had a much different steering arrangement than he was used to.

So, away we went, the natives in the bow to indicate the channel, the captain standing smoking his pipe amidships, and me at the engine and steering controls. We went into the inlet and waited till the tide was at the same stage as when Jack drowned. There was no wind. We went up, and I mean up, a slope of black polished glass. The bottom must be absolutely smooth because there wasn't a ripple as in a regular rapid. Before we started, the captain said to me, "I shall not give you any directions, you may use your own discretion as to the native's directions."

There were times when we were standing still under full power, and for a while we were actually going astern. The boat wasn't fast but she had a big engine and propeller and could buck a heavy current towing a loaded barge, but we hung there. I could feel the tension on the steering wheel and I knew if I let it slip, or if a chain broke, we'd be at the bottom of the slope upside down in jig time. You can be sure I tested the steering before I left.

After a long time we made it into the lake and ran up under the rocks to await the right stage of the tide to go down. The natives were very relieved to be up there and a bit apprehensive about going out again. The captain didn't seem concerned one way or the other. We stopped ashore for a while and he collected a few plants for a botanist back on the ship. Then we left to go out, as it was on the outward trip that Jack drowned.

I put on enough power to give me adequate steering, aimed at the centre of the slide, and we ripped down in seconds. I saw none of the scenery let me tell you. I had a little round hill as my mark and I fought that wheel all the way. The water was so fast that our engine was actually holding us back, and the buffeting on the rudder was something of an experience. Once or twice we were running just about level. In fact, the water looked even higher than the gunwale. We spun out of the eddy at the bottom and the Old Man said quietly, "Well, what do you think?" I said, "Anyone who went in there at that stage of the tide should have an awful good reason." He said, "I feel precisely the same way."

When we got back to the ship, the crew was glad to see us. They told me, though, they were so sure we'd never come back that they had drawn lots for my radio. It was a big special job and the best on the ship. The mate, a Scotsman, said it was "verra inconsiderate" of me to upset their arrangements. He must have won the draw.

Later on, the captain showed me his report to Winnipeg. He judged the place highly dangerous at the times we went through and unsafe at any stage, unless, and he twinkled a bit when he said it, the boat is under the control of a highly experienced man, and he believed few post managers could claim that experience. I wasn't very old at the time and was more than a little puffed up but came down quickly when Len Adey quietly reminded me that I'd gone there, not a very wise move in the first place. I asked if he would have gone had the Old Man asked him, and he grinned and said no, but I am sure he would have, as would the third mate. The mate had no experience in small boats, always been a steamboat man, and was uncomfortable in anything where you reach overside and touch water.

After all that, what I was trying to say is, that's one reason why the captain was a special man. Not particularly because he called me experienced. I was, or I'd not have been around and he wouldn't have asked me. But because he, quite as a matter of course, undertook to check out a place that only several days before had drowned a man who considered himself experienced. The Old Man was well aware of the risks he was taking, and he asked me to go, knowing that I'd never refuse. One doesn't meet that many people that he would willingly follow into any situation.

Winnipeg. I was still in Vanuatu, about to return home. The plan was to land in Vancouver and drive across Canada, visiting Len on the way back to Ontario.

December 22, 1988

Dear Claudia,

Sleigh bells ringing, are you listening? Be a good night for a walk in Winnipeg, lots of brand new snow, pure white. The trees look very modest in their white petticoats and the temperature is plus three, verily! Yes, this is Winnipeg. You probably have twenty-even degrees on us and you have the Southern Cross. But do you have a little bit of a lonely feeling for snow and for walking in a parka at this time of year? Wish you were here.

Unfortunately, the sleigh bells are only the commercial kind, though, you know, when I first came to this land they were not that uncommon, especially in the North. At La Ronge, they used Indian toboggans and horses with no shafts or poles, just two traces. The driver stood, and how he kept his balance over the drifts and hard snow, I'll never know, but he did. In fact one fellow, Colin Charles, there's a good Cree name now, was very lame but on a horse drawn toboggan he had no equal.

I was only doing a relief job at La Ronge but was there over Christmas. There weren't that many whites. School teachers, police, HBC (me), Forestry, missionaries and a wireless operator. They had a pretty regular run of weekend card games at various houses and of course the Christmas and New Year visitations. Well cards leave me cold, and that type of party colder, so I found an out in looking after the nurse's little girl, about three. I'd walk to the school, pick her up and take her to the HBC House, where she could do as she wished till she saw a light in the upstairs of the nurse's residence, then I'd walk her home.

We talked about serious things, and stuff like Santa and reindeer and how they come in the night and bring toys and things. Well, just before Christmas we had a lovely clear cold spell, and as there had been heavy snow, the land and trees were covered, and sound didn't travel well. So when I was taking the little one home, all wrapped up in a tiny cariole on her little toboggan, we suddenly heard sleighbells. We came to a sudden stop, and she stood up, and the expression on her face in the moonlight was something to see.

She breathed, "Santa, it must be Santa," and we stood there listening while the bells got louder and louder and then started to die away, and never a sign of a sleigh did we see. When we could no longer hear the bells, she sat down in the cariole and said, more to herself than to me, "I did, I heard Santa go by," and I took a very happy little person home, one who firmly believed in Santa and elves and reindeer who fly up into the sky at night. I stayed till she was in her bed and when I went to say a final goodnight, she said so seriously, "There is a Santa, I know because I heard him."

As I walked through the stilly night, I felt too that it was Santa that we'd heard and not old Hans and his long-suffering pony going by on the ice below the road, because when you look up at a million stars, you never look down. You hear what your heart, guided by a tiny little maid, tells you to hear. There couldn't be magic otherwise, now could there?

There are so many places, I would never know what to show you first, and how can I say that this or that was my favourite? They were all so different and all alike in their clear sky, clean land and quietness because, while you may sit and watch roaring rapids, you don't think of them as noisy. It's a natural sound, one that was there before you came, will be there when you are gone, and will be unaltered when you return.

I don't feel that noise describes natural sound. It's radio, cars, and the like that make noise. And voices … nothing more pleasant than a few friendly voices, nothing more disturbing than the clacking of a hundred tongues. Lady Job's Cove you would like, a calm sheet of water hidden from the sea by a bowl of hiss, an entrance so well hidden that even when your boat is almost in there, you feel that there is no place to go except slam into the rocks. But a turn this way, and immediately a turn opposite, and you are suddenly there and the storm that may be causing the ocean to beat madly at the cliffs outside is stilled. The water is smooth and the wind goes hurling over high above your head while the hills descend steeply to the shore, a shore not forested, but covered with pale reindeer moss, and here and there small streams leap down to meet the salt water, and everything is quiet and peaceful, "The haven where he would be." And if you take the trouble to scramble up the steep hills, when you reach the top the gale assaults you again and you can literally lean on the wind, and after a half hour of joyous tussle, you return to your boat, red of face, heartily tired, to eat a meal of satisfaction and sleep in content.

But there is another place, at first glance an ordinary place, a long lowish hill of black basalt, smoothed and worn down by the great grinding glaciers that once lay over all the land, and further polished by the wind-blown sand of the centuries since the glacier vanished. It looks like the back of an enormous whale open to the sea, and the east wind sends the breakers crashing ashore. The North Atlantic, as compared to the Pacific, has a short memory and no sooner has the wind gone than the waves diminish, and, after a few days of calm, are reduced to a slow gentle wash around the boulders strewn along the beach.

Then the water is clear and one may sit idly in his kayak and look down through many feet of clear water to the white bottom which is composed of billions of mussel shells crushed by the winter ice. There you may see the fish in their element, the sluggish cod, the flounder or sole, who will change his own colour to blend with the bottom. The spiny sculpin, with his resemblance to a rock, sits there with jaws agape and his whiskers of what looks like seaweed slowly waving in the current, till a small fish mistakes the mouth for sanctuary, darts in, and is forthwith swallowed.

If you are lucky, you may even see a seal engaged in his water ballet when the lumpish clumsy creature you see on land is transformed into a graceful and sinuous creature that dances across the sea floor in a breathtaking display of motion. If he should perceive the shadow of your boat, he immediately becomes a panic stricken torpedo that streaks out of your sight, but being the curious creature that a seal is, you may expect him to shove his round head out of the sea a few hundred yards distant where he seems to reproach you for scaring him half to death.

In spring, this ordinary place becomes very much out of the ordinary. Behind the basalt hill there is a marsh and it acts as a catchment for the snow that falls on the higher hills. Once the marsh is full, the water runs out over the basalt and down into the ocean, but due to the irregularity of the stone it forms into dozens of lacy little falls which are actually only a few inches deep where they run over the edge and fall into the sea. Imagine this place on a warm spring day when the shore seems to be one great drapery of fluid lace, when the ocean is a vast mirror stippled with the rings and wakes of hundreds of diving birds, the sea pigeon, the littlest auk, that six inches of arrogance clad exactly as his vaster cousins, and who seems to be almost impossible as he plays his «now you see me, now you don't» routine. If you can, get a glimpse of him underwater flying just above the bottom as competently as he can do above the sea.

You will see terns, just recently arrived from the Antarctic, fluttering above the water, ready to drop like a stone on any small fish that comes too close to the surface. You may sit there on the shore or in your canoe for hours and your attention is always engaged.

It is hard to believe that such a busy place could ever be deserted. But go there in winter when the hills and the marsh are covered with snow and the tumbling waters are still, when the ocean is a white blanket as far as the eye can see, then you may travel overland from the settlement in the bay to the north, and your ten to fifteen big furry dogs will romp along while you sit at your ease on the long narrow *komatik*. The last two miles are downhill through a snow filled valley and the pace can be fast and furious.

For a land that may look dead, there is surprising life. Perhaps a dozen ptarmigan will explode out of a snow drift where they have burrowed for shelter against the night frost, or you may see the dainty lines of foot prints that tell you a white fox had recently passed and, in fact, may even now be crouched by a rock looking like a snow drift while he watches you and your dogs rushing by. Or you may see the pits in the snow where Nanook the bear has hade his solitary way, minding his own business unless molested, when he can be a very morose individual indeed.

The last half mile downhill is so close to the perpendicular that the wise dogs fan out on either side and allow the *komatik* to take the lead while they race along behind in complete safety. They know that it is an unwritten law that once a team had crossed the "neck," as it is known, that there will be a rest period. The man will build himself a small shelter of snow blocks, if he happens to be me, where he can lie at his ease, drink a cup or so of tea from a thermos, and if the weather happens to agree, he will spend perhaps an hour or so there.

Any so-called experienced traveller who has written a book will tell you that Eskimo dogs are dangerous and unpredictable, and on no account should they be petted or indulged, which is one of the great misconceptions of Arctic life. To steal a phrase, "There are no problem dogs, only problem drivers." I've travelled miles and miles with fifteen huge furry bundles of good nature and willingness, I've slept with my head against a warm back and my feet against the stomach of another, warm and secure while knowing that either could tear my hand half off with one snap of his jaws, but confident that he would never. So when I stopped for my refreshment, I always gave my big fellows a bit of fresh meat or fish prepared in advance. After our wild slide down to sea ice, we'd take our bite and relax in our own way. Well, the mother of the rest of the team just might use her influence and crawl into my shelter where her soft fur and good nature added to my comfort.

If you were dropped there from the tropics, you might well think what a dreary, sterile place. But wait a moment, once the dogs have done with their rolling and stretching and cleaning the snow from another's eyes and faces, there is silence, absolute. On the right day, there's not even a whisper of wind. The sky is a pale blue canopy from horizon to horizon. Not a creature moves, not a sound is heard.

So you are shocked when you hear a metallic "dong," like a huge pure metal bell being gently struck. What is it? No other than your old friend the raven, the only bird save the ptarmigan and Arctic owl that stay in the Arctic all winter. Like the independent creature he is, he refuses to change his colour with the other Arctic creatures. He also refuses to sing his mellow note in the south, where his hoarse "roark" seems to be the only sound he makes. In the Arctic, especially in spring he delights in aerobatics. He will climb, dive, bank and wing over, it seems, for the pure enjoyment of just flying, and all the while sings his mellow "clonk."

Or, if the raven has business elsewhere, you may stare at the sky for minutes, but you feel that you have not passed through the country unobserved and that you will sooner or later be investigated, and sure enough, you will see a tiny dot away up over the hills. Watch it. It will circle and circle, and as it comes closer, it becomes an Arctic owl, gravely circling you and your team. Minutes seem to pass and the wings don't move. Finally he will be close enough that you may see all the details of his supremely efficient flight, the twist of a few wing feathers, or the adjustment of the tail, a complete and self-contained flying machine such as man will never make. If you and your dogs don't move, he will come so close that you can see his powerful hooded eyes and the great claws folded tightly against his breast to present least wind resistance, but ready to drop at an instant's notice to serve as brakes, or to scoop up an unwary ground squirrel or lemming or even a ptarmigan. If you should see fit to place a few scraps of meat on a high pinnacle of rock or ice, his Arctic majesty will undoubtedly see them and thank you for your offering. Meat or fish, he won't touch anything else.

I've driven or paddled to that place so many times just to see and feel the great quiet, just to lie there and realize how large the earth is, how many years it has existed, and how much more it may continue if only we are careful. The explorer said of Labrador that it was the land that God gave Cain. My thought has always been, "Lucky Cain." I've heard people say that they could never exist without trees and grass, but people can. I grew up in forested Labrador, but the call of the northern places was always strong, and I went. I've never regretted a moment of the time I spent there and no camera could record the things I carry in my mind. The places, the terrible beauty of the mountains, the elegance of the caribou, the seals, walrus, and beluga. And perhaps most impressive of all, the great kindly inoffensive humpback whales that may surface a few feet from your boat, and eye you with, you'd swear, a twinkle, before the massive head goes down and the great flukes point to the sky and your visitor is gone. He could destroy you and your boat with a flick of his tail, but you sit there in perfect safety. He may be mildly curious but he is never hostile.

Did I ever tell you how I once sighted from the land what I thought was a dead whale, probably crushed by ice? On paddling up to it I was convinced, because the water was bloodstained. I was almost near enough to touch the great creature when I noticed that the eye was alive. Then I saw that the whale was nursing a newborn calf. That was the reason for the blood in the water. She lay on her back, head half submerged. Her flukes were twisted at an angle to her body, and on them lay the calf partly supported by the water, partly by its mother. It was nursing and making much the same noises that a human infant feeding does.

My canoe was white, and whales don't have great vision, so she probably figured me for a piece of ice with a big raggedy gull sitting on it. In any event she didn't stir. The nipple of a whale is tiny, and the little one sort of hangs on to an area by some sort of suction or vacuum. He could have a couple of nipples enclosed. The amount of milk is stupendous and, from what I've seen of dead whales, easily released.

There was a killer whale born in captivity in Vancouver recently. The baby didn't seem to feed and the scientific people said whales do not suckle for days after birth. I am here to tell you I saw one feeding apparently very shortly after the birth if the signs in the water meant anything. In any event the Vancouver calf died and was found to be starved. So now I'm wondering, what those people did to prevent the mother from feeding the calf. Probably too much investigation, too little solitude for the mother, too many people around. In captivity, killers seem to be friendly creatures, but in the wild they are just what their name says. A baby would be devoured by the herd just as polar bear cubs are eaten by other bears if they find them. So obviously the killer mother would instinctively look for a quiet place to be till her calf was independent. This she was probably denied, and her calf may have died from neglect just as a ranch mink will ignore her kits if they are only touched by a human.

Perhaps the wrong creature got the name of killer. Like you, I feel strongly about animals being caged for their lifetime so people can see them. Who knows. If people couldn't see a lion in the zoo, they might grow up and go look for them in the right places, and that might be good for them.

FIFTEEN

Winnipeg, December 24, 1988

Dear Claudia,

I guess I'm still mad that Jackie Stevenson wasn't given her chance when I retired and that was strictly because she was a woman. Reminds me of when I took over at Île à la Crosse. There was a part-native girl hidden away in the marking room. She was a cripple, and standing for hours in front of a price-marking machine was obviously not right.

So I talked to her, found her to be very intelligent and that she spoke French, Cree, Chipeweyan, as well as English. So I asked her why she was stuck back there, and suggested she could be of much more use in the store and office. She was evasive, so I checked around and the RCMP corporal told me what I already knew. He said Florence was too smart and observant for anyone to risk having her where she could see any records. She would find out about serious merchandise shortages and other irregularities.

So I told Florence I wanted her to come into the office to do accounting, to look after the post office records, and keep an eye on the kid we had in the post office. I never did ask her to blow the whistle on anyone. I'd already found out all I needed to know, but she made such a difference in the store and office that my job was eased a lot. It's never easy to take a loss position and turn it round, but that is what we did, and Florence was as much responsible as I was. Her knowledge of the local people was complete, and she soon put curbs on the credit which was way out of hand.

The Company later offered me an assistant manager. I declined and asked that Florence get the job and the raise in pay that went with it. Head office agreed, reluctantly, but had to admit later that we (it's always we when things turn out, you when they go sour) had done the best thing. Florence stayed till a young family claimed her attention and that was long before maternity leave and childcare.

Guess I'm a bit of a freak because I've never had to regret any woman that I ever gave employment to. Except, to be honest, one. I had to fire a cook. She could make tea, coffee, and beans. Found out, too late, that she claimed to be a cook to get a job near a boyfriend. The Bean Queen, the boys called her, and after two weeks of beans in some form every day, they revolted. So I had a yarn with the Queen, who was a nice kid, but no cook. I paid her way home, which we were not obligated to do, as she was discharged for cause, and for a year I got letters from her telling me of all her adventures. The boyfriend was replaced without a broken heart as far as I could tell.

One of her last letters said, "Now, if I can get this fellow to marry me, I'll settle down and maybe learn to cook." I always hoped she did both. Shortly after, Uncle Ash came to cook and the boys were content. He wrote me last week saying he won't be going back to Moosonee. "I'll get sixty-five next year." They will miss him and will have trouble to replace him. He said, "Stop in touch, have a good New Year when he comes." "Stop" in Newfie is the same as stay. You stop with friends or relatives, but you "give up" fishing, or drinking or having kids.

Ash will have "Me tree bits of money": Old Age, his government pension, and the Company pension, which will be as good for him in Bonavista Bay as a university president's pension here. His butcher will be the sea and the land. He'll have his moose, caribou, rabbits, partridge, his ducks and geese and his cod, salmon, and trout. Delilah's garden will supply the spuds, carrots, cabbage, beets, and parsnips. There might be a goat for the milk. He will wander and hunt for days on end and he'll "give count to no man." He never said, but he probably carries a little of the blood of the vanished Beothics.

I hope so, because then every moose steak he filches from the under the white game officer's nose will be that much sweeter. Sure he'll break the law, the white man's law, but only enough to feed two little people. He might give you a salmon or a trout, but he'd never sell you one. He will never take more than he can use, and as long as wealthy Americans can come to his island and kill his game, he will agree with no one that he must not. Stop the sports hunters and explain to Ahaseurias[39] that it's necessary to conserve what is left, and he will obey you. But while a sportsman can put a gun to his face, so will Ahas. God bless him and may he live in peace and his own lifestyle for a thousand years. That merry little man gave me some of the most pleasant hours of my time in Moosonee. Ahas is every man's friend and thinks the same of the rest of us.

My great old friend and co-worker W.E. Buster Brown is back here. He was transferred from the Veteran's Centre in Vancouver to Deer Lodge. I've been out to see him. He is eighty-eight, and frail. He doesn't really know anyone but keeps a huge album of his life from the time he joined the Canadian Expeditionary Force in France at age seventeen till he was awarded the Order of Canada a few years ago. He didn't really recognize me, though he did ask if I were still going down the Mackenzie every spring. It is sad to see such an able intelligent man brought to this state. I prefer to think of him as I saw him once, sitting in a small airplane with Harry Winney and me, in a real blizzard on the way to Churchill for a mercy flight further north.[40] The weather had closed in behind us. Churchill was reporting no visibility in fierce winds with drift. We had enough fuel to reach Churchill, not enough to go back. One of our radios was out, due to us hitting a bump taking off from Norway House. Harry, the pilot, couldn't read Morse. He had the only pair of earphones, so I had to relay what Churchill had to say to him by putting my ear to one of the headphones which he turned inside out. Then I had to give Harry's message to Churchill via key. As Harry remarked, it was a hairy experience. All the time, W.E., fully aware, sat there reading a book, as calm as if he were at home. I'll send you the story.

I don't think of Buster as an old man in a wheelchair. To me, he's a self-possessed man reading a book with no apparent worry even though he might never finish that chapter. I might as well say that Harry, with a wartime RCAF career behind him, was also calm and collected. I guess I was the only scared one.

It will be so nice to see you again.

Take Care.

Winnipeg. I had visited Len and his family on my way across Canada the month before.

17th of Ireland, 1989

Dear Claudia,

I've been hearing about all the changes that have come to places like Sandy Lake and all the problems they are having, but wonder if the government people have been looking in the right direction. I get hit between the eyes for saying that I think the native people were much better off without us. The government says they have eradicated TB, but they don't see that it was the people who moved to places like

39 Ash Cutler's full first name.

40 An attempt to reach Repulse Bay in a canvas-covered Norseman aircraft. The story will be included in a further publication.

Sandy, where there were mines, lumbering or Hydro, who showed the first concentrations of TB. Those who remained out on the land rarely sent a person to the TB San, and even when that happened, it was usually the result of that person working with whites, or contact with them. I had many confrontations with the doctors of Sioux Lookout on the matter. The government persisted in putting up miserable temporary shack towns instead of good permanent housing, and soon every family had its incidence of the disease. The reserves are beginning to get better housing now, but the damage is done. Places like Pikangekum weren't affected much by the white man and his industries. They wore ragged clothes. Try to track a fisher through dense bush and keep the crease in your pants.

Now I gotta tell you about Kakegumik, D'moose someone called him, a cheerful mixture of Swampy Cree and wolverine, able to subsist anywhere. D'moose wasn't your white man's idea of a great trapper. He lived off the land, off fish, moose, caribou, ducks, geese, berries in their season, and sometimes he got a bit gaunt. He owned a trapline, registered like everyone else, and perhaps he owned a few traps. He was more the hunter-gatherer type, and when he felt like it, he could produce fur in some quantity, usually by cunning deadfalls of an ancient type, or, and this was his favourite, by running his quarry to earth, using his wits and speed to catch an animal blessed with equal or better wits and speed for the job on hand.

Adjusk, the fisher, was D'moose's ideal: fast, daring, wily, and possessed of immense stamina. If he were small and dark, he might be worth a hundred dollars in D'moose's ragged pockets. If he were large and brindled, he might fetch four or five dollars. Running after him through Northern Ontario underbrush for four or five days was, even at the best, not a well paid occupation. At the worst, well you see what I mean.

But when the smoke stick went out in the tent, when patches upon patches couldn't keep out the cold (D'moose had no wife so his hands must perforce handle the needle) then it was time to carefully repair the snowshoes, and make a few more willow toggles to close the rents in parka and pants. He'd eat heavily of meat and fish because food carries better in the basket nature provided, and go out, once more, to find and track a fisher, and to perhaps set deadfalls in likely places along the way. Because, while the fisher travels fast and furiously when pursued, he rests when his tormentor is otherwise occupied, in the finest of sporting tradition one might say, though I would guess that neither had any idea that Greenpeace might not approve. If they thought of it at all, it was possibly in the context of a predator and his prey, sanctioned and approved by Mom Nature her own self.

Anyway, one day D'moose arrived at Sandy Lake. He had a fine fisher and a few other pelts, so was rich. Tea, most certainly; tobacco, yes indeed. A watch would look fine on his bony wrist and serve no useful purpose for a man who took his time from the sky and the alternate light and dark, and who thought of the moon as a generous bonus. Well, the well-dressed man also required those comfortable undergarments which, in his society, have never earned the name (blush) of unmentionables, and a well-dressed man required a tweed cap, a parka, and durable (though the term is only relative to a man of D'moose's habit) overalls.

When D'moose left the post to run, and I say run advisedly, to his camp, only forty miles away, he was the acme of a well-dressed man. He wasn't a particularly handsome man by TV ideals. His nose was a bit prominent, his haircut was of the bowl type and not remarkably recent. His teeth perhaps lacked the regularity of a row of pearls, but handled hard tack and frozen moose and punched a hold in a milk tin when he indulged in that article, with force and precision.

But his homely mug was a mirror of cheer and good will. He would share the last morsel of tobacco he owned and right willingly build a fire and brew the last grains of tea he might have for weeks, just to accommodate a chance traveller, known or unknown, that he might meet on the road. He was weather-beaten, brown, rock hard. His arm and leg muscles and sinew and hip and midriff were so lean that no belt could keep his nether garments up. We sold ten pairs of braces, suspenders if you wish, to one belt, and that one belt had no function other than to droop languidly over the wearer's non-existent hips.

How you would describe D'moose would be according to your view of the man. If he worked for wages, which he might do briefly in summer, he'd be called lazy and irresponsible, unpunctual and disinterested. Right on the nail, because you see, Mother Nature created her tools to do the job, and neither the tools nor the job are interchangeable. You wouldn't use a glass cutter to chop firewood.

Now people like me would classify D'moose as a tough, self-reliant man, an extraordinary traveller. In a setting where every man was adept, he was even more adept at procuring his daily meat. I could never run or travel with him at his speed, nor could any white man I know or have heard of. He would laugh at the idea of a mile at top speed, he could never conceive of winning by a fraction of a second, and if he could, he'd consider it a most useless exercise. But if you needed a letter delivered a hundred miles away, he'd willingly step into his snowshoes and run there and back in a period that would leave you breathless just thinking about it. People like me would confess that we thought of D'moose with a great deal of envy because nature had bred him to do things which we could never aspire to.

So D'moose, in all his finery, stepped into his snowshoes in front of the store to amble, for him, at ten miles or so an hour till he got back to his camp.

The best laid plans of mice and men oft go astray. Not far from the post he crossed the trail of a fisher. Now he'd already run four days or more to catch the one that was responsible for his present state of worldly prosperity. He had not slept much in all that time, never under cover. One would expect him to utter the Cree equivalent of "Bad cess to you fisher" and carry on to his camp, only a possible thirty miles away to rest, sleep and enjoy the fruits of his labour.

However, this was D'moose, and the sight of that track was as the clamour of the Assembly Hall to Brian the Great himself. His packsack was hung in a tree, a few biscuits were thrust in his pocket, and D'moose was on the trail. Running through willow scrub, circling when his prey took to the trees, sleeping for short periods on his snowshoes when darkness hid the track, eating a dry biscuit now and then, and gulping icy water from rapids and steadies that he passed, he held the trail. One day a snowstorm slowed the chase to a crawl, but five days later he made his kill: a big brindled fisher, worth less than ten dollars.

His chase had led him far to the north of Sandy Lake, and one morning as I was standing at the door of the store admiring the view and the perfect day, a scarecrow man came around the corner, ragged beyond recognition except for the cheerful grin on his face. He laid a big ugly fisher pelt on the counter and laughed happily. Days of rushing through the thick bush had taken their toll. Parka and overalls, shiny new five days ago, were worn to a frazzle. His moccasins were bone-white from the chafing of his snowshoe slings, the jaunty tweed cap boasted a broken visor, and the sides were so chafed away that great tufts of black hair protruded. And he was as happy as if he'd earned a thousand dollars.

He hadn't eaten since the previous day. He'd sat all night beside a campfire to skin and partially dry the fisher, but no one ever accepted a gold medal with quite so much satisfaction as D'moose took a bit of tea, a tin of meat, and some biscuits that I gave him. He went to one of the local houses and had a yarn and a smoke. I expected he'd fall asleep for the next forty-eight hours, but he was back shortly, picked up a few odds and ends in trade for his fisher and again walked into his snowshoes and headed for home.

I walked a little way out on the lake with him. He accommodated his long strides to my short ones, and with snorts of laughter, he told me by pointing almost all around the compass where he'd been the last number of days. He shook hands and grinned when I told him, "For God's sake, go straight home. You can't afford another fisher hunt for a while." He stamped his snowshoes, pointed at the excellent walking, in his case running, conditions, pointed at the clear sky and the bright sun, and said *"Keespin,"* which is a wonderful word that says so many things, which can only be interpreted into our dull language as "If."

We have spent millions of dollars to take a superb craftsman out of that environment, put him in wooden box, given him an oil stove to replace his mobile camp fire, taught him to accept a monthly welfare cheque, turned his hand from making the snowshoes and canoes that he, by heaven, invented, even made our own models to be used as recreation items. I would like to know why, if the East Greenlanders and the Lappish people can live in their ancestral manner, why can't we, with miles and miles of empty forest, let the natives here do likewise. The Lapps follow the reindeer as they always have. They either go for medical help or it comes to them.

Blair Fraser, who was an editor of *Maclean's Magazine* before it became an echo and a copy of *Time*, came to Sandy Lake once. He stayed with us and remarked that Canada seems to have a record of fifty years of trying to get rid of the native population by neglect, then fifty years of trying to get rid of them by overindulgence. He was accompanied by Bill Cobb of Hudson's Bay Co. Bill was a clerk with my dad when I was a little shaver. He'd been around among natives for years, and so had I.

Fraser, when he first arrived, was a real white man. As he said, he felt like an evangelist when he came to places like Sandy, we knew so little of what went on outside. And he discussed Indian Affairs and the people he knew in the department and what they planned. All the while I could see Cobb's neck get redder and redder and I knew that mine was too.

Fraser, who was no fool, stopped talking and said, "Do I feel a resistance to what I am saying?" The dam broke and we hammered the poor man unmercifully, he whose weekly political broadcasts were listened to by thousands of Canadians. Finally when he got a chance he said, "Could I, could Ottawa, be so wrong?" and I'll never forget that Cobb said: "If you live for forty more years you will see just how wrong you are. You will see the destruction of two ways of life, two native peoples, in that time."

Fraser was drowned in a rapid on a canoe trip soon after. He never understood what we meant. Before he left, he put a book in my hands. He said that the reviews were good on this book. He said he felt that it was probably an accurate portrayal, also that he thought I would disagree. He wanted me to read it and drop him a note with my honest opinion. The book was *Top of the World*, by Hans Ruesch. It is back with me now after having been read by a host of Arctic men. The literary reviews may have been good. The Arctic men, however, described it in one graphic word, the kindest interpretation might be "garbage."

I tend to run on and on. Still, at Sandy I could see two populations emerging. Fr. Dubeau had a number of converts and, that they might be near and that their children might attend religious classes thinly disguised as school, he left no stone unturned to subsidize the families in living near the mission, and he left no stone unturned to get Indian Affairs to recompense him for the time and labour of his school teacher, and school. The teacher was usually a divinity student from on one the other of the RC colleges. The father's sister was the wife of a man very prominent in the business community, and father had no mean lever to press to get what he wanted from Indian Affairs.

He would sometime give the school children a few cents to come to the store, as he said, to use the English and Math they were learning at school, and to rub shoulders with the rest of the population who hadn't yet been converted. Since every other customer in the store spoke the native language, these kids naturally reverted, and I, for one, cannot recall one word of English being spoken.

But it was their appearance that could shake you. Fairly well dressed, they were thin, pale and always runny nosed. This is a constant condition with native kids who associate closely with whites. It doesn't clear up in hospitals even. These kids lived in permanent houses. They ate a lot of bannock, they had white fish and gold eye, they had rabbits, but those are starvation foods. The outlying camps had moose, usually lots of it. They had the oil fish, sturgeon, ling, trout. Rabbits, white fish, and the like were variety only. And, of course, in season they had beaver and muskrat, strong meats, both of them.

So it was like an invasion from another world when the camps arrived to meet the treaty party, the doctor and the RCMP. The kids living on the land in particular were round-faced bundles of energy. They'd march in with their bags of fur just like the hunters. A few minks, now and then a beaver, always muskrats, and all gained by his or her own labour. The parents might oversee and advise the boys but the kids did the work. In families where girls predominated, there was help given in cutting through heavy ice and in especially wet conditions, but they did a lot of the work and they cured their own fur. They were tough, sturdy, self-reliant kids who knew the snowshoe and paddle intimately. They could camp out in the face of a blizzard and survive.

No animal rights people destroyed the income they got from fur. Where they were closer to civilization, Natural Resources put a limit on their moose and caribou hunting so that there would be more for sport hunters. In my time, the sixty families at Pikangikum took about 150 moose yearly. There was always plenty. They hunted over a huge territory. Now, welfare and the benefits of civilization have collected them on a seven-by-seven mile piece of ground. This is not even what an original trap line, would have measured. They all live there. Firewood is harder to get, ski-doos and gas are expensive, and they have lost the desire to go afield and they get few moose.

When Angus Comber, my assistant and a long time Company man, retired, he wanted a trap line, as he is married to a native woman. His large and intelligent family have all gone as far as Toronto and BC, where they seem to be doing well. He applied, without, as he told me, much hope, for a registered trap line. The closer-in lines were still being held by natives, but the far out ones were open. He could pick and choose. He and a part-blood from Little Grand Rapids had always been friends and their wives were related, so they took over a trap line away out on Swan Lake, where they still live in a good measure of prosperity despite poor fur prices, and are completely happy.

This is excellent country. There is room for all on the large trap lines. Angus and Charlie are not "treaty," though their wives are. Indian Affairs cannot touch them. They have no children now, so welfare gives them a miss. The rest of the more than sixty families now live on welfare on the reserve.

When I left, everyone paid his own way. There was no welfare. In summer, the kids went to school and, I assume, learned how to protect themselves against the mean trader, me. In fall, with the first frost, the tents came down. The trappers came to the mean trader as they had done for years and were outfitted to go back to their winter camps and trapping. Those who were good producers, and most were, would ask for a certain amount of credit, which they usually spent wisely. That may not always agree with R.M. Ballantine.[41] Those whose production was lower, perhaps because of too much sitting around looked enviously at their more fortunate friends, resolved to do better. Those who, through illness, accident, or causes beyond their control, had done poorly last year, were treated in the same manner as the big producers. That may not be in accordance with some people's conception of HBC, but it worked very well for me. In justice to the Company, it must be remembered that come fall, from the Yukon to Labrador, the firm issued millions in unsecured credit, and in my time not a cent of interest was ever charged, no matter how long till repayment. Tell me of just one bank or financial group that trusted its customers so completely. That system suited D'moose, and Moses Keesik, and Johnny Turtle.

Some day perhaps someone will give me an explanation that I can accept as to why we brought progress to those people, progress that has destroyed them. I should live that long. Sure I live in the past, it was one hell of a good place to live.

The 1918 flu epidemic hit northern Labrador hard, more than six

41 Nineteenth-century novelist, *The World of Ice*, *Ungava: A Tale of Eskimo Land*, and other books.

hundred native people died. In the years between 1918 and 1930, the population recovered to some extent by new births, and to some extent by immigration from the Hudson's Straits area. The old Moravian custom of collecting the people in settlements at the good sealing places died out somewhat, as the natives could see that those who lived close together suffered more. They reverted to family groups, fairly widely spaced.

Of course, during the days of low population the wildlife also increased, and when I went up there, there was food for all. The depression was in full swing so there wasn't much cash money. We processed a lot of seal skins and oil for export, the meat and some of the fat we kept for man and dog. We processed a limited amount of char in brine for shipment to Holland. I was always afraid of overfishing that resource, and got lots of flack from my district manager about it too. He wanted more and more. We, of course, handled furs, mostly white fox which are so cyclic that it doesn't matter how heavily they are hunted. One year they'll be there in thousands and even if none were taken, they'd crash the next year anyway. I've known hunters to get several hundred one year and maybe ten the next. The cycle is about seven years from abundance to scarcity, but it works like this: the year after the crash there will be almost no white foxes, nor for the next several years. Then they become more abundant until by the seventh year they are everywhere and then they crash again.

No one knows where they go. In spring they are plentiful, by fall they are gone. You never see dead animals lying around. They just disappear. I've been told they die in the burrows which is why you don't see them. I don't accept that. Some sign would be visible. We know their cycle runs interlocked with the lemming cycle because the year after the lemmings crash, the white foxes do too. The coloured foxes in the same area don't seem to be affected. They don't seem to have a cycle of abundance or scarcity. So trapping of white foxes has no effect and natives take hundreds when they are around. But places that have no trappers, like the coast between Hebron and Burwell where none are taken by trappers, have the same cycle as those places that are heavily trapped.

Just to confuse us more, Mother Nature has decided that Banks Island won't have a cycle nearly as severe as other places. She doesn't tell us why, neither does she tell us why blue foxes, which are a colour phase of whites, born in the same family, are dominant in Greenland, while the incidence of blue to white in Canada's Arctic is about one blue for a hundred whites. Same way with geese. Snow geese have been predominantly blue in Greenland, white in Central Canada, and blue again in Western Canada and Siberia. Same birds, same eggs, different colours. Mrs. Nature plays her cards close to the vest. She doesn't talk much, or perhaps we don't listen much!

There is a dinky compass in a char's head. If he is hatched in a lake with two outlets, he will leave by the one his mom came in by. She's long gone so he doesn't follow her and learn the way like a bear or a rabbit. He gets left as a tiny egg, and when he grows up and it's time to head for the salt water, there is no ho-hum about it. He points his head toward the right exit and he's gone. If you prevent him from using Mom's exit he won't leave, even though another way out is available. He'll stay where he is and deteriorate into a wormy, snake-like fish, because only fresh salt water will clean him up.

Restocking overfished lakes ran into a lot of trouble at first. Then someone, my brother helped, figured out that if you take spawn from a lake with a northern exit, you must place the fingerlings in a lake with a northern opening, or a south or a west, or east according to where they came from. Why? No one knows. Well, don't we run in and out of doors marked boys or girls, his or hers, or cute ones like steers and heifers for our own set of reasons? Maybe fish aren't able to mark doors yet. I don't know.

I guess it's like old John Payne. He lived in an outpost all his life and fished for a living. He never got much schooling and in his job he never felt the lack. Anyway one day in comes a yacht, the Gospel Messenger, and people piled ashore to evangelize the Cove. John was polite, they came to his house and loaded him down with tracts and papers all about his soul and its salvation, and they left. Some time later they came back and dropped in to see John to see if the leaven was working, if the salt had savour. They found the books unread, exactly as they'd left them. And they asked John why. The fruit was for the taking and he hadn't put forth his hand. John said, "Well you see, I don't know much about anything, and if I look in those books there will be a whole lot more I don't know nothing about. Better to stay where I knows I'm to."

John lived all his life where he knew everyone, and late in life he shipped on a schooner to St. Johns where he might see his only brother, who had somehow found a way to leave the Cove years before. He arrived in St. John's at night, and was daunted by all the lights and people, but went ashore anyway. First man he met, he said as he would have said in any of the outpost he'd known, "Can you tell me where Frank Payne lives?" The man said "No," and John went on. Next several people gave him the same answer. John turned about and went back to the schooner. Said, "I been heard tell that people in St. Johns is smart, but not one knows where Frank Payne lives." He went ashore no more and when the schooner went back so did John. Never did understand why no one knew where Frank Payne lived. I guess you'd have to say he was a victim of his environment.

But the environment didn't get them all. There was McCarty who lived "out back a Fogo," meaning Cape Fogo, a merciless place of currents, reefs, continuous seas and heavy weather. A man had to be good to work there. He had to know the sea, his boat and himself. Well, McCarty didn't travel far afield either, but everyone knew him. He had the Irish of it on his tongue. He was the best of company, and, as he said, he feared no man on earth except his wife. He took every-thing as a joke but if he were bad mouthed, he could make a reply that sounded inoffensive but which had a barb under every word.

Well, one year he decided to take a trip to St. John's on the coastal mail boat, *The Prospero*. He may not have been a figure of fashion as he stepped on board. His sea boots were hand made and so were his trousers and sweater. He wasn't a big man and he wasn't handsome, but he was known and liked by everyone aboard. It happened that the regular old captain, a man of McCarty's own generation, was on relief duty some place and a young, "Johnny come lately" was filling in for him. This fellow saw McCarty in the saloon and decided to have some fun at his expense, though he was warned by Father O'Brien that he might find McCarty an unexpectedly quicksilver sort of target.

No matter, the captain roared, "Well Mr. McCarty has come to show us how to get around, dressed like a man from the grave and all." McCarty, who was one of the quietest men in a quiet breed, merely said that he had paid his money for the trip and that the captain got his money to get McCarty to St. John's and back on time, and there would likely be enough wind at sea so no more was required in the saloon.

To make a long story short, the captain badgered McCarty all the way south and back, while the little man made very little response. Father O'Brien tried to see fair play but the young captain was an insensitive brute, and things went pretty well his way. That is, until the last evening that McCarty was to be aboard.

It had been a dirty day, what they call a weather breeder, quite a heavy sea and fog patches. As they ran into Stag Harbour Run, the fog shut right down. Visibility was limited to a few yards, and these are dangerous waters with strong currents, reefs all over, and narrow channels. There was no radar in those days. As long as the captain had his echo sounder and his gyro compass, he could grope his way along slowly. This is an area of extreme magnetic disturbance and the standard compass is useless.

The captain was a worried man. He was in a bad place to have fog and an increasing wind and sea, but at least they were under control and moving. The sounder was faithfully sending back its report on the water depth and the chart was in agreement. It was then that a big drift log drifting with the current rammed its bulky top between the hull and the propeller. The engineer, with little to go on, cut the steam and the ship immediately lost speed, and with the drag of the tree soon commenced to swing off her course. The captain, as soon as he became aware of what was happening, tried to get rid of the log by moving his engine slowly ahead and astern. The only result of that effort was a burst steam pipe to the generators, and in a second the ship was without lights. No problem there. At that time all steam ships carried oil lights ready for use, and soon the ship was lit again albeit very dimly. However, there was no power for the compass and the sounder, those vital instruments without which the ship was blind and leaderless.

While this was all going on, McCarty and the priest were standing on the second deck, the priest more than a little agitated, and McCarty calmly looking over the side smoking his pipe.

The bosun rushed past with a deep sea sounding lead and line. There was a little platform on the starboard side of those ships that could be swung out from the wing of the bridge so that a sounding could be taken from there, right next to the wheelhouse, in the unlikely event that it was ever needed. As the bosun passed, McCarty took his pipe out of his mouth long enough to say, "Bose, sing out yer sounding and what you gits on tallow, good and loud, an I'll tell "ee whar we be to."

Shortly, the bosun cried so the captain could hear him in the wheelhouse where he was desperately trying to find some idea, from the chart and the sailing directions, where he might possibly be in that dark world of currents, wind and sea. "Thirty-six fathoms sir, with a nice bit of white shell and blue mud." "Ah," says McCarty. "Not past Bulldog yet, we'em fine yet, Father."

Well, thirty-five fathoms was something. At least there was water, and to spare, but on a chart showing dozens of places with similar depths, and on a ship that may have actually turned herself around, which thirty-five mark was he on?

Bosun said, "Where's we to McCarty?" and he said "Mile or so north of Bulldog and fair in the channel yet." The bosun swung his lead again called the sounding, and as a bonus added McCarty's advice.

The captain roared, "If you know so much, get in here and show me on the chart." Fairly caught, the bosun could only reply, "That's what McCarty says, sir." There was an awful silence from the wheelhouse and then the frantic captain roared, "Tell that damn McCarty to get in here, now." Looking calmly at the priest, McCarty said, "Father, Mr. McCarty would step into the wheelhouse and show that poor lost man where he's to, if he were asked, polite like."

Losing no time, the priest whipped into the wheelhouse and explained what was required to the distracted captain, who now had visions of losing his ship, his certificate, and perhaps some of his passengers at one swoop. He screamed, "I must be mad. Here I am, every damn thing against me, and I'm asked to be polite to some bloody outporter." Even in his present state of mind, and even if he managed to retain his certificate and title, it would be a long time before people forgot how he'd had to go, hat in hand, so to speak, and ask an outporter for help.

Needs must when the Devil drives, so out he went on the deck, and through tightly set teeth he asked Mr. McCarty if he'd step in the wheelhouse and see if he could be of any help. Graciously, Mr. McCarty agreed and, putting his pipe in his pocket, he stepped up to the Bosun and said, "Bose, don't strain yerself calling all them sounding. Just bawl out when you gets tween fifteen and twenty, hard bottom wi' a bit of white shell."

"Fifteen fathoms," the captain screamed, "We'll be ashore and broke up in seconds." Says McCarty, "Don't fret, me son. She'll float in two, so you still got lots of worrin' to do."

By now the mate had managed to get a boom up and swung over, and with no steam for a winch, he had all the crew and male passengers on a gang. With a lot of shouting and effort, they managed to free the propeller by dragging the tree out. Now they had power, but the captain and crew had completely lost any idea of how the ship was heading. The magnetic compass lolled in its gimbals pointing this way and that, useless, as McCarty said, as a goat's beard. However, he put his finger on where they were, and went out to join the bosun on his little platform to see how the seaweed and other flotsam was behaving. Years of fishing in foggy waters had taught him how to find his direction by the way things drifted in the currents he knew so well. A difference in the height or steepness of the sea told him what the bottom was like.

Shortly, the bosun yelled, "Eighteen fathoms, hard bottom, a bit of white shell." And McCarty murmured, "An' a good few fine fish down there, weather like this." Proceeding to the wheelhouse, he again laid a scarred finger on the chart. Said, "We'em thar, heading right across the channel now. Start her, come back to port. I'll tell 'ee when to stop." The captain said, "About ninety degrees?" McCarty said, "I dunno about any degrees. Just you haul to port and mind what I says."

The Prospero came back on course, and headed into the current. McCarty, who had now taken on all the airs of an admiral, with a twinkle at the priest, said to the anguished captain, "Now, me son, gi' her half speed. Mind your course careful. I'm goin' on deck for a smoke." Passing the bosun, he said, "Put that thing away, Bose, and git you some tea."

The priest swore this was all true, and I for one believe him. As McCarty calmly smoked his pipe and the good old *Prospero* headed into the maelstrom of tide and sea, the priest said to McCarty, "Do you really know where we are? Can you get her into Seal Cove?" McCarty said, "Father, sposin' you had no lights, would you be lost in your own church?" And father said, "No." McCarty said, "Nor in your parish?" and again father said "No." McCarty said, "Well, Father, dis be my church and my parish too. Sides, I got no notion to spoil my new boots crawling ashore from a wreck."

He went back into the wheelhouse, and for some hours he gave brief course changes, which the captain perforce had to obey. Then the wind and sea dropped, and the captain's heart began to pound again, sure indication that land was near. McCarty brought her to a slow bell and the poor captain sweated. Then McCarty said, "Stop her, and give her a kick back." The captain obeyed. McCarty said nothing and the distraught captain shouted, "Well?" McCarty mildly replied, "Well, you want to anchor her or go alongside the wharf."

The poor captain moaned, "Alongside," and Mr. McCarty went ahead on a slow bell until, a never forgotten sight, they saw a dim glow from a lantern and a few men grouped under it to take *Prospero*'s lines. The captain took over, gently put her alongside the dock and the lines went ashore. As the crew were about to belay them, Admiral McCarty shouted, "Hold them lines. Move her along two, three fad-doms." The bemused captain agreed, and she coasted about twenty feet more and finally tied up.

The priest followed McCarty down to the gangway. He said, puzzled, "Why that last move, McCarty?" McCarty pointed at his hand made boots, boots that the captain had noticed and sneered at so long ago. He said, "There was a big pond of water where we was about to tie up, Father. No outport man ever made a trip to St. John's to come home with dirty boots. I just moved her along to a dry spot, that's all."

It all happened before my day. Over time I'm sure the story will have been improved, but the captain was always known as the man who had to move his ship to spare McCarty's boots. There was never, as far as I know, any great surprise about Mr. Carty's feat in bringing a gravely endangered ship home in fog and darkness. That wasn't really so wonderful to people, who like McCarty, knew their own "church and parish" intimately. What counted was the fact that McCarty scored against the man who would put him down, who sneered at Mr. McCarty, and who had to swallow every word with a full garnish of pride.

My dad, who knew McCarty well, once asked him how much danger the ship was actually in, and with an angelic smile, Mr. McCarty said, "Not a smite, me son. That time of the tide, she'd ha' gone out past Wild Cove and been free and easy in deep water in half an hour. I could have told the skipper that but I needed to get home to Seal Cove that day."

Me? Well, once when we spent a winter in Fogo while my dad had

a holiday. A very old man came to our house for dinner one day. Dinner was at noon those days, in that place. He yarned away to my dad
in a rich Irish brogue and, in the short time we were allowed from
school, we were entranced. He opened his shirt and exposed his bony
chest, well-peppered with small black marks, evidence of a wound
from one of the old "Long Tom" sealing guns. He was ambushed
by some Protestants while hunting eider ducks early one morning,
"But they had drink in them and most of the shot spattered against
the rocks and he got it second hand as it glanced off the rock." The
doctors apparently foretold lead poisoning if he didn't die from the
wound, but McCarty was well alive and past the allotted span when
I saw him that one precious time. Whether he was ambushed or not,
I never knew. Looking back, it could have been an honest accident,
but thank God, McCarty, no, Mr. McCarty, was never one to spoil his
boots or a good yarn.

The old "hard do" fishermen are gone, the hand liners, the trawl
and trap men. They took their living from the water and they did it
with their hands. They never dreamed of half million dollar long liners, with radar, loran, fish finders, comfortable galleys and bunks, and
yes, the infamous monofilament nets and lines that are surely destroying the livelihood of those that use them. You have to see a lost net
or a long line floating on the surface, buoyed up by the bloated fish it
has trapped, followed by dozens of screaming herring gulls that have
also multiplied on man's garbage till they too project a problem. They
have increased to the point that when garbage is not available, they
attack the nests of puffins and other sea birds. They crowd out nesting birds from the sites they have occupied for centuries. And they
are protected and allowed to increase because, unlike many other sea
birds they claim part of the garbage man has mired himself in. They
go inland for their unlovely feasts and they have covered Canada from
coast to coast. They may well destroy the puffins and little auks, but
they do eat garbage so man conveniently forgets their disadvantages.

Speaking of fishing, we fished to earn a few dollars and we haunted
the hundreds of ponds for the justly famous Newfoundland brook

trout. When Greek or Italian ships were in, we cornered hundreds of big eels which their crews loved. We got lobster, at the time a fish of no value, for the British ships, and flounder by the washtub for the Scandinavian vessels. The very occasional Spaniard or Portuguese ship thanked us for cod. The Germans wanted halibut, a bit outside our reach unless some one had an older relative who was able to borrow a trap boat and take us off shore to where the halibut lay. Salt cod was the local medium of exchange. All other fish were seen as pot-fish only. No one would buy them except the foreign ships and they didn't pay high.

The schooners stayed afloat all winter and if ever a painter had an opportunity, it was on a lowering day in late fall when the sea was heavy with snow. The vessels were crusted with it, and through the broken cloud the sun could shine on the houses, all brilliantly coloured, clustered around the sleeping harbour, every rock with its cap of whitish snow and its sides black-black where the restless water had washed the snow away.

Though the life seemed to have gone out of the harbour, transferred to the cosy houses with their comfortably smoking chimneys, the waterfront still had an irresistible appeal for me. Our house was so close to the water that on dark fall nights when moon and tide combined to raise the water feet higher than usual, it used to run under our house, chuckling among the piles that lifted the house above the rocks. Lying on the kitchen floor, one ear tuned to the yarns and stories being told over my head, the other ear could hear the restless water surging about under me. I would feel that nowhere could there be greater content than where I lay.

At one time there had been a schooner wharf right in front of the house. The ship and its owner had long gone, and the wharf was in danger of falling down. We were given to understand that it was out of bounds for my younger brothers, but Max and I were exempted from that rule. We happily climbed in over and through the timbers and ballast beds with their collection of stone, old iron, and any heavy long lasting junk that served as ballast. Right on the front, where one could look down into clear deep water or across the mile wide harbour, were a few planks and one solitary wooden bollard. There I would perch for hours at a time and watch the sleeping harbour.

The noisy gulls and terns were gone. The silent head of a loon might break the water suddenly, and as suddenly disappear. The tiny round auklets would fuss back and forth, spending more time under water than above, and when they passed close to the front of the wharf one could see a demonstration of expert flying under water. And adept they were, turning suddenly to snap up a stray codling that perhaps thought himself the only fish in the ocean. Once in a while, from the wooded part of the island to the east and south, would come an osprey. He would circle and circle over the water till one felt that he must be blind not to see the dozens of rock-cod that were dimpling the water all around. But he knew what he wanted, and at exactly the right time, he would tip and side slip a couple of times, then fold his wings and drop like a stone. I never saw him lose a fish, and from the time he dropped till he was on his way home I'd forget to breathe. I can't tell you how good that next gulp of cold fresh air tasted.

Wait quietly long enough and a visitor that never came into the harbour during the summer would appear, a big spotted harbour seal. The first indication might be a line in the water as might be made by a not quite submerged object. This was the tip of its nose and long whiskers. Satisfied that nothing moved along the shore, the big round head would emerge, sometimes far out, now and then quite close. I would sit on my bollard and be convinced that only a deaf seal could fail to hear my heart pound. I have seen one fish for half an hour before finally submerging and heading back out among the reefs where it normally lived.

And this you might not believe, but I do, having had some acquaintance with harbour seals and their intelligence. Anyway, at Kippen's Cove there was only one church, and the bell rang several times every day on Sunday. No one, of course, would fire a gun or do any absolutely unnecessary work on the Lord's Day, and somehow the seal got to know that it was safe on the day the bell rang. It would come in, haul out on the warm dry rock in the middle of the harbour, and spend a lazy day there. The story had it that one day the bell tolled for a funeral, and the seal, thinking all was well, showed up and hauled out. But some one decided he wanted the seal and got as close as he could and shot at it with his old Long Tom. Fortunately he missed and the seal escaped. It continued to come on Sundays as usual, but no funeral bell could tempt it ashore again.

Folktales, stories, make believe, but try to tell a youngster with his head full of ospreys, and birds flying under water, who is listening to yarns twice as fanciful while he hears the water running under the floor. Try to tell that youngster that seals aren't that smart. He won't believe you, no matter how good your argument, because he has absolutely no intention of dropping his belief for anyone else's.

Many the night I would lie in my corner and listen to the yarns, to the slap of cards, smell the smoke and the odours from the stove. I knew the exact minute the pan would rattle out of the oven, the smell of the fresh buns, the capelin and the leggies (something between a kipper and a finnan haddie). Sometimes before this all came about, I would go to sleep and would wake to my dad's toe tickling my ribs. I'd get up and stumble off to bed with a head full of wonderful things to go back to sleep on.

SIXTEEN

Winnipeg, May 19, 1989

Dear Claudia,

When I was quite young, I had the measles.[42] Everyone did in those days and lots of people died from measles too. It wasn't just a childhood disease that you got and got over. In isolated places it was dreaded, especially by families with very young children.

Why measles just now? Well we have had visitors to stay a few days and everything had to be uprooted and scrubbed beforehand and I've cleaned windows and cars and shampooed rugs and stuff till I'm exhausted. For supper I cooked fish the way Mother did, but either the fish, or I, wasn't up to scratch, because I was told it was nowhere like my mother made it, so I've been taking a spell, and I've been staring at a patterned cushion, and finding out all the things I can see in it that aren't supposed to be there.

If you look long enough, you can see things in any intricate pattern,

42 On Fogo Island where the Budgells were on furlough.

like wallpaper, or our neighbour's tree branches. It's windy tonight and I can see in the branches a perfect dog on a leash trying to run, while a lady in a fearsome hat holds him back by brandishing a whip over his head. The neighbour, Mr. Tye, doesn't know that dog is there and is going to cut that tree down, and if he does he'll be sorry one day even if he does go to church regularly.

Where do measles come into this? Well, when I had them, my room, which wasn't mine but my cousin's (we had measles together), was kept dark because of our eyes. I used to lie there and see things in the seams of the ceiling that was put up long before drywall, plaster, or any of the things they use now to prevent kids from seeing all sorts of unimaginable things while they have measles. They did have wall-paper in those days though, and poor was the house that didn't change its floral patterns every twelve months. Geometric patterns weren't popular, though some of them did have neat things hiding in them. I was sure I was doomed to Hell and Damnation one time when I discovered something interesting in Aunt Mary Harnett's wallpaper.

Aunt Mary's sitting room, which in those days was only opened one, for special visitors, two, when the minister came, or three, when someone was finished with this mortal coil and qualified to be laid out in his probably one and only suit with his eyes closed and his mouth shut. See what crazy things kids notice? They buried one old fisherman with a button on his vest undone and I felt badly about him stomping along to the Throne in his heavy sea boots and getting sent to Hell for being improperly dressed, but my dad said not to worry. The old man, who was a bit of a case anyway, would likely catch it for other reasons, not the least of which was a fondness for black rum. I felt better, but I was about to tell you why I was personally on the way to H & D.

Well, Aunt Mary (she wasn't my aunt of course; it's an honorary title that anyone who lived to get grey hair was given), well, her sitting room with its heavy table with an even heavier Bible in the centre of it, had floral wallpaper. Roses I guess, not like roses I had ever seen, but fullblown roses on Fogo are a bit rare anyway.

In those days there were no bathing suits as you might see today, that are so low on the top and so high on the sides that one wonders how people stay in them, so kids had little idea of the Female Form Divine except that it consisted of a head, frequently very tired and harassed, at the top, and a pair of laced up boots on the bottom. Everything in between was mostly black with a white apron on the front. Strangely enough though, when small babies needed comfort and sustenance, mothers would deftly release a part of themselves that the babies liked very much. Little girls would go right up and touch the baby, but boys were taught that they must not look at this interesting display, and should avert the eye or leave the room.

Well one day, Sunday of course, visiting at Aunt Mary's with my dad and not being overly interested then in stories about people long dead (for which failing I have constantly reproached myself), I was looking at the roses in the wallpaper and suddenly I saw not one, but two of these interesting objects pertaining to my idea of the Female Form Divine wherever I looked. Perhaps the designer saw what I saw, I wouldn't know, but not only were they there, they were there in innocent profusion. I stared till Aunt Mary asked what was wrong with me. I was caught. Before I could think of H & D, I had blurted out my find, and the poor old lady was shocked beyond belief. Our visit came to an abrupt end. The sitting room door was locked and my dad and I walked home. He smoked his pipe and seemed to cough a good deal.

Word got around, of course, and Aunt Mary had a lot of kids to visit in the next days. The sitting room was locked, blinds drawn. Much later I heard my dad tell his friend Gilbert that once you looked the way I described, it was obvious enough. Roses for those who saw roses, and for those destined for H & D, stronger fare. And *Playboy* thought they started it all!

If you had measles, you probably had them at home, missed school for a while or lost some summer holiday days. Me? I had measles on the top of a cliff fronting the Atlantic Ocean, and if you sailed straight away from the front of my uncle's house, the next land after Funk

Island was Ireland. Made it seem quite close and homelike to know that over that line on the horizon was the old turf, black house people who hated Cromwell and somewhere the Boyne River, the name of which was never spoken without a sigh, even though many of us had no idea why the sigh till we went to school and read history.

If you are going to have measles then, the place to have them is in an old house on the top of a crag looking at the great swells coming in perhaps from Ireland itself. The time to have measles is when the ocean is angry and turbulent, when the grey rollers come crashing into the cliffs incessantly, trying to batter them down, when the rain clouds scurry by and water falls from the sky to meet the saltwater flung up by the sea. The old house should be so near the edge of the cliff that the front windows run with sea spray, and if there should be a crack in the glass you can hold a finger there and taste the salt, feel a strange emotion that is entirely unlike the emotion one feels when swimming in the sea on a sunny day. Spray from a south-east gale tastes different, more remote, foreign, unknown, as if it came from the very bottom of the sea, undisturbed for centuries.

So my measles were to the tune of the gale and the wind and the rain. I could not have asked for a better way to be ill. We had just arrived in Wild Cove, my father's home, a village struggling for half a mile along the top of the cliffs. The houses were small, so we went wherever there was room, and of course my brothers and sisters all had measles too, as well as the rest of the village kids. Despite the storm, my parents had to bring us food from house to house. They didn't enjoy our measles.

For two days, I didn't. I was too sick. But when I got a bit better and wanted out, of course I was refused, and I stayed indoors with my cousin, who had lived on the top of the cliff all his life and saw little to be ecstatic about. How I wanted to go out and be part of the wind, rain and sea. When I went to bed, the little brook that ran through the centre of the village and supplied the drinking water was a modest little stream with what looked like a ridiculously high wood bridge spanning it. Two days of constant heavy rain turned the brook into a torrent that not only reached the high bridge, but actually ran across the plank top. People wore rubber boots and walked to the middle of the bridge and dipped up their pails of water. From our room I could see how the usually peaceful little brook now tried to tear the pails out of people's hands. I wanted to be out there so badly.

Then my mother would come with my meal, scold me for having the blind up, though the days were so grey that one would wonder if there was a sun any more. So I'd go back to staring at the seams and the wallpaper, seeing all sorts of things in them, images born of the storm and the tumult outside and probably being just as hard on my eyes anyway. All in all, I enjoyed my measles, though I desperately wished I could be outside. One thing, though. The storm lasted so long that I was nearly recovered and my mother said I could go out first fine day.

I awoke early one morning. The rain could not be heard on the roof and the light in the room was different. I could hear the sea crashing against the land, and, when I raised the blind, the sun was just coming out of the sea and looking on a clean washed land. People tended to keep sick rooms closed and a week of storm hadn't helped. I dressed and went quietly outside, and the world was all my own. There was no one else. The sheep, horses, and goats were showing up from wherever they had sheltered. A few chickens were scratching around but not too hopefully. Everything was wringing wet. There was no wind and the air was like cool water on a hot day. Just to breathe was pure pleasure.

I came to the bridge, and the stream was still flowing across. Measles and complications or no, there was no way I could cross that bridge except in bare feet, and I did so. The water was cold, cold, but so unexplainably good. I walked along the top of the cliff watching the great combers come ashore. I saw beach rocks the size of grapefruit thrown high in the air, and as the wave receded, I heard the stones that had been thrown into the cliff rattling back into the sea only to be flung high again on the next wave.

Perhaps the confinement for the measles helped to make liberty that much sweeter. I can't say, but never again have I thought of measles as a thing to fear. Rather, the combination of measles, the great and unusual summer storm, and the brisk and beautiful day that followed has always seemed to be one of the truly wonderful experiences of my childhood.

If you round Cape Freels now, and head nor-west or thereabouts toward Stag Harbour Run, you will see the tidy little villages of Lumsden and Carmanville on your port hand. On your starboard is a line of cliffs, bare, uninhabited, given over to the horses and sheep, and perhaps the ghosts of the people who once lived there. The little graveyard is probably long overgrown with willow and alder, but I would bet that a few graves will show signs of recent care. People who have lived in such impossibly isolated and remote places don't just up and leave. They will go back and put their feet in the almost invisible paths where the long dead people walked. They will clear the encroaching brush away from a grave, and they will sit on the boulders at the top of the cliff and look toward Holy Ireland, and while breath is in their body they will never forget.

What is there to remember? Years of toil, years of poverty when the Great Depression crushed the fishermen almost into the very rock. They remember that, though there are fewer and fewer people who left to remember. They remember the days after a storm and they remember those who were taken by the sea. They remember the hopelessness of the widow with a young family and they remember the dazed look in a man's eyes as he stumbled away from a fresh grave, home to his family who now had no mother. And they remember the great kindness and spirit that gathered round to help the afflicted. They remember the bad days and the better days. They remember the sun lifting out of the calm water when the ocean is like a mill pond, and they remember the chill days when the Arctic ice crowded close ashore bringing the seal herds, and men went walking over the floating ice, so far out that the land was only a loom to the west, walking into the danger of storm or freezing, of being adrift on ice that moved even farther from land.

They accepted the hardship and danger as well, risked if there were a few skins to sell for cost, some meat for the family. Perhaps you will tell me that a man will not walk twenty miles over the ocean when at any moment his next step might be his last, and return rejoicing if he can figure that he made somewhere between one dollar and three, rarely more, in a day.

They will come back to the cliffs and they will feel the past and they will be happy to have been a part of that fearful struggle to stay alive and independent. And, one by one, they will go, never to return, and they will lay their bones elsewhere. And, one day, not too far away, no one will come back, except the odd tourist or someone looking for a lost horse. I like to think that the ghosts will meet near where their little church stood, and where they gathered on those rare days that a minister said prayers, that they will smoke their spirit pipes and yarn as they once did in the days before the world became small. The graveyard will disappear and the only memorial to those incredible people will be the cliffs where they chose to live, and this memorial will stand for all time to come, as long as the seas come thundering in from the old sod, which they loved and never saw. There is something inexpressibly sad about a deserted settlement, especially to one who saw it alive. There would be no point in ever going back, but I will never forget the sea the storms and the people.

Winnipeg, Tuesday, May 23, 1989

Dear Claudia,

It's been a strange week. We had visitors and saw Lower Fort Garry, the Selkirk Marine Museum, and all the things one shows visitors, but to me it was a time of grief and backward looking. My old friend Buster Brown died Friday evening.

It was a merciful release but one cannot experience such a thing without thinking about what it all means. Here was a man who at seventeen joined an army to go to France to fight in a war that he really knew little about. Wounded, he was invalided home, recovered, joined the RCMP and went to the Arctic where he travelled and explored for RCMP several years. He then joined HBC and, for the next forty years, worked in a variety of capacities, always following new and sometimes controversial ideas, always producing results for his Company.

The doctors said he wasn't aware, that he knew and felt nothing, but I know he did feel, that he had fears. I have been with him here at Deer Lodge when he seemed to be quite passive, when he didn't ever seem to know that I was there, and his face would twist with fear and he'd fight the restraints that held him in his chair and suddenly he would scream, "Help me, help me," and once he stopped screaming and looked at me and said, in a perfectly reasonable but terrified voice, "Can you help me to get out of here." I got an orderly and we put him in his bed and he reached out and took my hand and held it tightly till he went to sleep.

This was my best friend. Our paths first crossed in the Arctic where we worked together many years. Nature is a reasonable mother. She seems to have a plan, but why she takes a man who was mentally and physically way above the average and reduces him to this is beyond imagination. I am to be a pallbearer on Thursday.

I was asked to speak at the funeral. That I was unable and unfit to do. Can I stand before a church full of people, not one of whom knew Buster in the way I did, and talk about him while he lies there forever silent? Can I say in the time allowed what he did, what he meant. Can I say why it was one of the fiercest determinations of my life to see this man awarded the Order of Canada for his efforts on behalf of her and her northern citizens?

In my limited command of the language there are no words to express these things, and a funeral is not the place perhaps to say them. So I have passed that burden to Shirlee Smith who will say simple and compassionate words of goodbye to a man that she has always admired and respected, a man who was forceful and strong, a man that not everyone liked because of his absolute respect for law, order and loyalty, and a man that no one can ever say other than that he was completely and unreservedly honest in all his dealing. If a man ever stood on the earth who was equal in my affection with my own father, that man was W.E. Brown, who I would like to hope, left me a better man and his country a better place.

I am rambling. Old men tend to do that. Old men tend to grieve over things that cannot be altered. There are many rules that direct us and one rule is that people die. Another is that no one can ever stop it. Five years ago I actually said goodbye to Buster, in his apartment late at night, when we had talked of old times old friends, old events for hours on end. He knew of the malignant thing that had taken possession of him, and he said, "Len, there is something going wrong in my head. The doctors can't do a thing about it. When the time comes be patient with me. Above all, never leave me." That I could promise and I have seen him regularly and watched the terrible thing take his reason, take his speech, and now take his very life. If I could have said one thing to him before he died, it would be, "Buster, I have never left you." And that, Claudia, in this whole sad event, is the thing that gives me some comfort.

Buster was not a superstitious man. He had no problems with passing people on stairs, spilling salt or any of the silly things that people occupy themselves with. But long years ago, sitting half-frozen in a shack in Churchill, waiting out a storm, he said to me that while he had no use for such things, he had noticed that news of a death is often followed by news of two others. Why? He wouldn't guess. I guess I smiled because he said, just wait, you will see one day.

Well, I sincerely hope that Buster is now sitting some place yarning with two of his great friends, L.A. Learmonth and W.O. Douglas, and I hope that they can take a few seconds off as I write this, because Buster, as usual, you have the last word. Within hours of your death and of my knowledge of it, I was advised of two totally unexpected deaths. Now have your laugh and go back to your yarns, but before you go, Buster, best of friends, I meant every word I wrote a few moments ago.

Now I'm away. Will phone you soon, and find out when it will be convenient for me to drop by.

Best of everything, Len.

Len has visited me in southern Ontario, and returned to Winnipeg.

July 29, 1989

Dear Claudia,

One must thank one's hosts for the kind and considerate things they do for a guest and one may search his mind for the proper words. They never are quite what he wants to say, but I have a special window in my fortress of recollections through which I can see the very special things that happen. I have a new and precious addition to that recollection: a parrot, hummingbirds, chipmunks, a furry masked man at the door for a handout,[43] long soul-soothing conversations, and the friendship of cherished people.

So what else? Well a bear, perhaps two years old, in blueberry country. He was feeding along the road. A porcupine trying to cross the road. He was almost halfway when I saw him, so, stubborn like all porky's, he stopped and shook up his quills. I tried to be reasonable, said, "Why don't you keep going. A car can hit you here." He said never a word. Just looked at me. So I got a stick and tried to prod him along. What do you think he did? Went back to the side he started from. Of course he did. He was a porcupine, wasn't he?

Shirlee Smith wants the Repulse story. I sent it to you as a piece

43 A raccoon.

called "Mercy Mission." The reason she wants it is that it never got much publicity at the time. HBC was a bit embarrassed at letting their stocks fall so low, a bit more embarrassed about clearing the store out in favour of a camp trade at Wagar Inlet so as to have clean shelves at Repulse for the goods which never came. The people who made or agreed to those events played their cards close to their vest and there was never much that got to the archives or Mrs. Smith. The then-personnel manager advised me when I came out that Buster Brown had told him that he felt I was due a bonus, but they were not giving me one because officially I hadn't done anything remarkable, only what I was paid to do. He also said he would take a dim view if I spoke to the media or did anything foolish in that direction. It didn't bother me because generally I felt the same way, though I would have been glad to accept the bonus.

So Shirlee wants the Repulse thing, though she won't find any HB House gossip there. Obviously a certain amount got into the papers. Some place we have the clippings and it's easy to see how the information was restricted as much as possible. It was a bad few years for HBC from a publicity point of view: the Fort Ross evacuation, the Repulse incident and the loss of the *Nascopie*, one following closely on the other.

The wreck of the gallant *Neophyte*, on the other hand, received little or no attention. Too bad, because it, in its way, was quite a story and goes to show that a man will sometimes go to sea in an unseaworthy vessel and survive, when as Capt. Shaw says, he has to have the heart of a lion just to board the ship.

Briefly, *Neophyte* was a Dutch canal barge, with an ancient hot-bulb diesel that could help the horses get her around the canals, but for use in open sea she was useless. Somehow she arrived in Churchill in several pieces during the construction of the port. She was put back together, and because of her long deck that was mostly hatch, she was to be used to carry dredged material out to sea and dump it. She didn't work well in that trade, as they couldn't get a clam down her hatches without tearing her half apart, so she was tied up, used for storage and, as usual on government jobs, she had a skipper and an engineer to live aboard and keep her painted and polished for no earthly reason.

So when the war came, and freights became heavier and heavier, the HBC bought the *Neophyte* to carry cargo around Hudson's Bay. A mistake to be sure, but needs must when the devil drives.

She actually made several voyages. She could snort along at four or five knots in good weather and going downhill. When she hit headwinds, she was lucky to stay in the same place, just bobbing up and down. Usually, she wasn't lucky, and with full power ahead, she drifted astern. Eric Carlson was her captain and a braver man never went afloat.

The wreck? Glad you asked. Well she left Churchill bound for Severn. The weather was bad, heavy winds, fog, high seas. The winds were behind her and for once she scooted south at a fair rate, though her decks were continually awash. When Eric figured she was somewhere abeam of Severn, he headed her into the wind, hoping to be able to hang around till the visibility improved so he could find Severn. You see, at the time, none of these rivers were properly buoyed or marked. At low tide, the HBC managers would send men out in canoes and they'd stick small spruce trees in the sand to mark the channel. Honest. On the ship they had all the complicated navigational aids you would expect on a canal barge, plus a slightly more modern magnetic compass, which in that area of variation is slightly more useful than a straw in the wind.

Anyway, the gale increased. *Neophyte* was driven south past Severn, and by the time the gale blew itself out, the crew were exhausted. So when Eric managed to claw back to the Severn area, he was ready to take most any risk just to find shelter. And in a way, luck was with him. He managed to find one of the spruce trees still standing. I should mention that the land is so flat in that area and the shoals and sandbanks extend so far off, that even when one finds the trees he still had a long way to go before he even sees land, and the channels are by no means straight. While generally heading west, you are pointing every which way as you follow the forest to land.

Well most of the trees were gone, but with a much higher than usual tide, the *Neophyte* and her crew staggered from tree to tree, sometimes going aground, but always making some sort of progress. At last they could see land. Success was nearly in their grasp when suddenly, in all those miles of sand, *Neophyte* found the only large boulder for miles and miles, and she sat squarely on top of it, in fairly rough water. The inevitable happened. *Neophyte* was heavily loaded, her bottom could not stand the strain. The plates ruptured and the boulder entered, since it is a fact that two objects of the same size cannot occupy the same space at the same time. Eric saw the hatches bulge upward and as the strain became heavier on the falling tide, the hatches gave way and cases of canned goods, oranges, spuds and the like erupted through the deck.

Neophyte was a gonner. At dead low tide, there was no water to be seen except that in the channel, but *Neophyte* wasn't in the channel, she was half a mile off. That's what happens when you lose the trees. We went there to pick up the crew shortly after, and Captain Barbour of the *Fort Severn* and I went to see the wreck. She was submerged at high water except for the pilot house and masts. At low water, one could stand on the boulder that had wrecked her. It stood inside the hatches and level with their top. It just about filled the whole cargo space of the vessel. Today there are huge self-unloading and loading bulk carrying vessels. Way back in 1947, *Neophyte* actually unloaded herself, though not to anyone's advantage, but as far as I know, she never made the national news. Buster Brown had the old hot-bulb removed and we hauled it back to Churchill in the *Fort Severn*. He thought it would be a museum piece, but no one was interested and it sat in the pier shed in Churchill then disappeared. Too bad. They are not to be found on this side of the water now.

Winnipeg, January 10, 1990

Dear Claudia,

As usual, your letter was a delight. I can see you with the snow and the woods at Clarendon all wrapped cosily about you. You know when I was small and we lived at Rigolet, our house was on slightly higher ground than the rest of the HBC post, which was all that was there. The hills ran back quite steeply but were covered with a dense forest of spruce, fir, birch, tamarack and willow. We had lots of snow so close to the Atlantic. A single fall of four feet was normal, so usually it looked like a Christmas card. The green trees would be all heaped with snow. There were white buildings with red roofs and trim, and little pathways from house to house. The ice pans drifted silently past on the outgoing tide only to return on the next flow. I may have been bitterly cold but Claudia, it looked warm.

The sleigh dogs would curl up their tails over their noses and sleep the winter night away, only awakening now and then for no apparent reason, to howl in response to a howl heard from another team probably ten miles away north some place. Their howl was passed from team to team all along the coast miles and miles to the south. After they had howled, they carefully trod their beds again, then settled down to sleep. If it snowed, all that could be seen when daylight came was a hump here another there, but the first rattle of the door had them on their feet and they too looked warm.

After a calm night of frost the harbour was frozen. Will or my father would take an ice chisel and test the ice, marking the limits of safety with little clumps of the ice they chipped out when testing. Then we could go skating on this great big outdoor rink that never needed shovelling. That's a luxury.

Sometimes mild weather prevented the ice from freezing immediately. So what? In every direction there was a hill. A few passes up and down with snowshoes, and overnight it was ready to slide on.

We used miniature Eskimo *komatiks*, homemade toboggans with only half curl, easy to make but the hard upper edge accounted for many a nose bleed for the careless. We also used barrel or puncheon staves. If the cooper was in a good mood, perhaps we'd get a four-and-a-half-foot oak stave that could be planed and polished to a mirror finish. We never stood or sat on them, always knelt on one knee. Imagine it, a kid perched on one knee, the other leg held straight out behind, like Katerina Witt, though hardly as graceful. Hands in pockets, again the careless ones, and we'd go down hill like rockets. When one knee got sore from kneeling on the hard wood, substitute the other knee.

When both knees were sore and cold, head for the old dog feed house, where there was a fireplace five feet long, and perhaps half a dozen men, trappers and hunters, in to buy supplies, busily cooking meat and seal fat to feed their hungry teams. There were ten or so irons to hang the big iron pots on. The size of the fire depended on the number of cooks. There was never a problem in getting a warm-up. Most of the light was provided by the fire but there was a coal oil lantern hung high on the rafters. It was always lit, but the glass was so smoked up that all that could be seen was a sulky glow among the smoke from the fire, the steam from the pots, and the fumes from half a dozen black pipes stuck in their owners' faces. They smoked plug tobaccos, hard as a rock, black as Satan's heart.

If sliding and skating palled, though they never did for me, the older kids could follow the hard-packed dog team trail across the portage path about a mile, to a lake where we'd fish for trout through the ice. The trout were not large and not very plentiful, but we had fun and were proud when our catch appeared on the table.

But I do remember the frosty fall mornings when everything was so beautiful that it was an exquisite pain in the chest to see it, and I'd get up early so that I could go check my rabbit line. Perhaps have time to climb the highest hill where the migrating ptarmigan used to stop to feed on the millions of black berries, (service berries) that grew here. If one could get a few of those astonishingly quick and shy birds, he felt rewarded for the work he had put in, and doubly rewarded when they were the main course for Sunday's dinner.

The customs officer at Rigolet was Capt. William Parsons, old when I first remembered him, and ancient when he finally quit the job. He was a small man with a white goatee and he was peppery too. He must have been in his eighties when I first remember him. He lived in the customs house and, with his equally ancient tidewaiter, ate all his meals at our house. With our family, the HBC clerks and Pappy, as everyone called him, and John Smith, there were fourteen or fifteen people sitting at our big table for every meal.

It was not easy for my mother to prepare meals for such a crowd.[44] Almost all vegetables had to be imported and we ate venison, seal, cod, salmon, birds of all sorts, and trout and smelt when they were available. Pappy liked his "country meal" and except for bear, which he refused to touch, he ate anything. Well, to be exact, bear too, if it were referred to as venison. Anyway, when "fall meat" was on the table, he'd enquire which of us was responsible for the rabbits or partridge. Once when I'd made a fairly adequate donation, he remarked that some day I might amount to something. Since Pappy doted on my two sisters and apparently loathed all boys, I figured that was as close to the old man's heart as I'd ever get and was suitably impressed.

Newfoundland governments had a way of changing rapidly in those days, and when it changed, it really showed. All patronage appointments were terminated immediately after an election to make room for the incoming recipients. Well, one time Pappy's luck ran out. His powerful friends couldn't help him. Anyway, he was nearing ninety, and for years my father had done all his work, which wasn't much anyway, for him. Pappy's son, Ralph Parsons was the last fur

44 Usually Phyllis Budgell had help preparing these huge meals.

trade commissioner of the HBC. He happened to be at Cartwright when the election results came through.

The men to replace Pappy and John were already on their way to Rigolet. So to save Pappy unnecessary strain, R.P. sent a boat from Cartwright to Rigolet to warn Pappy to be ready to go. The boat came late at night, long after Pappy had gone to bed. The orders were that he was to be awakened and given the telegram, no matter what the time might be. So, with some misgivings, my father walked over to the customs house to awaken Pappy. The old man had a dicey ticker and Dad was a bit apprehensive as to how Pappy might react. But he woke him anyway. The old fellow immediately feared that his equally ancient wife had had an accident and asked my dad to read the telegram to him. When he got it, he laughed and said, "If John Snow (the new customs officer) wants this bed he's going to wait till I get my sleep. Tell the missus that I'm going to be late for breakfast," and he rolled over and went back to sleep. Snow arrived the next morning and waited forlorn while the old man took his time, had his sleep, his breakfast around eleven, then calmly packed up his belongings and left the place to John Snow. He chuckled when he told my mother that he'd accidentally broken the big teapot that morning, and that John Smith had "clean forgot" to stack the fire or to get in a supply of wood. Poor Snow and his tidewaiter landed in a cold rain to a cold house. Later, my father went to see him and asked him for supper till he could get established.

The patronage thing biggled on Snow too. There was no need for a customs officer at Rigolet really, and after a year he was laid off. He could never replace an institution like Pappy anyway. The old man was so well known that people would drop by the post just to leave smoked salmon roe, or a special trout, or something else the old man liked. He always came early in spring, left late in fall, and there was something missing when Pappy stopped coming.

He had a bunch of cronies who usually came down on the coastal steamer with him in spring and who went back with him come fall. They were Tom Dawson, the fish warden, who had lost both feet in the Greenland sealing disaster, and Father Edward O'Brien who came to Labrador for twenty-five years to visit the Naskapi Indians, to bury the dead, marry and baptise and do all the things their regular priest from Quebec never seemed able to do. There was another customs man at Cartwright, who had been sworn to a temporary Justice of the Peace position to make some seizure of property legal, and who forever after, signed himself Judge Murphy and who was called that by an amused and indulgent community. He never did get another chance to act even as a J.P. and his self-imposed judgeship hurt no one and kept the old fellow happy. There were also Jack Smokum, Stan Brayirl and a host of others who would each need a whole book to him justice.

Together they were a crew such as you'd never find again or anywhere else. Only on Labrador in the twenties I guess. These old fellows went to great lengths to outwit one another. They resorted to barefaced robbery on the ship coming and going to get hold of one another's rum supply. If one could steal his roommate's liquor supply and generously share it with him in another cabin, that was a triumph to crow about until the pirate was himself victimized.

It was before radio or TV, and these old scamps, and others, were our entertainment. There are many who would never agree that radio and eventually TV brought us more laughs. One of Pappy's favourite stories was about how he smuggled several bottles of rum aboard the coastal steamer SS *Kyle*. It was during the prohibition and the ship's cabins were frequently searched before sailing. The rules of good sport dictated that the police search cabins only.

So Pappy, as was customary, wrapped his cache in oilskin and stowed it in one of the lifeboats. He had a suspicion that he had been observed by another of the group, so he watched that man carefully, and was rewarded by seeing him put an oilskin package in another boat. So, expecting that his cache was known, he moved his bottles to the other boat and put the other fellow's bottles where his had been. He was gratified to see the other man shove his arm into the boat several times to check that his liquor, now actually Pappy's, was safe, and at a suitable time he removed what he thought was Pappy's cache.

One oilskin parcel looks much like another anyway, and he invited his buddies, including Pappy, down to his room as soon as the ship sailed to have a snort. When all the available space on bunks and seats was filled, he gleefully hauled out the oilskin parcel, prepared to give Pappy the bird. And by golly he did. Unwrapped, the supposed liquor turned out to be a couple of deceased chickens addressed to a nurse up the shore and placed in the boat by a steward as that was the closest thing they had to refrigeration.

In seconds, there was a mad scramble up to check the two boats. Alas, not only they had been observing the actions of others. Both parcels were gone. The bereft owners held hasty council and decided that the only way to ever recover part of the loss was to visit as many cabins as they could and drink what was available, but it was a dry voyage. Somewhere along the way, someone asked Pappy's opposite number, a good Catholic, if he'd perhaps brought along a little holy water. The good man, entirely misunderstanding the question in his grief, said, "Well, I did have a couple of bottles or so, but some thief stole them and drank 'em." When Pappy told the yarn to my father at our dinner table, Father O'Brien was present and he laughed as heartily as anyone else.

The father, a good man, and loved by everyone on the coast, was not teetotal, and there was a story about him and a parishioner who used to drop in now and then, confess to a few mistakes and take a little punishment. Well, one time the father's basement needed cleaning, and the parishioner's penance included doing a little work there. In the course of his duties, he found several or more empty bottles which, being a thrifty man and opposed to waste, he was examining in the hope that a little fluid might be left behind. The father came up behind him quietly and said, "You are wasting your time Tom. They are all dead soldiers." To which Tom replied, "Yes, and thank God, every one saw a priest before he died." The story is now a regular in Newfie joke books, but it was a word of mouth thing when I was young.

Winnipeg, April 1, 1990

Dear Claudia,

Poor old Bert Swaffield died at eighty-eight in February. In a way I'm not sorry; he wasn't happy. Bert was like me, born in the HBC. He started, like me, on Labrador, where his father was manager at Cartwright. He was sent to Rigolet as an apprentice where my father was manager, and later went into the Eastern Arctic. He was ahead of me by fifteen years but I took over posts where Bert had served, and his mark was always there.

He was a bachelor most of his life, and to read his journals was to see a very particular little man quietly working away in the Arctic with one thing in mind, to do as much as he could to further his Company's interests. He rarely had a white apprentice or assistant. He preferred one man posts. Every window had a little ticket showing the date, in red, when it had been cleaned, and the date, in blue, when it would be cleaned again. Ditto the stovepipes. The journal recorded when the floors were done, when the dogs were fed, when ice was brought in to ꞏꞏꞏꞏꞏꞏ fꞏꞏꞏ wꞏꞏꞏꞏ. Dꞏꞏꞏy dꞏꞏꞏil. The store shelves, in his time, all behind the long counters that separated customers from goods, no self-serve there, were all neatly ruled off, and the item that would occupy that space was neatly printed therein. Bert was no mean penman. If he ran out of that item, then the space remained bare till next ship time.

You know, despite modern computer stock checks and modern ordering procedure, Bert's system was about as effective, and had the benefit of complete visibility. He only had to glance around his shelves and in his warehouse to know what he had and what he needed. Granted, he didn't have as many items, and only one re-supply per year, but his methods, laughed at now, were singularly effective in his time, and he operated in the Arctic, as we all did, an unheated store. Let Mr. Modern Merchandise work that one out, standing on a bearskin to keep his feet from freezing and using painted sticks for money.

So I feel for Bert in his last days. All he wanted really was to be near his old buddies, to retell all the old yarns, tell all the old fables, grin at the old jokes and be concerned at where the fur trade was going or gone, and he retired here to get that. When Bert picked a retirement spot, it was as much because it was his company's headquarters as anything, as long as he could visit the office. He grieved with the rest of us when our old fur trade department became the Northern Stores and was horrified with the rest of us when Northern Stores was sold to become North West Trading Company, and not a part of HBC any more.

Some one said to me about Bert, how stupid it was to allow a company to rule one's life. I couldn't explain it, I didn't ever try. It wasn't Bert's company as much as it was his family. He was happy. I think all his life he was happy. He reached a place in his Company that he wanted, a post manager in the old sense. He worked alone for years before radio and air transport. He made decisions regarding many things because there was no one else. He was protective and paternal of his native customers and they came to him for advice and help. He could have been wrong sometimes, but he always acted in what he figured were the natives' best interests.

Bert was hired by the same man who hired me, Ralph Parsons, sometimes referred to as the King of Baffin Island. He was probably told the same thing that I was: "You will be in charge of an isolated post. You will not be able to call for help or advice and you would not be going there if we did not feel that you could handle it. We do not expect miracles. We do expect you to use the goods and materials we send in to you to good purpose. You will not list those goods out in "lashings and leavings" (his exact words), but if one of our people (the natives) suffers hunger from your actions, I will see that you are discharged as quickly as I am hiring you now."

Bert never forgot that, nor have I. I would wish that people who have written false and misleading things about HBC methods could have lived and worked with Bert for a year.

Bert's books balanced to a cent. We were all expected to do that. Bert would hunt for a week for a one cent error. Wasted time we are told. Just write it off and get on with business. That wasn't the point. Bert was just as accurate and fair in all his dealings, dollars and cents involved or not. You could say his life balanced to the cent. He never worked for anyone but HBC. He ran post offices, he kept vital statistics. He wore a dozen hats, but no matter what hat he wore, it had the HBC flag on it. Everything he did was with the approval and authority of his Company, and where his old bones lie, that is a tiny bit of HBC land. He would never want it otherwise.

What am I trying to say? Well, I think that little Bert, in a very quiet way, left some large and enduring footprints, and I regret bitterly that he could not spend his last days in the place he would have chosen, with those few people remaining from the country and life he loved. There will be a little file in the HBC Archives, a few contracts, a few letters, the record of a man who lived his life, did his best and caused no problems, and in perhaps a hundred years some person will pick up that file of a remarkable man. That person probably will never understand that file, with unknown harbours on Mansel Island, Swaffield Harbour, and he will never know that this man, so long dead was, in his way, a great man, because even in his lifetime there were very few like him. And perhaps we should see that a note to that effect is placed in Bert's file, so that what the official file does not say will be known.

My back door just opened gently and no one came in. The cats are asleep in the living room. Muriel is at a rummage sale. I could say perhaps she didn't close it properly when she left, but she went out the front door. Anyway, a reasonable solution isn't so exciting. Perhaps I disturbed a few HBC ghosts in the previous pages. Fitz has come to look. He is sitting at the top of the stairs looking from me to the open door. Too bad, but in this case there is a reasonable solution. During a long cold winter, the doors are rarely left open. When they are, it's because groceries are coming in, fish even. So he likes to be there. Who knows, he might get more than just the smell. In any case, there are apparently no chills running up and down Fitz's spine, nor mine, so the ghost, if any, is friendly.

It seems that recently nearly everyone I talk to has a new ghost yarn, some fairly responsible people. Of course, I don't believe in ghosts except the ones no one can explain. My mother and the old midwife who helped me into this world agree that there was something around when I was born, well yes, beside me. They both maintained that all their lives. Never put a lot of stock in it myself, even though I was there. You see, I was pretty young at the time. But last summer, seventy some years after I came into the vale, I was visiting some people in St. John's, Newfoundland. The wife of my friend casually mentioned that she had been in North West River many years before. She was a member of a religious group at the time and she had had a strange experience. Guess where. In the very house where I was born. She said it couldn't have been association of ideas, because she hadn't had any idea that anything had happened there before. And to cap it all, her young daughter, about six I think, had also seen the same apparition. See what I did just getting born? I ghosted up a whole house.

Still not convinced? Well Gino Watkins, an Oxford explorer, and J.M. Scott, also of Oxford, spent a year in Labrador doing a survey for the proposed British air route. They rented a house in North West River and apparently saw or heard nothing out of the way. However, in J.M. Scott's fine book, *The Land that God Gave Cain*, he mentions that one of the men they employed slept in the house one night, and then moved elsewhere because the ghost would not let him sleep. Guess what again? That was the house where I was born.

Only thing I remember about that house was the beautiful clear drinking water that could be pumped up into the kitchen. There was an old farm style hand pump there, and we used to go in just for a drink. The house was empty at the time but was later used by a HBC employee who, as far as I know, never saw or heard anything.

But last summer I visited a sister in St. John who had been with my mother shortly before she died, as had my other sister Marge. They both tell me that Mother always said that she and old Aunt Lizzie had heard strange and unnatural sounds in that house.

I lived in a house in Hebron, and slept in a room that no one would use because of a ghost, but in four years, he or she never appeared to me, though several times there were strange happenings that could be traced by very human foot prints outside.

Gotta tell you this one, too good to miss. A man now in his eighties told me, perhaps forty years ago, and told me again in practically the same words again this year, and he isn't fooling. Both times he became very agitated when he told me.

Many years ago he was sent to Dundas Harbour on Ellesmere Island for the winter to see if the place might be a good area to relocate natives who were going hungry in Amajuak. A landslide there had stopped up a small river where they used to get lots of char to feed themselves and their dogs. At the same time, the RCMP decided to send a constable to Dundas to check on the Greenland natives coming across, and particularly to see if they were hunting musk ox. It was decided to house both men in the same building.

There was little to do, and there were absolutely no natives over there, so the two men took turns in running trap lines. One would stay home to keep the house warm, and prevent the food from freezing, while the other would go away trapping for a couple of weeks.

Well, one time my friend was home and the policeman was away. It was a cold blustery night, and he was sitting with his back to the table, reading by the light of a lantern hanging overhead. He sensed that he wasn't alone, and looked around, and there on the other side of the table was a man Ches had never seen before. Not a native, a white man.

Ches says he dived for his sleeping bag and huddled there till morning. The fire went out in the coal stove and the lamp burnt dry. He doesn't remember much about the night. It was uneventful except for his terror.

By morning he had a grip on himself, and was able to believe that it was a vivid nightmare. In any event, when the policeman came back, they talked about it and agreed that it was all the result of isolation and being housebound too much. They agreed also, on a schedule of one week there and one week away, with at least a week together between times. There were no further incidents. Dundas didn't measure up as far as seals and walrus were concerned, so the place was closed again.

Some years later, Ches was some place, I forget where, but an RCMP inspector was showing some official photos of RCMP activities in the Eastern Arctic. He handed Ches a photo of a man standing facing the camera with a smile on his face. Ches says he felt the same terror he felt in Dundas Harbour, but he'd never seen this man except across a table on that unforgettable night years before. He said he was about to ask the inspector not to explain anything more, but was too late. The inspector said, "This is one of our very early men in the Eastern Arctic. He shot himself accidentally at Dundas Harbour many years ago and is buried there. As I said, Ches becomes terribly agitated when he talks about it, but has some sort of compulsion to do so every so often.

What is the answer? I wish I knew. One doctor said perhaps Ches was shown the picture before he went to Dundas and told about the shooting, but his mind refused to accept it, just banished it. Perhaps something in the book he was reading started the memory again long enough for him to think he saw the man whose features were imprinted some place in his brain from the picture. When he saw the same picture years later it might have triggered what he thought was a face he'd never seen before except in that dream or nightmare.

Except Ches isn't the sort of person you'd expect to have illusions. He's one of the most solid unimaginative people you could ever meet, but he is convinced there was a man there that night. As a ghost story, it's a good one, but what actually happened? I guess the doctor could be right. After all, Ches wasn't that old at the time. He was one of the two farthest north men in all Canada. Perhaps some place inside his mind he didn't care to be going where one of the few white men ever to get that far had died. Perhaps his mind refused to believe that there was a third man there, frozen solid, but except for being dead, was exactly the same as he had been before the bullet killed him. Again I can't see Ches being the type to worry about that, but there is a lot of machinery inside the human head that no one has directions for.

I don't believe that ghosts talk. Sometimes I think it would be sort of neat if they did. A yarn with Franklin or Parry would be a good way to pass time, and incidentally clear up a few points.

The other day Charlie Reiach told me that years ago, when he was in Tuk, they lived in the same little house that I used when I was there. He told me that one day after a heavy rain, some earth slipped and exposed a grave of an old woman. She had been buried without a coffin, and was completely frozen, having been in permafrost. He said her features were quite clear of ice and most of her shoulders. The rest could be seen through an ice covering. So he had her covered up again, but as she was in an area where there was quite a lot of weather movement, she had to be reburied several times while he was there. Charlie said she was a kindly looking old soul and he got sort of fond of her, especially since she was only yards from the house door.

Well, many years later I was in Tuk. The sand spit where the house stood was being eaten away by the Beaufort Sea. Global warming, greenhouse effects, you name it. Anyway, it was getting to the point where my bedroom window was right on the edge of what was left of the bank. The house must be moved. I knew nothing of Charlie's old friend. So I got the borrow of a bulldozer from N.T.C.H., laid out some long stringers, and was about to move the house to a new location, when an old fellow came along and asked me not to let the dozer go over a certain part of the yard. I wanted to know why, and he said his father's mother was buried there, and offered to show me.

He stripped the back the turf, and there was a wooden deck, put there, as I know now, by Charlie, and under that a few more shovels full of dry sand, and there was the old lady just as she was when she was put there many years before. We couldn't abandon her to the hungry Beaufort, so we took her out, still encased in her ice coffin, and we buried her on the highest ground we could find. We put her right back into permafrost, and if all of Tuk eventually goes under water, that unnamed old lady will likely be last to go. Her name? I don't know. I asked her grandson who was perhaps sixty-five. He scratched his head but couldn't get a name for me. In my mind, since last spring, she's "Charlie's friend." I guess she'll have to be satisfied with that.

One thing about the permafrost, it's so clean about things. Also at Tuk, the Dew Line people opened a gravel pit to get material for their airstrip, and far down they found a man's body. Big excitement. There was a local graveyard. Why wasn't he buried there? RCMP got into the act. Planes came down from Murvik with fingerprinters and all the science fiction stuff. The two churches overhauled their lists to find out who might be missing. As these fellows used to change names more often than socks, that didn't help much.

One day, old Portuguese Joe strolled over to the pit in the permafrost where they were keeping the old fellow, and pointed out that the buried man had been there a long time before any whites ever entered the country. On his hands were mitts of sea otter, once a trade item from Bering Straits, but not seen in any area east for a hundred years or more. He wore ivory labrets in his lips. His clothing, all animal skins, had been made with bone needles, his boots were nothing like the type presently worn.

Joe was no mean detective. He pointed out that the man was wearing light fawn clothing. He must have died soon after the caribou calved, as there was little wear on the garments. Any fawnskin clothing that passes a winter is very well worn. This wasn't, so he died in the spring. Joe pointed out too, that while pingos[45] usually erupt upwards, they sometimes go the other way and leave pits. The pits are usually full of gravel due to frost action on the limestone that usually fractures to form the pingos. Joe's idea was that this fellow had probably been walking across the pit formed by the reverse pingo on the ice, had fallen through, and had frozen in at the bottom among the gravel. If he had been buried, it would have likely been near the sea and some tools or weapons left with him.

Over the years the ground moved again, the water drained away, and our friend lay quietly in his permafrost bed till the Dew Line tractor broke his rest. Last I heard, there was a squabble about who owned him. Dew Line was then mostly American. They wanted him too. He was still in his frozen pit when I left. Don't know who got him, or if they ever found out what his last meal was.

---

45 A pingo is a mound of ice found in the Arctic, subarctic, and antarctic that can reach up to 60 metres in height and hundreds of metres in diameter. It can only happen where there is permafrost. When they collapse they leave pits.

SEVENTEEN

June 10, 1990

Dear Claudia,

Did I ever tell you about the little ship called *Perseverance*? No? Well, she was a little North Sea lugger or sloop. I heard a tale about her first in 1938, but had never seen her.

Maybe it's all strange and far away now but in the 1930s there was a lot of interest in Labrador not only by our own Newfoundland government, but by Canada, and especially Quebec, by the USA, by Britain, by Germany and by Finland. Italy also displayed interest in a big way. Why? Well there was a gang of bad guys who expected war. Labrador had several things they wanted: unlimited iron ore, airfield sites, and a weather factory that sent its product all over, especially to the continent of Europe.

As far back as 1929, Britain had Gino Watkins surveying in Labrador for airfield sites for what was then Imperial Airways. He finished there and moved to Greenland to do further work. The story of the operation is told in two well-done books by J.M. Scott.

Eric Fry, a Canadian surveyor, spent much time in the interior of

Labrador in the thirties. He was flown in and out from the Gulf North Shore and was never seen on coastal Labrador though his presence was known.

Walter Averil, an American surveyor and, he said, prospector, spent a lot of time around Knute and Sandgirt lakes where the first inland weather stations were eventually built.

A German WWI flying ace, Father Schultz, joined the RC Oblate fathers and flew all over Hudson Bay, East and West Hudson Straits, Baffin Island and the West Hudson's Bay Barrens. He was able to skip the country, but his gas caches were found and destroyed and his papers disappeared into the USA with him at the beginning of the war when the USA was not yet committed. I have no idea where he went from there. Back to Germany?

Then there was the German effort, by far the most fruitful. They established several automatic weather stations on Labrador and a fully manned station in East Greenland. The unmanned stations were not found until comparatively recently. Hang on and I'll tell you what happened to the manned station.

First I have to tell the story I heard in 1938. I was in Hebron, hunting with a very nice family called Millie. On stormy days, as is usual, we chatted and told stories of our own experiences and those of others. One night, sitting in a tent in remote Natchvak, Millie told me about an experience that he had had before I came to Hebron, earlier in the thirties.

Three Finnish scientists had hired him and his boat to take them north from Hebron. They were supposed to be looking for traces of prehistoric natives, but seemed to be more interested in capes and headlands. They took frequent soundings and climbed up the headlands with instruments, and would sit way up on a hill by a small box that looked like a radio. Sometimes they sat all night with the small box in their tent. They never allowed Millie anywhere near when they were doing this. Otherwise, they were completely friendly. In passing, I'd like to say that many of us who knew the Finns and who had worked with them never saw any sign of a radio.

Anyway, one day after they had sat up all night over the black box, the leader told Millie that he could take the boat and go on a deer hunt if he wished. They were quite insistent that he take his wife and family. Well, they had had no caribou for a while. It would be a nice change from seal and char, so away they went.

Millie left his family on the beach about five miles up the fiord and climbed the hill, as the deer would be up there, out of the flies.

He could see back out the fiord and was surprised to see, through his brass telescope, a small black ship anchored at the Finns' camp. He could see that it was not a Newfoundland fishing schooner and it was a rig that was strange to him.

But there were caribou, and he got what he wanted, so instead of staying there overnight, he headed back to the main camp.

Now Millie spoke a few words of English but had a much better knowledge of German, picked up when he went to the Moravian school at Nain. He couldn't understand the Finns when they spoke among themselves but he and the leader, Dr. Tanner, could get along in a mixture of German and English. Dr. Tanner, however, would have nothing to say about the black boat.

Unknown to Dr. Tanner, not far from his camp there was an old and simple native who was left there with a large number of dogs that he cared for while the rest of the group were away hunting. He had his badly handicapped but very intelligent son with him.

On another day while the Finns were busy on other matters, Millie took his kayak and went seal hunting. He stopped at the old man's camp and heard a funny story.

It seems the old man had also seen the black boat and decided to find out if someone aboard would exchange ivory carvings, done by his son, for tobacco and tea. On his way he saw another ship come in sight. We figured later it may have been Commander Forbes doing an American survey, or Commander McMillan, one of Peary's polar group, also doing work for the USA. In any event, the black ship got up her anchor in a great hurry, started her motor, and ran in among the islands and hid.

The old native reached the black ship with the little boat he used to tend nets, and he took his son with him. There were three men on board. One, Karl, a very kind man, took their ivory and gave them "much" for it. He also gave them medicine and bandages for the son. He spoke some Inuit, but of a greatly different kind, which the old man had heard from the German missionaries who had worked with Greenland people.

The men told the natives that they were hunting hood seals off the coast. This was strange, as the northward seal migration was long over for the year, and in any case, hoods have a different migration route from the harps and are very rarely seen on Labrador. Another thing, the sharp-eyed boy saw no evidence of seals or pelts on the ship, which he said was remarkably clean. There was also no hunting equipment to be seen. Seals sink in spring, and one must have floats and harpoons.

The old man could not say what the name of the ship was, but one of the men was from Norway, the man named Karl had told him. The other, Nois, was a trapper from a big island. We gathered later, from a book by Karl's wife, that this was the famous hunter Nois from Spitzbergen, and the other man was Karl Ritter's trapping partner from the same place.

The next time Millie visited the old native, Millie's wife went along. She talked to the boy who, not being able to get around, had developed keen powers of observation. He drew a picture of the vessel with a sharpened .22 rifle cartridge on a bit of paper, and beneath it he wrote the ship's name as he saw it.

When I heard the story, the paper was long gone, but Millie's wife, also a very intelligent person, drew a rough likeness of the ship the boy had drawn. It resembled a sloop-rigged vessel, the shape and shear reminiscent of a Colin Archer North Sea pilot boat.

She also printed out the letters she remembered but, while she was adept at Eskimo syllabics, she was not too familiar with Roman letters. John Piercy and I worked some time on it and finally got the name, *Perseverance*.

Back to the Finns. They were Dr. Tanner, Dr. Husliche, and Dr. Kranke of Helsinki University. They came to Labrador well recommended by the HBC and various government departments. They did some work on native peoples, but their main job was spy work for the German navy. It was they who provided local information and soundings so that German ships and subs could come in, well before the war, to make the sites ready for weather stations, and to land oil and other supplies for the sub wolf packs that were to operate in the North Atlantic.

They were three very nice men. When war broke out, they left their equipment with HBC at Cartwright, Labrador. Dr. Tanner and Dr. Kranke were able to board a neutral ship in the Straits of Belle Isle and got home, where Dr. Vino Tanner became prime minister of Finland before the Russian invasion. Dr. Husliche was caught at Battle Harbour and spent the war a prisoner as far as I know.

The "Karl" on the *Perseverance* was Karl Ritter, a German natural history scientist, and pacifist. He had worked on Spitzbergen, supporting himself by trapping while he studied its natural history. His wife was Austrian. She spent a year on Spitzbergen with Karl, and wrote a remarkable book which has been translated. It is called *Woman in the Polar Night*. She went back to Germany to have a child and the war broke out.

Karl, who at one time had had naval training, was contacted during the war by the German government and ordered to Greenland to take charge of the manned weather station. He had probably not been too concerned about visiting in peacetime. After all, just about everyone else had people there, but this was war. The information I got was that he was reminded that his wife and daughter were in Germany. So he went to Greenland.

The manned station was then discovered by a sledge patrol organized by the Danes. One native was shot and killed by the German soldiers who operated the station. The other man on the patrol, also a native, was taken prisoner.

Karl was absolutely overcome by the shooting of Jens, the young

Eskimo. One day Karl took the prisoner and the sledge patrol dog team on what he said was a northern patrol, a good excuse because the Germans were not able to go far, not having dogs. They went a few days north. They built a snow house, and Karl did some hard thinking.

Finally, he handed his weapons over to the native saying, "I am now your prisoner. Take me to the Danes at Cape Farewell."

The Americans at Thule later bombed the station out of existence but most of the personnel had been previously airlifted out by JU52 aircraft from Norway. A ship that the Germans had frozen in was also sunk.

One man, the camp doctor, was away when the station was attacked. The departing crew left supplies for him hidden nearby. In the summer, the Americans landed there to see the results of their bombing, and noticed marks of recent occupation. They knew no natives were or had been anywhere near, and they could hear music. They finally located the doctor, holed up happily nearby. He was taken to the USA for the duration of the war.

Karl spent the winter in Greenland, where he was called on to operate on a USA civilian worker to remove a bad appendix. Then he went to the States as a prisoner. I heard that the Red Cross was able to reunite him and his wife and daughter after the war.

The *Perseverance*, yes we were talking about her. Well, two years, or was it three, ago, I went to Sidney, BC, to visit some people. One day I walked down to the docks, and there was a North Sea pilot boat tied up. Millie's wife's drawing was like a photograph in my mind. It had had a distinctive shape because of modifications to house an unusual engine. Here was a ship with the same lines, same rig. I was almost scared to look, but around her polished oak counter, in gold letters, it said *Perseverance*.

A man, a little girl, and a big black dog were on deck. The man and some friends had bought her years ago in a ship's graveyard. She was still sound, and the massive hot-bulb Polar Atlas diesel could be made to work. They spent much time and effort. One by one, work, marriage, the world, claimed the rest of the friends till only he was left. And so he crossed the Atlantic, through the Panama, saw Japan, and came to Canada to earn money for the next leg. Where next? Well, he thought New Zealand, and wife and daughter agreed. The *Perseverance* wasn't there when I went to check the following year. Interesting world, when I can see *Perseverance* in Labrador and half a world away in Sidney, BC, with nearly half a century in between.

Len is writing from on board the MV Cygnus. *After the first leg of the voyage, he left* Cygnus *to fly home to Labrador to visit his brothers in North West River, then rejoined* Cygnus *on July 16.*

July 6, 1990

Dear Claudia,

The evening is wonderful, the sea flat, calm except for a gentle swell that lifts the ship ever so lightly as she goes, and as gently lets her down again. The westering sun is bright, and, in the shelter of the deckhouse, is positively enchanting. In the open deck areas, the wind is cool and brisk.

From the engine room I ascended to the bridge, by elevator, if you please, and yarned with the mate in the intervals that he paused from his duties at the radar and instruments. Everyone is friendly and pleasant. Someone has turned on the radio to a soap opera. Pardon me, I'll close the door. The only thing I shall allow into my cabin is the sea air through the port.

MV *Cygnus* was originally built for German interests, so all the doorplates, signs, etc., are in English and German. The ship was actually built in Japan, and at the end of my alleyway, there is a large board with the ship's building number in plain numerals, and a lot of Japanese writing around the board. I assure you that I have read it carefully and will take a picture of it to prove same. Not just now though. We are heading north-east and the evening sun is about to go down into the ocean. When did I last see the sun go down in salt water? Heavens no, it couldn't be that long ago.

I am going back, if only for a short time, to Newfoundland and Labrador, a trip to memory. In some ways the changes that have come since I first left will not bother me. The land is there, much of it bare, people might say barren, but it is there, much of it exactly as the Vikings first saw it six hundred years ago. How much of the granite face of Cape Spear will have fallen to the ravage of the sea, the rain and the wind since I last saw it? Indeed, how much has fallen since the Vikings looked up at it from their longboats? How much is left to be eaten away in the eons which must follow? The granite is there, patient and almost everlasting. It will give up a little to time, but there is so much to give before the island and the Labrador escarpment are milled to the level of the sea on both its sides.

From the bridge, we saw whales, not heads, but living, talking real whales. The low sun glistened on their jet black backs as they rolled and dived. There are no birds, not even a lone gull. I would guess that many are on the nest, far from where we are and that the little blue-backed capelin are finning on a thousand beaches. We are in relatively lifeless waters at the moment, not near the Banks, but tomorrow it will change.

Next day:
Sunday morning, ship's necessary work only, so the mess room is quiet. At first I am one of two early birds. The first one left, and I am alone with the mess attendant, who does not need to open his mouth to let me know he is my countryman. I say, "I guess the blueberry pancakes are good," and he says, "Me darlin' man, they are that." The ice, which was never there, having been broken, we establish our respective corners of the rock and yarn. He once fished for a living on Labrador at a summer station that tended, as they all did, to be primitive. I remarked on the difference. He stared at the walls, mahogany

panelling, and attractive wallpaper, and reflectively he said, "If dey lef us even a little of de fish, I dunno but I'd be at it yet, but me son, dere ain't near fish lef for we. The draggers got "em all." I said, "God's curse on the draggers," and he said, "Right on, me man."

The captain sat down, remarked on the fog, as all the others had done. The logs show fourteen days of fog in this area in the last three weeks, yet each man has mentioned it as rather surprising. The talk turned, as it always does, to ship's affairs. The mate is perturbed; he asked for carpet shampoo for the wheelhouse and got some sort of solvent for cleaning up grease.

Our captain is a practical sea man. He operated the bow thrusters and the remote controls to the engine room when we left. One small malfunction was noted. It was corrected, that was logged. Every small thing duly noted.

July 16, 1990

Dear Claudia,

I am again aboard the *Cygnus*, on D deck this time. I took Air Nova to Goose Bay. Mother Nature laid out her best white cloth all over the Island of Newfoundland, but good friend that she is, she twitched it aside so that I could see the Straits of Belle Isle as we crossed over. Amazingly, she had set three huge icebergs in a pattern just where we always crossed going north. They looked like they could have been there sixty years ago when I crossed in the lovely schooner, *Fort James*.

The green woods of Labrador have not changed. The lakes are still unspoilt, not a sign of man for miles and miles. The Mealy Mountains still wear their caps of white reindeer moss and, from above, one can see the narrow paths that the caribou have woven over the hundreds of years. Game trails, the guidebooks say. What a pedestrian name for those fairy warps and nufts that knit the sturdy mountain tops. Game? Caribou are not game, they are the windblown thread that forms the lace that decorates the high places. I, who was once a hunter, now believe firmly that the Mealy Highlands should be preserved, forever inviolate, and that beyond a certain point in the footlands, no human should be allowed to ascend. The snap of the rifle and the stain that spreads over the fairy moss should forever be forbidden.

Met at Goose Bay my brothers George and Jack, both retired but busy. We drove the twenty miles to North West River in George's car. There the changes were apparent. When I last saw it, there was one row of neat little and big houses along the river bank. The North West River is not like the Moose. There is little fall and rise of the tide, and you can walk down to the river edge along a very gentle slope. There is no brush or scrub, it is all sand or grass.

The Grenfell Hospital that once provided employment is closed; only a small clinic is operating. Closed buildings do nothing for a place. I can't help but feel the Grenfell Hospital should be activated as a home for the aged, as people are now taken to Goose, where they don't have the river and the lake and the community.

There is one especially delightful road that runs at right angles to the river, up a shoulder, then up a hill and across the top. The view from the top is magnificent, and there, in the best spot of all, my brother Dick (short for Eric, but who knows why) has his house. His wife served a lovely supper and took herself to church. When she got back, we were still there, looking, talking of the old days, old folks. Claudia, I wish I could have given you that view, that sunset across Grand Lake, the smoky distance over the water in Lake Melville till the eye refuses to go any further. The absolute contentment in the time and company of my brother.

There were a lot of poignant moments. After all, it was the first time in fifty years that five of the six surviving brothers were together. Of all the moments, the one when I stood at the side of my parents' graves was the most affecting one. That hilltop, with the ancient land, still largely untouched, lying before us, stirred an emotion in me that said I was born here, in this small place. I belong to it forever, even though it's possible that I may not see it again.

Once, many years ago, I found an old, sick, and injured caribou on the top of a great bare hill. He could look for miles in any direction and see only the land that had been his. I could never believe that he had gone there by accident. If I had a choice, I would a thousand times rather die on a hilltop than in any other place under the best of care. The original Arctic people often laid their dead on hilltops where their spirits might see the land. Since man must eventually return to the earth, why not on a high, clean, windy hill, instead of in a murky grave.

To pause for a moment, I asked the third mate to buzz me when we are abeam of Cape Race. I have three bottles with the names and addresses of all my grandchildren and Marilyn's[46] two, who consider me in the light of a grandparent. They are to go into the sea at Cape Race and from there who knows where? Marilyn and I sat till way past midnight. She wants me to promise to visit every year from now on, and I'll do my best, but you see, fortune has given me another chance at joy. Kathy is expecting again. I am ecstatic of course. Kaleigh and I had a long talk. She says it will be a girl and it will be hers and mine. Josh says it is to be a boy. Keira says she wants a baby too, but right now she wants a baby rabbit more.

Now, where were we? At North West River. Four of my brothers are retired there, Norman, George, and Jack live on the sand beach at the east end of the river; Dick lives in his castle on the hill. The beach is about twenty yards from George's house, perhaps ten from Norman's fence, and a bit more from Jack's. My brothers are retired but busy. They work so well together and the community is lucky to have them. They often collect in one or the other's workshop at least once a day to ponder over a repair job, a local problem or just to sit on the benches and yarn. I have my compensations, but I still feel a bit of

46 Marilyn Lewis, a friend from St. Johns, Newfoundland.

envy. I would like to be there and part of it, but my orbit, my family and grandkids, is outside theirs.

In North West River, though there have been several people who came to live there from the south, the original native strain is still predominant. I could still tell a Michelin from a Blake, and a McLean from a Goudie, by the shape of their faces. Often I was wrong in the name, which could be Hawkins or any other that did not exist when I was there, but I would find out that the mother was a Michelin or a Goudie.

I went to see an old lady, Aunt Edna, who used to babysit me. She was a grown woman when I first remember her. She lives with a grandson who is unmarried and keeps house for them both. Her love for all the Budgells is so evident, even now. As George said, the little "aunt" is not just honorary in her case, and I agree.

Of course, I was at a disadvantage; everyone knew I was there and could call me by name. I met a man on the beach, much younger than I. He grinned as we met and he said, "You don't know me?" I said, "Not your face perhaps, but you are a Chaulk and when you opened your mouth, your speech told me you were from Mulligan I'd guess Percy Chaulk's son." And he laughed and said, "Right on."

He was on his way to see George to have him make an axe helve. That lovely word says so much more than the ugly "handle." The people who are his ancestors once lived in canoes, and they caress the word "canoe" so that it is delightful and slow, and becomes "kinoo." The spelling does not begin to convey the pronunciation. Things are not ripped or torn, they are "libbits," literally little bits. Boots become "buts" and a boat is "bow-at." The speech, unfortunately, will change. Many youngsters don't have it now. Too bad; it was interesting and communicative.

Some of the old ways prevail. Fibreglass boats that need no maintenance are painted because that was how it used to be done. Outboard motors can be tilted to go over shoals, but they are stopped, and the boat is poled over because the old motorboats had to go that way. Jack is a purist. He fixes dozens of outboards and owns a couple, but he will not use a Fibreglass boat. He has a large one that is built of wood in the same way our grandfather made his boats. He shapes them for outboard motors but he also has a little wooden rowing boat exactly like one we had as kids. He uses it only rarely, but he has it, and as long as he can handle a boat, he will have one that depends on oars or sail only.

He has a rifle I gave him many, many years ago. He has no sons, so no one has ever put that gun to his face except Jack. He will give you almost anything he has, but don't ask him for that rifle or the little .20-gauge double-barrel shotgun made by HBC that was Dad's favourite and is now his. There are still no regular butcher shops, and people rely on game for meat: moose, caribou, partridge, ducks and geese. The other brothers shuffle firearms around as required. Not Jack. These are things he cannot share. I know because I was the same. I could not lend my dog team or my canoe and guns. I just couldn't.

One more memory brought on by my visit...I told you about old Captain William (Pappy) Parsons. I can still recall a twinkle in his eye once as he listened to a very righteous schoolmarm of mine telling, with appropriate horror, of the probable fate of a young woman thought, and I'd guess only thought, to be having too close a relationship with a young man. Old Pappy, then in his seventies, said, "Maid, I wonder what you and I might do if we were nineteen and no one to see us." Miss Bright must have had a good imagination, or previous experience, because you never saw anyone turn so red do fast, and Pappy chuckled for half an hour.

Yes, Miss Bright, she shoved one of my illusions down the drain and started me on my way to being a cynic. You see, I was saving to buy a small boat. Tom Coombes would build her for me, one dollar per foot of the keel. I'd get her unpainted for ten dollars. I can't buy a paddle for that now. So every cent was hoarded.

Then Miss Bright, the teacher, a self-styled missionary who sold the used clothing given her for the poor, honest, I mean, honest she did, not that she was honest. Okay, just explaining. Anyway, she decided that all the kids should have a Bible of their own. In "them days," teachers were supported by parents, so part of my hoard had to go for a Bible. Miss Bright got the books, I suspect at less than we paid. She probably read in the same book about the fellow who got ten talents and doubled them.

Anyway, we eventually got them. Not being, to my shame, much of a Bible opener, I handed mine to my dad and he opened it and his eyes popped. The inscription read, "Presented to Leonard Budgell by his teacher and well wisher, E.R. Bright." My father said, "Well I'll be damned," and my mother said, "You will be, swearing with an open Bible in front of you." I was angry. I probably needed the Good Book as much as anyone ever did, but I wanted my boat.

Only a few days ago, Norman's wife handed me a small Bible. I had no recollection that I'd ever seen it before, but when I opened it and saw that inscription, I felt the same anger that I'd felt more than sixty years ago. The word "Presented" hit me just as hard. Yes, I got my boat. The Bible? I guess my mother kept it. Sona asked me if I wanted it now and I gave it to her. I don't want to be mad at a person who has been dead so many years.

The fog hangs on. I was on deck for a while after lunch. It's not really cold, not like it was coming up from Halifax.

July 18, 1990

Dear Claudia,

We are in Cornerbrook. At dawn we were entering the bay of islands and the scenery there has to be the equal of any in the country.

There was a big Russian ship loading paper, a Canadian Coast Guard training vessel and some sort of research vessel all tied up as we approached. It looked as though no one, much less a ship this size, could ever get into the space left for us, but Captain Herring played his console like an organ, and that large vessel was positioned at the dock in that tiny space as accurately as a polished driver would park a car between two others. I am deeply impressed with the captain who alone can jockey this ship, and in the meantime joke with the third mate who is learning this job.

The bosun of the ship studied my face for a while today, and said, "Are you from Labrador and is your name Budgell?" I confessed, and he said he and Dick worked together at Twin Falls power station twenty-two years ago. That Budgell face will get me hanged one day.

Claudia, you should be here. Twelve miles off the Cape Breton shore, I awoke around six and the sun was a great red ball rising out of the sea. I was watching it through the port and wondering if a world could be more perfect when a huge bow head whale surfaced between me and the sun, close enough to the ship that I could see the shine on his black skin as he slowly submerged again. The last I saw was his flukes outlined against the sun in that distinctive way they have.

The sun is shining warm on the paper as I write. The ship is steady as a rock. We should arrive in Halifax tomorrow morning when I will go ashore with anticipation to meet my family, but there I will be leaving this ship with some regret.

After time at Kathy's, I'll go to see my sisters at Moncton and St. John, also Capt. Shaw and Forrest McLelland at Parrsboro, then it's back to Winnipeg.

Later:

Soon I will get into my berth for the last night aboard. I have to pack my things and shall probably not write any more in this till I get to Winnipeg. The old grey Atlantic has been good to me. There are many things that I shall save from the last month, many things to blunt time and age. But I want to give you a few things for your own. The whale in the sunrise. The green of the Labrador forest standing sentinel along a quiet shore. The great still wings of two ospreys circling a lake. The bright sunlight and clear, clear water on a beach of perfectly rounded stones in a remote cove on Newfoundland, and the whisper of the waves as they roll gently ashore, a place to be alone with all the spirits of the past and future.

Now I will say thanks for coming along on my journey into memory.

I am looking forward to seeing you soon.[47]

Best wishes, much love. Len.

47 These excerpts are from a 77-page letter. The rest of the letter was about Len's family, his old friends Captain Shaw and Forrest McLellan, the ship itself, the captain and crew of the *Cygnus*, and people met on board. We continued writing until Len died in the year 2000.

LEONARD BUDGELL
Genealogy

Len Budgell's family traces its roots in Newfoundland back to the latter part of the eighteenth century. In the 1700s, when fishing companies recruited fishermen from England and Ireland for the Newfoundland fisheries, either Len's grandfather, John Budgell, or his great-grandfather had come to Newfoundland. There is a record of a Joseph Budgell with the Slade Company from 1790 to 1792 at Fogo Island. The Slade's employees usually stayed for three years before returning to England. These Budgells were from Dorset, and the Slade Company owners, originally from Dorset, had been recruiting from that area for a hundred years. As time went on, more of the Slade's servants began staying on in Newfoundland and bringing their families to the colony rather than returning to England. By 1850 almost all employees were recruited locally from those who stayed.

In an oral history taken by Jocelyn McKillop for The Hudson's Bay Company Archives in 1982, Len says that two Budgell families originally came and stayed in the area. Some settled around Point Leamington. In the 1836 census for Shoe Cove, there appeared an Elias Budgel, then over sixty, and a Giles Budgel, under fourteen. The same year, at Flurry's Bight, a John Budgell was recorded in Twillingate District, as well as a Joseph Budgell, over sixty years of age.

These may have been the Budgells in the Slade reports from forty-five years earlier. Many Budgells are also recorded in the Exploits Valley of central Newfoundland at that time. Whichever branch he was from, John Budgell was fishing from Fogo Island when he married for the first time in 1866.

John wed Rebecca Harnett and the couple had seven or eight children while at Island Harbour on the west side of Fogo. There is no record for the death of Rebecca, but Len's family knew that their father had older half-brothers and half-sisters from an earlier marriage. When he subsequently married Emma Jane Foote in 1885, John Budgell settled on the other side of Fogo Island at Wild Cove, near Seldom Come By. John was listed as a fisherman on the wedding certificate. Both John and Emma Jane signed with an "X."

Their third child, George, was born in 1887. Four years later, John died in 1891. No specific record for Emma Jane's death has been found, but the unidentified "Budgell" death recorded on a page titled "1891 or '92" may have been that of George's mother.

Young George was the last of many children from the two marriages, and upon his parents' deaths, he and one of his sisters were sent to stay at White Bay, near Hampden, in Newfoundland, where Parson Charles Woods of the Church of England undertook the care and education of orphans. This development was the break from tradition that would mean George, unlike his father and brothers, would not become a fisherman, but a schoolteacher. George completed Grade 9 in 1903. For further successful studies, he was awarded the Victory Medalct in 1905, a special medal made of copper from Admiral Nelson's ship, the *Victory*, which was sent to every part of the British Empire to commemorate the Nelson centennial.

Some time after 1910, George was given charge of teaching in Labrador. This was an itinerant position in the Cartwright area, which meant spending roughly three months in one place, then travelling on to the next group of homes. In the winter, it sometimes meant walking on snowshoes for up to a hundred kilometres as he could not afford to own a dog team.

A few years later, George Budgell was sent to be the teacher/catechist responsible for the area around Hamilton Inlet. At Dove Brook, he met Phyllis Painter and married her on October 4, 1914. Phyllis Painter was born in Dove Brook to Mary Brown, daughter of William Brown of England and Marth Smith of Carbonear, Newfoundland. Silas Painter, born in Dove Brook, was the child of George Painter of England and Margaret Brown of Petty Harbour, Labrador. Margaret had been married to Richard Bird.

George Budgell and Phyllis would have ten children; one child died at the age of four months and is buried at Davis Inlet. In 1915, when he was twenty-eight years old, George was hired by The Hudson's Bay Company to serve at Rigolet as clerk and postmaster. Leonard Gordon Budgell was the couple's second child, their second son.

Len wrote of Labrador and his yearning to return there in nearly every letter he wrote in the last years of his life. His family travelled to North West River to leave Len's ashes by his parents' graves.

LEONARD BUDGELL
Hudson's Bay Company
Record of Service

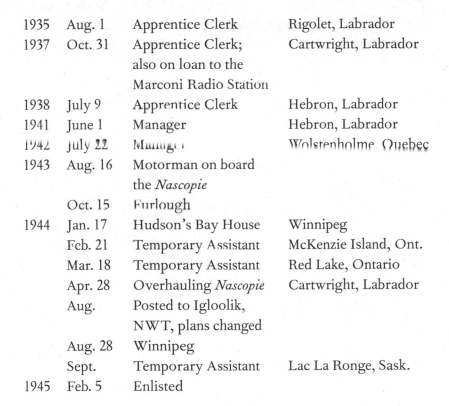

1935	Aug. 1	Apprentice Clerk	Rigolet, Labrador
1937	Oct. 31	Apprentice Clerk; also on loan to the Marconi Radio Station	Cartwright, Labrador
1938	July 9	Apprentice Clerk	Hebron, Labrador
1941	June 1	Manager	Hebron, Labrador
1942	July 22	Manager	Wolstenholme, Quebec
1943	Aug. 16	Motorman on board the *Nascopie*	
	Oct. 15	Furlough	
1944	Jan. 17	Hudson's Bay House	Winnipeg
	Feb. 21	Temporary Assistant	McKenzie Island, Ont.
	Mar. 18	Temporary Assistant	Red Lake, Ontario
	Apr. 28	Overhauling *Nascopie*	Cartwright, Labrador
	Aug.	Posted to Igloolik, NWT, plans changed	
	Aug. 28	Winnipeg	
	Sept.	Temporary Assistant	Lac La Ronge, Sask.
1945	Feb. 5	Enlisted	

	Dec. 1	Temporary Manager awaiting discharge	Repulse Bay, NWT*
1946	Sept. 16	Winnipeg	
	Oct. 1	Spare staff, Fur Trade Dept.	Winnipeg
	Nov. 7	Relief Clerk	Minaki, Ontario
1947	Jan. 13	Spare staff	Winnipeg
	June 1	Chief Engineer	Fort Severn, Ontario
	Oct.	Fur Trade School	Montreal
1948	Feb. 6	Manager	Sandy Lake, Ontario
1951	Sept. 7	Manager	Pikangekum, Ontario
1955	July 8	Manager	Île à la Crosse, Sask.
1956	Aug. 27	Manager	Beren's River, Man.
1958	Nov. 16	Manager	Fort Resolution, NWT
1959	Feb. 15	Transport Dept. Agent	Tuktoyaktuk, NWT
1963	May 1	Transport Dept. Agent	Moosonee, Ontario
1976	Jan. 1	Moosonee Transport, General manager	Moosonee, Ontario
1982	Aug. 31	Retired	

*Northwest Territories at the time; now Nunavut

SOURCES

One of the greatest resources is *Them Days Magazine: The History Magazine of Labrador*, based in Goose Bay, Labrador. Len Budgell wrote several pieces for the magazine. *Them Days* continues to collect the oral and written history of Labrador. Back issues and special issues are available. See www.themdays.com.

Baikie, Margaret. *Labrador Memories: Reflections at Mulligan*. Happy Valley (Newfoundland): Them Days Inc., n.d.

Barbour, Job Kean. *Forty-eight Days Adrift*. St. John's: Breakwater, 1981.

Buckle, Archdeacon Francis, ed. *Labrador Teacher: Clara Gordon's Journal*. St. John's: Transcontinental, 2005.

Bursey, Marilyn. *Trekking Through Northern Labrador: A Woman's Odyssey*. St. John's: Oceanside Publishing, 1998.

"Census for the Labrador Coast, 1863–64." *Them Days Magazine* 16.2:50, 1991.

Davidson, James West, and John Rugge. *Great Heart*. New York: Penguin Books, 1988.

Davey, Rev. J.W. *The Fall of Torngak: or, The Moravian Mission on the Coast of Labrador.* London: S.W. Partridge & Company and the Moravian Mission Agency, 1905.

De Poncins, Gontran. *Kabloona.* New York: Time Life Books, 1941.

Fitzhugh, Lynne D. *The Labradorians: Voices from the Land of Cain.* St. John's: Breakwater, 1999.

Goudie, Elizabeth. *Woman of Labrador.* Toronto: Peter Martin Associates Limited, 1973.

Merrick, Elliott. *Northern Nurse.* Woodstock (Vermont): The Countryman Press, 1994.

Moody, Dr. Joseph P. *Arctic Doctor.* New York: Dodd, Mead & Co., 1955

Peacock, Rev. F.W. "The Moravian Church in Labrador." *Them Days Magazine* 1.3:3, 1975 (article excerpted from book).

Mowat, Farley. *Walking on the Land.* Toronto: Key Porter Books, 2000.

Provincial Archives of Newfoundland and Labrador. "Slade & Co.: Fogo, Twillingate and Labrador." PANL, MG 460 (unpublished paper).

———. "Slade &Co. Records." PANL, MG 460 # 23, 34, MG 244, Reel 1–3 (ledger books and microfilms).

———. Census, Birth, Marriage and Burial records for Newfoundland and Labrador.

Ritter, Christiane. *A Woman in the Polar Night.* New York: Dutton, 1954.

Rompkey, Ronald, ed. *Labrador Odyssey: The Journal and Photographs of Eliot Curwen on the Second Voyage of Wilfred Grenfell, 1893.* Montreal: McGill-Queens University Press, 1996.

Ruesch, Hans. *Top of the World.* London: New English Library, 1967.

Saunders, Doris. *Alluring Labrador.* Happy Valley (Newfoundland): Them Days Inc., 1980.

Twomey, Arthur C., and Nigel Herrick. *Needle to the North.* Boston: Houghton Mifflin, 1942.

Villiers, Alan. *Cruise of the Conrad*. New York: Charles Scribner's Sons, 1937.

———. *The Quest of the Schooner Argus*. New York: Charles Scribner's Sons, 1951

Wallace, Dillon. *The Long Labrador Trail*. Whitefish (Montana): Kessinger Publishing. Reprint of 1907 book.

———. *The Lure of the Labrador Wild*. Guilford (Connecticut): The Lyon's Press, 2004.

INDEX

CREDITS

The first person I would like to thank is Len himself. When I first envisioned a book from his letters, he didn't think he had written much that was worth a wider readership. He suggested it might be more interesting if my letters were included, but with a few exceptions, my letters were of mundane things, of interest to him as a friend, not much more. Once he realized that publication could give his story to his children and grandchildren, Len supported me in every way, helping to win a Canada Council grant so that we could have relevant portions of the letters put into a computer.

A keen and accurate typist, Diane McCullough of Sharbot Lake, sat for many hours in the tiny under-the-roof office in Oskar Graf's home in Clarendon. Len's writing, though clear, was tiny, and I commend her for staying with the project for as many hours as it took. My gratitude also to Oskar.

There were so many who were enthusiastic about Len's writing. Inie Platenius, who read an early version of the manuscript, Rufus Stewart of Vancouver, luthier and sailing master, who met Len and organized Len's much-dreamed-of sailing trip along the Labrador coast. That dream was never fulfilled as Len's wife, Muriel, became ill at the time and he would not leave her.

Dr. Graham Rowley, anthropologist and honorary member of the American Polar Society, a researcher in northern and native studies at Carleton University, took time out between his commitments in the Arctic to read and comment on an early manuscript.

Dr. Susan Rowley, curator of public archaeology at UBC's Museum of Anthropology and assistant professor in the Department of Anthropology and Sociology, for reading and commenting on the manuscript. From her experience working extensively with Inuit elders on historical and archaeological research in Nunavut, she knows the truth of his words.

Patty Way, Labrador Historian and writer, and Shirlee Anne Smith, former Keeper, The Hudson's Bay Company Archives, caught my mistakes and tactfully suggested edits.

With comments and suggestions, readers of the manuscript shepherded *Arctic Twilight* towards publication. Dr. Frits Pannekoek, historian and Principal of Athabasca University; Dr. Brian McKillop, author, Chair of History at Carleton University; Mike Earle, manager and resource curator of Battle Harbour Historic Trust; Shirlee Anne Smith, former Keeper of The Hudson's Bay Archives, and author Bernice Morgan of Newfoundland Labrador, read and commented on the manuscript within the framework of their knowledge of history, writing, and/or locality. Special thanks go to historian and author Karen Molson for her enthusiastic and perceptive response to the letters, and for our ensuing insightful discussions about Leonard.

Everyone who is connected in any way to *Them Days, A Magazine of Labrador History*, deserves my deepest gratitude. Judy Pardy, Lorne Hollett, Aimee Chaulk, Susan Felsberg, chairperson, and Robin McGrath, chair of the research and reproduction committee made me feel welcome at the Archives and took time to help locate photographs and articles with any reference to Len and his family.

My thanks to many at The Hudson's Bay Company Archives, Archives of Manitoba: Bronwen Quarry, archivist; Kathy Mallett, archivist; Marcia Stentz, archivist acquisition and access, textual records and moving images and sound; Debra Moore, archivist,

Head, acquisition and special media; and Denise Jones, head of client services for their patience, consistent good humour and guidance.

I would like to extend my appreciation to the National Library and Archives in Ottawa, always a sanctuary for a beleaguered writer. Thanks to its gracious staff and researchers who eased my way through that source of material, maps and photographs.

For the Budgell family roots, I appreciated the help of Phyllis Fawcett and Connie Morrell, Richard Budgell, and the researchers in the genealogical section of The Rooms in St. John's. Bert Riggs of the Memorial University of Newfoundland's North Atlantic/Newfoundland and Labrador studies department, and Linda White of their photographic archives found the wonderfully appropriate images of the Torngat mountains taken in 1939, just about the time Len would have been travelling there by dogsled.

Others along the way contributed the time to listen and discuss the letters, found information, or met with me and shared their memories of Len. Among these are Dr. William C. James of Queen's University; Tim Schobert, librarian, Joseph Casserly, MA, who read an early manuscript, and Jocelyn McKillop, archivist for The Hudson's Bay Company Archives, the recorder of many hours of Len's oral history.

Len's immediate family have been gracious, forthcoming, honest, generous. I would like to thank Kathy Anstett and her family for a roof and food when I visited her father at her home. I value their warm hospitality, support and friendship. I would like to thank Len's son Patrick for talking with me. For sharing photographs and memories, their stories and emotions, I will always be grateful to his daughters Kathy, Maureen, and Shelagh. Len's brothers Dick and Jack, and their wives, opened their homes to me, and fed me. I thank Jack's daughter Jenny Gear for easing communication between Carleton Place and North West River. Halden, Len's youngest brother, took the time to speak with me and to send photographs. Len's nieces Phyllis Fawcett and Anne Budgell, his nephew Terence Budgell, and Connie Morrell have supported this project in so many ways.

In Winnipeg, Wulf Tolboom met with me and shared early memories of Len at Hebron. Jocelyn McKillop expressed what it was like to be included in Len's circle of friends. Many thanks to Christine Wigglesworth and Michael Cobus for opening their home to me while I researched at the archives. Shirlee Anne Smith has been invaluable. Her historical background and expertise with The Hudson's Bay Company Archives, her experience of Leonard Budgell as a co-worker and friend was so important when I was writing the foreword.

For photographs, I am indebted to Mary Voisey, and to George S. Cotter, to Dick Budgell, Anne Budgell, to Phyllis Fawcett and to Max Blake of North West River. Janice and Michael Bowie of Lux Photographic Services in Carleton Place have always been there for me when I needed them. At the Museum of Science and Technology in Ottawa, Bryan Dewalt and Sharon Babaian are responsible for an exhibit at the museum concerning the development of radio communications in the North. Len is an important part of the exhibit. His photo is there, and his voice can be heard describing those early radio experiences. Sharon Babaian was a friend of Leonard's and shared her memories of their time together; her sister Artena Babaian took the author photograph.

Visiting Moosonee gave me insight into Len's world there. The hospitality of those who worked with Len, the people at the lodge, Bishop Hennessey of Two Bay Enterprises and his pilots, guides and staff, Freddy Moore and his wife, Asheurias, who cooked such hearty Newfoundland-style meals, Cal and Ellsworth, Jackie who ran everything so efficiently, all made those visits more precious than the grandest world tour.

My thanks go to Dr. Thomas E. Brown not only for giving me the best introduction possible to the world of history, but for his long-time interest in, and enthusiasm for this project. My son Paul Driscoll, my sisters Margaret, Carol and Diane, my brother Paul, friends Terry Ann Carter, Philomene Kocher, and Grant Savage have listened to excerpts about Len and his letters for years, helping to clarify for me the content of most interest, and sustaining me during the times when

I thought this project might never reach publication. Special thanks must go to my husband, Ted Radmore, for without his loving support in these past few years, I would not have had the freedom to travel or to complete the work on *Arctic Twilight*.

In September 2004, on a tour down the Labrador coast on the little red ship *Explorer*, guides took us to shore by zodiac. Several landings were at places Len had described, and in the evenings, tour organizers let me read excerpts from his letters about Hebron, Saglek Harbour, and the Iron Strand to the passengers. I am grateful to Adventure Canada and its staff for being the first to let Len's letters see the light of day. Their eventual publisher, Patrick Boyer, was on board. In the past three years I have had many requests from my fellow passengers about a publication date. I would like to thank them. Their faith and interest in the project carried me through many a busy day. Special thanks to one of those passengers, Peter Jennings, who has passed on comments and messages through his benlo.com site.

The most important elements in getting the letters out into the wider world are the editors and the publisher. Thanks to Catherine Whitehouse as an early editor. However, the best thing that could have happened to the manuscript was for it to go through the hands of Dominic Farrell. From the many hundreds of pages sent to him Dominic sculpted a literary armature that would work, and suggested, as remedy for a lengthy manuscript that no one wanted to shorten further, that a second book was the answer.

Patrick Boyer has been every writer's ideal of the publisher to work with. From the time he first heard Len's writing on board the *Explorer*, he has guided every aspect of the manuscript to its completion in this beautiful and fitting publication.

I also wish to thank the Canada Council for its support.

—*Claudia Coutu Radmore*

October 2008

CLAUDIA COUTU RADMORE first met Len Budgell in Winnipeg when he was about to retire from The Hudson's Bay Company. Their friendship led to a written correspondence when she went to Queen's University for a B.F.A. degree.

Claudia is a Montrealer who writes and paints in Carleton Place, Ontario. A former teacher who has taught in Quebec, Ontario, Manitoba, and China, Claudia trained teachers in the South Pacific for three years. Her first publication was a pre-school manual in Bislama, one of the national languages of Vanuatu.

As a member of The Canadian League of Poets, Haiku Canada, and Kado Ottawa, she writes and edits prose, lyric poetry, and Japanese-form poetry, and has been published internationally in these fields. She is the author of *a minute or two/without remembering*, lyric poems spoken in the voices of her French-Canadian ancestors who settled in New France.

INTERVIEW
WITH THE EDITOR

*When did you first realize the stream of letters from Leonard Bud-
gell were of historic importance?*

CLAUDIA COUTU RADMORE: Years went by before I looked
at the letters in this way. Len and I were simply enjoying the back
and forth of stories and news. I often found myself reading parts
of them to anyone around, and would bring the most recent out to
share with friends.

Only after I came back from the South Pacific in 1990 did we
start to think others might be interested. Len proposed publishing
the complete correspondence but I was reluctant. My letters were
of daily happenings, family news, descriptions of travel and travel
experiences, and while Len found them interesting, I doubted my
side of the correspondence would interest a wider audience.

*People are intrigued by his friendship with you, the unique bond
you shared. How do you explain it?*

COUTU RADMORE: We listened to each other, and were patient with each other. Len was the kind of father figure one reads about in fiction and I admired him, admired his respect for people. I was captured by his stories, but captured even more by his understanding of humanity.

Anyone who knew Leonard Budgell well knows that when he was with you, he was completely yours, and he spoiled you in the old-fashioned way. You came away rested, content, feeling that you had spent an interesting afternoon with a person who was consistent in his values, considerate, helpful and interesting. There wasn't much we could do about it so we allowed the friendship to blossom. I felt privileged to know Len well enough for him to share his thoughts and his family with me.

You've written about him in this book, and edited his letters for a much wider audience. Yet wasn't Leonard Budgell a shy man, a very private man?

COUTU RADMORE: Yes, on one level Len was a shy man until he decided that you were worth knowing. Once that happened, he was committed to a friendship. If you wrote to him, a correspondence was started until you ended it. He never would. Once a friendship was established, even with the woman down the block who needed help carrying groceries, he treasured it.

He was not shy with your friends either, for they were part of you, and he was never too shy to stand up for a cause, or for his family.

Len would not have enjoyed talking about his own book, calling attention to himself. I am so glad to be able to present his writings for him. Otherwise they would have been lost.

What are some of the other books you've written?

COUTU RADMORE: This is fun to tell about. The first book I wrote, *Kindabuk*, was in the language of Bislama and has been the official manual for pre-school teachers in Vanuatu since 1989.

When I came back to Canada, I began to practise writing because I wanted eventually to write a novel. I self-published *The Pond and Boxes*, my earliest poems, *Moonbeam*, a collection of poems and prose pieces, in the nineties, then a book of haiku-like poems called *White on White*. Terry Ann Carter and I published *Callalilypepper-words*, poems about Mexico, and with Joy Hewitt Mann, we put together *"3"*, a book of poetry.

I have just completed *a minute or two/without remembering*, lyric poems in the voices of my earliest ancestors in New France, and I have finally begun that novel I wanted to write, which is based on my mother's life.

You've lived and worked overseas, seeing other cultures. How might that have made you more appreciative of these unique stories of the northern culture in Canada?

COUTU RADMORE: With the organization known as Canadian University Students Overseas or CUSO in Vanuatu, I worked with people who were not yet too damaged by our so-called more progressive civilizations. I saw the effects of our various intrusions into their culture, many well-intended, by missionaries and aid workers. Benefits were evident, but couldn't we all have been more intelligent about it, more empathetic towards their cultures and values? When I returned six years later, the damage was out of control.

In China as recently as 2005 I felt the fears that citizens lived with every day. I saw a people who had no say in restrictions and laws by which they had to live, yet who were by nature generous, kind, and outgoing.

Travelling the Labrador coast brought home how much the indigenous peoples have lost, how much is now inaccessible to them and to the descendents of the early settlers. In some way, Len's writings will give some of that back to them.

 How would you describe your work as an artist?

COUTU RADMORE: In my art as well as in my writing, I am interested in process as much as in the finished work. Often I could not afford art materials so fell back on things that I had learned from my mother who always made do. I like to recycle materials and ideas and am using natural materials and green products where possible. Figure drawing always interests me for its necessary accuracy yet its range of possibilities. Much of my work is based on landscape and is often abstract.

 As a published poet yourself, did you find something "poetic" in Leonard Budgell's letters?

COUTU RADMORE: Perhaps the underlying poetry of Len's writing subconsciously captured me. There had to be a reason I kept every one of the 4000 pages he wrote me in the ten-year span covered by this book. It was so I could pick them up and reread them whenever I wanted or needed to. That is one of the reasons we buy books of poetry, and I think I got out of Len's words much of what I get today from good poems.

I write haiku and other Japanese poetic forms. There is an insistence on immediacy, on the moment, but with a great deal of silence, description, capturing that moment. Len spent so much time alone and it is evident in the power of his writing. He took it all in: the landscape, the experiences, the people. It seems as if everything he saw and heard was treasured and subconsciously honed, so that when he told someone it came out seamlessly. That someone happened to be me. What poured out was perfect in its natural rhythm, perfect in its chosen words.

I am sure that if you took many of his passages, broke them up into shorter lines, spaced them as he would have breathed them, you would have beautiful poems. Long, yes, but beautiful. Something along the lines of the early sagas.

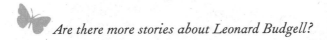 *Are there more stories about Leonard Budgell?*

COUTU RADMORE: It would have been a worthwhile project to record stories about Len. It wasn't done while he was alive, and there are not so many now who knew him well enough to explain the effect of having Len in their lives. His writing can be found in several issues of *Them Days*, a magazine of oral and written history of Labrador. There are others who have kept his letters to them, many of which could be published. He also wrote to me for another eight or nine years after we put this manuscript together, though these later letters are quite different from the earlier ones. There is a wealth of material on the tapes in the Manitoba Archives that he recorded with Jocelyn McKillop under the auspices of The Hudson's Bay Company Archives.

Fortunately, more amazing stories written by Len exist, some taken from the letters, but others created separately. Seven or so of these stories, true-life episodes and adventures in Labrador and the Canadian north, will be published in another book I am now preparing for Blue Butterfly.

ABOUT THIS BOOK

LEONARD BUDGELL saw the Canadian North like no one else. As a "Servant of the Bay" he ran Hudson's Bay Company trading posts for decades in isolated communities up the Labrador coast and across the Arctic, and served on the Company's supply ship *Nascopie*. He witnessed episodes and heard stories that would have been lost forever—except that he wrote of them in articles and in letters.

Intact for centuries, Northern ways changed with the advent of rifles and motorboats, radios and electric generators, new foods and different medicines. Budgell bridged the aboriginal and southern cultures. In his youth, he took nurses and doctors to distant settlements by dogsled, hunted in the Mealy Mountains. Later, he was one of the earliest to operate radio stations at places like Hebron and Wolstenholme.

In *Arctic Twilight*, Leonard Budgell chronicles a traditional way of life that was changing forever, through an outpouring of remarkable letters to a much younger friend, Claudia Coutu Radmore. His pen memorably portrays everything from dancing northern lights and the nesting practices of primal birds to astonishing human adventures and predicaments. Now edited and organized by Claudia, this unique memoir sees the light of day for the first time.

GR
Oct 16

MB
Oct/21

Scenes in the Torngat Mountains, Labrador, a region that
greatly impressed Len Budgell.

Above Cape White Handkerchief. MUN

Opposite, top Cape Mugford. MUN

Opposite, bottom Bishop's Mitre. MUN

Leonard Budgell at Cartwright, Labrador, 1935.
THEM DAYS / HERBERT HARDY COLLECTION

Speaking of Joe Michelin and lies, he once told my dad that when he first came to Labrador the curlew were so numerous that a man could fire one shot and get enough to give him a curlew every Sunday for a year. He said, as a matter of fact, that once he had fired one shot and picked up ninety-nine birds. My dad said, "Might as well say you got a hundred." The old man looked shocked. "What, tell a lie for one lousy curlew?" So there was Uncle Joe Michelin, who wouldn't tell a lie but could spin yarns of his days in the lumber woods in Quebec that rivalled Paul Bunyan. In fact, they were so close to the Bunyan yarns that you'd think they were the same. They couldn't have been, Uncle Joe didn't tell lies.

You guessed it, yarn spinning was a favourite evening entertainment where there was no radio or TV and only a limited number of records for the few old wind-up gramophones. Old Uncle Jesse Flowers, one of our principal yarn spinners at Rigolet, used to say, "Now I can't guarantee this is true, but a man who never in his life told a lie, told me."

Was to the market this morning. Have to admit the market does have lovely blueberries. They should, at the prices they charge. One of my favourites too. Rigolet was a great place for berries of all kinds, and the late fall blueberries were a great target for the fall geese. We'd try to get what we needed before the hungry young geese came to the coast from inland. They soon scoffed the blueberries and went after the low bush cranberries, marshberries and bake apples too.

Greed did get the best of them though and a good few ended up in the oven because they were too busy eating to watch for hunters. We always kept the biggest fattest goose for Christmas. We had a special airtight box to keep fall meat in. Using a mixture of ice and salt we could freeze a bird early in the fall and have it in perfect condition for Christmas. My dad insisted on goose for Christmas and salted salmon for Good Friday. The other holidays got what we happened to have.

I wasn't very old when a lucky shot got me a big Canada goose.

Can I really remember it? Not only can I remember the actual stalk and shooting, I can remember how my breath hurt in my chest, how my hands shook with excitement. I knew I could never hold the gun steady, but at the last moment I found that I could. As I've said so many times, we were brought up to hunt. We had to, and because it was a necessary part of living, there was a wonderful joy in bringing home a Sunday dinner.

I can still taste that first goose. My dad carved at the table and he served the meat from the platter. My mother served the vegetables. I can see him now as he laid that crusty gold slice on a plate and passed it to my mother. "First cut to the hunter." There were several clerks and employees and my dad at the table, all adults, all hunters, but it was my goose, my first one. I was alone when I got him and he was a heavy lug back home over the hills and through the marshes.

I put a good many more on the table later on, but that is the one that I remember. I got home late, after dark. My mother always worried. They had just about finished supper when I turned up. Mother heard the door and came out, relieved that I was back alive, and in her relief inclined to scold me for being late. "What kept you?" I can't tell you the pride that was in my heart and in my voice when I said, "This old fellow, I think he weighs twenty pounds," and I dropped him on the floor as if I'd brought a hundred others home. I got a wash and went in to the dining room and got seated.

My dad started serving whatever there was and old Mr. Parsons, the customs officer, who ate all his meals at the house said, "Any luck, boy?" I said as modestly as a ten-year-old who has just got his first wild goose can, "Oh, I got a goose." The old man, a retired ship master said, "You did, well I'll be damned," then quickly to my mother who wouldn't have swearing in the house, "Saving your presence my dear," and he had to know where I got him, how, and all the details. He said to my dad, "We got a coming hunter here. Remember that when you have no further use for the rifle."

That almost brought tears, because the rifle in question was one

Young J.M. loading truck

The Herr children in 1959

Herr Family at the Greenbrier, summer of 2011, with 57 of the then 59 family members in attendance

Inducted into the Small Business Administration Hall of Fame, 2004

The NFIB honored Jim and Mim for many years of contributions to the free enterprise system. The plaque in the photo reads: "THE JIM & MIM HERR FREE ENTERPRISE CENTER. In recognition of Jim & Mim Herr's dedication to America's small businesses and to the free enterprise system."

Jim with Herr's truck, 1956

Jim with Herr's truck (same location), 1992

Newest Truck, 2012

SBA Names James S. Herr State Small Businessman Of The Year

James S. Herr of Nottingham, President of Herr's Potato Chips, Inc., has been named Pennsylvania's "Small Businessman of the Year".

Herr was honored Friday in an award ceremony held at The Red Fox Inn, near Kennett Square. Prior to the combined award ceremony and luncheon, a tour of the facilities of Herr's Potato Chips, Inc. was made by representatives of the Small Business Administration and officials representing Philadelphia area banks: First Pennsyl-vania National Bank, Philadelphia National Bank, Continental Bank and Trust Company, Industrial Valley Bank, The Fidelity Bank, Lincoln National Bank, Frankford Trust and Delaware County National Bank.

This award is presented annually by the Small Business Administration to the small businessman in the state who has had more than routine success, and has made a recognizable contribution to the economy of the community. northeast Pennsylvania and South Jersey. They also cover the northern portion of the state of Maryland and the state of Delaware; also parts of New York and West Virginia.

In 1946, at the age of 21, Herr bought a small potato chip business for $1,860. To make the purchase, he borrowed $1,700 from a friend, $200 from his father and used his savings of $200 for working capital. The annual sales of this small business at the time of purchase were approximately $1,500. The

As the company expanded, Jim Herr's reputation as an exceptional businessman grew as well. In 1969, he was named Pennsylvania's Small Businessman of the Year by the U.S. Small Business Administration.

Early packaging

Packaging, 2012

Tobacco Shed on the Herr Family Farm

First Plant in Nottingham, 1952

1956

1963

1963

*J.M. and Jim in front
of the new corporate office
in 1990*

1990

Plant #2 in Nottingham was opened in 2008.

Herr's Visitors' Center

Plant expansion through 1999. Distribution Center is in foreground

Herr's Christmas Lights

Herr's Summer Social

Jim's favorite hobby allowed him to meet some famous golfers like Tom Watson.

Jim and Mim help Billy Graham celebrate his 90th birthday.

Early Chipper mascot at Phillies game

Jim and Mim have always been avid Phillies fans.

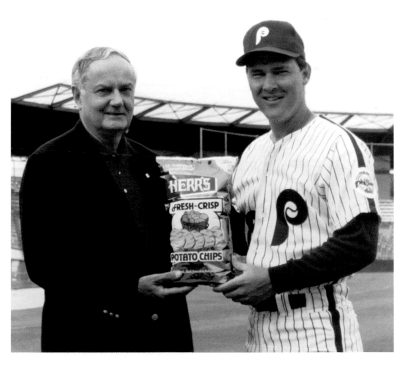

When Tommy Herr (a distant relative) played for the Phillies, he also helped advertise Herr's Chips.

Jim with President Gerald Ford

Jim with President Ronald Reagan

President George H. W. Bush greets Jim on Far East Trip

*President Bush is the keynote speaker at
the 2000 Snack Food Convention in Philadelphia.*

Jim and Mim with then Governor Bill Clinton

Jim and Mim with President George W. Bush and First Lady, Laura Bush

Air Force One

Jim with Governor Tom Ridge

In 1994, Jim became a familiar face in TV advertising for Herr's.
Here he and Mim are taking a break from filming a commercial.

candy. She would order all kinds of raw nuts, which my father would roast in a kettle of hot oil until he felt they were "just right." She would then cover these roasted nuts with chocolate and pack the candy in small white boxes labeled "Mrs. Herr's Chocolates." They were delicious, and our salesmen always had more orders than she could produce. That was the problem—she was the only one who made them and as she got older she could no longer keep up with it. Sometimes I think one of our family members should revive that line for us!

Expansion always involves a construction company, and I wanted to be able to count on one person to work with, rather than dealing with various subcontractors. That person was Paul Risk, a builder I met through my brother-in-law. He began working with me in the early 1960s, and his company continues to do work for us to this day (his son Steve now runs their company).

Paul was willing to take some time to get to know our industry, so he could understand our building needs. I asked him to visit some plants in New York and Canada, to see how they functioned. I also wanted him to get to know our key production employees, so they could work together on what we needed. I really didn't want to have to think all that through myself and I knew they would do a better job planning what we needed because they were involved with the details every day. The only request I made of Paul was that his company would not work for a competitor, and that didn't seem to ever be a problem for him.

When we had about a dozen trucks I talked with Paul about needing a building that would handle at least 25 trucks and a larger cooker.

At the time we were operating out of the 4,500-square-foot plant that had been expanded from our initial building in Nottingham. I also told him I thought we could grow 10 to 15 percent for the next 10 to 15 years. Paul did some figuring and then came back and asked if I really believed Herr's would experience such growth, because if I did we were talking about a much greater project. He said we would need to start in the middle of the property (just like my uncle had suggested years before!). I said, "But what will we do with the existing building? Shouldn't we use that?" Paul told me that if we really grew as projected, it wouldn't matter about the existing building. He was right; eventually it became a truck garage, then a maintenance shop, until it was razed to make space for our Visitors' Center.

In 1963 we quadrupled in size by building a 21,000-square-foot production facility in the middle of the property. In 1968 we added an additional 23,000 square feet for more cooking, packing, and potato storage space. A few years later we added 8,000 square feet of new stock rooms. I've always been grateful for Paul's close work with our engineers and production teams to build whatever we needed to accommodate our growth. Paul was a good listener and he worked well with our people.

In 1964, our sales really jumped when we embarked on a new packaging venture. For years we had sold chips in wax paper bags for 5, 10, and 15 cents a bag. We also offered a twin pack (two bags inside a larger cellophane package) for 49 cents. A packaging salesman convinced me that we should try selling chips in a 20-ounce cardboard barrel. The barrels resembled the popular wax-lined ice cream cartons and could be assembled affordably on site.

"King Style" barrels in production

The sturdy barrels would prevent chips from breaking and protect them from light (which causes them to become stale).

We called them "King Style" barrels and sold them for 99 cents. They became so popular, one of our salesmen told me that he was having trouble building a store display because customers pulled most of them from his cart as he was taking them from his truck into the store.

In 1966 our company hit a significant milestone when sales reached $1 million.

Ben Fenninger was the force behind our sales. He was so good at building routes that I asked him to train others and manage them. He trained some aggressive salesmen and routes expanded. One time Ben came to me and said we needed to expand into New Jersey. One of our good customers in Chester, Pennsylvania, wanted to open a store in New Jersey and wanted to sell our products.

I thought it was a little far out, but Ben convinced me we should do it. He had found a salesman who would drive from Nottingham to New Jersey, and he thought the area had a lot of potential. Sales grew there, and we rented a warehouse to store the chips, so the sales people could avoid the long drives. By 1968 we operated 35 sales routes out of Nottingham and five from New Jersey. Eventually we purchased a warehouse in Egg Harbor, New Jersey; it was our first branch and we operated 20 routes out of that location. We later built a larger warehouse in the same town to accommodate our growth.

Around the same time that we expanded to New Jersey, we began selling our products to the first Wawa convenience store. Over the years we have had the pleasure of growing with them and now serve over 500 of their stores.

The late 1960s marked the beginning of rapid territorial expansion that resulted in our opening new branch warehouses, purchasing trucks, and hiring people. In the 20 years after 1968, we grew from 35 routes to nearly 300, opened 12 new branches, and hired more than 500 people.

In the 20 years after that, 1988 to 2008, we added another 200 routes, opened eight additional branches, and hired another 500 people.

To support all this growth, we built a new plant in 1980 that allowed us to more than double our potato chip capacity and to create space for manufacturing other products as well.

Business Principles

Delegating is important to growth. Employees will make mistakes, but so will you! Remember that you are paying them for all the good things they are doing for the company. If they make a mistake now and then, forget it.

Always keep your word. If you can't make a payment on a loan, tell the person the reasons and make arrangements to repay it as soon as you can. Don't just ignore the problem. Make sure you pay your bills and treat people fairly.

Love forgives mistakes; nagging about them
parts the best of friends.
Proverbs 17:9

Herr children, 1961

Board of Directors, 1981

Chapter 8

DEVELOPING AS A FAMILY BUSINESS

You can tell from previous chapters that Mim and I have always operated as a team. As our family grew, she became less visible in the running of the company, but our home was always the source of my strength and support in business.

∽o∾

A worthy wife is her husband's joy and crown; the other kind
corrodes his strength and tears down everything he does.
Proverbs 12:4

∽o∾

That naturally carried over into the way we raised our children. Early on, our children were exposed to the day-to-day decisions and issues we faced, just because they were at the same dinner table or in the same car as we discussed things. They also grew to know the employees, watched the buildings being built, avoided delivery vans when they rode their bikes, and smelled the chips cooking each day. There was very little separation between the Herr family and the Herr business.

I liked the idea of the family continuing to run the business, though I didn't want anyone to feel obligated to do so. Our oldest daughter,

June, went to college and became an English teacher and I don't think she ever thought seriously about working here full time. Our oldest son, J.M., said that he always thought he would be a part of the business and never considered doing anything else. After high school and two years of college, J.M. was unsure about continuing his education and I thought he would learn more by actually working in the business, so I encouraged him to become my apprentice instead of continuing. I know that J.M. regrets that he never finished college, but I guess I was influenced by my father's idea that experience was better than "book learning." Anyway, that's what we did, and it worked out OK for us, but J.M. and the rest of the second generation now have a program for the third generation entering management, requiring a bachelor's degree and at least two years of working successfully for another company before entering our management track.

When J.M. came on there were fewer than 100 employees and he knew everyone. He and I shared a small office and he learned a lot from listening, discussing issues, and observing people. Of course he had worked throughout his childhood by washing trucks, cleaning packing machines, and sweeping floors.

Gradually I turned some of the management over to J.M. One of his first responsibilities was overseeing our purchase of the Price & Englehart Company in Reading, Pennsylvania, manufacturers of a lard potato chip. The owners were a lot older than J.M. was, but he did a good job of working with them and trying to merge our two companies. We kept the Reading business going for some time, but eventually J.M. decided it was more cost effective to have this product made for us by another company.

J.M. began doing some hiring and worked with our advertising and purchasing departments. As people began reporting to him and I saw him growing in experience, I turned over the operations of the company to him, and then eventually he went from my assistant to Executive Vice President. In 1989 he became President, and in 2000, Chief Executive Officer.

Before J.M. came on board, I don't think we even had a budget. I certainly didn't know the words "strategic planning." That is not to say that we didn't have sound accounting and legal services from outside sources. Jack Ross, of Ross Buehler & Associates, has been invaluable to Herr's over the years; in fact, he is Mim's and my personal accountant to this day. Another professional, attorney Clarence Kegel, who began his career at a Lancaster law firm and later began his own firm, has offered legal advice to our company and our family for many years. In addition to their expertise in accounting and legal areas, part of Jack's and Clarence's effectiveness has been the result of their understanding and appreciation of our family culture.

But in addition to these outside specialists, J.M. saw the value of hiring an employee who could take our financial planning to a new level. He hired Gerry Kluis, who has now been our Chief Financial Officer for many years. We are very grateful for Gerry's guidance, not only in the financial area, but also as a senior leader in our company.

J.M. and I have always worked well together, perhaps because we have different management styles and we each respect what the other brings to Herr's. I am much more entrepreneurial and I tend

CEO & President

to make decisions more intuitively, whereas J.M. is better at planning and strategizing. We are both conservative in our business approach, being careful not to jeopardize the stability of our company. We want our employees to have a solid, healthy company to work for, so they don't have to worry that they're going to lose their jobs to a buy-out or a poor business decision.

Herr's has thrived under J.M.'s leadership. On our fiftieth anniversary in 1996, we employed 1,100 people and our annual sales had grown to $130 million. By the year 2000, sales increased to $150 million and, in addition to our geographic growth in the mid-Atlantic region, we grew in international markets such as Latin America.

Our middle son, Ed, became president in 2005, when J.M. became Chairman of the Board of Directors and I took the title of Founder. Ed had worked in the manufacturing area for a number of years, and then opened his own business for a while, before returning to the company to assist J.M. Among his many duties as President, Ed serves as our company spokesman, a role that I had enjoyed before handing it over to the next generation. Ed brings a fresh energy level to the management team, and he and J.M. are now close partners in running the business.

Our youngest son, Gene, has the responsibility of handling our most essential raw material—potatoes. People don't realize how important this job is to our whole operation, because if we're out of good quality potatoes, we're out of business! All the planning in the world can't alter that fact. I'm so glad that he has focused on that area of our company and provides that stability to the production process.

Gene Herr

Daryl Thomas

I have enjoyed more time to pursue personal interests such as charitable giving and travel, but I still love going to the office every day. I want to be available to Herr's as long as I am able to make a contribution, in whatever way people want me to.

Martha's husband, Daryl Thomas, started his career at the company operating a route truck before he served a few years in the Navy. When Daryl returned from the Navy, I asked him to start up and manage the Quality Assurance department, which served the company well and gave Daryl some great experience. He then moved into the marketing department and was eventually asked to head up Sales and Marketing. He was the first family member on the management team to earn a graduate degree, and he brings a lot of knowledge and good will to the position. He is a good mentor to several of our grandchildren and their spouses, who also are learning the business and getting their MBAs. It's encouraging to see the adventure continue through these young people! I think they will be good leaders in their time.

You might wonder what all this has to do with your career. Maybe you don't have the opportunity to develop a family business and you want to build an enterprise and then sell it when you retire. That's fine too, but I would just like to make the point that there is a tremendous advantage to running a business as a family. I've read that more than 90 percent of the companies in North America are family-owned, and that over two-thirds of all people starting businesses today grew up in a family business environment [*Encyclopedia of business.com. 2ed*]. That early exposure makes it easier for kids to learn the value of money management, of dealing with customers, of relations with employees, and just general knowledge of how to operate a business, such as working long hours.

Family businesses have a shared sense of traditions and values that often provide a stable foundation for decision-making. Also there's a strong commitment to making the business work, because your family cares about it, too. In addition, I think one of the biggest reasons we've decided to stay privately held is the control factor. We can make a decision to do something that reflects long-term thinking—something that may be expensive in the short term but will pay off later. This would not be possible if we had to answer to outside stockholders about our profits each quarter.

In 1981 I decided to expand the Board of Directors to include all five kids. One of the lawyers I mentioned this to said, "Go ahead and put 'em all on the board and watch 'em fight!" Well, I'm still watching, and so far there's been nothing but benefit to having all five on the board. June and Martha are not working in the business, but they

In 1996, the top management team consisted of: (Seated, left to right) J.M. Herr, President; Jim Herr, Chairman and CEO; Ed Herr, Vice President. (Standing, left to right) Richard White, Vice President - Sales and Marketing; Gerry Kluis, Vice President - Finance; and Harold Blank, Vice President - Manufacturing.

Jim Herr passed the Chairman's gavel to J.M. Herr as J.M. assumed the position of Chairman & CEO at the company's Board of Directors meeting on January 7, 2005. Directors, left to right: front row – John Stanton, Ed Herr, J.M. Herr, Jim Herr, Mim Herr, back row – June (Herr) Gunden, Bill Alexander, Jay Carr, Gene Herr, Martha (Herr) Thomas.

bring insights that we value and we feel that our business needs the interaction of all of its family members, not just those who work here every day.

∽◦∾

Pride leads to arguments; be humble,
take advice and become wise.
Proverbs 13:10

∽◦∾

Conventional wisdom says you should also have outside directors, and in 2001, we began adding folks to the Board who could give us direction from their expertise in business—some from higher education and some from other industries. They have been a great asset to us.

Going forward, I think our strength as a family is in our ability to work together and get along, despite differences. We now have 20 grandchildren and 18 great-grandchildren. I call Mim the "Queen," but she says her role is "Social Director" for the family, because she loves to plan get-togethers and family trips. The family bonds are crucial for the well-being of our family and of our business and we pray that they will stay strong.

Business Principles

Good relationships are a key to your success. The ability to get along with others, whether family or others, is vital.

If you have children who are interested in the business, give them the opportunity to learn and grow in the business. Be willing to turn your responsibility over to them, as they are able to handle it.

*The fool who provokes his family to anger and
resentment will finally have nothing worthwhile left.
He shall be the servant of a wiser man.*
Proverbs 11:29

Chapter 9

DECISION POINTS

∽◦∾

Any enterprise is built by wise planning, becomes
strong through common sense, and profits
wonderfully by keeping abreast of the facts.
Proverbs 24:3, 4

∽◦∾

I've already told you about some of the major decisions we had
to make in our past—like rebuilding in Nottingham after the fire
and choices about expanding. I'd like to elaborate on a few more
decision points, because the success of any business depends on the
incremental effect of day-to-day decisions.

In 1961 we decided to incorporate. There are many reasons why this
is beneficial to a company, from tax benefits to liability issues. But
for me, the whole impetus was so that we could start a profit-sharing
plan for our employees. We needed the vehicle of shares of stock in
order to best accomplish this.

With my farm background, I knew that farmers normally have
a source for cash in their retirement years by capitalizing on their
appreciated land values. I wanted to create something for our

employees that would enable them to profit in their retirement from the increasing value of our company. The profit-sharing plan that we developed includes stock ownership of some of the company, so that as the stock rises in value, so do their assets. In addition to our profit sharing, which consists of company contributions only, we also have, as do most companies, a 401k plan. Between the two plans and Social Security, I believe our employees, especially those with a long tenure here, will have sufficient funds for retirement.

Usually, and fortunately, you have some time to ponder big decisions. One decision I had to make quickly involved whether or not to sell our products in the western Pennsylvania and eastern Ohio area. Around Christmas time in 1974 we got a call from a distributor who sold another brand of chips, saying that the other company was on strike and he couldn't get product. He had route salesmen who couldn't make a living if they didn't have chips to sell. Would we supply chips to them?

On the surface this looked like a golden opportunity, but we also wondered where it would lead in the long term. When the other company resolved its labor issues, where would this distributor's loyalty lie? We had to make a decision fast—they wanted product the next day— but clearly this had long-term implications. We decided to say yes, we'd help them out, but we sure didn't know how it was going to turn out. I put Curt Jones in charge of this project. A former Marine, at 6'4" Curt was imposing and could get right to the point, but he also worked well with people. He oversaw this uncharted venture into brand new sales territory, and with our first distributor of any size, at that. He did a great job and eventually we ended up with our own distribution facility in the Pittsburgh area. (Curt, after involvement in a number of other important projects, eventually left the company to become an entrepreneur/owner himself.)

On the heels of this decision, in 1976 someone called me and told me a company was for sale in Chillicothe, Ohio, about 50 miles south of Columbus. Because we have been able to grow without making acquisitions, and because that growth took capital, we never looked to purchase other companies. But J.M. and I went out to take a look at the facility and meet the owners. The company had been in business for quite a while, and was owned and operated by two brothers and one of their sons. They had their own brand and a clean, if not modern, facility. With our new distribution in the Ohio and western Pennsylvania area, we thought this made some sense.

We decided to purchase the company, and we knew who we wanted to run it. A man named John Thomas (son of our Mount Vernon friends) had started with us in route sales, then moved up to district manager, then branch manager, and we felt he could oversee both manufacturing and sales for this new operation. We changed their brand name to Herr's and that plant has been very helpful, especially now, as the Nottingham facility is often filled to capacity. John later moved back to Nottingham, served as our first Human Resources manager, and eventually retired after 42 years of service.

Many of our business decisions had to do with expenditures. Buying potatoes was always a determining factor in whether we made a profit, since potatoes are the raw material most basic to our company. I tried to become an expert on potatoes, learning the different varieties, how they grow, potato diseases, and where to purchase crops depending on the season of the year. Some potatoes are good for "table" use, but are not suitable for chipping.

When we were still in Willow Street, we met Bob Bare, an 18-year-old farm boy from Bird-in-Hand, Pennsylvania, when he and his younger brother, Jake, came to deliver a load of their farm's potatoes to us. At that time most farmers in Lancaster County grew a few acres of potatoes and Herr's would buy from the local farms when potatoes were in season. Bob suggested to his father, Elvin K. Bare, that they purchase a truck and become brokers for the local farmers. We developed a relationship and I saw that I could trust them to help keep us supplied with good potatoes.

When the Nottingham operation began we were using one and a half tractor trailer loads of potatoes a week. By the time of our major plant expansion in 1963, our needs had risen to several trailers a day, and I contracted with E. K. Bare & Sons to supply all our potatoes. They worked with us to develop growers in a number of states in the eastern U.S., and I was counting on them to keep our supply strong. After I made that deal with them, I began to worry about the consequences if something happened to the Bare brothers. What if there was an emergency? That's putting a lot of pressure on one source.

I leveled with Jake one day. I told him, "We're using an awful lot of potatoes, and what if something comes up that you can't supply them? Could we adjust our deal to allow others to supply some of

Unloading potatoes

them?" He graciously agreed, but they still supply the majority of our potatoes.

Currently we use up to 15 trailer loads of potatoes daily (over 75,000 tons annually). Our son Gene oversees the contracting for them, as well as the logistics, quality, and budgeting for this whole area of the business. He attends regional and national meetings with growers, fellow processors, and industry representatives from across the U.S. and Canada.

In addition to decisions about the potatoes, we have taken some bold steps in packaging. In 1974 we decided to change our bags from a glassine bag to a foil bag. Foil prevents light penetration, which is so important for keeping chips fresh over a long period. As you can imagine, one of our great challenges in chip sales is to keep the product fresh. Although the changeover was difficult and expensive and the additional cost for the foil was significant, we were convinced that it was important to consumers. Eventually packaging companies developed a metallized material that was cheaper than foil but had similar qualities for keeping the product fresh.

Only two years later we were faced with the difficult decision to discontinue the popular 99-cent barrel. The purchase price of the barrels had nearly quadrupled since ten years earlier, when we began using them. Reluctantly, we searched for a replacement. At first, we went to another type of round container, then a rectangular carton, and eventually discontinued that type of package altogether.

It was about the same time that we debated whether we should try to produce some of the products that were being made for us by other companies. We knew that we could make more money if we produced them ourselves, but should we venture into making other products? Could we sell enough to justify the cost of the equipment? What if the quality wasn't as good? We decided to try it and we began with cheese curls, followed by popcorn.

Foil Bag

In 1981 we decided to make pretzels, a process which requires a large baking oven rather than frying equipment. This was a major step for us and required a large learning curve for our production staff, but they were always eager to learn and try something new. In 1983 we began to manufacture corn products, such as corn and tortilla chips, and in 1984 we began making our own Onion Rings. Our latest venture was to make baked potato crisps, as well as extruded products made from corn or potato flour.

To make these latest new products, we were forced to face the biggest financial decision in our history: to build a whole new plant for the purpose of producing baked potato crisps as well as extruded snacks, like cheese curls. The plant was eventually completed in 2008 at a cost of nearly 20 million dollars, including equipment, but we delayed it several times due to a leveling off of sales, as well as cost pressures on raw materials. We finally decided to move ahead and we're glad we did—the plant is running nicely and growing in output every year. The plant was built in such a way that it can be easily expanded; hopefully we'll need to do that someday.

Our employees seem energized by new products—either ones we make or those we re-sell. It's fun for the sales force to have something new for their customers, and it keeps our production and marketing folks busy, creating new ways of handling products and new slogans and styles for packaging. In 1983 we changed our name from Herr's Potato Chips, Inc. to Herr Foods Inc., to reflect this commitment we have to our whole line of products.

When I think back over other decisions I've made, one comes to mind that occurred numerous times: whether or not to sell our company. Any company with a long history of growth will attract would-be buyers who like the idea of purchasing an established company. We often get calls from companies (or organizations working on behalf of a company) to see if we would be interested in selling the company.

For the longest time I'd tell them "No, my children are interested in running the business, and besides, I still enjoy what I'm doing." Now, as my children start to near retirement age, they are saying, "No, some of our third generation is interested, involved, and learning to run the company, and we're committed to keeping the business independent and family owned." Frankly, it takes a lot of work to keep a business independent. From a financial standpoint I would be better off to have sold it, but money and "things" are not as important to me as the continuation of a dream. Also, for our employees and our community, I believe we're better off being family and locally-owned. I know my children agree with that.

One of the business decisions that I'm proudest of came from a problem that gave me the most headaches. In 1983 waste disposal was a mounting concern for our growing company. The water from our production contains starch and other residue from the potatoes which makes it difficult to treat to the extent required for stream discharge. In addition to the waste water, we had potato peelings and other solid wastes to dispose of, such as product that doesn't pass quality control specs.

Through the years the company had purchased farmland in the vicinity of the plant, and we were using the waste water, from which most of the starch had been removed, to spray irrigate the land. I've always thought it would be neat to see cattle grazing on those fields, and I got to talking with one of our friends at church, Dennis Byrne, who is educated in the field of cattle, particularly Black Angus. I asked him if he thought Angus cattle would like to eat potato peelings and under-spec potato chips. Also, could they be fed crops grown on the farm if it was being irrigated with the waste water from the plant? Dennis began researching and worked with a nutritionist; they found an appropriate feed mix that would include not only corn and haylage grown on the farm, but our edible waste products.

Today Dennis Byrne runs the Herr Angus Farm, near the plant in Nottingham. Any product that we manufacture that does not meet quality standards is used to feed 500 head of cattle (the farm staff calls it "steer party mix"). Nearly one million gallons of water a week, which is used in our manufacturing process, is pumped to the farm to irrigate fields.

Because our business uses so many natural resources to produce and distribute our products, it's important that we stay sensitive to protecting our environment. It is very gratifying for Herr's to have found a solution to our waste products that contributes to the preservation and stewardship of our renewable natural resources. In addition to the Angus Farm, I'm also pleased that we found other ways to be careful with resources. For example, we reuse our corrugated shipping containers before selling them to be recycled. We use steam from our cooking process to heat water. And we've learned that the starch that is removed from the water in the potato processing area can be sold for fine paper manufacturing.

Business Principles

Solutions to business decisions take wisdom. If you reverence the Lord, He gives you ideas that you can't attribute to any other source.

The Lord helps you through the advice and insights of others He puts in your path.

∞∘∞

Get all the advice you can.
Proverbs 19:20

Chapter 10

SOME FLAVORFUL EXPERIENCES

In 1957 I listed a used 800-pound cooker for sale, and a man from Ohio bought it, with the purpose of taking it to Morocco, in North Africa, where he also had a home. When we finalized the sale, I told him to let me know if he ever had trouble with it—all he'd have to do is buy me an airline ticket to Morocco and I'd come help him. He said he knew all about machinery and certainly wouldn't have any trouble running this cooker.

Six months later he called and told me he had purchased a ticket for me to come to Morocco, that he needed help with the cooker. Never having been out of the country, I was enthused to go and I bought a ticket for Mim to go, too. We knew it would be a fascinating experience to travel in a culture so different from our own.

When we got there and looked at the cooker, it was squeaky clean, just like when we sold it to him. The man explained that he hadn't been able to use it, because whenever you try to start it, it jerks, and all the employees run out of the building expecting it to explode! I soon saw that there was a leak in the gas line, and when we fixed that the cooker worked like a charm.

We had a memorable trip to Africa, all because of that little gas leak. Another memorable experience took place in Latin America.

In the early 1960s I received a phone call from a business person I knew in Delaware. He told me that President John F. Kennedy was initiating a federal program called "Alliance for Progress," for the purpose of establishing economic cooperation between the United States and Latin (and South) America. Part of the program involved asking U.S. business owners to invest time and money in building businesses in other countries, to help that country's economy and to forge an alliance with our country. Specifically, the caller asked, would I be willing to partner with a Panamanian to start a potato chip operation in Panama City? There were five Delaware partners who said they would contribute money, if I would just provide the expertise.

Mim and I thought about this for a while and decided we liked the idea, because of the adventure it offered and also the thought that we could help our country—even if it was a small contribution. We traveled to Panama and met our Latin partner, whose wife and children graciously invited us into their home. He was excited about the opportunity ahead, and I made plans to send our plant engineer, Charlie Temple, to help put together the plant and equipment.

It wasn't long before the cost of the venture increased beyond the expectations of the Delaware partners, and they got cold feet and backed out. I decided to continue and became co-owner with our Panamanian partner. Over the next few years, Mim and I made quite a few trips there, even taking our two youngest children with us to live in Panama City for a short time.

At one point when the operation was going pretty well, I saw that they had extra capacity in the plant that wasn't being used and they needed to generate more sales. I agreed to provide some additional funding so that the business could purchase another truck, to be used to develop sales. The next time I arrived in Panama I asked about the truck, and it turned out the money was used to purchase a boat. Our partner was convinced he could get more customers by taking them fishing! I told him we couldn't *afford* to take anyone fishing— we needed a truck to deliver product to the stores. This was one of several cultural differences that we didn't know how to handle.

A major problem vexing the Panama operation was the length of time it was taking to get potatoes to the plant. We started out buying potatoes from the same broker we used in the States and made a deal with the container shipping company to keep the potatoes cool during transit. If they weren't kept cool, the potatoes would rot and run out of the container like water.

The shipping agreement didn't solve the problem. Sending potatoes by boat from Florida just took too long. If potatoes aren't used within a day or two of taking

Panama potato warehouse in Boquete

them out of the ground they must be stored properly or they will turn brown, making a very off-color product.

Realizing we would need a local source for potatoes, we were put in touch with another Panamanian, who had a degree in agriculture and knew a lot about the soil and farming conditions locally; he also spoke English very well. We felt confident he could help us, and we partnered with him to buy a 200-acre farm in the fertile, mountainous region of Boquete, about an 8-hour drive north of Panama City. Our new partner was excited to be able to grow a crop for which he had a ready market, and we trusted his ability to get us good potatoes for the plant. And the colorful, endearing locals were somewhat curious to see what we Americans were doing there. They watched as our partner engineered an irrigation system from the top of the mountain to the potato growing areas, and the indigenous Indians who lived in the steep parts of the mountains would shyly come to apply for work in the fields. The women, with their colorful handmade dresses, would silently watch from the shelter of coffee trees nearby. We so enjoyed the pristine beauty of that place. At one time we took our five children and their spouses on a unique vacation there.

I soon learned that my partner was very full of ideas, not only for growing potatoes, but for any other business venture that captured his attention. He was very gregarious and well-known, and at one point, with his contacts in government, he thought he could control the entire vegetable market for the country. As he got more involved in these bigger deals, he lost interest in the potato growing business. I could see that he was thinking too big and had too many irons in the fire.

One day I learned that the farm had been sold, without anyone letting me know! I never received any money. I asked how the farm could be sold without my consent, since I was co-owner, and I was told that my signing off on the sale wasn't needed in Panama, that I would probably get paid someday. Needless to say, I'm not holding my breath.

I'm not sure what they did with the chip plant. It was functioning for a while, but I know it was a headache for them, so I don't know if they kept it very long. Eventually, I learned that my farming partner got into the bed-and-breakfast business.

We lost money on the Panama venture, but I wouldn't trade the experience for anything! I'm not sorry we did the project, but it did make me realize that culture plays a big part in the way we do business. It gives me great respect for successful international companies.

Another experience that lost money, but was "flavorful" for our family, took place right in Nottingham. It started when I saw an ad in the newspaper for a herd of ponies. The cost was $7,000 for ten mares and two stallions, which was expensive, but I thought we could breed them and make some money. I also enjoyed the thought of presenting them to the kids, because we already had one pony, Jenny, at the time, and the kids loved her, but she was getting old. One Saturday I told the kids that I had twelve surprises for them coming that day. It was so much fun to see their excitement when ponies started arriving!

True to my plan, our ponies multiplied and we had as many as forty at one time. But, not according to my plan, many other people were raising ponies as well, and the prices dropped to almost nothing. The children outgrew the ponies and we almost gave the ponies away to get rid of them. We even used them as prizes for some contests at Herr's. We hired a promotional firm to help devise a win-a-pony contest that we put on the back of chip bags.

I guess if there is a silver lining to that cloud it is that two of our children, J.M. and Martha, have a life-long love of horses as a result of this experience. In fact, Martha has built a career on this passion of hers: she and a partner are brokers who buy show horses in Europe for American clients. They also run a training program on the horse farm that Daryl and Martha own.

Business Principles

Every company has a "culture." Identifying your values and staying true to them helps give your company a firm footing.

Not all your ideas will work out, no matter how well-intentioned you are!

Shown here, the former Mira-Pak offices and manufacturing facility.
Herr plans to sell the building, keep the operation small in the early stages of growth.

James S. Herr

On October 15, 1980, James S. Herr, President of Herr's Potato Chips, announced that he had purchased the assets of the Houston firm with the expressed intention of returning it to its former prominence.

The first step has already been taken. Mira-Pak's first new packaging machine will roll off the line in April. But Herr admits that the rebuilding will be slow.

"We've started with about 23 people (compared with 200 previously)," explains Herr, "many of them former Mira-Pak employees. For now, we're looking to assemble a team of well-qualified people to put Mira-Pak back to its original status in the industry.

Report on Mira-Pak purchase from a trade journal, 1980.

Chapter 11

MISTAKES ARE PART OF IT

S ometimes I think people get the impression that if you have a successful company, you must have done everything right. Well that certainly isn't true of me, as you know from the Panama venture and my idea to raise ponies. I think mistakes are just part of life, especially if you tend to take risks. The key is what you do after you've made a mistake. My father-in-law, a man of succinct speech, gave me some wise advice about that: "In a bad situation, just make a deal and settle."

If we learn from our mistakes, they aren't totally wasted. I'll tell you about a few of mine.

The first was with a packaging company. One of the major suppliers of packaging equipment in our industry (and for our company) was Mira-Pak, a company based in Houston, Texas. In 1980 it went into bankruptcy and the common reasoning for it was that they had simply not made the changes necessary to compete with other companies in the industry. However, they still had some good people, and several of the members of Mira-Pak's sales force approached me about buying the company, saying that it would be a blessing to the whole industry if I would purchase it. We would run the business with the current employees.

I was somewhat intrigued by the idea and went to the court's bankruptcy auction and took along my banker. We learned that it would take a million dollars to buy the company. My banker was a free spirit. Having just returned from vacation, he hadn't checked in with his bank superiors, but he said loaning me a million dollars wouldn't be a problem. He also suggested that I buy a condo in Houston for about $30,000, so I'd have a place to stay when I went to Houston. I thought it was interesting that a banker was trying to spend more of my money, but it did make some sense since it was close to the Mira-Pak company.

The purchase of the company included two buildings—one big, nice building and a smaller one—and I didn't feel we needed both. To raise capital, I sold the larger structure to a company who made motors for drilling companies (they put electronic components on gas and oil drilling rigs). The drilling industry in Houston had been booming prior to this, but the bottom fell out shortly after they purchased the building. The people I had sold it to called and told me they had to back out of the deal and they were going to file for bankruptcy. I took the building back and eventually sold it to the city of Houston.

I still had the Mira-Pak business in the second building, and for a while it looked like we were going to make it. But then some of the engineers decided to quit the company, and they had been a big factor in my decision to buy it.

To add to the Mira-Pak debacle, the production people at Herr's began telling me that even *they* didn't want to keep buying Mira-Pak equipment. They had learned of a better weighing process offered by a Mira-Pak competitor and they felt it was in Herr's best interest to change vendors.

Finally, I just had to admit it was time to pull the plug on the effort to save Mira-Pak. I eventually sold the buildings, our condo, and chalked the whole thing up to a learning experience. The lesson? Probably that we should have done better due diligence and evaluated the situation less emotionally. I am by nature quite inquisitive and there are many different things I'd like to try. When I see a business opportunity, it's very tempting for me to jump in with both feet and not spend a lot of time thinking about it.

Secondly, I have made some mistakes in the oil and gas well industry, which I've been involved with for more than three decades.

During the 1970s, the man who ran the advertising agency our company was using invited J.M. and me to dinner at a fancy Philadelphia restaurant to introduce us to a friend of his. He thought we'd be interested in his friend because he was a Christian and was very philanthropic.

There were about ten people at the dinner. The man we were all being introduced to was a smooth-talking, charismatic Texan, who promptly told us he didn't believe in banks but he believed in helping his Christian brothers make money. That comment alone should have made us question whether what he was about to suggest was a good idea. But he knew his Bible inside and out and talked a lot about religious themes, which I guess dispelled some of our reservations.

He told us he wanted to help people invest in the oil and gas business. He had a connection with a well-known Texas family, who made a lot of money in the oil business, and it was his aim to use his connections "to help God's little people." We were impressed enough that we went to Texas to see him, and I remember he had a Lincoln with no license plates—he said he didn't believe he needed them, that he had a right to drive. That should have been another red flag.

Still, he sounded as if he knew what he was doing, and both J.M. and I believed him. Well, he knew what he was doing all right: he was getting us to invest in his oil wells, and we ended up losing most of that money. The sad part was that he had also convinced a number of missionaries with little money to invest in his company, telling them that he wanted to provide an income for them. They lost their investments.

This guy was also involved in wells in West Virginia, and when his business failed, I received some equity in the West Virginia gas wells. I decided to join several other people to start a company, the Interstate Drilling Company; we thought that at least we could recoup the money for the missionaries. Eventually I took control of the company and became chairman of the board and saw to it that those debts were repaid.

I remained involved in the Interstate Drilling Company until 2001 when I sold my share of the company.

And finally I'll tell you about a costly mistake from trusting someone who turned out to be involved in a Ponzi scheme. In the 1980s I learned of an organization that helped non-profits with fundraising and also advised corporations about charitable organizations they considered especially worthy of funding. The man who ran this organization came very well recommended by some influential people, and I'm always interested in how to best handle our charitable giving.

The head of this organization told me that he knew quite a few people who were very wealthy and very philanthropic, but who just didn't have the time or inclination to do a lot of research into which organizations they wanted to contribute to. So they told this "facilitator" that if he found people who were also contributing large sums of money to good causes, they would match, or essentially double, that contribution.

I would need to deposit my money with the organization for six months, proving to the other contributors that the money was available for gifting, and allowing the organization to match up donors. Then the donor would make their contribution and the organization would send the doubled amount to whatever charity I wanted to fund. The story sounded somewhat plausible to me, because I know that charitable giving, if you are conscientious about it, does take a lot of time and effort.

It was exciting to me, of course, to have my charitable giving doubled! The more I saw this happen, the more money I wanted to give through the organization. I also knew others in the Philadelphia area who were experiencing the same benefits, and momentum seemed to be building. The organization boasted that it was giving away more money than the Carnegies, Mellons, and Rockefellers.

We didn't know that the facilitator had begun siphoning off funds for his personal use, which eventually totaled millions of dollars. We did know that the time period of the initial deposit had gone from six months to nine and ten months; later we learned that he had begun using current deposits to pay off earlier charitable contributions, instead of sending the money to the intended charity.

Eventually the house of cards fell and our facilitator went to jail. The judge ordered that those of us whose target charities received the doubled money had to pay some of it back to those whose charities had not received any of the benefits they were promised. Several of us went further and made a commitment to pay back everything that was lost to those charities whose donors we personally had introduced to this organization.

Looking back, it's easy to see that this really was "too good to be true" and as the saying goes "when it looks that way, it probably is." It was a hard lesson to learn.

Business Principles

If you make a mistake, admit it, learn from it, and move on.

Be careful about entering into a new venture; do your homework and don't invest more than you can afford to lose.

A man who refuses to admit his mistakes can never be successful.
But if he confesses and forsakes them, he gets another chance.

Proverbs 28:13

Jim with Franklin Graham of Samaritan's Purse

Chapter 12

MONEY!

∽∘∾

Trust in your money and down you go!
Trust in God and flourish as a tree!
Proverbs 11:28

∽∘∾

I didn't tell you that when I was 15 and I read that verse from Psalm 37 about "the desires of your heart," I had a pretty elevated desire in my heart. I told the Lord that I would like to earn a million dollars and that I would like to give a million dollars away. I guess I was tired of being poor.

Money has motivated me, there's no doubt about it. Companies need to be profitable to thrive, and I want our employees (including me) to earn a good living. I enjoy the challenge of taking a struggling entity and making it profitable. The goal of being profitable is what keeps our company disciplined and focused.

I think that the reason the word "profit" has become a bad word in some circles today is that the desire for money can easily take precedence over higher goals. Money, instead of being a tool, can become an end in itself, a slave driver that takes away your good judgment and moral values. It can rob you of your joy. It can truly become your master, rather than your servant.

Mim has a few quotes from people on our refrigerator door, and for years she has had this one there: "The only way to avoid the tyranny of money is to ruthlessly give it away" (Vernon Broyles, pastor at North Avenue Presbyterian Church, Atlanta, Georgia). I think it's good to remind ourselves that money can become a tyrant, and it is a ruthless one that destroys people. Instead we need to be "ruthless" (in the sense of being unrelenting) in giving it away.

You might think, "That's something I'll worry about when I have more of it," but I would like to encourage you to give some of your money away even when you are earning very little. This was a principle that our church taught us early on, that tithing (giving a tenth of your income to the Lord) was a discipline a Christian should practice. So Mim and I were careful to do this, even when we were still living on my brother's farm. We learned over the years that there is great joy in giving money away, regardless of the amount you give.

∞∞

Honor the Lord by giving him
the first part of all your income.
Proverbs 3:9

∞∞

About twenty years ago I formed the James S. Herr Foundation as a vehicle for more intentional giving. While the foundation serves primarily as a charitable organization that supports the interests of Mim and me, occasionally there is some overlap between the foundation and the company. (The company has its own charitable giving program, which disperses support to hundreds of local organizations.)

Funding for the James S. Herr Foundation comes primarily from my own funds and our focus over the years has been to spread the good news that Jesus is the Master of the Universe and that He cares about each person in His creation. He cares so much that He died to provide for each person a way to be forgiven and to become part of His family. In my opinion, there is no better way to use money than to get this message out, and there is no better way to live than to become involved in His cause.

Years ago Mim and I were introduced to the ministry of Stephen Olford, a dynamic preacher who we felt was doing a great job of getting the gospel message out. We wanted to support this work, and I have enjoyed many years of serving on the Board of Directors for the Stephen Olford Center for Biblical Preaching in Memphis, Tennessee.

Some of the other ministries that have meant the most to us are Sandy Cove (a Christian camping ministry in North East, Maryland), Lancaster Bible College, the John Edmund Haggai Institute for Advanced Leadership Training in Atlanta, Georgia, and Samaritan's Purse, in Boone, North Carolina.

More than 50 years ago I was influenced by a group of Mennonite business people who had a heart for using their business skills to help others around the world. One such person was Erie Sauder, who started Sauder Woodworking Company, in Archbold, Ohio. He was a founder of an organization called MEDA, Mennonite Economic Development Association. His passion was to develop the wasteland of Chaco, Paraguay, into habitable and profitable land. Sauder made 18 visits to Chaco, working with the native Paraguayan Indians to develop their colonies. Other founders of MEDA were Sanford High, who started the High Welding Company, Orie Miller, who ran a shoe factory, and Ivan Martin, who had a limestone business. They were service-oriented Mennonite business people who wanted to use their business skills to create solutions to poverty.

I've been particularly interested in Africa, and have taken five trips there for MEDA causes. Once we went to Somalia to help a man who wanted to start a hammer mill in his little hamlet. I remember eating on a plate in his hut that was made of cow dung, and really it was OK! It was so invigorating to me to see someone get a start who could then develop a small business to help others make a living. I'm still involved in MEDA, though I don't travel as much anymore.

There are so many other good organizations and causes that it can take all your time just trying to absorb the information about them. I thoroughly enjoy this season of my life, when I can use the resources we've been given and figure out ways to be a blessing with them.

I have said many times that you can never outgive the Lord. He always gives back more, not only in more earnings, but in a richer quality of life. You don't have to be a millionaire to know this. Perhaps you have already found that when you give your time or money or efforts to help others, you get back so much more.

∽∘∾

It is possible to give away and become richer!
It is also possible to hold on too tightly and lose everything.
Yes, the liberal man shall be rich!
By watering others, he waters himself.
Proverbs 11:24, 25

∽∘∾

I have enjoyed serving on boards of various ministries and community organizations, because it's a way I can contribute, in addition to giving money. I also think it's healthy for a company to be involved in the life of their community. As a company, you are a citizen and there may be ways you can help your local neighbors to enjoy a better quality of life.

Jim presents a check to Larry Spaid, of the local hospital

One of Herr's projects that we enjoy most is that we light up the trees on our campus for Christmas so that people can drive through with their families (without charge) and be blessed during that special season of the year. Our granddaughter's husband is in charge of it, and Mim, who loves Christmas anyway, gets excited every year when they start putting up the lights.

We also team with Chester County at July 4 to put on a "Freedom Fest" at Nottingham Park. We bring in music and we have fireworks and food and over 10,000 people attend. It's something we can enjoy with our community while we also celebrate and honor our great country.

In addition to giving to the community, we always want to be sure to treat our employees fairly. We attempt to adjust wages with the cost of living increases, but, much as you would like to, you have to be careful not to promise too much. Unexpected increases in the cost of goods and other factors can diminish cash reserves and undermine the health of the company. The best gift you can give your employees is to keep the company good and solid, so they don't have to worry about their job security. It's gratifying that in 65 years, we have had no lay-offs due to a lack of business.

In recent years management has instituted more programs for Herr's employees. Dick White, a long-term senior management member who is now Vice President of Human Resources, has been diligent about making the best programs available to our employees. A *Helping Hands* program aids employees with unplanned emergencies or financial setbacks. A *Partners in Service* program pays those who want to donate time to charitable organizations. A ministry staff is available to provide confidential religious counseling for those who ask. Also, scholarships are given to children of employees. This is all in addition to a very competitive fringe benefit program.

I've seen business owners who take a lot of money out of their businesses, even from the start, but our philosophy has been to be conservative and plow as much as we can back into the company. That way we're prepared if we need to expand or if we need a new piece of equipment.

Although we have taken on debt over the years to purchase new equipment and buildings, I have tried to be prudent about it and not allow the company to become too leveraged. More than once banks have encouraged us to take on more debt because we had a strong balance sheet (after all, that's what they're in business to do), but you have to be careful not to get overextended.

∽o∾

The wise man saves for the future,
but the foolish man spends whatever he gets.
Proverbs 21:20

∽o∾

There is a proverb that says "He who gathers money little by little makes it grow" (Proverbs 13:11, NIV). I think one of the pitfalls people fall into is that they try to get too big too quick. I like the idea of "plugging away" at something, not trying to make an impression or get rich quick, but being more methodical and careful about growth.

Steady plodding brings prosperity;
hasty speculation brings poverty.

Proverbs 21:5

∽∘∾

There are times when this doesn't feel exciting or glamorous, but that has to be OK. I remember times over the years when I wondered "What in the world am I doing making potato chips?" There were other people doing things I thought were a whole lot more significant or impressive. But we just went to work every day, regardless of those occasional thoughts. I don't think anyone feels positive all the time, and you have to just go on and do what you know you need to do. I also felt a lot of responsibility for those whose livelihood now depended on Herr's. It wasn't just about me—it was about all of us together.

I mentioned earlier that in my teens I enjoyed playing in Mr. Simmons' orchestra, and here is a song we used to sing (I still sing it to myself):

There are many things I'd like to do
As my journey I pursue.
I would like to be a leader
As any normal man would do.
I would like to be a millionaire
With a million to bestow.
But I'd rather be an old-time Christian, Lord,
Than anything I know.

Business Principles

Be careful with your money. Don't let it master you.
Don't spend it all. Keep your business good and strong by
having a solid financial foundation.

Give to others, both as a company and as an individual. Learn
the joy that comes from being generous.

Avoid the temptation to try to get "big" quickly. Just concern
yourself with doing the best you can with what you're given to
do *today*, and your company's size will take care of itself.

Jim and Mim with 2nd generation family members in the business. Left to right: J.M. Herr, Gene Herr, Ed Herr and Daryl Thomas (married to Martha)

Chapter 13

LOOKING AHEAD

People ask me what I see when I look forward—for myself, our family, our company, and our industry. Also, what message would I offer you, as you look ahead in your own life?

For myself and my family, I just want us to always keep moving forward in this adventure of living for the Lord. Even though there are days, at age 87, when I have health issues, I want to always be energized by the things that matter in life: the value of making a difference in someone else's life, either by giving financially or by helping in the myriad of other ways we can serve. Business and service should never be separated.

As for Herr's and for the industry, I know that we are operating in a very competitive environment these days. While consolidation in the snack food industry has resulted in many fewer companies than when I first began, it doesn't mean that it is less competitive. The companies that have survived and thrived have done so because they're good at what they do. In addition to the traditional snack food companies, other large food companies have also entered the market with various snack-like products. The truth is the market overall is more competitive than it's ever been.

The future of Herr's will depend on our leadership, on the work ethic of our employees, on the political climate of our country, and on our use of resources. It will depend on our ability to weather the storms that will inevitably come and our willingness to look for opportunities that will also come.

As I envision the future, I see the need to continue our growth through expansion of our sales territories and product innovations. We will need to pay constant attention to details in every department of our business and always be willing to learn. We need to do everything in our power to keep our country from over-regulating business and therefore destroying personal initiative. Hard work and high goals have never been more important.

People are our most valuable asset and we must continue to encourage and empower our employees. Several years ago Don Cartusciello, who was new to our company at the time, asked me to jot down what I consider to be "Laws of Good Business." As you can see on the following page, my main concerns are that we treat our employees and our customers well and that we manage our finances properly.

෴

Watch your business interests closely.
Know the state of your flocks and your herds.
Proverbs 27:23

1 Follow the Golden Rule.
Treat others the Way you would
like to be treated.

2. Start out with Integrety

3. Have a good business model

4. Be Honest and always pay
your bills on time.

5. Have good financial Controls.

6. Earn the respect of your lenders
or financial institution.

7. As you grow try to have the
employees involved so they are a
part of the team.

8. Make sure employee's have good
working Conditions.

9. If everyone works hard to achieve
the quality products you desire
Share profits with them some way.

10. We are all in this together.

11. Try to assess our Customers
needs and make sure they are
Pleased with the product at the end
of the day.

12. Hope everyone is Happy.
And can smile.

Jim Herr's "Laws of Good Business," 2009

I think the best chance of long-term success for Herr's is for us to remain an independent, family-owned business. At this time we already have ten of the third generation active in the business, including both descendants and spouses, and I wouldn't be surprised if that number grows. That is very encouraging to me, and I have high aspirations for our business and our family. I pray that they will continue our values and culture.

Most of my values have come from my faith, and it would be dishonest to take personal credit for them. All I can tell you is that I have seen how Biblical truths have played out in my life, and that it is God who directed my paths. Financial success is a very small part of being successful. The most satisfying way to live is to know you're in a relationship with the Creator and that you are pleasing God. Delight yourself in Him by reading His book and by seeking His wisdom. See what desires He plants in your heart and how He goes about giving those to you. Learn to see life as an adventure!

Starting a business may not be what God wants you to do—it just happens to be what He called me to do. Your gifts may be in creating a wonderful home environment for your family, or using an innovative idea as you teach school, or beginning a ministry of some kind. Perhaps you are working for a company and you can make a difference by being open to new ideas for doing your job better. I encourage you to use the creativity you were born with to find your passion and work hard at it.

I see this in our own family. While our three sons are active in our snack food business, our two daughters have chosen very different career paths. Both have started a business in the area in which they are gifted: one in the equestrian field and one in editorial services. Also, in our third generation (our grandchildren) I am delighted to see many varied interests, in fields like ministry, drama, education, finance, nursing, homemaking, dietetics, marketing, and engineering. In addition two couples of the third generation have started their own businesses.

We have stressed all along that while family members are welcome to join the business, what we truly desire is that they'll be happy doing whatever they choose to do. For those who do choose to join the company, we have written rules that govern all aspects of getting and keeping a job, requirements for moving up to take on more responsibility, and so on. We have a "family constitution" and a Family Council made up of our second generation siblings. The key to success in this area is good communication, fairness, and transparency. Mim and I are so pleased, not just with those who have joined the company, but also with those who haven't.

I'll leave you with my definition of success: Success is finding out what God wants you to do, and then doing it. Simple, but it takes a lifetime of work!

God bless you!

Business Principles

If you have a family business, be careful not to assume that everyone in the family will want to make it their career. After all, I didn't continue working on my father's farm, but I pursued something I personally wanted to do.

Never stop looking for opportunities to be a blessing to someone else!

Epilogue

(I asked Mim to write this epilogue, since many folks who know us best think she is our "better half"!)

MIM'S NOTES

What's it like to have been married to Jim Herr for 64 years? It's been a career of its own, in a sense. It never occurred to me to pursue anything other than being an encourager and supporter to my husband and our children. That's what my mother, his mother, and all my aunties did.

Our five children were born before the advent of epidurals, but I *was* in a hospital, which is more than my mother could say. When I was five years old, my mother gave birth to identical twin girls (so identical she tied a pink ribbon around the wrist of one of them). My older sister and I were helpful (that's the way we remember it) in changing diapers, feeding them, and rocking them to soothe them. I chose to respond primarily to the younger twin. Two years later Mother gave birth to identical twin boys. This time I was responsible for cuddling and caring for the older one. So I did have experience in taking care of infants by the time our own children came along.

My heart never ceases to praise God for answering our on-the-knees prayers for safe deliveries of healthy babies—five wonderful, varied, lovable children, who continue to bring us much joy. I tried to use Proverbs 14:1 as a guide: "A wise woman builds her house, while a foolish woman tears hers down by her own efforts." I repeat "I tried," but not all of my judgments and priorities were as good as I wish they were. I tell the children that what I didn't do right they could use as a learning experience—lame logic, huh?

Our household was always in a state of "managed bedlam" while the kids were young. The big mongrel house dog shed hairs, the little pink Easter chicks had free roaming, the kittens were born in the house, an effort was made to hatch duck eggs in a warmer on the kitchen counter—and then there was Tojo, the monkey. His cage rested on the table between the recliners in the TV room. He'd put his little claw through the cage and hold Jim's finger while they watched the evening news together. Our enjoyment of him waned over the months, especially after he escaped from the cage and raced around the house. Since it was summer we thought he would enjoy living in the trees outdoors and hopefully make his way south by winter. NO, he *liked* us and sat on the door knob looking in, or snatched a half sandwich from our picnic table, or landed out of nowhere on an unsuspecting visitor's shoulder. We finally resorted to paying the SPCA to find a home for him. Our German shepherd pup never did learn to obey. His name was Prince, but he didn't act very princely when he threatened to bite our guests. The Shetland ponies we had didn't involve me, thankfully.

At my present age, I can't believe I put up with such a menagerie in addition to five children—not to mention gardening, canning, freezing, and doing bookwork. But I had energy then.

Meals were predictably regular and around the kitchen table. Sometimes Jim would call in the afternoon and ask what was for supper—could he bring Urb Anzmann (a packaging rep) or another business associate to the house with him? I can only imagine some of their thoughts as we just put out one more place at our simple kitchen table. But they kept coming back, and the kids and I learned to know many of Herr's business associates this way.

At evening meals our practice was to read a Bible story from *Egermier's Story Book* (given to us by Jim's mother) and have a prayer. Then quite often Jim left for a meeting—school board, church committee, etc. There was usually quite a lot of household activity when he hurried off, but by the time he got home the kids' schoolwork was done and the cafeteria change was laid out for the next day. Toys were put away, the kitchen was clean, and all five were in bed. It was then that we had a chance to converse without interruption.

In later years, Jim sometimes questioned whether all his church and community involvements (in addition to his time at the business) were detrimental to the kids, since he did not have long hours in the evenings to be home with them. It's a question with no definitive answer, but I don't remember ever sensing that the children felt resentful or deprived because he was at a meeting. I know they were proud of their father; in fact, there's a proverb that says, "A child's glory is his father" (Proverbs 17:6). I'm sure they could sense that I was positive about what he was doing, and I think a mother's attitude is often "caught" by the children.

I also don't remember ever resenting that I was so "occupied" at home, while Jim was on the move. He felt a responsibility to be involved in local community work (later branching out into national and international involvements), and I was contented in my role. He encouraged me and expressed appreciation often. Besides, I wasn't as gregarious and outgoing and self-confident as he was. He is the one who has brought me out of my timidity and helped me find that I did enjoy stepping outside the role of homemaker (though "homemaker" is still my favorite classification).

Anyone reading this who is from a large family, even a family wholly dedicated to God, knows that everything is not always peaches and cream. A large family means a lot of doors opening and closing, some quarreling between siblings, teenagers sometimes choosing a temporary detour from what they were taught, illnesses, and disappointments. And I lost patience, chose improper discipline, disagreed with Jim on financial indebtedness (I was always leery of *any* indebtedness)—I certainly wasn't perfect! However, the strange but happy truth is that now I have to deliberately *try* to recall unpleasant memories (because I was told that I have to be realistic in this book). When I think back, honestly all that I remember is good.

When our youngest started school I began volunteering for the Red Cross. At the time we were called "Gray Ladies," for the color of our uniforms. I volunteered once a week at the local hospital in West Grove. Toward the end of the 20+ years I limited my time to helping at Bloodmobiles. (I even donated a couple gallons of blood during that time.)

Another outside-the-home activity was attending Lancaster Bible College. Upon applying I learned that in order to attend daytime credit courses I needed a high school diploma—duh! So I first tested out and got a GED diploma. It was a one hour drive one way to the college each day. I only took three courses, but I really enjoyed them even though I was old enough to be the mother of the rest of the students.

I began giving addresses at banquets, church services, or community clubs, but mostly at women's meetings. I have no idea how it came about that I could make an inspirational speech that would bless others. I found I was pretty good at memorizing and inserted poetry and stories into the speeches (maybe because my father gave us pop quizzes on math or Bible verses during meal time all through my childhood). In any event, I spent quite a bit of time preparing for speeches and accepted invitations for many years—until I felt I was too old to be gallivanting around the country, especially for night meetings. At the same time, Jim was invited to speak at business functions; I guess we were on a roll.

When our firstborn was six months old, Jim wanted me to go with him to a Potato Chip Institute convention in Cleveland, Ohio. (This would be the first of many conventions and the beginning of his many involvements with the organization.) Now I had never been more than a two- or three-hour drive from my home until our honeymoon! So to think of leaving the baby with a grandmother and go to a *convention* was a big decision. Obviously I survived and learned to relax and be comfortable in crowds. Throughout the years we were blessed with the availability of trustworthy people who would move in and take over the care of our household. Our travels took us pretty much around the world. Quite often the travel was for Jim's work within the snack food industry, his interest in economic development connected to the church, and his role with the National Federation of Independent Business. Our participation in the Alliance for Progress program took us to Panama repeatedly for several years.

When our "favorite five" were between the ages of 8 and 18 we began family trips, the first being an extended motor home trip across the U.S. Then there began the weddings and grandchildren, and we developed planned family vacations once a year. These were most often in the States (particular memories stand out of dude ranches in Idaho and Wyoming, as well as a cruise in Alaska), but we did go to Israel for a Holy Land tour, to a favorite resort in Acapulco, to South Africa on safari, and to Scotland for a golf holiday. A couple of missions-oriented trips were to the Dominican Republic with Hope International and to Maui, Hawaii, with the Haggai Institute. By God's good graces we enjoyed health and safety in all our travels. The trips abroad were ever so exciting, but possibly the most relaxing and simplest vacations are the times we've spent at the Greenbrier Resort in West Virginia. In the summer of 2011 fifty-seven of our then fifty-nine family members were able to join us there. (Since then our number has grown to sixty-one, and we've learned of another one on the way.) Jim and

I say that one of our happiest times in our advanced years is to "sit back" and watch the family interacting in such a happy way.

We live in the same house we started in when we came to Nottingham. It's old, but it's *familiar*. We can still host the family for outdoor picnics (with the help of everyone), but we *have* outgrown room for seating at dinners and I have started this last year to use a caterer and the tour center next door for dinners. Family gatherings are the moments I cherish!

At age 85, I am thankful for the richness of life, the *flavor*, if you will. Jim and I pray that your life will be just as rich, just as seasoned with the blessings that will come as you follow your own personal calling.

APPENDIX

Family Tree of
James S. & Miriam Herr

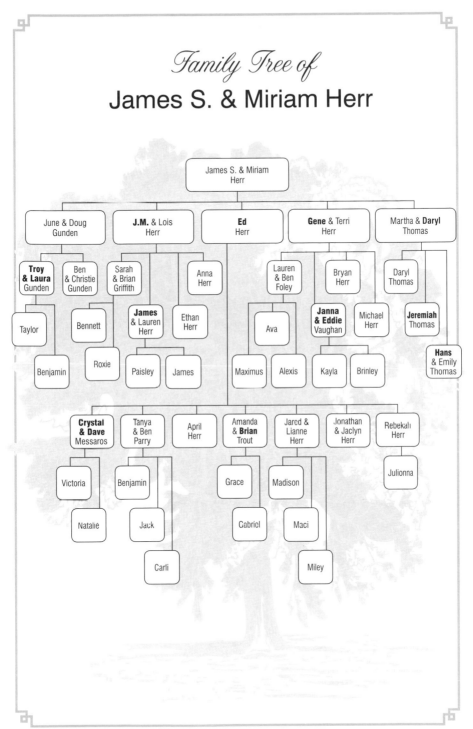

James S. & Miriam Herr

June & Doug Gunden

J.M. & Lois Herr

Ed Herr

Gene & Terri Herr

Martha & Daryl Thomas

Troy & Laura Gunden

Ben & Christie Gunden

Sarah & Brian Griffith

Anna Herr

Lauren & Ben Foley

Bryan Herr

Daryl Thomas

Taylor

Bennett

James & Lauren Herr

Ethan Herr

Ava

Janna & Eddie Vaughan

Michael Herr

Jeremiah Thomas

Benjamin

Roxie

Paisley

James

Maximus

Alexis

Kayla

Brinley

Hans & Emily Thomas

Crystal & Dave Messaros

Tanya & Ben Parry

April Herr

Amanda & Brian Trout

Jared & Lianne Herr

Jonathan & Jaclyn Herr

Rebekah Herr

Victoria

Benjamin

Grace

Madison

Julionna

Natalie

Jack

Gabriel

Maci

Carli

Miley

Bold denotes employed at Herr Foods, 2011

177

MILESTONES

1946	Bought Verna's Potato Chips for $1,750
1947	Moved business to a farm in Willow Street, PA
1949	Moved business to a bakery in West Willow, PA
1951	Fire destroyed the bakery
1952	Bought property in Nottingham, PA and constructed building
1956	Built addition for warehouse
1961	Incorporated
1962	Developed Panama business relationship
1963	Built new plant in Nottingham
1963	Employees Profit Sharing Trust was started
1966	First $1,000,000 sales year
1966	Opened 1st branch, Egg Harbor, NJ
1968	Built new plant in Nottingham
1973	Somerset, NJ branch was opened
1976	Began cheese curl production
1977	Purchased Carroll's Potato Chips in Chillicothe, OH
1977	Perryopolis, PA & Chillicothe, OH branches were opened
1978	Began popcorn production
1979	Jim Herr became President of the Snack Food Association
1980	Built new plant in Nottingham
1980	Wilkes-Barre, PA branch was opened
1981	Hampton, VA & Hatfield, PA branches were opened
1981	2nd generation family members join the Board of Directors

1981	Began pretzel production
1983	Name changed to Herr Foods Inc.
1983	Elkridge, MD branch was opened
1983	Began corn chip & tortilla chip production
1985	Herr Angus Farms was established
1986	Oakland, NJ branch was opened
1987	Camp Hill, PA, Lakewood, NJ & Seaford, DE branches were opened
1988	S. Philadelphia, PA branch was opened
1988	The James S. Herr Foundation was established
1989	Bedford, PA and Ona, WV branches were opened
1989	J.M. Herr was named President
1990	Corporate Office Center was built in Nottingham
1991	Jim Herr became Chairman of the National Federation of Independent Business (NFIB)
1992	Visitors Center was built in Nottingham
1992	New Castle, PA branch was opened
1993	Warehouse additions in Nottingham
1994	Jim Herr stars in TV Ads
1994	Newburgh, NY branch was opened
1996	Reach $100,000,000 in sales
1996	50th Year Anniversary celebrated
1997	Allentown, PA branch was opened
1997	Jim Herr receives the Circle of Honor Award from the Snack Food Association in recognition of outstanding contributions to the industry

1997	Jim Herr was named Business Leader of the Year by the PA Chamber of Business and Industry
1998	N. Philadelphia, PA branch was opened
1999	Addition to the Nottingham plant & 3rd chip line
2000	J.M. was named CEO; Ed Herr became company spokesman
2000	Concordville, PA branch was opened
2001	First non-family member joins Board of Directors
2004	Back to the future — began kettle chip production
2004	First national shipment to Wal-Mart
2005	Jim's title changed to Founder; J.M. Herr was named Chairman
2005	Ed Herr was named President
2006	60th Year Anniversary celebrated
2008	Plant II opened in Nottingham, with two production lines — one for extruded snacks & one for Baked Crisps
2009	Hainesport, NJ branch was opened
2010	The Nottingham Inn, an adjoining property & restaurant / lodging business, was acquired
2011	65th Year Anniversary celebrated
2013	Ten 3rd generation family members are working full time at the company
2013	Company purchased controlling interest in Silk City Snacks

SALES GROWTH

Year	Annual Net Sales Exceed ($)
1946	1,500
1956	150,000
1966	1,000,000
1976	10,000,000
1986	50,000,000
1993	100,000,000
2007	200,000,000
2013	250,000,000+

DISTRIBUTION ROUTES

Year	Number of Routes	Estimated Average Cost of Fuel/gallon ($)
1946	1	.15
1956	5	.22
1966	30	.32
1976	80	.59
1986	250	.89
1996	434	1.22
2006	505	2.96
2013	500+ Company owned routes; 250+ Distributor routes	3.45

PERSONNEL GROWTH

Year	Number of Employees*
1946	1½
1956	20
1966	75
1976	201
1986	630
1996	1,100
2006	1,366
2013	1,500+

*Full and Part Time

JAMES S. HERR, founder of Herr Foods Inc., has served as International President of the Snack Food Association, Chairman of the Board for the National Federation of Independent Business, Chairman of the Board of Interstate Drilling, Inc., Chairman of Sandy Cove Ministries, and President of the Oxford Area School District Board of Directors. He was named Outstanding Pennsylvania Businessman of the Year by the Small Business Association in 1969 and in 1997 he was named Businessman of the Year by the Pennsylvania Chamber of Business and Industry. He has received the highest honor bestowed on an individual by the Snack Food Association, in recognition of his contributions to the industry. In addition he has served on various community and ministry boards and has been active in his church all his life. On April 5, 2012, the 65th anniversary of his marriage to the former Miriam Hershey, James S. Herr died from complications of pneumonia. Together they had five children, twenty grandchildren, and twenty-two great-grandchildren.

BRUCE E. MOWDAY is an author of books on history, business, sports and true crime. He began his writing career as a newspaper reporter, columnist, and editor. He has won awards for investigative journalism, and hosted radio shows on three stations. He also regularly contributes to several magazines. Since 1997 he has been President of The Mowday Group, Inc., a full-service media relations firm headquartered in Chester County, Pennsylvania. For more information on Bruce Mowday, his books, and The Mowday Group, Inc., visit www.mowday.com.

JUNE HERR GUNDEN is a daughter of James S. Herr. Collaborating with her husband Doug, she helped her father create his autobiography. June and Doug are the owners of Peachtree Editorial Service, which specializes in serving Bible publishers worldwide. The company employs 25 people and is located in Peachtree City, Georgia.